# The Cosm

Jami,

The wider your perspective
is, the more hope you
will have.

Respectfully,

Paul K. Chappell

# The
# Cosmic Ocean

NEW ANSWERS TO BIG QUESTIONS

by Paul K. Chappell

PROSPECTA PRESS

WESTPORT AND NEW YORK

Prospecta Press
P. O. Box 3131
Westport, CT 06680
(203) 571-0781
www. Prospectapress.com

*Book and cover design by Barbara Aronica-Buck*
*Cover image based on an iStock photo of the Fountain of Neptune by Robert Pavsic.*

Paperback ISBN: 978-1-63226-009-3
eBook ISBN: 978-1-63226-010-9

For the unsung heroes of peace and justice

# CONTENTS

# AUTHOR'S NOTE

*The Cosmic Ocean* shares the treasures I have extracted from trauma. To explain how these treasures—which take the form of timeless truths—can help us solve our personal, national, and global problems, this book uses personal stories and extensive research to journey through time, around the world, and into every facet of the human condition.

To survive and progress as a global human family, we need a paradigm shift that can transform our understanding of peace, justice, love, happiness, and what it means to be human. But to create such a massive paradigm shift, we must voyage far beyond sound bites. We must look deeply into the nature of reality, resisting the dumbing down of information that has become so common today.

To help create this paradigm shift, the following chapters explore diverse subjects such as empathy, rage, nonviolent struggle, war, beauty, religion, philosophy, science, Gandhi, the *Iliad*, slavery, human sacrifice, video games, sports, and our shared humanity. It is important to understand these subjects, because to effectively wage peace we must strive to increase the quality and quantity of our understanding, just as generals who wage war strive to increase the quality and quantity of their soldiers.

Understanding allows us to humbly recognize truth. Every human community—including our global community—needs truth, because peace and justice are built on the foundation of truth. When we extract truth from trauma, we can uncover a road that leads to hope, happiness, and human survival.

# The Human Condition

## *Finding Light in Darkness*

Trauma has been my greatest teacher, and it has a message all human beings need to hear. If we do not listen to what trauma has to tell us, humanity will not be able to solve problems such as war, nuclear weapons, and environmental destruction. If we ignore the teachings of trauma, these problems we have created may cause our extinction.

Just as diamonds are buried in the darkness of the earth, the solutions to our human problems are jewels hidden in the darkness of trauma. If we listen to what trauma has to say, we will learn how to heal a wide variety of problems that affect our personal lives, country, and planet. If we uncover the secrets buried in the darkness of trauma, we will even learn how to navigate our most urgent problem of all—human existence itself.

Although trauma has been my greatest teacher, I have also been transformed by other sources of wisdom. This book expresses the essential life lessons I learned during four years at West Point and seven years in the U.S. Army. I also discuss what I learned from studying humanity's greatest peacemakers. And I share the wisdom I received from the unsung heroes of peace and justice. These people are not famous on a national or global scale, but are among the best teachers humanity has to offer.

Martial arts philosophy states that an opponent can become our greatest teacher, because struggle can make us stronger. In this way my trauma has been both an opponent that has tormented me and a teacher that has molded me. Throughout history countries have used armies, mountains, and oceans to keep foreign aggressors off their soil, but trauma is an opponent that can easily bypass these barriers and invade our communities. My father was a veteran of the Korean and Vietnam Wars, and neither large oceans nor locked doors could stop the trauma he carried with him from invading my childhood home.

When we think of shadows we often think of the shade cast by buildings and trees, but war can also cast a shadow. Unlike a building that casts a shadow in a city, war casts a shadow in the human mind. The *shadow of war* is a metaphor for the trauma caused by war, and by understanding this form of trauma we can better understand all forms. War casts a terrifying shadow on those who are unfortunate enough to stand in its shade; I experienced this during my childhood when my father and I spent many years living in the shadow of his war trauma.

In this book I share the life-changing insights I learned as a child in a violent household, a West Point cadet, an active duty soldier, and a student of trauma. I express these insights through metaphors that help us see the world in new ways, practical lessons we can apply to our daily lives, and stories that provide realistic hope. The army taught me that stories are one of the most powerful communication tools. To explain how this book came into existence, I must tell you a story that began before my birth. It is the story of my father.

My father, Paul B. Chappell, was born in 1925 and grew up in Virginia during the Great Depression. Half black and half white, he lived under segregation. My father was a career soldier who served in the army for thirty years and retired as a command sergeant major—the highest enlisted rank. He met my Korean mother while he was stationed in Korea. They married in 1975, and I was born in Maryland in 1980 when he was fifty-four years old. My parents moved to Alabama when I was a year old. I was their only child.

Most African Americans born in 1980 are five generations removed from slavery, but I am only three generations removed. My father was old enough to be my grandfather when I was born, thus a generation was skipped between him and me. Furthermore, my grandfather was raised not by his parents, but his grandparents, two former slaves named Wyatt and Frances Chappell; thus another generation was skipped. According to the 1870 census, Wyatt Chappell was born a slave in Alabama in 1835 and Francis Chappell was born a slave in Virginia in 1842.

Because my mother is Korean and I inherited the shape of her eyes and texture of her hair, I grew up looking Asian rather than black or white. Although I look Asian, I was raised to see the world like a black person living before the civil rights movement. The U.S. Army had desegregated during the early 1950s prior to the major civil rights victories, and throughout my childhood my father constantly told me, "The army is the only place in America where black men are given a fair chance. You'll never be able to get a decent job unless you're in the army."

As a child I tried to hide the fact that I was part African American, because to me it was bad enough being half Korean, since I was often bullied because of my Asian eyes. No matter how hard I tried to hide my African American blood, however, my parents reminded me that people would eventually find out. According to them, the army was the only place where I would be accepted despite my racial background.

In 1990 when I was ten years old, General Colin Powell was chairman of the Joint Chiefs of Staff, the highest-ranking position in the military. One day when General Powell was on television, my father said, "Just look at Colin Powell. He is the highest-ranking soldier, and he is black! Where else in America is such a thing possible? Have you ever seen a black president?" My father died in 2004, before the first African American president was elected.

If two of the generations separating me from slavery had not been skipped, perhaps I would have grown up with a different attitude toward my racial background. My attitude was not based solely on what my father told me; it was also reinforced by the racism I experienced as a child in Alabama. When I became an adult, my mother tried to protect me by reminding me that racism would continually threaten my well-being. When I told her in 2009 that I was leaving the military, she shouted, "Are you out of your mind? Nobody is going to hire you. It's bad enough you look Asian, but you're also part black. Nobody is going to give a job to a black man who looks Asian." My parents did not tell me lies. On the contrary, they told me their truth. They were describing life as they had experienced it and trying to protect me from the suffering they endured.

Interracial marriage did not become legal in all U.S. states until 1967, when the Supreme Court ruled in *Loving v. Virginia* that laws banning inter-racial marriage were unconstitutional. Although interracial marriage was illegal in nearly all the southern states prior to 1967, white people were not the only ones opposed to it. Marrying when interracial marriage was still controversial in many parts of the country, my parents did not feel welcome in African American or Korean communities. Many Koreans did not like that my mother had married a black man, and many African Americans did not like that my father had married an Asian woman.

The fears we develop in childhood can dominate our behavior as adults. As an adult I tried to keep my racial background a secret, because my father said people would hate me if they discovered that a person who looks Asian is part black. Since I also felt alienated from the Korean, African American, and white communities—where many people saw interracial marriage as an abomination—I was afraid of how people would react if they knew I was a product of this abomination. I felt like I was carrying a horrible secret within me. Eventually I reached a point where I could not carry this secret any longer.

When people asked me about my racial background, I would lie by say-ing, "I am half Korean and half white." But when I was a twenty-two-year-old army officer I decided to no longer keep my racial background a secret. When I began to tell people the truth that I was half Korean, a quarter white, and a quarter black, their responses surprised me in a way I never expected. Instead of being horrified, they seemed oddly pleased. One southerner I told responded by saying, "That's a really cool mix."

Responses like this shocked me at first, because it was difficult for me to believe that anyone could see my multiracial background as positive. But attitudes about race had in fact changed. According to a Gallup poll, in 1958 only 4 percent of Americans supported interracial marriage between blacks and whites, and by 2013, the amount of support had grown to 87 percent.[1]

Racism still exists in America today. I have experienced it firsthand and so have many other Americans from various racial backgrounds. Just because a black president was elected does not mean racism in America is dead. But if we have made progress on the issue of race, why can't we make more progress? I have met some people who say African Americans are not any better off today than they were under slavery two hundred years ago. Whenever I hear this it reminds me of the pro-slavery and pro-segregation propaganda in the South that claimed black people were not treated badly and most slaves were happy being slaves.

To understand what state-sanctioned slavery truly was in America, a more accurate name for it would be *state-sanctioned rape and murder upon a country's own people.* It was common for slave masters to rape slave women and murder rebellious slaves, and these crimes were tolerated by the legal system. Under the system of state-sanctioned slavery, an ordinary white person could murder a black person, admit to the murder without claiming self-defense, not even accuse the black person of committing a crime, and not be put on trial.

William Lloyd Garrison, an American white man born in 1805 who dedicated his life to ending slavery, tells us: "Let it never be forgotten, that no slaveholder or overseer can be convicted of any outrage perpetrated on the person of a slave, however diabolical it may be, on the testimony of colored witnesses, whether bond or free. By the slave code, they are adjudged to be as incompetent to testify against a white man . . . Hence, there is no legal protection in fact, whatever there may be in form, for the slave population; and any amount of cruelty may be inflicted on them with impunity. Is it possible for the human mind to conceive of a more horrible state of society?"[2]

Frederick Douglass, who was born in 1818 and rumored to be descended from his white master and a black slave, describes the complete lack of legal protection for slaves in the part of Maryland where he lived, and he debunks the myth that slaves were happy being slaves:

> I speak advisedly when I say that in Talbot County, Maryland, killing a slave, or any colored person, was not treated as a crime, either by the courts or the community. Mr. Thomas Lanman, ship carpenter of St. Michaels, killed two slaves, one of whom he butchered with a hatchet by knocking out his brains. He used to boast of having committed the awful and bloody deed. I have

heard him do so laughingly, declaring himself a benefactor of his country and that "when others would do as much as he had done, they would be rid of the damned niggers."

Another notorious fact which I may here state was the murder of a young girl between fifteen and sixteen years of age, by her mistress, Mrs. Giles Hicks . . . This wicked woman, in the paroxysm of her wrath, not content with killing her victim, literally mangled her face and broke her breastbone . . . The offense for which this girl was thus hurried out of the world was this: she had been set that night, and several preceding nights, to mind Mrs. Hicks's baby, and, having fallen into a sound sleep, the crying of the baby did not wake her, as it did its mother. The tardiness of the girl excited Mrs. Hicks, who, after calling several times, seized a piece of firewood from the fireplace and pounded in her skull and breastbone till death ensued. I will not say that this murder most foul produced no sensation. It *did* produce a sensation. A warrant was issued for the arrest of Mrs. Hicks, but incredible to tell, for some reason or other, that warrant was never served, and she not only escaped condign punishment, but the pain and mortification, as well, of being arraigned before a court of justice . . .

One of the commonest sayings to which my ears early became accustomed, was, that it was "worth but a half a cent to kill a nigger, and half a cent to bury one." While I heard of numerous murders committed by slaveholders on the Eastern Shore of Maryland, I never knew a solitary instance where a slaveholder was either hung or imprisoned for having murdered a slave . . .

Slaves were expected to sing as well as to work. A silent slave was not liked, either by masters or overseers. "Make a noise there! Make a noise there!" and "bear a hand," were words usually addressed to slaves when they

were silent . . . It was a means of telling the overseer, in
the distance, where they were and what they were about
. . . The remark in the olden time was not unfrequently
made, that slaves were the most contented and happy
laborers in the world, and their dancing and singing were
referred to in proof of this alleged fact; but it was a great
mistake to suppose them happy because they sometimes
made those joyful noises. The songs of the slaves represented their sorrows, rather than their joys. Like tears, they
were a relief to aching hearts. It is not inconsistent with
the constitution of the human mind that it avails itself of
one and the same method for expressing opposite emotions. Sorrow and desolation have their songs, as well as
joy and peace.[3]

Racism is still a problem in America today, but African Americans are
no longer subjected to the full horror of state-sanctioned slavery, which
denied slaves basic education (it was illegal to teach slaves to read and write)
and gave them no legal protection against being beaten, murdered, raped,
worked relentlessly without pay, bought and sold as property, and stolen
from their mothers as infants. If someone looked white but inherited a small
amount of African American blood from an ancestor, that person could also
inherit the status of a slave and be denied basic education and any legal protection against being raped and murdered.

For example, if a boy's father was white and his mother was a biracial
slave, he could be treated as a slave even though most of his blood was European. Frederick Douglass said a man "could sell his own child without incur-
ring reproach, if in its veins coursed one drop of African blood."[4]

In a January 1864 issue of the magazine *Harper's Weekly* there appeared
photos of three mixed-race children who looked white. Their names were
Rebecca Huger, Rosina Downs, and Charles Taylor. *Harper's Weekly* also
printed a letter about the children written by Colonel George Hanks.
Colonel Hanks commanded a northern unit of black soldiers, and he was
trying to raise money for the education of freed slaves. The three mixed-race

children were slaves who had been freed when a northern army led by General Butler entered New Orleans. In his letter Colonel Hanks described the white appearance of the children:

> Rebecca Huger is eleven years old . . . To all appearance she is perfectly white. Her complexion, hair, and features show not the slightest trace of negro blood . . . Rosina Downs is not quite seven years old. She is a fair child, with blonde complexion and silky hair. Her father is in the rebel army. She has one sister as white as herself, and three brothers who are darker . . . Charles Taylor is eight years old. His complexion is very fair, his hair light and silky. Three out of five [white] boys in any school in New York are darker than he. Yet this white boy, with his mother, as he declares, has been twice sold as a slave. First by his father and "owner," Alexander Wethers, of Lewis County, Virginia, to a slave-trader named Harrison, who sold them to Mr. Thornhill of New Orleans. This man fled at the approach of our army, and his slaves were liberated by General Butler . . .
>
> These three children, to all appearance of unmixed white race, came to Philadelphia last December, and were taken by their protector, Mr. Bacon, to the St. Lawrence Hotel on Chestnut Street. Within a few hours, Mr. Bacon informed me, he was notified by the landlord that they must leave. The children, he said, had been slaves, and must therefore be colored persons, and he kept a hotel for white people.[5]

Since it was illegal to teach slaves to read and write, Colonel Hanks wanted to provide former slaves with a good education. This issue of *Harper's Weekly* included other photos of former slaves, such as a black man named Wilson Chinn and a black boy named Isaac White. In his letter Colonel Hanks wrote: "Wilson Chinn is about 60 years old . . . When 21 years old he was taken down the river and sold to Volsey B. Marmillion, a sugar planter about 45 miles above New Orleans. This man was accustomed to brand his negroes, and Wilson has on his forehead the letters 'V. B. M.' . . . [Of the 105 slaves who entered the Union camp] thirty of them had been branded like cattle with a hot iron, four of them on the forehead, and the others on the breast or arm . . . Isaac White is a black boy of eight years; but none the less intelligent than his whiter companions. He has been in school about seven months, and I venture to say that not one boy in fifty would have made as much improvement in that space of time."[6]

As slave owners controlled their slave populations by using violence and forbidding them to learn to read and write, enormous governmental powers were also used to keep slaves in captivity. To better understand how unjust state-sanctioned slavery truly was, imagine if the role of American law enforcement officers was not to punish people caught with slaves, but to return their escaped slaves to them. According to the Fugitive Slave Act of 1850, any U.S. marshal who refused to arrest a runaway slave should be heavily fined, and any person helping an escaped slave by providing food, shelter, or any form of assistance should be heavily fined and imprisoned.

The fact that a descendant of slaves is able to write these words today, and the fact that attitudes toward mixed-race children have changed so much since the era when a few drops of African American blood could condemn a child to slavery, are proof that progress does happen. But this progress did not happen by itself. It requires struggle. Frederick Douglass said:

> If there is no struggle, there is no progress. Those who profess to favor freedom, and yet depreciate agitation, are men who want crops without plowing up the ground. They want rain without thunder and lightning. They want the ocean without the awful roar of its many waters. This struggle may be a moral one; or it may be a physical one; or it may be both moral and physical; but it must be a struggle. Power concedes nothing without a demand. It never did, and it never will.[7]

One of the most effective forms of struggle is the *art of waging peace*, which was successfully used by Frederick Douglass, Susan B. Anthony, Mahatma Gandhi, Martin Luther King Jr., Wangari Maathai, and many others. Waging peace applies pressure through protests, boycotts, and other democratic means. Waging peace also attacks ignorance and hatred at their root in order to transform how people think for the better.

Two hundred years ago women could not vote, own property, or go to college, and those who advocated women's rights were ridiculed and threatened for challenging the oppression of women. American women did not gain these rights by fighting a war. Instead, they waged peace during the women's rights movement. And although the American Civil War kept our country together, African Americans did not truly gain their human rights until they waged peace during the civil rights movement.

Unjust policies are always supported by inaccurate beliefs. For example, American opposition to women's right to vote was supported by the inaccurate belief that women are intellectually and morally inferior to men. As long as the vast majority of Americans believed in women's intellectual and moral inferiority, it was easy to think women would endanger society if allowed to vote, own property, and go to college. Slavery in America was supported by the inaccurate belief that African Americans are subhuman, born to be slaves, and happy being slaves. As long as the vast majority of Americans believed that black people were racially inferior, it was easy to view them as objects with no human rights.

People have had many different kinds of inaccurate beliefs. For most of human history the majority of people believed the world was flat and the sun revolved around the earth. These people were not stupid, but had based their views on the information most readily available to them at the time. Just as people had inaccurate beliefs about our external universe, most people today have inaccurate beliefs about our internal universe—the human condition. Again, these people are not stupid, but have based their views on the information most readily available to them right now. If we do not offer people accurate information about the human condition in a way that appeals to a variety of worldviews, we cannot solve problems such as war, injustice, oppression, environmental destruction, and trauma.

A widespread view today is the inaccurate belief that human beings are naturally violent. This book offers abundant evidence to show that human beings are *not* naturally violent. Furthermore, this book explores the hidden causes of violence.

In my other books I write extensively about the many causes of violence; this book identifies additional causes and provides more insights into curing the virus of violence. When someone gets malaria, cancer, or HIV, I have never heard anyone say, "Oh, that's just human nature," because people realize something has gone wrong within the human body. But if someone becomes violent, people often say, "Oh, that's just human nature," which assumes that violence is an essential part of being human (like eating and sleeping), rather than the result of something that has gone wrong. But what if violence, like an illness, has a cause that we can understand and prevent? This book will offer abundant evidence to support this claim.

Today it is common knowledge that war traumatizes the human brain. This is so noncontroversial that even pro-war people now say war is hell. But if human beings were naturally violent, why would war traumatize the human brain, and why wouldn't people go to war and become more mentally healthy? If human beings were naturally violent, why would raising a child in a peaceful and loving environment be good for the human brain, and why would raising a child in a violent and abusive environment be bad for the human brain?

This book will challenge the inaccurate beliefs about violence that prevent us from creating a more peaceful world. Injustice benefits from the inaccurate belief that human beings are naturally violent, because if violence is as much a part of our nature as eating and sleeping, then I can look at gang violence among impoverished youth and say, "That's just their human nature. It's natural for them to murder each other. There's nothing I can do about it, so why should I care?"

But what if human beings are *not* naturally violent? If violence is not an essential part of being human like eating and sleeping, but is more like an illness that occurs when something has gone wrong, then we can proactively do something about the causes of violence. Just as preventable problems such as malnutrition and lack of clean water can cause physical illness, preventable problems such as poverty, desperation, injustice, dehumanization, ignorance, bullying, and trauma can cause violent behavior.

According to Gary Slutkin, a medical doctor and founder of the program Cure Violence, which works to stop gang violence: "Violence is like the great infectious diseases of all history. We used to look at people with plague, leprosy, TB, as bad and evil people . . . What perpetuates violence can be as invisible today as the microorganisms of the past were."[8]

This book is part of The Road to Peace series, a seven-book series about waging peace, ending war, the art of living, and what it means to be human. As the fifth book in this series, *The Cosmic Ocean* provides new answers to big questions about violence, peace, trauma, joy, oppression, war, environmental destruction, spirituality, the human condition, and humanity's future. Just as inaccurate beliefs support unjust policies, realistic answers enable progress.

Like the other books in this series, *The Cosmic Ocean* shows how the road to peace is also the road *of* peace. In other words, the road that leads to peace is made of our dedicated efforts to wage peace. Because *The Cosmic Ocean* revisits a few of the central ideas from the other books, this book series can be read in any order. Each book journeys deeper into the human condition by expanding those central ideas in new directions and also introducing a lot of new content.

The Road to Peace book series journeys through dark places such as trauma, war, and racism, like passing through a foreboding cave, shadowy forest, or winding tunnel. But we will emerge on the other side with larger hope, stronger empathy, greater understanding, and practical tools we can use to improve our lives and communities. The stories in this book show how the brightest light shines in the deepest darkness, and how the answers human beings are searching for can be found in the darkest places of the human mind where many are afraid to enter.

## The Problem of Purpose

The military taught me a secret about the human condition that many people do not know. By learning this secret as a West Point cadet and active duty soldier, I clearly saw how Gandhi, Martin Luther King Jr., and other great peacemakers became so influential as leaders and visionaries. They also knew this secret.

Psychologist Erich Fromm described this secret when he wrote about how Sigmund Freud had been incorrect; Freud mistakenly believed that biological urges such as our desire for food and sex cause most human problems. Even today, I hear some people claim that most conflicts, wars, and injustices around the world are caused by human cravings for food and sex. According to them, if everyone had easy access to food, sex, and other physical comforts, humanity would live in peace.

But Erich Fromm had a more realistic understanding than Freud of our human problems, because he knew what the military, Gandhi, and King also knew. Fromm realized that when we have easy access to food and sex, our problems as human beings do not end. Instead, when these biological urges are easy to feed, our human problems truly begin.

For example, conquerors such as Alexander the Great and Napoleon had easy access to food and sex. Their motivations ran deeper than this, however, because although they had access to more food and sex than one person could possibly consume in a twenty-four-hour day, this could not stop them from conquering. In Europe and other parts of the world, many kings and even queens also became obsessed with conquering, despite having easy access to food, sex, and other physical comforts.

The U.S. military, Mahatma Gandhi, Martin Luther King Jr., and Erich Fromm all taught me a secret about the human condition. The secret is that our greatest human problems do not result from biological cravings for food and sex, but our search for purpose and meaning. The craving for purpose and meaning, more than any physical craving, drives people to conquer, to become fanatics, to produce great art, to feel alienated and alone, to suffer from addiction, to descend into madness, and to commit suicide. Erich Fromm explained:

Even if man's hunger and thirst and his sexual strivings are completely satisfied "he" is not satisfied. In contrast to the animal his most compelling problems are not
solved then, they only begin. He strives for power, or for
love, or for destruction, he risks his life for religious, for
political, for humanistic ideals, and these strivings are what
constitutes and characterizes the peculiarity of human life.
Indeed, "man does not live by bread alone."[9]

The saying "man does not live by bread alone" is from the Bible, found
in the book of Deuteronomy and the Gospel of Matthew. Jesus says, "Man
shall not live on bread alone, but on every word that comes from the mouth
of God."[10] Although this saying has been interpreted in different ways, its
core message expresses a basic truth about the human condition that religious
people and atheists can both agree upon. This truth is that food alone is not
enough to satisfy a human being, because we have other needs. Some people
call these religious needs. Others call these spiritual needs. And some call
these psychological needs. But whatever we call them, these needs include
*humanity's craving for purpose and meaning.*

The *McGraw-Hill Dictionary of American Idioms and Phrasal Verbs* says
"man does not live by bread alone" is a proverb that means that "in order to
survive, people need more than physical things like food and shelter; people
need mental or spiritual things like satisfaction and love."[11] The McGraw-
Hill dictionary also illustrates the meaning of this proverb through a dialogue
between two people:

Alan: I'm so miserable.
Jill: How can you be miserable? You've got a good place to
live, plenty to eat, nice clothes . . .
Alan: But man does not live by bread alone.[12]

At West Point I learned that effective leaders provide people with purpose and meaning, because the human condition causes us to crave purpose
and meaning like plants crave sunlight and water. If people are given a deep

sense of purpose and meaning, they will work hard and even willingly die for a cause. Throughout history countless people have died for causes that give them purpose and meaning, such as their freedom, family, country, religion, and ideals such as democracy. Gandhi and Martin Luther King Jr. died for peace and justice, while many soldiers and activists died struggling for the rights and freedom of others.

The more I thought about it, the more I realized this secret was common sense. Human beings, no matter what racial or religious background they come from, want a reason to get out of bed in the morning. They want their work to be rewarding. They want life experiences that give them emotional fulfillment. They want to feel that their existence matters. And they want to feel connected to something larger than themselves, whether it is their friends, family, country, planet, God, a mission, or an ideal. They want something worth living for, and even something worth dying for.

We can better understand humanity's craving for purpose and meaning by exploring the story of Sisyphus from Greek mythology. Sisyphus had been condemned to hell, which was called Tartarus in Greek mythology. The book *Mythology*, edited by C. Scott Littleton, describes Tartarus, where people who committed evil and many of the Titans who rebelled against Zeus were tortured for eternity:

> The real terror that assailed the dying was the thought of being condemned to take the road to Tartarus, increasingly thought of as the destination of sinners. Tartarus was a pit so deep that it was said that an anvil dropped from Earth would take nine or ten days to reach the bottom. Much of it was in total darkness. Within its bounds, wrong-doers faced eternity under the worst torments. One was Ixion, who had killed his future father-in-law, then tried to carry off Zeus's own wife; his fate was to be stretched forever on a wheel of fire . . . Sisyphus, who had seized his brother's throne and betrayed Zeus's secrets, had to keep pushing a huge boulder up a steep hill, only to see it roll down each time he neared the top . . .

Tartarus's horrors endured in a long lineage of colorful accounts. They were described by the Roman poet Virgil in the first century BC. Thirteen hundred years later, Virgil's poetic vision was in Dante's mind when he wrote his *Inferno*, although by then Tartarus had been subsumed into Christian notions of hell.[13]

In the *Odyssey*, written by the Greek poet Homer nearly three thousand years ago, the warrior Odysseus sees Sisyphus in Tartarus. Homer's description of Sisyphus gives us important insights into the human condition:

> And I saw Sisyphus too, bound to his own torture, grappling his monstrous boulder with both arms working, heaving, hands struggling, legs driving, he kept on thrusting the rock uphill toward the brink, but just as it teetered, set to topple over—time and again the immense weight of the thing would wheel it back and the ruthless boulder would bound and tumble down to the plain again—so once again he would heave, would struggle to thrust it up, sweat drenching his body, dust swirling above his head.[14]

Greek mythology is filled with brilliant metaphors, and the punishments in Tartarus reveal that the Greeks knew some important truths about psychology and the human condition. They knew that torture could consist not only of extreme pain inflicted on the body, but also the loss of all purpose and meaning. Sisyphus experiences hell not because of the strain he feels from pushing the heavy boulder uphill, but the sense of futility he feels when the boulder refuses to go over the top of the hill, rolling back downhill despite his best efforts. His repetitive actions serve no purpose. They have no meaning, and all of his work seems in vain. Imagine struggling with every ounce of your strength to push a boulder uphill, only to see it roll back downhill, and repeating this meaningless cycle for eternity. You would go insane.

Victor Frankl, a psychiatrist and Holocaust survivor who was imprisoned at the Nazi concentration camp Auschwitz, realized that finding purpose and meaning is important not only for our sanity, but also our survival. Rabbi Harold S. Kushner described Frankl's contribution to our understanding of the human condition:

> Frankl approvingly quotes the words of Nietzsche: "He who has a Why to live for can bear almost any How." He describes poignantly those prisoners [in Auschwitz] who gave up on life, who had lost all hope for a future and were inevitably the first to die. They died less from lack of food or medicine than from lack of hope, lack of something to live for. By contrast, Frankl kept himself alive and kept hope alive by summoning up thoughts of his wife and the prospect of seeing her again, and by dreaming at one point of lecturing after the war about the psychological lessons to be learned from the Auschwitz experience. Clearly, many prisoners who desperately wanted to live did die, some from disease, some in the crematoria. But Frankl's concern is less with the question of why most died than it is with the question of why anyone at all survived.
>
> Terrible as it was, his experience in Auschwitz reinforced what was already one of his key ideas: Life is not primarily a quest for pleasure, as Freud believed, or a quest for power, as Alfred Adler taught, but a quest for meaning. The greatest task for any person is to find meaning in his or her life. Frankl saw three possible sources for meaning: in work (doing something significant), in love (caring for another person), and in courage during difficult times. Suffering in and of itself is meaningless; we give our suffering meaning by the way in which we respond to it . . .

My own congregational experience has shown me the truth of Frankl's insights. I have known successful businessmen who, upon retirement, lost all zest for life. Their work had given their lives meaning. Often it was the only thing that had given their lives meaning and, without it,

they spent day after day sitting at home, depressed, "with
nothing to do." I have known people who rose to the challenge of enduring the most terrible afflictions and situations as long as they believed there was a point to their
suffering . . . Having a Why to live for enabled them to
bear the How.[15]

Discussing his experiences as a prisoner at Auschwitz, Frankl explained
how prisoners who found purpose and meaning in the midst of suffering were
better able to endure the tremendous hardship of the concentration camp:

Nietzsche's words, "He who has a *why* to live for can
bear with almost any *how*," could be the guiding motto
. . . regarding prisoners. Whenever there was an opportunity for it, one had to give them a why—an aim—for their
lives, in order to strengthen them to bear the terrible *how*
of their existence. Woe to him who saw no more sense in
his life, no aim, no purpose, and therefore no point in carrying on. He was soon lost.[16]

When suffering has no purpose and meaning (which is symbolized by
the psychological torture of Sisyphus in Tartarus), it feels like a senseless hell.
But when we find meaning in our suffering, we can "bear the cross" with
courage and dignity. Christian philosophy teaches that suffering becomes
redemptive when it serves a high moral purpose. This is symbolized by Jesus,
whom many Christians believe was able to carry the cross despite its heavy
weight, because he knew his suffering was for the benefit of humanity.

Gandhi applied this to leadership by giving people a purpose for their
suffering. In *The Art of Waging Peace*, I explain how Gandhi was more strategically brilliant and innovative than any general I have ever studied. In his
struggle against colonialism, he used nonviolent tactics such as protests, boycotts, and "going to prison for a just cause" to undermine the authority of
the British Empire—the most powerful empire in the world.

Throughout human history, people have dreaded going to prison.

Because Gandhi had an ingenious understanding of the human condition, however, he realized people will voluntarily suffer if they know it serves an important purpose. How incredible was Gandhi's leadership ability? He was the first leader in history who motivated tens of thousands of people to *want* to go to prison. Gandhi did not even pay these people. Unlike presidents and generals, Gandhi had no official authority, instead having to rely on his moral authority.

Gandhi motivated people to voluntarily suffer for a cause by first leading by example (he spent many years in prison himself), and by giving them a noble purpose they felt strongly about. Gandhi scholar Michael Nojeim describes how Gandhi's understanding of the human condition allowed him to transform prison from something people dreaded into something they desired:

> Ordinarily, going to jail was supposed to be a shameful, peril-riddled experience that no self-respecting Hindu, and surely not one from Gandhi's social status, could ever imagine or countenance. But Gandhi changed all that because he was able to convince other Indians that going to jail while fighting for a just cause could be a point of honor and even prestige. He made going to jail "the hallmark of integrity and national commitment rather than an experience of degradation and public shame" (Brown, 1989, 117). Moreover, Indians having served time in jail for taking principled, nonviolent stances often increased their political stock among their nationalist brethren, which added to their qualifications to become high-ranking members of the Indian Congress Party . . .
> Gandhi's repeated incarcerations in South Africa (in 1908, 1909, and 1913) for conducting civil disobedience campaigns provided an excellent training ground for other reasons. He learned to court and face prison sentences with pride and resilience and for the sake of conscience.[17]

Describing how Gandhi's leadership transformed perceptions in Indian society, Narayan Desai discusses how he reacted when his father—who served as Gandhi's secretary—was arrested by the police:

> A batch of policemen came to arrest my father, and some of us young children were following the police van and instead of saying "Bye bye papa" or something like that, I was telling him, "Papa, this time no less than two years," which means I want you to be in prison for no less than two years. You see, it was a [source of] pride to have your father sentenced for two years and not for three months or so. So Gandhi's idea is what had touched even the children in that atmosphere.[18]

Applying Gandhi's tactics and understanding of the human condition to the civil rights movement, Martin Luther King Jr. gave many people a high sense of purpose and meaning that motivated them to confront physical danger, go to prison, and even die for their cause. Civil rights leader and congressman John Lewis, who was beaten and imprisoned as a young activist during the civil rights movement, said, "Growing up in the rural South, it was not the thing to do . . . to go to jail. It was bringing shame and disgrace on the family. But for me, I tell you, it was like being involved in a holy crusade. It became a badge of honor."[19]

Civil rights leaders knew that when people have a high sense of purpose and meaning, they become stronger when facing a variety of dangerous situations, such as being kidnapped. Civil rights leader Bernard Lafayette said the movement taught people that "in order to remain strong during a kidnap situation, you must maintain a clear sense of purpose in life, and have a motto that states what your life means or some particular value that you have chosen."[20]

The U.S. military teaches the same thing. Soldiers are required to learn the Code of Conduct, which states: "I am an American, fighting in the forces which guard my country and our way of life. I am prepared to give my life in their defense . . . If I become a prisoner of war, I will keep faith with my fellow prisoners . . . I will never forget that I am an American, fighting for freedom, responsible for my actions, and dedicated to the principles which made my country free."[21]

Of course, being kidnapped or becoming a prisoner of war are terrible situations that can break even the strongest minds after a prolonged period of time, but the more purpose and meaning people have, the longer it can take for them to be broken. As Victor Frankl said in the earlier quote, "Woe to him who saw no more sense in his life, no aim, no purpose, and therefore no point in carrying on. He was soon lost."[22]

Just as food and water can nourish and strengthen our body, purpose and meaning can nourish and strengthen our mind. Victor Frankl referred to our craving for purpose and meaning as the "will to meaning." He realized people of all races and religions experience this kind of hunger, because it is part of our shared humanity. In a world where so many are starving for purpose and meaning, how can we best feed ourselves? According to Frankl, people often feed their craving for purpose and meaning with activities that are empty and unsatisfying, just as eating dirt does not satisfy our stomachs and drinking salt water does not satisfy our thirst.

Frankl realized that when we base our purpose and meaning entirely on greed, for example, it does not satisfy us as much as the psychological nutrition found in a life devoted to deep empathy and service to others. Frankl said, "Sometimes the frustrated will to meaning is vicariously compensated for by a will to power, including the most primitive form of the will to power, the will to money. In other cases, the place of frustrated will to meaning is taken by the will to pleasure."[23]

In this book I show how empathy is a powerful source of psychological nutrition, capable of satisfying our craving for purpose and meaning in ways few other things can. I also discuss what happens when the will to meaning collides with the storm of childhood trauma, like a ship caught in a ferocious hurricane. Furthermore, this book questions much of what we have been told about happiness. What if happiness is not the absence of struggle—as I have often heard—but finding purpose and meaning in our struggle? What if a struggle that gives us a deep sense of purpose and meaning is more fulfilling and rewarding than a life that lacks meaningful struggle?

Bernard Lafayette said, "Martin Luther King Jr. believed voluntary suffering builds character."[24] The U.S. military and many of the world's greatest religious and philosophical traditions teach the same thing. Realizing that struggle can strengthen the human mind, Nietzsche said a person can cultivate an attitude toward life where "that which does not kill him makes him stronger."[25]

This book will address many of the questions people have about happiness, while debunking common misconceptions. For example, people often associate smiling with happiness. Although people certainly smile when interacting with those they care about, people usually do not smile when engaged in an activity they love. How often do you see professional athletes smile when they are deep in concentration and completely focused? None of the great violinists perform while grinning ear to ear. If they smile at all while performing it is rare. This is because when human beings are deep in concentration, when they are "in the zone," they almost never smile.

During a *60 Minutes* interview, the father of world chess champion Magnus Carlsen told journalist Bob Simon how much his son enjoys chess. Since Carlsen almost never smiles while playing chess, Simon reacted with surprise and said, "When I look at him, enjoyment is not the word that comes to mind." Carlsen's father responded, "It should. Maybe you have to compare it to a writer or a painter. Probably if you see them at work, they are not smiling or having an easy time. They are exploiting their mind to the utmost, and the same with the chess players."[26]

In addition to gaining a deeper understanding of joy and suffering, perhaps the most important tool I have gained from exploring the human condition is the ability to increase my empathy for all human beings. In order to build our empathy for humanity, the first step is recognizing what we have in common with all people, regardless of their racial or religious background.

For all people, working for something feels fulfilling when it gives us purpose and meaning. And all people can feel hurt and even betrayed when what they worked for loses its purpose and meaning. When Al Qaida captured the Iraqi city Fallujah in 2014 after the withdrawal of American forces, a U.S. Marine staff sergeant, whose comrades died so that American forces could gain control of Fallujah in 2004, explained his reaction: "It brings back a lot of anger . . . I feel like it's been a big waste of time. It's kind of like, why the hell did my buddies die there for? *There's no purpose to it* [emphasis added]."[27]

When I learned that we all crave purpose and meaning, it became easier for me to find common ground with people, whether they call themselves liberals or conservatives, whether they are fellow American citizens or fellow citizens of the world. We are all vulnerable to the problem of finding purpose in our lives. We are all searching for meaning, and many of us remain psychologically and spiritually starved. The following chapters will offer more insights into the human condition, revealing other aspects of our shared humanity that can further expand our empathy.

Cynicism can interfere with empathy. Today it has become trendy to trash-talk humanity. It has become fashionable to say in a cynical tone, "Humanity sucks. We are like a cancer upon the earth. We are a stupid, inherently violent, and bad species." But the following chapters will explain why I respect and love humanity, despite the traumatic upbringing that has given me reasons to hate the entire human race. When we derive purpose and meaning from nutritious sources such as empathy, we can all find reasons to respect and love humanity.

But what happens when we are unable to find purpose and meaning in our lives? What happens when we feel like Sisyphus day after day, and this emptiness lasts year after year? When this happens we will either "lead lives of quiet desperation"[28] as philosopher Henry David Thoreau said, or self-destruct and likely hurt others in the process.

The road to peace leads away from desperation and destruction. As we journey together on the road to peace in the following chapters, we will explore the deepest mysteries of the human condition and the universe we inhabit, searching for answers, finding light in storms and darkness.

# PART I

# Our Primordial Past

# CHAPTER I

# A Dark Night Filled with Predators

## *Predators in the Home*

Long after a war has ended, it can cast a shadow not only in the minds of veterans, but also in the lives of their children. Growing up as an only child in Alabama, I have fond memories of being three years old and watching my father tend to his garden, feed the birds in our backyard, and chase away a spider that almost frightened me to death. But when I was four, everything changed.

I was sleeping peacefully late one night when I felt someone grab my leg and drag me from my bed onto the floor. My leg was pulled so hard I heard my pajama pants rip down the middle. Looking up and seeing my father, I began to panic as he pulled my hair and told me he was going to kill me. His cursing and my screaming woke my mother, who ran into the room and bear-hugged him until he finally calmed down.

When I was four something else occurred that I could not understand at the time, but that I later attributed to my father's war experiences. One evening I heard him screaming at my mother and threatening to shoot himself with his pistol. This was the first time I heard him threaten to commit suicide, but it would not be the last. Throughout my childhood, I watched my father lose his grip on reality, and his frightening behavior caused me to struggle with my own sanity. Rage overshadowed his once peaceful nature, and when I heard him complain about violent nightmares, I realized something called war had taken my gentle father from me.

During these early years, I internalized my father's despair and longed for an escape from his violent behavior. When I was five, this trauma led to my lifelong obsession with war and suffering—when I had a vivid dream that I killed myself. I still remember the dream clearly: I walked through the front door of my house, where I saw both my parents lying dead in coffins. Without thinking, I went to the bathroom cabinet with the intent of stabbing myself in the heart. I opened a drawer and saw a large pair of scissors, but their menacing size frightened me. Next to them, I saw a smaller pair of scissors that my mother used to clip my fingernails. I picked them up, stabbed myself in the chest, and watched as blood covered my hands. Then I walked to my mother's coffin and laid in it with her, where I waited to die so that my anguish would finally end.

What did this suicide dream mean? When I grew older, my need to understand its meaning caused me to question the nature of all dreams. As I explored my unconscious mind and read books on psychology, I learned that dreams communicate in an ancient language that predates English, Spanish, Latin, and even Sanskrit. This primordial language is not composed of nouns and verbs, but metaphors and symbols.

We have abundant evidence that our brains are hardwired to understand the language of metaphors and symbols. Metaphors are a common form of expression in every culture, and they are used all over the world in daily conversations. For example, if someone in America says, "We must get to the *root* of the problem,"* the metaphor of a root makes it easier for us to understand the meaning behind the words. By helping us visualize ideas in our mind, metaphors can also create a form of visual learning.

This is why Socrates, Aesop, Jesus, Buddha, Lao Tzu, and other great spiritual teachers used symbolic language (in the form of metaphors) to express complex philosophical ideas. Symbolic language can help us understand a wide variety of dangerous behaviors, such as arrogance and hypocrisy, which West Point taught me were two of the most dangerous traits a leader can have. When discussing hazards such as arrogance and hypocrisy it is easy to get lost in an abstract academic debate, but Aesop and Jesus were master teachers who used metaphors to make ethics easy to understand.

In the Aesop's fable The Tortoise and the Hare, a slow tortoise competes in a race against a much faster hare. Halfway through the race, the arrogant hare is so certain he will win that he decides to take a nap. Oversleeping, the hare wakes up in shock and hurries to the finish line, where the tortoise has

---

* There is a lot of overlap between metaphors, analogies, fables, parables, allegories, and idioms. "Root of the problem" is an idiom that contains a metaphor.

already won the race. Although this fable also contains lessons about per-
sistence and determination, the hare loses the race because of his arrogance.
At West Point I learned that arrogance caused the downfall of characters in
Greek mythology and Shakespearean tragedy. Furthermore, Alexander the
Great, Napoleon, and many other conquerors became victims of arrogance.

In addition to arrogance, hypocrisy is another dangerous characteristic
that causes leaders to harm themselves and those they are supposed to serve.
A hypocrite is someone who criticizes the vices of others while ignoring his
or her own vices. West Point taught me that hypocritical leaders are dangerous because they do not practice what they preach or lead by example. Jesus
described hypocrisy with a simple metaphor: "Why do you look at the speck
of sawdust in your brother's eye and pay no attention to the plank in your
own eye? How can you say to your brother, 'Let me take the speck out of
your eye,' when all the time there is a plank in your own eye? You hypocrite,
first take the plank out of your own eye, and then you will see clearly to
remove the speck from your brother's eye."[1]

Although the metaphors used by Aesop and Jesus may sound simple,
concepts such as arrogance and hypocrisy are complex ideas that help us ana-
lyze unethical behavior. Metaphors can make complex ideas sound simple
without oversimplifying them, and this is why humanity's great spiritual
teachers often communicated their wisdom through metaphors. When I
learned how to interpret my dreams metaphorically, I saw that they also contained wisdom. Our dreams become spiritual teachers when we know how
to read their metaphors. As I became a young adult, I realized that my childhood suicide dream contained a metaphor about something more dangerous
than arrogance and hypocrisy—the destructiveness of trauma.

Many people in our society do not realize how destructive trauma truly
is, and even psychologists can believe common misconceptions about
trauma. In an article written by Eric Jaffe for the Association for Psychological Science, I saw numerous misconceptions about trauma that often go
unnoticed. Here is an excerpt:

> [Psychologist George] Bonanno has demonstrated
> through statistical modeling that humans are actually quite
> resilient in the face of disastrous events. While disasters
> can cause major psychological trauma that can't be fixed
> with a quick and easy solution, over time most people
> demonstrate an impressive ability to rebound from a
> frightening incident . . .
> 	The most common response [to trauma] is actually
> resilience, Bonanno said. Roughly 35 to 65 percent of peo-
> ple who experience a disaster return to their normal rou-
> tine shortly after the event and stay there. A recent study
> of war veterans, for instance, not only demonstrated that
> roughly 7 percent of soldiers who were deployed devel-
> oped PTSD, but that 83 percent showed exemplary men-
> tal health in the face of potentially traumatic combat
> situations. Recent research has shown that resilience has
> also been the most common documented response to
> events such as a nightmare mudslide in Mexico or the 9/11
> attacks.[2]

Are people really as resilient to trauma as this article suggests? This short
excerpt contains many misconceptions about trauma. To explain these misconceptions, I have listed seven factors that increase the severity of trauma:

## 1. Cause

The article's first misconception is not distinguishing between different
causes of trauma. The article says, "Roughly 35 to 65 percent of people who
experience a disaster return to their normal routine *shortly after* [emphasis
added] the event and stay there." The article then discusses soldiers in war,
a mudslide in Mexico, and the September 11 attacks. However, a person's
ability to recover psychologically depends on the *cause* of the disaster, because
a disastrous event is far more traumatizing when caused by a human being.

For example, what is more traumatizing, falling off your bike and break-ing your leg or a group of attackers holding you down and breaking your leg with a baseball bat? Even though the physical outcome—a broken leg— is the same in both scenarios, harm inflicted on us by a human being is much more traumatizing than an injury resulting from an accident or natural dis-aster. What is more traumatizing, being a black family in the South and hav-ing your house burned down by a wildfire, or being a black family in the South and having your house burned down by the Ku Klux Klan? Even though the physical outcome—a destroyed house—is the same in both sce-narios, the Ku Klux Klan exceeds natural disasters in the ability to inflict psychological trauma on human beings.

If you and your family were hospitalized due to injuries caused by a tor-nado, it would be less traumatizing than a gang breaking into your house, tying up you and your family, and viciously beating you, your spouse, and children to the point where you all end up in the hospital. You might recover psychologically from a tornado after a few weeks, but it might take years or even your entire life to recover psychologically from the gang invasion sce-nario.[3]

In his groundbreaking book, *On Killing*, Lieutenant Colonel Dave Grossman tells us:

> The *Diagnostic and Statistical Manual of Mental Dis-orders* (*DSM-III-R*), the bible of psychology, states that in post-traumatic stress disorders "the disorder is apparently more severe and longer lasting when the stressor is of human design." We want desperately to be liked, loved, and in control of our lives; and intentional, overt, *human* hostility and aggression—more than anything else in life—assaults our self-image, our sense of control, our sense of the world as a meaningful and comprehensible place, and ultimately, our mental and physical health.
>
> The ultimate fear and horror in most modern lives is to be raped or beaten, to be physically degraded in front of our loved ones, to have our family harmed and the sanc-

tity of our homes invaded by aggressive and hateful intrud-
ers. Death and debilitation by disease or accident are statistically far more likely to occur than death and
debilitation by malicious action, but the statistics do not
calm our basically irrational fears. It is not fear of death
and injury from disease or accident but rather acts of personal depredation and domination by our fellow human
beings that strike terror and loathing in our hearts.

In rape the psychological harm usually far exceeds the
physical injury . . . far more damaging is the impotence,
shock, and horror in being so hated and despised as to be
debased and abused by a fellow human being.[4]

In fact, we are so vulnerable to human-induced trauma that a person
does not even have to physically touch us to traumatize us. A person can
harm our long-term psychological health by betraying us, humiliating us,
calling us a racial slur, spitting in our face, verbally abusing us, spreading
malicious rumors about us, and even shunning us. Many people would prefer to break their leg in an accident rather than be publically humiliated or
betrayed by those closest to them. People crave nurturing relationships,* and
abusive relationships are a significant source of trauma.

In 2013 I attended a nonviolence workshop with participants from
many countries. To help us understand the differences and similarities
between our various cultures, the workshop organizers had us break into
small groups and discuss how our culture responds to the death of a loved
one. All of the participants in my group said that when a relative dies, the
person's life is remembered and celebrated with compassion.

I interjected, "But doesn't it depend on the cause of the person's death? If
a grandmother dies of old age, the funeral might be a celebration of the person's
life, but what if a family member is kidnapped, tortured, and murdered?
Doesn't that tend to be more difficult to celebrate and far more traumatic for
the family? What if a loved one is killed in a terrorist attack? Some people may

---

* Low self-worth, which I discuss later in this book, can cause people to get stuck in a cycle of
abusive relationships. Low self-worth can cause us to look for characteristics in relationships that
are abusive rather than nurturing.

react to the death not with compassion, but with a desire for revenge."

This changed the nature of the discussion. We began to talk about how most people—regardless of their race, religion, or nationality—would be devastated if a loved one was kidnapped, tortured, and murdered. This helped us see our shared humanity, and how the violent death of a family member can traumatize people regardless of whether they are American, Vietnamese, Japanese, British, Russian, Iraqi, or Iranian.

War propaganda often tells us that people in other countries don't love their children or value human life.* General Westmoreland, who commanded U.S. military forces in Vietnam, said, "The Oriental doesn't put the same high price on life as does a Westerner . . . Life is cheap in the Orient. As the philosophy of the Orient expresses it, life is not important."[5] To see this propaganda refuted, a useful place to start is the film *Hearts and Minds*, which won the Academy Award for best documentary feature in 1974. By understanding trauma and our shared humanity, we can all work to refute the illusions of war propaganda.

Trauma will be more severe if we see any human being as the cause of the traumatic event, even if the human being is ourselves. If a family member dies in an accident and we blame ourselves for the accident, the trauma will be more severe because forgiving ourselves can be as difficult as forgiving another person. When we blame ourselves for a tragedy or feel like we should have suffered instead of the victims, this is known as survivor's guilt.

People can experience survivor's guilt when someone is hurt or killed by a natural disaster, illness, accident, animal attack, or human attack. When any tragedy occurs, survivor's guilt can be very difficult to overcome. Many soldiers who survive a war blame themselves for the deaths of their comrades, and survivor's guilt can be so painful that many people wish they could die and take the place of their deceased loved one.

---

* Later in this book I discuss some of the reasons that can cause people in any country to sacrifice their children to a government or god.

## 2. Intimacy

The article's second misconception is not taking into account how intimate the violence is. In his book *On Killing*, Grossman says most of the people who survived the London bombings in World War II have less psychological trauma (because the violence was less personal and intimate) than those who were beaten and tortured in Nazi concentration camps:

> Those in concentration camps had to face aggression and death on a highly personal, face-to-face basis. Nazi Germany placed a remarkable concentration of aggressive psychopaths in charge of these camps . . . [Journalist and historian Gwynne] Dyer tells us that concentration camps were staffed, whenever possible, with "both male and female thugs and sadists." Unlike the victims of aerial bombing, the victims of these camps had to look their sadistic killers in the face and know that another human being denied their humanity and hated them enough to personally slaughter them, their families, and their race as though they were nothing more than animals.
>
> During strategic bombing the pilots and bombardiers were protected by distance and could deny to themselves that they were attempting to kill any specific individual. In the same way, civilian bombing victims were protected by distance, and they could deny that anyone was personally trying to kill them . . . But in the death camps it was starkly, horribly personal. Victims of this horror had to look the darkest, most loathsome depths of human hatred in the eye. There was no room for denial, and the only escape was more madness.[6]

The article I quoted earlier seems to underestimate the harm caused by trauma, because it does not take into account more intimate forms of trauma such as being beaten, raped, and tortured. The article says, "A recent study of war veterans, for instance, not only demonstrated that roughly 7 percent of soldiers who were deployed developed PTSD, but that 83 percent showed exemplary mental health in the face of potentially traumatic combat situations." However, the article does not mention that most veterans of modern war have never been in combat, and that the violence soldiers experience in war can vary widely. As I explain later in this book, if a group of soldiers were forced to commit extremely intimate violence, such as massacring children they know at close range, the rate of trauma among the soldiers would be much higher than 7 percent.

## 3. Age

The article's third misconception is not taking into account the age of the person experiencing the trauma. An adult's brain is more resilient to trauma than a child's brain, especially if the adult had a healthy and loving childhood. Psychiatrist Bruce Perry describes a common misconception about childhood trauma that was widespread when he began working with abused children in the 1980s, and how this misconception persists today:

> Unfortunately, the prevailing view of children and trauma at the time—one that persists to a large degree to this day—is that "children are resilient." . . . If anything, children are more vulnerable to trauma than adults . . . The developing brain is most malleable and most sensitive to experience—both good and bad—early in life. (This is why we so easily and rapidly learn language, social nuance, motor skills and dozens of other things in childhood, and why we speak of "formative" experiences.) . . . Consequently, we are also rapidly and easily transformed by trauma when we are young. Though its effects may not always be visible to the untrained eye, when you know what trauma can do to children, sadly, you begin to see its aftermath everywhere.[7]

## 4. Helplessness

The article's fourth misconception is not taking into account how helpless the traumatic event makes a person feel. What is more traumatizing, successfully defending yourself against two knife-wielding attackers but getting slashed across your face as you frighten them away, or two knife-wielding attackers holding you down and cutting your face as you remain completely helpless to stop them? Even though the physical outcome—a permanent scar on your face—is the same in both scenarios, the feeling of being empowered to protect yourself is far more desirable than the feeling of being completely helpless.

There are also varying degrees of helplessness. If a man's wife is raped and murdered while he is not at home, that can certainly be traumatic for him. But if the man is tied up and forced to watch someone rape and murder his wife while he remains completely helpless to protect her, he would probably experience more severe trauma. In war zones there have been instances where parents were forced to watch soldiers rape their children, and children were forced to watch soldiers rape their parents.

Jocelyn Kelly, director of the Women in War program at the Harvard Humanitarian Initiative, describes the trauma caused by the ongoing war in the Democratic Republic of the Congo:

> Perhaps nowhere in the world is rape as public as it is in DRC [Democratic Republic of the Congo]. In many cases, family members are forced to watch, and sometimes forced to participate in, the rape of a wife, sister or mother. Other times, rapes are carried out in public areas where neighbors and community leaders can see. This creates family- and community-wide trauma, just as it is intended to do. Husbands feel helpless as they are unable to stop the attack and children see that their parents are powerless to protect them . . .
>
> Couples that do stay together [after the rape] still face deep-seated trauma and cycles of blame and shame within

the home. Some men may use drugs and alcohol or per-petrate physical violence against family members as [a] result of their own trauma . . . In eastern DRC, children are often the first to suffer the effects of war. Not only are children the direct victims of sexual violence, but they are also often forced to witness horrific acts of violence against family members. Cycles of violence emerge as children who have been deeply traumatized by violence join armed groups, street gangs or live on the street because their family networks cannot support them.[8]

Human beings do not like feeling completely helpless, preferring to have some control over their lives. When children are physically or sexually abused by an adult, the feeling of being a helpless child who is too weak to resist the adult can have negative psychological consequences that last for a long time. Helplessness by itself is often an uncomfortable experience, and when a high degree of helplessness is combined with a traumatic human attack, it can cause psychological wounds that do not heal easily.

## 5. Unpredictability and Period of Time

The article's fifth misconception is not taking into account the kinds of trauma that occur unpredictably over a long period of time. I know some people who were spanked a few times by a parent, yet they do not show obvious signs of trauma. The way my father attacked me was far different from spanking. An army psychiatrist told me that in addition to sexual abuse, the most traumatic experience a parent can inflict on children is to "subject them to violent and out of control attacks in an unpredictable way over a long period of time." According to this army psychiatrist, children who grow up in an unpredictably violent household have symptoms similar to trau-matized war veterans.

Unlike a controlled spanking, when my father attacked me he would become so enraged that he seemed completely out of control. He would sometimes threaten to kill me, and during the worst beatings my mother had to restrain him to stop his assault. I remember my mother yelling at him, "If you keep hitting him in the head, you are going to give him brain damage!" When my father beat me to the point where I feared for my life, the size difference between me and him was truly terrifying. Imagine being beaten up by a man who is ten feet tall. That is how I felt as a child when my six-foot-tall father was stomping on me.

Although my father often made me fear for my life, this terror was magnified by the unpredictable nature of his attacks. Sometimes I would make a serious mistake (such as getting in trouble at school for having behavioral problems) and he would not punish me. On other occasions he would attack me for making a very small mistake or when I did not make a mistake. Sometimes he would assault me in the middle of the night when I was sleeping. When these unpredictable attacks occur over a long period of time throughout most of someone's childhood, it can rewire the brain in dangerous ways that I will discuss throughout this book.

According to psychiatrist Daniel Siegel, "When an attachment figure [such as a parent] is the source of terror, the child's brain has two processes going on at once. One is the inborn attachment system which says, 'I am in a state of alarm. I need to go to my attachment figure for soothing.' But if that attachment figure *is the source* of the distress, and I don't just mean being upset and you don't get ice-cream before dinner, I mean *terror*, then what happens is . . . another track in the child's brain will state, 'Do not go to that figure. That is the cause of your distress.'"[9]

What happens when a child's brain experiences the confusion described by Dr. Siegel? When the people who are supposed to protect us make us fear for our lives, it can rupture our ability to trust not only them, but all human beings.

## 6. Rupturing of Trust

The article's sixth misconception is not taking into account the forms of trauma that rupture our trust in human beings. A traumatic event that damages our ability to trust human beings will increase the severity of our trauma, because we all want to be around people we can trust. Even Adolf Hitler wanted to be around people he could trust. Nobody ever says, "One quality I value in a friend, spouse, boss, coworker, or employee is betrayal. I love being around people I can't trust." One of the most painful events we can experience in our fragile human existence is betrayal.

Why can betrayal be so devastating to our psychological well-being? Human beings are social creatures who rely on cooperation to survive, but true cooperation cannot exist without trust. When we lose our ability to trust human beings, we can feel like we are going insane. Paranoia is often associated with insanity, but what does it mean to be paranoid? Psychiatrist Jonathan Shay, the author of *Achilles in Vietnam*, says paranoia can be best understood as "the inability to trust human beings."[10]

The ability to trust human beings is crucial to both our psychological health and survival as a species. Zebras don't trust lions who hunt them, but imagine what would happen if zebras lost the ability to trust other zebras. Bees don't trust bears who want their honey, but imagine what would happen if bees perceived every other bee in their hive as a threat. What would happen if wolves lost the ability to trust the members of their own pack, and elephants could no longer trust the members of their own herd?

Countless species must deal with their fear of predators, but human beings are the only species that contend with predators in their homes, in the form of family members who are supposed to protect us but instead make us fear for our lives. Nadine Burke Harris, founder and CEO of Center for Youth Wellness, described how this contributes to behavioral problems in school when Ira Glass interviewed her on National Public Radio:

> If you look on the molecular level, you're walking through the forest and you see a bear, right? So you can either fight the bear or run from the bear. That's kind of your fight or flight system . . . And that's really good if you're in a forest and there's a bear. The problem is when that bear comes home from the bar every night. Right? And for a lot of these kids, what happens is that this

system, this fight or flight response, which is an emergency response in your body, it's activated over and over and over again. And so that's what we were seeing in the kids that I was caring for . . .

[If a teacher asks a student living in a violent household], "Oh, could you please diagram this sentence? Or could you please divide two complex numbers?" You'd be like, what are you talking about? And so that's what we were seeing in the kids that I was caring for, is that a lot of them had a terrible time paying attention. They have a hard time sitting still . . . For our kids, if they had four or more adverse childhood experiences, their odds of having learning or behavior problems in school was 32 times as high as kids who had no adverse childhood experiences.[11]

Ira Glass added:

When the brain does something over and over and over again, it creates pathways that get more and more ingrained. So this kind of repeated stress affects the development of these kids' brains. And especially affected in this situation is a specific part of the brain that's called the prefrontal cortex, which is where a lot of these non-cognitive skills happen—self-control and impulse control, certain kinds of memory and reasoning. Skills they call executive functions.

If you're in a constant state of emergency, that part of your brain just doesn't develop the same. Doctors can see the differences on brain scans. Dr. Burke Harris says that for these kids, the bear basically never goes away. They still feel its effects even when they're just trying to sit there quietly in English class . . . And you hear about this in lots of schools. Head Start teachers in one survey said that over a fourth of their low income students had serious self-control and behavior problems. Nadine Burke Harris says that it's true for her patients, the ones with adverse childhood experiences like neglect, domestic violence, a parent with mental illness or substance abuse.[12]

Like many children who grow up in unpredictably violent households, I had serious behavioral problems as a child in school. I had great difficulty paying attention to the teacher, concentrating, and controlling my impulses. I was kicked out of elementary school for behavioral problems, almost kicked out of middle school for similar reasons, and suspended in high school for fighting. I actually love to learn; I just hated school. When a child is miserable and terrified at home, these feelings do not go away just because the child is at school.

In high school I did well on the SAT and had good enough grades to get accepted into West Point, but my behavioral problems as a student did not go away just because I left my parents' house. At West Point I still had problems concentrating and paying attention to the teacher. My mind was often lost in daydreams while the teacher was talking, and sometimes an entire class period went by without me listening to anything the teacher said. Instead of doing my homework at West Point, I read books on philosophy that had nothing to do with my classes, hoping to find answers to my agony. My grades suffered because of this, but not as much as I suffered.

## 7. Lack of a Support Network

The seventh factor that increases the severity of trauma is *lack of a support network*. Although the excerpt I quoted from Eric Jaffe's article contains numerous misconceptions about trauma, later in his article he skillfully addresses how the presence of a support network can reduce trauma. He says, "Silvia Koller of Rio Grande do Sul Federal University in Brazil, studies the concept of resilience as it applies to her native country . . . [Koller and her colleagues found that] promoting these positive social elements might increase resilience even among a very disadvantaged population."[13]

To better understand how a support network can counterbalance trauma, let's consider animal attacks. When a child is severely bitten by just one dog, that child may develop a fear of all dogs that lasts for many years. A Rottweiler bit me when I was twenty-one, and although twelve years have passed since then (I am thirty-three as I write this), I still get a little nervous around big dogs. In a similar way, when we are violently attacked by just one human being, this can damage our ability to trust all human beings.

However, if we have positive experiences with many other dogs, this can counterbalance the negative experience of being bitten, just as having many loving and trustworthy human beings in our life can counterbalance the trauma caused by those who hurt us. I call these people *counterbalancers* because their positive influence can counterbalance the negative effects of trauma. A counterbalancer can be a relative, coach, teacher, neighbor, or friend.

Counterbalancers create a support network and provide nurturing relationships. When they do not exist in a traumatized person's life, the trauma becomes much more severe. A support network does not have to consist of many people, because sometimes the presence of just one loving and trustworthy person can have a significant positive impact on someone suffering from trauma.

The following diagram illustrates the seven factors that increase the severity of trauma:

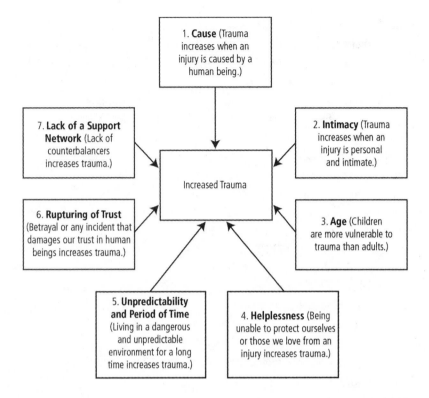

Figure 1.1:  Seven Factors That Increase Trauma

Because my father ruptured my ability to trust human beings, I have difficulty trusting all people. If my father—the man who was supposed to protect me—could beat me to the point where I feared for my life, who could I really trust? Someone once asked me, "Your father hurt you, but he is just one person. How can you let one man influence your perception of all human beings?"

I responded, "Toward the end of elementary school, my father stopped letting me visit with friends, and as a child I had very little contact with extended family and neighbors. My father did not socialize with people because his trauma caused him to view everyone around him as a threat, so my social group growing up was mostly just two people—my parents. How could I trust my father when he threatened to kill me, and how could I trust my mother when she could not protect me? When the only two people closest to you make you feel unsafe, it can affect how you see all human beings." Later in this book I will discuss the counterbalancers I met much later in my life, and how a lack of human counterbalancers during my childhood reduced my resilience to trauma, allowing trauma to shape my brain in dangerous ways. George Bonanno's research into people's resilience to traumatic events is useful, because he shows that natural disasters and illnesses are not as traumatizing as the harm caused by human beings. Bonanno may never have intended for his research to result in inaccurate generalizations about resilience to all forms of trauma, but it is important that I clear up these misconceptions, because a society that does not understand trauma is at great risk.

However, I must emphasize that people can still experience trauma, even if their trauma does not contain all seven factors in the diagram shown. No matter what kind of trauma we are experiencing, there are helpful and harmful ways to acknowledge it. It is harmful to let our trauma trap us in a "helpless victim mentality" where we blame all our problems on our trauma and constantly look for pity, and it is also harmful to turn our trauma into a competition where we denigrate the suffering of others. In his book *Achilles in Vietnam*, Jonathan Shay explains the dangers of turning trauma into a competition:

> One would think that severe psychological injury would give rise naturally to shared compassion and mutual respect among the many diverse groups of trauma survivors, such as have lived through genocide, political torture, domestic battering, incest, war, abusive religious cults, and coerced prostitution. Unfortunately, it has not. Veterans call it "pissing contests" when one veteran denies the validity of another veteran's war trauma. Different survivor groups eagerly start these competitions as well, each claiming that their experience is the only significant one.
> An intern in our [veterans] program approached a battered women's shelter for further training opportunities;

when she spoke of her experience with combat veterans, the person at the shelter scoffed and said, "That was twenty years ago. This is now!" Holocaust scholars have disparaged the writings of incest survivors as merely "confessional." These pissing contests only serve the interests of perpetrators, all perpetrators. It gives me great pain whenever I hear such disparagement among veterans or among survivor groups. No person's suffering is commensurable with any other.[14]

These seven factors should not be used to compare our trauma with other people's trauma, because other factors unrelated to the traumatic event and its aftermath (such as upbringing and personality traits) can make some people less resilient to trauma. Instead, these seven factors can help us understand the human condition, our shared humanity, and the nature of trauma.

Exploring trauma also offers additional evidence that humanity is not naturally violent. When a child is raised in a peaceful and loving environment, it is good for the human brain. That is a scientific fact. When a child is raised in a violent and abusive environment, it is not good for the human brain. That is also a scientific fact. But if human beings were naturally violent, why wouldn't the opposite be true? Later in this book I will discuss why violence can have such a seductive scent, despite its traumatizing taste.

The suicide dream I had at age five gave me an early glimpse into the trauma that would later become both my fiercest opponent and greatest teacher. The dream contained metaphorical insights that have increased my understanding of trauma, the human condition, and the road to peace. In the language of metaphors and symbols, my dream seemed to be saying, "The parents who once protected you are dead. Now you must die with them, because life has become terrifying and confusing and no one can protect you anymore."

In the suicide dream I stabbed myself in the chest with a pair of scissors, but I did not die. I woke up in my bed, surrounded by darkness, alone and afraid. The suicide dream had ended abruptly, but the real nightmare was being alive.

## *Two Ways to Drown*

It was difficult being half Korean, a quarter black, a quarter white, and growing up in Alabama. As a child I felt like I was not Korean enough to be Korean, not black enough to be black, and not white enough to be white. Living in a world where so many people defined their identity by race, I felt like an outcast.

People have asked me, "What race do you see yourself as?" That's a complex question, because is my race determined by how I look or how I think? My father conditioned me to think like a black man living before the civil rights movement, and my mother reinforced this view. My parents did this because they wanted to protect me from the racism that had harmed so many black men from my father's generation. As a mixed race couple, they were not naive about racism in America.

During my childhood my mother frequently told me, "People will call you 'Chinese-face,' but when they find out your father is black they will treat you like you are black. When you buy something from the store always make sure you hold on to the receipt, because people often accuse black men of stealing. Be careful around women, because they often accuse black men of rape." This was the reality for my father and other black men living during segregation, and although the civil rights movement achieved many important victories, much work remains to be done.

In the midst of these dark and painful experiences, I began to see light. After all, being an outcast can have its advantages. Because I did not belong to just one racial group, I taught myself to see beyond our differences and perceive the light of our shared humanity. As a young adult I realized that all people, regardless of their race, nationality, or religion, want purpose and meaning in life. And all people, no matter what their skin color, want to be around people they can trust.

Furthermore, although a broken leg can be caused by an accident, natural disaster, animal attack, or hateful human being, the greatest amount of psychological trauma will result if a hostile person assaults us, makes us feel helpless, and breaks our leg out of malice. This is true whether we are American, Vietnamese, Russian, Chinese, German, or Iranian.

Reading philosophy allowed me to find other thinkers who realized there is really only one race—the human race. Over two thousand years ago, Socrates said, "I am not an Athenian or a Greek, but a citizen of the world."[15] Many religions also express the idea that we are part of one human family. Only recently has science caught up with Socrates, when geneticists found physical proof in our genetic code that all human beings are actually related.

Spencer Wells started contributing to this groundbreaking genetics research while earning his PhD at Harvard and doing his postdoctoral work at the Stanford University School of Medicine. Wells is currently the director of the Genographic Project of the National Geographic Society in Washington, DC.[16] As Wells explains, countless people throughout history believed that some races were intellectually and morally inferior to others, but modern genetics research has proven there are no intellectual or moral differences between the races. The myth of racial inferiority was used to justify slavery, colonialism, and other oppressive systems, and many people still believe this myth today. Wells tells us:

> The American pro-slavery lobby embraced an extreme form of the Linnean view [of racial division] in the nineteenth century. The view that human races were actually separate, inherently unequal entities made it easier to justify the brutal oppression practised in the United States. The theory that human races are distinct entities, created separately, is known as polygeny—from the Greek for "many origins." This theory clearly contradicted the biblical story of the Garden of Eden, inhabited by a single Adam and a single Eve, and thus raised the hackles of the church. Most biologists also objected to the polygenist view, noting the extensive hybridization among human races.[17]

Genetic testing shows that all human beings on the planet today descended from a common ancestor who lived within the past several hundred thousand years in Africa. When I mentioned this genetics research during one of my talks, someone responded, "Why does it matter if human beings are all related? Family members fight with each other all the time, so the knowledge that human beings are one big extended family will not end human conflicts."

I replied, "Great point, and I think you are right. Conflicts certainly exist within families, but I am not discussing the end of conflict. Martial arts and the military taught me to see conflict as an opportunity, because it can allow us to arrive at greater clarity and understanding. What causes so much harm is not really conflict, but *destructive conflict resolution*, where I try to solve our disagreement or misunderstanding by punching you in the face. When family members have a conflict, should they resolve it by massacring each other? Most people would say no. Looking at history allows us to see how war, genocide, slavery, and oppression rely heavily on propaganda that dehumanizes people as being inferior and subhuman. It's harder to justify massacring or enslaving a group of people when we transform the knowledge of our shared humanity into empathy for all human beings."

The person then agreed that although the knowledge of us being one human family will not end conflict, this knowledge makes it more difficult to dehumanize people just because they have a different skin color. We can move the world closer to peace if we combine the truth of our shared humanity with waging peace skills that allow us to effectively resolve conflict.

Science confirms the truth of our shared humanity. Stanford professor Marcus Feldman led an international genetics study, which showed that human beings share about 99.9 percent of the same DNA.[18] When a baby is born anywhere on earth, even to people whose skin color differs from yours, about 99.9 percent of your DNA is passed on. In the ancient era of Socrates, our shared humanity was a philosophical idea. Today it is a scientific fact.

What else does modern genetics research reveal about the truth of our shared humanity? In an article for *Vanity Fair*, Spencer Wells explains that because all people on the planet today share a common ancestor who lived hundreds of thousands of years ago in Africa, we are all technically African: "What if I told you every single person in America—every single person on earth—is African? With a small scrape of cells from the inside of anyone's cheek, the science of genetics can even prove it."[19]

Genetic evidence shows that humanity almost went extinct during the past several hundred thousand years. The reason we are all related is because we descended from the relatively few who survived. Going extinct is not unusual, because nature has driven most species to extinction. Many scientists estimate that over 99 percent of the species that ever existed have gone extinct. To understand how difficult survival can be, let's discuss how our human ancestors lived hundreds of thousands of years ago.

Our nomadic ancestors were the most vulnerable mammals in Africa. We are too slow to outsprint predators and too weak to quickly climb trees. Lions and leopards can climb trees much faster than the average human. We are also too big to burrow underground for safety, and because our large brains take so long to develop, human children remain helpless for a longer period of time than the offspring of any other mammal. To make matters worse, we have no natural weapons such as fangs, claws, tusks, or horns.

With no natural weapons, relatively weak bodies (in comparison to chimpanzees and gorillas), and the inability to outsprint much faster predators, how did our early ancestors survive on the African savannah hundreds of thousands of years ago?

Imagine a pride of lions hunting an early human tribe. A tribe of ten to twenty people* would have included elderly, children, infants, and probably some pregnant women. When lions hunted early humans, how would our ancestors have reacted? Would they have thrown grandma to the lions and run away? Would the adults have fled, letting the children fend for themselves? If lions threatened your grandmother and children, what would you do? Military history reveals that when our loved ones are in danger, people often use tools as weapons and react with an emotion I call *fury*.

To understand fury, we must first understand every army's greatest problem. As I explain in my first book, *Will War Ever End?*, the greatest problem of every army in history has been this: when a battle begins, how do you stop soldiers from running away? Where our fight-or-flight response is concerned, the vast majority of people prefer to run when a sword is

---

* Groups of ten or twenty nomadic hunter-gatherers are often referred to as a *band*, but I am using the word "tribe" because the word "band" has become associated with musical groups, and my use of tribe matches dictionary definitions of the word.

wielded against them, a spear is thrust in their direction, a bullet flies over their head, or a bomb explodes in their vicinity. In the U.S. Army a complex system of conditioning trains soldiers to stay and fight—but the ancient Greeks discovered a more effective method still used today.

The Greeks realized that one simple thing could give soldiers endless courage when their lives were threatened and convince them to not only stay and fight, but to sacrifice their lives. At first glance the Greeks' solution might seem like a contradiction, because the most powerful motivator that convinces people to stay and fight is not a natural propensity for violence or killing, but their capacity for love and compassion. Halfway around the world, Lao-tzu, a Chinese philosopher who lived during the sixth century BC, also acknowledged this fundamental truth about human nature when he said, "By being loving, we are capable of being brave."[20]

The military taught me that when soldiers bond as comrades and view each other as family members, they will more likely fight and die for each other. This is why the military puts so much emphasis on camaraderie and the ideal of being a "band of brothers." The military does not do this because it is sentimental, but because of military necessity. Soldiers who view each other as family members will fight harder and be less likely to retreat from the battlefield.

At West Point I learned a famous passage from Shakespeare's *Henry V* that reads: "We few, we happy few, we band of brothers; for he today that sheds his blood with me shall be my brother."[21] In *The Art of War*, written over two thousand years ago, Sun Tzu says, "Regard your soldiers as your children, and they will follow you into the deepest valleys; look upon them as your own beloved sons, and they will stand by you even unto death."[22]

When I give lectures around the country I often ask, "If our flight response is stronger than our fight response when we are threatened by lethal violence, what is the most effective technique ancient armies used to encourage soldiers to fight and not retreat?" The audience immediately realizes the answer to this question when I ask them another question, "What would all of you die for? Raise your hand if you would risk your life to protect your family." All of the audience members will raise their hand.

In my book *Peaceful Revolution* I describe a radio interview I heard in

2002. The interview was with a seventy-three-year-old woman, Margaret Hargrove. Her story reinforced what the military taught me about love creating courage. She described how she had been walking in her neighborhood when she saw an aggressive pit bull running toward her. What would you do in this situation? Because our flight response is more powerful than our fight response, most people would rather run to a safe place than fight a large animal.

But Mrs. Hargrove was not alone. She was walking Alex, her small nine-month-old Scottish terrier. Reaching them, the pit bull latched its jaws onto her tiny dog. Mrs. Hargrove, driven by concern for her loved one, bent down and bit the pit bull on the neck until it let go.

How would you react if you saw a large animal attacking your dog, child, spouse, parent, or friend? Would you not feel compelled to protect your loved one? Although our flight response is usually more powerful than our fight response when violence threatens us, our instinct to protect our loved ones is usually stronger than our flight response. Protecting those we love can even be more powerful than self-preservation, and military history confirms this. When we see our loved ones in danger and our concern for them fuses with adrenaline, causing us to rush to their aid, I call this emotion fury.

When asked if she was afraid for her safety during the attack, Mrs. Hargrove said, "I wasn't scared. I was scared my dog was dying. I wasn't afraid of danger. I will never get over the look in Alex's eyes while I was trying to get him loose . . . I'm fortunate not to have been killed. I'm very lucky, and Alex is very lucky. I hope he knows how much I was willing to do for him."[23]

Imagine a pride of lions hunting an early tribe of humans, and these people experiencing the fury that erupts when our loved ones are in danger. If lions threatened to kill your children, spouse, and parents, how would you react? You would probably become extremely aggressive. Imagine an early tribe of humans throwing rocks, shouting, and shaking large sticks or spears. Now the lions must contend with a much more dangerous prey.

How do we know that our earliest ancestors were hunted by predators on the African savannah, and that our instinct to protect our loved ones is a primordial part of our psychology? Many scientific fields offer evidence to support this and, surprisingly, war propaganda also offers evidence. When we study military history we see that war propaganda works the same way in every country and time period. Every war in history has been enabled by propaganda that *dehumanizes the other side*, and there has never been a war where both sides saw each other as human beings who are just like them. By dehumanizing the other side, war propaganda portrays the "enemy" not as human beings who are just like us, but as dangerous animals or an evil force. War propaganda basically tells us, "Evil predators (in the form of barbarians, terrorists, etc.) want to kill our family or hurt another group of innocent people, and we must fight out of self-defense or in the name of peace."

There are certainly dangerous people in the world, but as I explain in my book *The Art of Waging Peace*, war is always framed, even by the aggressor nation, as a moral crusade necessary to defend one's country, liberate oppressed people, or protect a noble ideal such as peace, freedom, or justice. In a speech Hitler gave in 1939, he explained why Germany invaded Poland. The speech, which is full of propaganda, describes the Polish people as "sadistic beasts":

> The Polish Marshal . . . said that he would hack the German Army to pieces. And martyrdom began for our German nationals [living in Poland]. Tens of thousands were dragged off, mistreated, and murdered in the vilest fashion. *Sadistic beasts* [emphasis added] gave vent to their perverse instincts, and this pious democratic world watched without blinking an eye . . . At a certain moment England herself offered to bring us into direct discussion with Poland. I was ready. Of course it was the Poles who did not come . . . Then came the next day and nothing occurred except for Polish general mobilization, renewed acts of terror, and finally attacks against Reich territory.
>
> Now in the life of nations, patience must not always be interpreted as weakness. For years I patiently looked on these continuous provocations [from Poland]. What keen

suffering I underwent in these years only few can imagine
... In the last six years I had to stand intolerable things
from States like Poland ... If peoples go to pieces it will
not be the German people, who are fighting for justice,
who have no war aims and who were attacked [by Poland]
... England, with lies and hypocrisy, already has begun
to fight against women and children ... I hope then they
do not suddenly begin to think of humaneness and of the
impossibility of waging war against women and children.
We Germans do not like that. It is not in our nature. In
this campaign I gave an order to spare human beings.[24]

By using dehumanization to depict the enemy as predators, war propaganda manipulates the primordial part of our brain that protected our loved ones from predators on the African savannah. Because our fear of predators is such a powerful instinct, every war in recorded history, without a single exception, has relied on propaganda that dehumanizes the enemy as subhuman or evil. The propaganda that depicts people as predators has worked quite well in all cultures and time periods.

In this chapter I am just scratching the surface of dehumanization and war propaganda. Later in this book we will journey much deeper to learn more about the propaganda techniques that hide our shared humanity. We will also learn how we can combat the illusions of dehumanization by increasing our awareness, understanding, and empathy.

More evidence of early humans being hunted by African predators can be found in the fact that these predators usually hunt at night, and human beings have an instinctual fear of darkness. It is no coincidence that religions, philosophies, and mythologies around the world depict darkness as a metaphor for danger. In modern epics such as the *Star Wars* film series, the villains are "Dark Jedi" who use the "dark side of the force." In *The Lord of the Rings* trilogy, the villain Sauron is known as the "Dark Lord." In the *Harry Potter* series, the villains are "Dark Wizards" who practice the "dark arts." And in a famous African folk tale, the hero Mwindo must journey underground into darkness and danger to confront Muisa, the lord of the underworld.

Unlike human beings, lions have excellent night vision and do most of their hunting at night. Night is the best time for lions to fill their bellies, and they also do not have to endure the blazing African heat when the sun goes down, so why would a lion pride consisting of a large male and many females be afraid of darkness? But when human beings are concerned, sources as diverse as religion, science fiction, and even modern horror films depict darkness as a symbol of danger to us. In horror stories from long ago, it is no coincidence that vampires and werewolves come out at night.

Adults may read this and think, "But I'm not afraid of the dark." If we look closer, however, we realize that nearly all children are naturally afraid of the dark. Pediatrician Sue Hubbard tells us, "Nearly all children go through a phase when they're afraid of the dark. It's interesting to see a toddler who happily goes to bed in his crib in complete darkness turn into a 2-year-old terrified of shadows and monsters in a dark room . . . Fear of the dark is called 'nyctophobia' and is amazingly common. Even as an adult, my worries and anxieties seem to be worse at night, in the darkness, than the same issues are during daylight hours."[25]

Adults may not fear darkness when they are sleeping in a house with a lock on the door, but put an adult in a dark alley or in a jungle with no flashlight, and many will be afraid of the dark. Isn't it common sense that human beings, who have such poor night vision, would be afraid of the dark when so many predators hunt at night?

Wildlife documentary makers have filmed lions hunting fully grown African elephants at night. They have even filmed large groups of hyenas hunting female lions to the point where the lions had to climb trees to escape the attacking hyenas.[26] One purpose of the male lion is to protect female lions from hyenas. If hyenas will hunt animals as dangerous as lions,* and if lions will hunt an animal as dangerous as a fully grown African elephant, these predators would certainly have hunted our vulnerable early ancestors.

Although my books show that human beings are not naturally violent against other human beings, this does not mean we did not come from a warlike environment. The African savannah has many warlike characteristics,

---

* Hyenas are predators of lion cubs, and are more likely to hunt a lion pride when a large male lion is not present.

because predators were relentlessly hunting us. Lions and hyenas need to feed their offspring after all, and will provide for their young at all costs, just as we would. When our early ancestors discovered how to use fire, it shifted the balance of power on the African savannah.

Our ancestors had to endure dark nights filled with predators; our incredible intelligence, willingness to protect and die for our loved ones, and enormous capacity to cooperate enabled us to survive this threat along with catastrophic changes in climate. Predators and changes in climate have driven countless species extinct. According to leading scientists, the dinosaurs were not driven extinct merely by an asteroid, but by the climate change that resulted when the asteroid struck the earth and threw vast amounts of dust and debris into the sky, reducing sunlight and lowering global temperatures.

The cosmic ocean is a metaphor for the universe, and there are two ways to drown in the cosmic ocean. The first way is extinction. Most of the species that ever existed have drowned in this way. The second way is to lose our sense of purpose and meaning. This form of drowning seems unique to human beings. Due to our heightened craving for purpose and meaning, we are the only species on the planet that can sink into self-destruction, quiet desperation, and suicide when we have access to safety, food, community, and freedom.

In fact, when we do not have a solid foundation of purpose and meaning, our freedom can feel empty because our lives lack direction. As we discussed in the preface, "man does not live by bread alone." For human beings, which form of drowning is worse? This book will explore that question and discuss ways to navigate the dangerous waters that threaten to drown us.

When our early ancestors lived in small tribes, how did they find purpose and meaning? Purpose is like satisfying food that fuels our zest for life, and meaning is like fresh water that quenches our thirst for a life worth living. Humanity has always dealt with two major struggles, the struggle for survival and the struggle for purpose and meaning. But for most of human history these two struggles were combined into one, because our nomadic ancestors found purpose and meaning in protecting and providing for their tribe.

In an early human tribe every person was needed to help the tribe survive. Everybody mattered. In our society today, millions of people feel like they are not needed, and many elderly feel alienated, shunned, and discarded. But in early human tribes everyone was essential for the continued survival of the tribe, from the youngest child (who would ensure the future of the tribe) to the oldest adult. Elders could teach the young and help raise children, and also use their experience and wisdom to guide the tribe. Spencer Wells explains why elders were important in early human communities:

> Old people are good to have around. A reliance on teaching and learning, rather than instinct, is one of the things that distinguishes humans from other animals. Most of our early lives are spent learning, and it isn't until we are well into our twenties that most of us feel that we are in command of sufficient knowledge to be able to synthesize and teach others. The older we get, the more knowledge we accumulate, and the more we can help our offspring to benefit from our experience. Grandparents . . . have "been there and done that"—and, crucially, lived to tell the tale. Having grandparents around also allowed higher fecundity, since (as any new parent can tell you) they can care for children while younger generations go about their lives. This includes continued childbearing . . . Anthropologist Kristen Hawkes has suggested that grandmothering—the act of a child being cared for by its grandmother—may have played a substantial role in the population expansion of modern humans.[27]

We may have different national identities, but just as every river flows into our world's interconnected oceans, every nation is part of the interconnected universe I call the cosmic ocean. The metaphor of our universe as an ocean has been used by other philosophies and religions before me,* but we will use this metaphor as a tool for solving the twenty-first-century problems that threaten our country and planet.

Although the perspective of being an outcast helped me perceive the

---

* The metaphor of the universe as an ocean can be seen in Judaism, Christianity, and Hinduism. The phrase *cosmic ocean* has been used by Carl Sagan and others.

truth of our shared humanity, this perspective revealed another vital truth. Because problems such as environmental destruction, nuclear weapons, and war threaten human survival, we must learn to navigate these dangerous waters as a global human family, or we will drown. To save ourselves from drowning into extinction, we must journey deeper into darkness to reveal what makes humanity so powerful, vulnerable, and unusual.

## The World's Most Unusual Predator

When I was twenty-nine years old, I went to a therapist who works with traumatized veterans. She was aware of my violent upbringing and put me in a light hypnotic sleep, saying this would reconnect me with the fourteen-year-old boy I used to be. By the time I was fourteen, I had lived in terror for ten years, afraid that my father might kill me, unable to trust the parents who were supposed to protect me, suspicious of all human beings.

As her soothing words put me into a light hypnotic sleep, the therapist asked me to imagine myself standing in a room with my teenage self. She said, "The fourteen-year-old boy you used to be is handing a gift to the twenty-nine-year-old man you are today." She described how the gift was elegantly wrapped like a Christmas present, with festive wrapping paper and an ornate bow. Then she said, "This gift is a peace offering from the child you used to be. You carefully remove the beautiful wrapping paper and lift the lid on the box. What gift do you see, and what does this gift represent to you?"

I replied, "I see my father's decapitated head." After pausing for a moment, I added, "To me the decapitated head represents safety. After living in terror for ten years, the only way I could feel safe was if my father was dead, and the only way to make sure a human being is dead is to remove the person's head."

Some people may look down on me with condescending judgment when they read this, believing that their lack of childhood trauma makes them morally superior to me. But I will explain how extreme trauma can cause anyone to fantasize about violence, just as extreme hunger can cause anyone to fantasize about food.

Imagine if a giant snake—five times your size—had slithered into your home when you were four years old. This snake randomly bites you with its massive fangs, often when you least expect it. Sometimes it bites you in your sleep. Sometimes it coils its huge body around your tiny frame, squeezing without mercy until you think it will kill you. Imagine living with this dangerous snake for ten years of your life, from the ages of four to fourteen. Your parents cannot protect you from this predator in your home. No one can.

Imagine spending your childhood with a dangerous and unpredictable snake that goes wherever it wants. It slithers into your bedroom, through the living room, and across the kitchen floor, biting you randomly, strangling you repeatedly, making you fear for your life continually. You cannot always see the violent serpent because it usually hides deep within your father's mind. But you know it could show up at any moment when you least expect it, on Thanksgiving Day or Sunday afternoon. And you are helpless to stop it.

If your parents cannot keep you safe from this predator, at what point do you take your protection into your own hands? After living with this snake for so many years, you would probably fantasize about killing it. Then you might fantasize about cutting its head off, just to make sure it is dead. Eventually, you could develop fear and hatred for any creature that resembles a snake, causing you to fantasize about killing all snakes, not just the one in your home. If growing up in these terrifying circumstances caused you to lack empathy for snakes, would anyone blame you? Would anyone judge you?

If you were at school, would all your fear of the giant predator living in your home miraculously disappear just because you are taking a test? Wouldn't your frightening, unpredictable, and confusing home environment—which you must return to every day after school—make it more difficult to concentrate in class? Wouldn't the terror that haunts you make it harder to pay attention to the teacher? If you felt that no person on earth was willing or able to protect you, if your agony had to remain a secret, and if the snake was not a snake at all, but was in fact a human being whom you had once trusted with all your heart, a part of you might begin hating the entire human race.

When my father died in 2004 from a stroke, my terror did not magically go away, because childhood trauma can leave wounds in our mind, like metaphorical scar tissue etched across our brain. When fire burns our flesh, a scar can remain on our body long after the flame has died. In a similar way, when human beings betray our trust in traumatizing ways, a scar can remain in our mind long after those who hurt us have perished.

When people quote Nietzsche's attitude, "That which does not kill us makes us stronger,"[28] they often do not acknowledge how severe psychological trauma can maim and scar our mind, just as a severe physical wound can maim and scar our body. It is possible to heal our psychological wounds when we embark on the challenging spiritual journey that allows us to find light in darkness. My lifelong spiritual journey has allowed me to find the light of empathy in the darkness of trauma.

Although I felt indescribable terror for much of my childhood, I have used these painful experiences to increase my empathy for the suffering of others. Today I can feel empathy for people from all walks of life, and I can perceive our shared humanity that transcends skin color, national identity, and political viewpoints. My empathy grew strong because of my trauma, but I had to work hard to find the light of empathy in the darkness of trauma. The light did not appear automatically; through great effort I gradually uncovered more and more of its radiance.

Just as the pain of lifting a heavy weight can strengthen the muscles in our arms, we can use the painful experiences from our past to strengthen our muscle of empathy. Transforming my agony into empathy gives purpose and meaning to my suffering, which has helped me heal. When we use the weight of trauma to strengthen our muscle of empathy, the painful experiences from our past can still hurt occasionally, but we may find that the pain becomes easier to carry.

Later in this book I will share many more insights that reveal how I found light in darkness. For now, I must emphasize that we don't have to experience extreme trauma to strengthen our muscle of empathy, because we can also grow our empathy by improving our understanding. For example, learning about the *causes of aggression* has dramatically increased my empathy, and all people can benefit from a deeper understanding of aggression. Before we can explore what causes aggression, however, we must first discuss the psychology of predators.

The most powerful predators on earth can be afraid of becoming prey to other animals. Many grizzly bear cubs have been killed by wolves, and many lion cubs have been killed by a variety of mammals on the African savannah. I once saw a wildlife documentary where a herd of African buffalo spotted several lion cubs in broad daylight. Even though buffalo are herbivores, they went after the lion cubs and used their horns to kill them, while the adult lions ran around frantically, unable to stop the attacking buffalo. Lions kill countless buffalo every year, but this time the lion cubs had become the prey.

Many people in our society do not know how predators usually deal with other dangerous predators in the wild. When I give lectures around the country I often ask the audience, "When a hungry grizzly bear and hungry pack of wolves both want a dead deer carcass, what usually happens?" Most people in the audience either say "they fight" or "they share," but the grizzly bear and wolves usually do something else. They *posture*.

Posturing happens when an animal makes noise or tries to appear larger in order to frighten away a creature it perceives as a threat. In my book *The End of War* I use the term *warning aggression* to describe posturing. Warning aggression can be seen when a bear roars, a wolf growls, and a cobra lifts its body and spreads its hood. Warning aggression is a nonviolent form of aggression that tries to *prevent* violence.

When a rattlesnake expresses warning aggression by shaking its tail, we know it is trying to tell us "leave me alone" rather than "come over here and pet me." An animal that expresses warning aggression is basically communicating "I don't want to get in a fight with you, so I am giving you a fair warning that will allow you to safely walk away." If you ignore this warning, the rattlesnake will be forced to retreat or bite you (the act of biting is an example of *hostile aggression*).

Most animals, including those that are not predators, use a form of warning aggression as their preferred method of self-defense. Gorillas are not hunters, but they posture by beating their chest, and when elephants feel threatened they posture by making loud noises or charging.

In our society, many people have the misconception that predators in the wild are constantly killing each other. But when predators are not hunting out of necessity to feed themselves and their young, they are actually far more risk averse than many of us realize.* The reason for their aversion to danger is because *there are no hospitals in the wild.* If a predator is injured and loses the ability to move at full speed or overpower its prey, it cannot go to an emergency room where a doctor will treat its wounds. It will starve to death.

Most carnivores and herbivores posture when they feel threatened, and so do human beings. Our nomadic ancestors were omnivores, a combination of carnivore and herbivore that gave them greater access to food resources in the wild. Just as posturing animals will make noise and try to appear larger when afraid, two men will usually posture before getting into a fight by raising their voices, standing tall, and puffing out their chests.

If human beings were naturally violent, why would warning aggression—which tries to prevent violence—nearly always precede lethal combat between human beings (except in cases of psychotic behavior, which I discuss in chapter 3). In ancient Greece, soldiers wore big helmets and screamed when going into battle. Like posturing animals, soldiers in ancient armies tried to appear larger and made noise as a form of warning aggression.

Because our posturing instinct is stronger than our killing instinct, the inaccurate musket became more popular than the deadlier longbow and crossbow. In his book *On Combat,* Lieutenant Colonel Dave Grossman explains:

> Napoleon said that in war, "The moral is to the physical as three is to one." That is, the psychological factors are three times more important than the physical factors. In combat, one of the most important of these "moral" factors—or morale or psychological factors, as we would call it today—is noise.
>
> In nature, whoever makes the biggest bark or the biggest roar is most likely to win the battle. Bagpipes, bugles and rebel yells have been used throughout history to daunt an enemy with noise. Gunpowder was the ultimate "roar,"

* In chapter 2 of *Peaceful Revolution* I discuss how animals usually fight over mates by using a "less lethal" form of combat that can cause minor and sometimes severe injuries, but is not intended to kill.

since it had both a bark and a bite. First used as fireworks by the ancient Chinese and later in cannon and muskets, gunpowder was a noisemaker that provided sound and concussion. The concussion was felt and heard, and gunpowder provided the visual effects of flash and smoke. Since a gunpowder explosion and its drifting smoke could be tasted and smelled, it provided a powerful sensory stimulus that could potentially assault all five senses.

This is one of the primary reasons why the early, clumsy, smoothbore, muzzleloading muskets replaced the longbow and the crossbow. The longbow and the crossbow had many times the rate of fire, more accuracy and far greater accurate range when compared to the early smoothbore muskets. Yet these superior military weapons were replaced, almost overnight (historically speaking) by vastly inferior muskets. While they were inferior at killing, they were not inferior at psychologically stunning and daunting an opponent . . . If you are in a battle going *doink, doink* with a crossbow and the other guy is going *Boom! Boom!* with a musket, all things being equal, the doinker will lose every time.

Some observers, not fully understanding the all-important psychological aspect of combat, have assumed that the longbow disappeared because of the lifetime of training required to master it. However, this logic does not apply nearly as well to the crossbow. If training and expense were the real issues, then the tremendous expense and lifetime of training needed to create a mounted knight or cavalry trooper (and his mount) would have been sufficient to doom those instruments of war. If a weapon system provides military dominance (be it the knight, the frigate, the aircraft carrier, the fighter jet, or the nuclear missile), then a society will devote the resources needed to get that weapon system. But if a more effective weapon is

found, then the merciless Darwinian evolution of the battlefield will doom the older weapon and embrace the new.
    Thus, with the invention of the first crude muskets,
the longbow and the crossbow were doomed, and the psychological reasons for this are, in Napoleon's words, "three
times more important than the physical . . ." You have
probably heard of the Big Bang Theory. I call this the Bigger Bang Theory, which states that, "all other things being
equal, in combat whoever makes the bigger bang wins."[29]

How can a deeper understanding of aggression increase our empathy
for human beings? When I was in the army a colonel told me, "In order to
think strategically, you must be able to see the world from the other person's
point of view." This reminded me of a principle from Sun Tzu's *The Art of
War* where he said, "Know your enemy."[30] If you can put yourself in your
opponent's frame of mind during a chess match and see the board from the
opposing point of view, then you have a much better chance of winning.

When waging peace is concerned, the only way to truly know our
enemy is through empathy, which causes us to realize they are not really our
enemy. As Elinor "Gene" Hoffman, founder of the Compassionate Listening
Project, said: "An enemy is a person whose story we have not heard."[31] Empathy tells us our true enemies are hatred and ignorance, not a particular group
of people. The most effective way to fight enemies such as hatred and ignorance is with the techniques of waging peace.

Using hatred against hatred is like throwing gasoline on a fire, but when
empathy is applied strategically, it has the potential to extinguish hatred like
water dousing a flame. As I explain in my other books, the civil rights movement is an example of the strategic application of empathy, and waging peace
gives us many effective ways to resolve conflict, which are more reliable than
the last resort of violence.

Since empathy and its higher expression of unconditional love offer us
the deepest insight into another human being, when Sun Tzu said, "Know
your enemy" and Jesus said, "Love your enemy" they were essentially saying
the same thing. The deepest way to know another human being is through

the unconditional love that Jesus, Gandhi, Martin Luther King Jr., Elinor "Gene" Hoffman, and many other spiritual teachers taught us to embrace.

Gaining a deeper understanding of aggression taught me that warning aggression (also known as posturing) in all animals is caused by fear or another form of discomfort. The same is true for human beings. When people behave aggressively toward me, I can have more empathy for them if I perceive the fear, frustration, confusion, or other painful emotion causing their aggression. It is easier to have empathy for a fearful, frustrated, or confused person, rather than an angry person.

Psychologist Erich Fromm said, "There are many layers of knowledge; the knowledge which is an aspect of love is one which does not stay at the periphery, but penetrates to the core. It is possible only when I can transcend the concern for myself and see the other person in his own terms. I may know, for instance, that a person is angry, even if he does not show it overtly; but I may know him more deeply than that; then I know that he is anxious, and worried; that he feels lonely, that he feels guilty. Then I know that his anger is only the manifestation of something deeper, and I see him as anxious and embarrassed, that is, as the suffering person, rather than as the angry one."[32]

The more deeply you perceive another human being and embrace our shared humanity, the better you can understand the other person's point of view and the more strategically you can think. By giving us the deepest form of knowledge into the perspective of another human being, empathy creates the strongest foundation for strategic thinking.

Human beings became predators at some point in our primordial past, and we share the posturing instinct with other predators. But we are the most unusual predator in the world, because as far as we know, we are the only predator that is troubled by killing its prey. We do not know of any other predator on earth that displays empathy, appreciation, respect, and reverence for those it hunts.

Every nomadic tribe of traditional hunters we know about, from the San people (also known as Bushmen) in Africa to the Native Americans, performs rituals to express empathy, appreciation, respect, and reverence for the animals they kill. These rituals can also serve as a way to seek forgiveness from the animal and atone for the guilt that may arise from killing. During an interview with mythologist Joseph Campbell, journalist Bill Moyers asked him, "Do you think [hunting] troubled early man?"

Campbell replied:

> Absolutely, that's why you have the rites, because it did trouble him. [These rites included] rituals of appeasement to the animal, of thanks to the animal . . . And some kind of respect for the animal that was killed. That's the thing that gets me all the time in this hunting ceremonial system, the respect for the animal. And more than respect . . . [The buffalo] was the sacred animal for the [American] Indians. These [European] hunters go out with repeating rifles and shoot down the whole herd and leave it there, and take the skin to sell and the body is left to rot. This is a sacrilege . . . Can you imagine what the experience must have been for a people within ten years to lose their environment, to lose their food supply, to lose the central object of their ritual life?[33]

No other predator in the world kills its prey and then performs ceremonies to express respect and gratitude. No other predator transforms its prey into a sacred creature that becomes the spiritual center of its nomadic tribal life. No other predator creates art by painting depictions of its prey on cave walls, as Europeans did tens of thousands of years ago when they lived as nomadic hunter-gatherers. No other predator has spiritual traditions encouraging it to extend empathy beyond blood relatives, local community members, and even its own species.

No other predator has spiritual teachers who encourage universal love. Saint Francis of Assisi, Buddha, and Gandhi taught us to have compassion for other living beings who share this planet with us, and Christian theologian Albert Schweitzer taught us to have "reverence for life." (Later in this book I will explain the philosophical, spiritual, and scientific meaning of reverence, and I will also discuss why we have lost reverence for human beings, animals, and nature.)

Furthermore, no other predator in the world transforms another predator, the wolf, into "man's best friend," the dog. And no other predator in the world transforms the cat, yet another predator, into a beloved family member. Our extraordinary human capacity for empathy makes us unusual predators indeed.

But we are the world's most unusual predator in other ways, because trauma can turn us into predators of our own family members. My father could be kind and gentle, but his unhealed trauma caused him to unpredictably transform into a metaphorical serpent. No other predator in the world torments its own children with the fear of death.

As I share more insights about the reality of trauma in later chapters, I will reveal how I almost became an even more unusual kind of predator, who was once a helpless child but was transformed by trauma into a ticking time bomb. Why did I not explode in rage and slaughter my fellow human beings, as trauma made me capable of doing? By sharing my story, I will uncover secrets about trauma, violence, and empathy that remain buried in our unconscious mind and primordial past. By discussing how I learned to love humanity despite having reasons to hate the entire human race, I will reveal how I created a path out of darkness.

# CHAPTER 2

# Poseidon's Wrath

## *Freaks of the Universe*

When I was a child I felt like a freak. I hated this feeling back then, but today I consider it a gift, because it allowed me to see the human condition in a way that can help us solve our greatest problems. As I mentioned in the previous chapter, I grew up in Alabama feeling like an outcast because of my mixed-race blood. My sense of alienation grew worse due to several factors: my father's paranoia caused him to socially isolate me, I was an only child, and my home environment was violent, unpredictable, and terrifying.

What is the difference between an outcast and a freak? Outcasts are treated by their community like they don't belong. Based on my experiences, freaks are outcasts who have experienced such a high degree of alienation that they think they will never belong. After feeling like an outcast for so many years, I began to feel like a freak. But feeling like a freak can have its advantages, because it allowed me to see the world from a unique perspective.

We begin to grow as human beings when we work to expand and deepen our perspective. As I observed the world from the viewpoint of an outsider, I made an effort to see farther and deeper, like an explorer who journeys to see what is over the next hill or a scientist who peers beneath the shallow surface. When I looked farther and deeper into the human condition, I saw surprising features on the landscape of our shared humanity.

Some of the features that make us more similar than different as human beings truly shocked me. During my junior year at West Point, as I was contemplating suicide after a lifetime of agony, I thought, "What if all human beings are freaks, even if they don't realize it? What if I am not alone?"

Although my traumatic upbringing gave me a unique perspective, I am certainly not alone in my suffering. I used to stare in the mirror and hate the shape of my Asian eyes, wishing I looked white so that I could belong. But haven't most people shared an experience similar to mine, even if it was not with the same intensity? How many people, especially in our society, have stared in a mirror and wished they could change how they look? How many have wanted to be taller, slimmer, more muscular, or younger? How many have gazed at their reflection and desired a nicer head of hair, clearer skin, less wrinkles, a flatter stomach, or the ability to change the shape and size of their facial features and body parts? How many have been tormented by the feeling that they are not pretty enough, handsome enough, or good enough?

Human beings are unusual, because no other species on the planet, as far as we know, stares in the mirror and thinks, "I hate my body. I hate my face. I hate myself." No other species suffers from self-destructive eating disorders because it perceives itself as being too fat. No other species hates its body because it does not look like a supermodel, or feels so ugly that it ponders suicide.

I will discuss how mass media influences our perception of beauty in a later chapter. In the meantime, it is important to understand that mass media influences us so powerfully through images because it understands the human condition. Human beings gather more information about the world through our eyesight than any other sense, and our large brains give us a level of self-awareness so high it is often painful. Our heightened self-awareness is a blessing that made us more adaptable on the harsh African savannah, but it is also a curse.

Many other species also demonstrate self-awareness, but as far as we know, no other species can become depressed, addicted to drugs, and suicidal as a result of being tormented by its self-awareness, even when it has freedom, good physical health, companionship, and a belly full of food. No other creature is so tortured by its ability to think that it searches for escape in alcohol. A female friend once told me, "I get drunk to stop my mind from worrying, to stop my thoughts from racing, to stop feeling anxious about the future, to stop feeling regretful about the past, to stop my brain from thinking. These are some of the ways alcohol allows me to relax and have fun." Of course, alcohol can also amplify emotions in some people, causing them to become more regretful, depressed, and angry when they are drunk. A male friend told me something similar, but added, "Alcohol makes me less self-conscious. I often feel nervous and anxious, but alcohol makes me brave enough to talk to women, which is why it is called 'liquid courage.' Because I am self-conscious and worried about people judging me, I can be more social and carefree when I am drunk." As far as we know, no other species has such trouble calming and relaxing its mind that it searches for peace in outlets such as alcohol, meditation, and music, just to name a few.

All animals fear dying when their lives are in immediate danger, but they seem at peace with nature's laws such as the inevitability of old age and death. As far as we know, only human beings are haunted so much by the fear of old age and death that they can desire plastic surgery to appear younger, worry if there is life after death, and see themselves at war with nature's laws. I remember being around seven years old and lying in bed late one night, unable to sleep, overcome with a sense of dread and meaningless-ness, as I realized that my parents and every single person on earth would someday grow old and die. I thought, "Why does the world have to be this way? Why does everyone have to die? Why is life so painful? Where did the world, death, and pain come from? Why am I here? Does anyone know the answers to these questions?"

Since then I have been searching for answers to those questions. When I became a teenager I realized that virtually all people, at some point in their lives, ask themselves these same questions. These questions bind us together as human beings, but the way we attempt to answer them can divide us. When two religions answer these questions in different ways, it can create conflicts that are not easily resolved.

Every other species on the planet seems to know its purpose and does not need to find a meaning for its existence, but our large brains have made human beings into the most unusual creatures on the planet. We must seek purpose and meaning as other animals search for food and water. When we are unable to find purpose and meaning in the midst of our suffering, the pain can be unbearable.

As a result of our craving for purpose and meaning, human beings seem to be the only organism in the world capable of committing suicide because life feels meaningless. Even more unusual, we seem to be the only organism capable of hating itself and its entire species due to trauma. Psychologist Erich Fromm described human beings as "the freak of the universe," because our large brains make us aware of our inability to change the laws of nature and our powerlessness to stop the inevitability of death. Fromm explained:

> Self-awareness, reason, and imagination have dis-rupted the "harmony" which characterizes animal exis-tence. Their emergence has made man into an anomaly, into the freak of the universe. He is part of nature, subject to her physical laws [such as the aging process and death] and unable to change them, yet he transcends the rest of nature . . . Being aware of himself, he realizes his power-lessness and the limitations of his existence. He visualizes his own end: death . . .
>
> Man is the only animal . . . that can feel evicted from paradise. Man is the only animal for whom his own exis-tence is a problem which he has to solve and from which he cannot escape.[1]

When Fromm said human beings are the only animal "that can feel evicted from paradise," he was referring to the Garden of Eden. In the Bible, the story of the Garden of Eden depicts humanity as an oddball among all other animals. In the story, Adam and Eve eat a piece of fruit from the Tree of the Knowledge of Good and Evil. Consuming the fruit gives them a new awareness that causes them to feel embarrassed about their exposed genitals. Their embarrassment symbolizes a feature of the human condition we just discussed, when we explored how human beings are the only creatures who can feel deeply insecure about a natural aspect of their physical appearance.*

---

* All human tribes wear some form of clothing or body decoration (modifying their natural appear-ance with an object or color, often in the form of jewelry or face painting). We do not know of any other animal on the planet that does this. Even the few tribes that seem comfortable with full nudity use some form of body decoration to symbolize belonging, and can be self-conscious about aspects of their appearance.

This new and heightened human awareness expands the thinking of Adam and Eve in other ways, resulting in their eviction from the Garden of Eden, which is a paradise where old age, suffering, and death do not exist. Exiled to the harsh and unforgiving wilderness, they must grow old and die against their will.

In addition to the story of the Garden of Eden, countless stories from cultures all over the world depict human beings as oddballs different from other animals, outcasts from nature, or freaks of the universe who suffer because of our heightened human awareness. The San people of Africa (also known as "Bushmen") are one of the oldest human populations, and they have a story similar to the Garden of Eden. In this story, fire is a metaphor for humanity's heightened awareness. Religious scholar G. R. Evans explains:

> A Kalahari bushmen's creation story tells how once people and animals lived beneath the surface of the earth with the Lord of Life, Kaang (Käng). This was a golden age, an age of happiness, when there was no quarrelling or warfare and everything was bathed in a light which did not come from the sun. Then Kaang decided to make a more wonderful world above ground.
>
> He created a great tree whose branches stretched out across the whole world. Under its roots he made a passage-way down to the place where people and animals were living comfortably together. Then he led the first man up to the surface, followed by the first woman, and then all the people. After that he brought up the animals, who rushed out eagerly, and some of them swarmed up into the branches of the tree.
>
> Kaang gave them all instructions. They were to continue to live together peacefully, people and animals. He gave especially firm instructions to the people not to build fires. If they built fires evil would come. They promised

and he left them to their lives, moving away but continuing to watch over them.

In their underground world it had always been mysteriously light, but above ground the sun set and it grew dark. The people were frightened because they could not see what was happening and, lacking the fur the animals wore, the humans felt cold. Someone suggested building a fire to give light and heat, forgetting Kaang's warning. But the fire frightened the animals, who ran away to live in mountains and caves, and people and animals lost the ability to talk to one another.[2]

These primordial stories about human vulnerability, along with the large amount of psychological problems in the modern world, show that the primary difference between human beings and other animals is not that we drive cars or go to the moon, but that human beings can perceive themselves as cut off from nature and be deeply troubled by their very existence. In the ancient Greek epic the *Iliad*, written by Homer nearly three thousand years ago, Zeus says, "There is nothing alive more agonized than man of all that breathe and crawl across the earth."[3]

Although our heightened human awareness can cause us to feel like outcasts from nature, which is symbolized by the eviction of Adam and Eve from the Garden of Eden, our heightened human awareness also strengthens us by expanding our ability to think, enabling us to conceive of things that were once inconceivable. The heightened awareness and expanded thinking of our large brains allow us to change aspects of nature to a degree that exceeds the ability of any other species. This gave our nomadic ancestors a powerful survival advantage.

For example, we can change animal skins into warm clothes that protect our bodies during winter. We can change raw meat into cooked food through the use of fire. We can change sticks and stones into a wide variety of tools. We can change wild wolves into loyal and loving dogs. We can change wild plants into cultivated crops. We can use irrigation to change dry land into moist soil. We can combine copper and tin, changing them into bronze. We can combine iron and carbon, changing them into steel. We can change the ink that flows from a pen into words, sentences, and ideas. We can create ideas that change the world.

But despite all our brilliance, we are unable to change basic laws of nature such as the irreversible flow of time and the inevitability of death. We can change wrinkles into smooth skin through plastic surgery, but it is only an illusion. We cannot truly change time and death, which gradually consume all that is alive. Worst of all, we are aware of our powerlessness to change the laws of nature. Although we can use weapons to stop lions and hyenas from killing our family, we are aware of our inability to stop time and death from eventually killing us and everyone we love. Indeed, our incredible capacity for self-awareness is a blessing, but it is also a curse.

Our powerlessness to change the laws of nature, despite our vast intelligence that allows us to change so many aspects of nature, makes us fragile and vulnerable as a species. Like a tragic Greek hero filled with hubris, we may believe we have total mastery over nature, but Thor reminds us of the truth. In Nordic mythology there is a story about Thor, the mighty god of thunder, participating in an odd wrestling match.

When Thor visited a royal palace in the land of the giants, the king challenged him to wrestle an old, tiny, toothless woman. Thor accepted the challenge. Walking across the large hall where the king sat watching from his throne, Thor wrapped his muscular arms around the old woman, trying to throw her to the ground, but she would not budge. To Thor's surprise, the old woman gradually overpowered him, subduing the powerful Nordic god. The king who issued the challenge was not surprised, however, because the old woman was actually a clever disguise for time and death. Not even a god as strong as Thor could defeat time.

Understanding our fragility and vulnerability as human beings increases my empathy for humanity. The story of Thor is a metaphor for our inability to stop time, and one thing all human beings (and all forms of life) have in common is that time wrestles with us all. Economist and social theorist Jeremy Rifkin explains how our understanding of human fragility and vulnerability is essential for empathy:

Around eight years of age a child learns about birth and death . . . that they have a one and only life, that life is fragile and vulnerable, and one day they are going to die. That's the beginning of an existential trip, because when a child learns about birth and death and they have a one and only life, they realize how fragile and vulnerable life is. It's very tough being alive on this planet, whether you're a human being, or a fox navigating the forest.

So when a child learns that life is vulnerable and fragile and that every moment is precious and that they have their own unique history, it allows the child then to experience another's plight in the same way, that [other] person, or other being—it could be another creature—has a one and only life, it's tough to be alive, and the odds are not always good. So if you think about the times that we've empathized with each other—our fellow creatures—it's always because we've felt their struggle . . . and we show solidarity with our compassion.

Empathy is the opposite of utopia. There is no empathy in heaven . . . There isn't any empathy in heaven because there's no mortality. There is no empathy in utopia because there is no suffering. Empathy is grounded in the acknowledgement of death and the celebration of life and rooting for each other to flourish and be. It's based on our frailties and our imperfections, so when we talk about building an empathic civilization, we're not talking about utopia, we're talking about the ability of human beings to show solidarity not only with each other, but our fellow creatures who have a one and only life on this little planet.[4]

In addition to the biblical story of the Garden of Eden and Jeremy Rifkin's scientific perspective, many philosophical and religious traditions also recognize that human beings are oddballs—freaks of the universe who can brilliantly change so many aspects of nature, yet remain powerless to change the laws of nature. People may try to repress this awareness by pretending they will never grow old and die, but deep in our unconscious mind, we realize death eventually comes for us all, whether we are male or female, European or Asian, rich or poor. Realizing that death is a part of our shared humanity, philosopher Marcus Aurelius said death made the Macedonian king Alexander the Great and his lowly stable boy equal in the end, by reducing them both to atoms.[5] As the Bible says, "For dust you are and to dust you will return."[6]

However, this book is not about death. It is about the mystery and beauty of life. Many people perceive the inevitability of time, old age, and death as a source of darkness, but later in this book we will uncover abundant sources of light hidden in this darkness. In the first chapter I explained why human beings are the most unusual predators in the world. In this chapter I discuss why human beings are the most unusual creatures on the planet. And later in this book I will reveal why human beings are the most unusual form of dust, capable of choosing to drown in darkness or bathe in light. Understanding our unusual human condition has made me proud to be human, allowed me to walk the hidden road to peace, and strengthened my empathy for humanity and all life.

My other books explore human nature in ways that empower us to solve our national and global problems. But in this book we will explore the nature of reality itself. We will explore the nature of existence and the universe. My other books focus on the understanding and tools we need to create peace between human beings. But only by exploring the nature of the universe, which I call the cosmic ocean, can we learn to make peace with our delicate ecosystem, the unchangeable laws of nature, and even death. Human survival in our fragile future will depend not only on our ability to create peace between human beings. It will also depend on our ability to make peace with the problem of human existence.

## *Why Humans Ask Why*

In the previous Erich Fromm quote, he said animals live in harmony with nature. What did he mean? His statement seems absurd at first glance, because animals in nature suffer from hunger, thirst, fear, pain, physical injuries, old age, and death just as we do. Many of them also experience the terror of being hunted, which is certainly not a harmonious feeling.

Furthermore, scientific evidence shows that many animals can form deep emotional bonds with other creatures. Since elephants can bond deeply with members of their herd, how can an elephant experience harmony with nature while seeing its family members die from drought? And since animals fear being eaten alive, how can a panicking zebra experience harmony with nature while being killed by hyenas?

Although animals in the wild are vulnerable to many of the same forms of suffering experienced by human beings, what Fromm meant is that these animals live in harmony with a *certain part of nature*. They live in harmony with the *purpose and meaning of their existence*. As I mentioned earlier, human beings must seek purpose and meaning as other animals search for food and water. If human beings are unable to find purpose and meaning in their lives, they can suffer enormously, even if they have food, safety, good health, and freedom. Because other species live in harmony with the purpose and meaning of their existence, we have never seen an animal in the wild experience a midlife crisis, the need to explore religion, or the desire to scientifically explain the origin of the universe.

All organisms except human beings live in harmony with another part of nature—the mystery of life and death. As far as we know, only human beings are troubled by the following mysterious questions: Why are we here? Where did the universe come from? Where did life come from? Is there a God? What is death? Is there life after death? What is the meaning of life? These questions are central to human existence, and both religious people and atheists feel a need to answer these questions, often in different ways. People can attempt to answer these questions through religion, science, philosophy, a fanatical ideology, or some other means.

The Tree of the Knowledge of Good and Evil is a metaphor for our *heightened human awareness.* In the story of the Garden of Eden, Adam and Eve live in paradise where there is no old age or death. In the garden they experience harmony, happiness, and innocence, but when they achieve heightened human awareness by eating the tree's forbidden fruit, their harmony with existence becomes disrupted and they are evicted from paradise. All adults have had an experience, or series of experiences, that disrupted the harmony of their childhood, causing them to feel evicted from the happiness of their youth.

Before my father attacked me in my sleep when I was four, I remember being such a happy child. I remember my kind and gentle father carrying me on his shoulders when we went to the store and being a protective force in my life. Back then the world seemed magical, beautiful, and full of wonder. But when my father made me fear for my life, the happiness and innocence of my childhood became disrupted. The traumatic experience of being attacked by my father gave me a new awareness that evicted me from the metaphorical paradise of my happy childhood.

Many different kinds of experiences can disrupt the happiness of our childhood. When Adam and Eve lived in the Garden of Eden they were not vulnerable to old age or death. Today science has revealed that very young children are not aware of the inevitability of old age and death. Becoming aware of these laws of nature can disrupt the harmony and innocence of our youth. Puberty can also disrupt our harmony.

When I was in the army, a sergeant I worked with told me, "When I was a child I used to be so happy. I didn't seem to worry about anything. I was so carefree, and every day seemed like an adventure. But becoming aware of sex during puberty messed it all up. During puberty all I could think about was sex, nearly all the time, to the point where it stressed me out." Like many people, this sergeant was more content before puberty than he was as a confused, insecure, and hormonal teenager.

Many women experience a disruption of their childhood happiness when they grow older and people in society value them based on how they look. One of my female friends told me, "At the age of eleven, breast size became a pressure. Girls would harass each other over who was able to fill out a bra and who could not."

When I was in eighth grade, I was sitting in science class with the other students, waiting for the teacher to show up. Sitting in the back of the class was a girl who some called "flat-chested." In front of all the students, another girl yelled across the room at her, "If you didn't have feet, would you wear socks? Then why do you wear a bra?"

Most young children are not as self-conscious about their appearance as teenagers and adults. Most three-year-old girls experiencing the innocence of childhood are more carefree than a teenage girl who is picked on because of the way she is dressed, or an aging supermodel who has to compete with younger supermodels constantly flowing into her industry. Boys can also become painfully self-conscious about their appearance. When I was three years old, I did not hate my Asian eyes, but my youthful innocence was shattered when I grew older and people insulted me because of my race.

If we contemplate our lives, we may remember an experience, or series of experiences, that disrupted the harmony of our youth. Perhaps our parents were divorced, and this shattered the happiness and innocence of our childhood. Perhaps it was the death of a family member, and this made us painfully aware of human mortality. Perhaps it was puberty or being bullied. Philosophy, religious traditions, and scientific evidence all agree upon a basic fact of the human condition: achieving a new and heightened awareness about our world can cause us to feel confused and disillusioned, like a metaphorical eviction from paradise. To quote the old adage, "Ignorance is bliss."

Ignorance may seem like bliss during the harmony, happiness, and innocence of our childhood, but when we make peace with the problem of human existence and learn to live in harmony with the mystery of life and death, we can achieve a *higher bliss than ignorance*. Although philosophers, religions, and growing scientific evidence reveal the possibility of a higher bliss than ignorance, we will question if this is true by first exploring something rarely talked about today: the wrath of Greek gods.

The Greek gods Poseidon, Zeus, and Hades were brothers. After Zeus overthrew his father, the titan Cronus, the brothers drew lots to decide who would rule the various parts of the world. Zeus gained dominion over the sky, Hades became ruler of the underworld, and Poseidon became lord of the ocean. In the Greek epic poem the *Iliad*, Poseidon says, "The world was split three ways. Each received his realm. When we shook the lots I drew the sea, my foaming eternal home, and Hades drew the land of the dead engulfed in haze and night and Zeus drew the heavens, the clouds and the high clear sky, but the earth and Olympus heights are common to us all."[7]

To understand why so many ancient Greeks worshipped these gods, imagine living in Greece three thousand years ago. Imagine having no scientific explanations for why earthquakes, tsunamis, and other natural disasters happen. Furthermore, no one has ever seen a virus because the microscope has not yet been invented, so when a plague kills a large number of people in your city, you don't know why it happened. You don't even know what causes lightning and thunderstorms.

Now imagine you are a kind and generous person, living in ancient Greece, who takes care of your family and provides for your community. Suddenly, without any warning, a massive earthquake destroys your house and kills your child. How would you explain the destruction of your house, death of your child, and cause of the earth shaking beneath your feet? Why did these bad things happen?

A feature on the landscape of our shared humanity, something we all have in common, is that we ask *why* when bad things happen to us. But why do we ask why? When the September 11 attacks occurred, causing thunderous explosions and the sky to fill with smoke, we do not know of any other species that debated "why did this happen?" When a murder or mass shooting occurs, the people affected by the tragedy, along with many not affected, will ask why. The question "why did this happen?" results from humanity's *craving to understand underlying causes.* I use the word "underlying" because this craving searches for causes that go beyond the immediate range of our senses.

Not only do we want to know the underlying causes of tragedies, but we also want to know the underlying causes of natural phenomena. When I was a child I asked countless questions such as "why does it rain?" and "why does the sun go away at night?" Children possess innate curiosity that leads to these kinds of questions. When our nomadic ancestors lived on the harsh African savannah, their craving to understand underlying causes allowed them to make complex connections between cause and effect, empowering them to control many aspects of nature. For example, the question "why did this happen?" allowed our early ancestors to discover the underlying causes of fire, empowering them to create fire and use it for light, warmth, and protection.*

When a plant sprouted from the ground, the question "why did this happen?" allowed our ancestors to comprehend how plants grow when seeds are put in a certain kind of dirt. If they planted seeds in the right kind of soil, they could create and control their own food supply. When Sir Alexander Fleming noticed a mold had inhibited the growth of bacteria in a Petri dish, the question "why did this happen?" began an intellectual journey that allowed him to discover penicillin. Asking "why did this happen?" can be extremely useful for human survival, but this question can also be dangerous.

To understand this danger, we must recognize a basic fact about the human condition: human beings yearn to know.** We need answers that help us make sense of our world. When bad things happen to us, we search for explanations. These explanations can assume many forms.

For example, when a tragedy happens and people say things such as "everything happens for a reason" or "God works in mysterious ways," these vague answers serve as explanations. Or when people say a tragedy was caused by "fate" or "bad luck" or "bad karma," these are also explanations for the underlying cause of the tragedy. When people say crime is caused by "evil" or "original sin," they are trying to explain the underlying cause of crime. When people say human behavior is a product of "nature" or "nurture" or a combination of both, they are trying to explain the underlying

---

* Earlier humans such as *Homo erectus*—who may have known how to use fire—had some ability to understand underlying causes, but this ability seems to have increased in later humans. There are also different layers of causes. The makers of the samurai sword understood how to make strong steel on a manufacturing level, but they did not understand the underlying atomic cause of strong steel.

** As I explain later in this book, our craving to understand underlying causes can vary in intensity from person to person, and some people may repress their urge to know. Sometimes people will repress their urge to know if the knowledge could increase pain and trauma. Our yearning to know can compete with and lose to our notion that "ignorance is bliss."

cause of human actions. As far as we know, no other species searches for scientific and religious explanations for the underlying causes of events. We do not know of any other species that debates concepts such as fate versus luck, the existence of evil, or nature versus nurture.

Like two arms emerging from the human body, science and religion both emerge from humanity's yearning to know—our craving to understand underlying causes. Like two arms searching for objects in darkness, the arms of science and religion search for answers in the mysterious world around us. Human beings are unusual, because all other animals seem at peace with the causes of nature. When scientists observe their behavior, other animals exhibit a deep connection with nature that many human beings aspire toward. Other animals can better protect themselves in the future if they observe a catastrophe and learn what to avoid next time, but they don't search for underlying scientific and religious explanations that transcend what they can observe.

Our craving to understand underlying causes gives us an immense survival advantage, because it makes us want to know at a deep level why harmful and helpful things happen to us. This makes us more effective at preventing those harmful things and creating the conditions for those helpful things. Because our yearning to know is so powerful, if we do not have enough evidence to find accurate answers for how our world works, we can feel tempted to invent an explanation. This is why ancient Greeks explained the existence of lightning by saying Zeus hurled lightning bolts across the sky. This is why every ancient culture had mythological explanations for the forces of nature.

When our ancestors lacked the scientific evidence to arrive at accurate answers for how our world works, their craving to understand underlying causes tempted them to create stories that most people no longer believe today. How many people in the twenty-first century literally believe that Zeus causes lightning bolts? Our ancestors did not make things up due to a lack of intelligence, but because the human yearning to know is a craving that must be fed.

The question "why did this happen?" becomes dangerous when we arrive at inaccurate answers. If you lived in ancient Greece three thousand years ago and an earthquake destroyed your home and killed your child, the question "why did this happen?" could lead to strange answers when you lacked a scientific explanation for natural disasters. To understand how our brilliant reasoning ability and vivid human imagination can cause us to arrive at odd conclusions when we lack scientific evidence, consider the following logic.

An earthquake seems like a violent and destructive act. After all, earthquakes destroy things and kill people. When human beings become angry, they can also destroy things and kill people. So maybe an earthquake happens because nature is angry, similar to how an angry person might shake a table, smash a piece of furniture, or knock someone down. But why would nature be angry? People often become angry when someone does something hurtful and offensive to them. Did we do something hurtful and offensive to nature? If we change our behavior, can we stop nature from being angry, and will nature stop hurting us with earthquakes?

In ancient Greece and many other parts of the world, gods were personifications of nature. Instead of saying an earthquake was caused by "nature," most people living thousands of years ago would have said the name of a deity who symbolized nature. Many ancient cultures believed violent gods caused earthquakes, but because our vivid human imagination can invent many different explanations for earthquakes, numerous ancient cultures believed gigantic divine animals were the underlying cause of earthquakes. Among the Tzotzil people in southern Mexico, a story emerged that a cosmic jaguar caused earthquakes by scratching itself against the pillars of the world. And in Mongolia many believed that a massive frog that carried the earth on its back caused earthquakes by twitching.[8]

Today science has revealed that earthquakes are caused by shifting "tectonic plates" rather than angry Greek gods or gigantic divine animals.* In addition to creating inaccurate divine explanations for the causes of earthquakes, our ancient ancestors also created inaccurate natural explanations. Journalist Andrew Robinson tells us:

---

* Tectonic plates are the most frequent cause of earthquakes, but earthquakes can also have other causes such as volcanic eruptions, and there is growing evidence that "fracking" can cause minor earthquakes.

In classical antiquity Poseidon, the Greek god of the sea, was usually considered to be responsible for earthquakes—perhaps not surprisingly, given the destructive power in the Aegean and Mediterranean of earthquake-induced tsunamis. Poseidon was said to cause earthquakes while striking his trident on the ground when he became annoyed. However, some Greek philosophers proposed natural, rather than divine, explanations for earthquakes. Thales, for example, writing around 580 BC, believed that the earth was floating on the oceans and that water movements were responsible for earthquakes. By contrast, Anaximenes, who also lived in the sixth century BC, proposed that rocks falling in the interior of the earth must strike other rocks and produce reverberations.[9]

According to Greek mythology, Poseidon caused earthquakes because he was angry, using his massive trident to violently shake the earth. The *Iliad* refers to Poseidon as "the god of the quakes who grips and pounds the earth."[10] In Greek mythology, Poseidon was a personification of the ocean that caused earthquakes, floods, droughts, and storms.

Why was Poseidon portrayed as angry and violent? Imagine if you did not have a scientific understanding of the ocean or the causes of weather, and you believed the ocean had a human personality. How would you describe the ocean's personality? The ocean can be calm, gentle, and generous. It can give us fish to eat and the means for travel and commerce. Many ancient societies built their economies on professions that relied on the ocean.

But the ocean can also be a destroyer. It can sink ships, drown people, and devastate the land with storms and other natural disasters. If you lacked a scientific understanding of the ocean and imagined it behaved like a human being, and you tried to describe its personality, you would probably say it was fickle, moody, and prone to anger and violence. It could be generous today and destructive tomorrow. This is the way many ancient Greeks viewed Poseidon, a god who was known for his abundant gifts and terrible wrath.

Classics scholar Walter Burkert explains why the ancient Greeks saw earthquakes and storms as violent acts of wrath: "Poseidon remains an embodiment of elemental force; *sea storm and earthquake are the most violent forms of energy directly encountered by man* [emphasis added]."[11]

Why did the ancient Greeks believe that a violent god, rather than the innocent movements of a divine animal, caused earthquakes? Perhaps environmental, architectural, and cultural reasons made the Greeks more likely to believe in violent gods. Environmentally speaking, earthquakes and tsunamis were especially destructive in ancient Greece. According to the *Encyclopedia of Ancient Greece*, "The maximum intensity [of earthquakes] is much higher in some parts of the Aegean because they lie close to the edge of tectonic plates."[12] Because of the catastrophic earthquakes and tsunamis that affected the Aegean, nature may have seemed more "violent" to a person living in ancient Greece than a person living in many other parts of the ancient world.

Architecturally speaking, the ancient Greeks constructed stone buildings that could collapse and crush people during an earthquake, and entire cities could be devastated when the ground shook. Consequently, earthquakes posed a greater threat to the ancient Greeks than to many other cultures. Professor Amos Nur tells us, "The nomadic people who dominated most of North America in the distant past were probably affected only slightly by any but the greatest earthquakes. Their lightweight construction materials made their homes neither particularly dangerous in earthquakes nor particularly difficult to rebuild."[13]

Culturally speaking, perhaps the religious views of the ancient Greeks shaped their attitude toward natural disasters, although it could be that severe natural disasters in Greek prehistory actually shaped their religious views. Nevertheless, the bottom line is this: if the ancient Greeks saw nature as violent and dangerous because of the devastating earthquakes and tsunamis that killed their families and destroyed their cities, can we really blame them?

To appease Poseidon's wrath, the Greeks often sacrificed animals. Why did they do this? One reason is because Poseidon could seem like a psychopath who might murder you and your family when he was upset. Helen

Scales explains: "Sailors and fishermen made sure not to incur the sea god's wrath; they built temples to worship him, drowned sacrificial horses in his name, and implored him for safe passage across the seas."[14]

When we project a human personality onto the destructive forces of nature, then nature can seem psychotic. Although some ancient Greeks such as the politician Pericles, playwright Euripides, and poet Diagoras seemed to believe Poseidon was a metaphor rather than a real personality, many believed if they spilled blood on Poseidon's behalf, perhaps he would not massacre their families. Many ancient Greeks believed that their gods expressed anger through natural disasters and plagues. Hesiod, a Greek poet who lived around the seventh century BC, wrote, "But for those who practice violence and cruel deeds far-seeing Zeus, the son of Cronos, ordains a punishment. Often even a whole city suffers for a bad man who sins . . . [Zeus] lays great trouble upon the people, famine and plague together, so that the men perish away."[15]

Many ancient Greeks also believed that Poseidon and other Greek gods could become so enraged that they would slaughter children. Just as natural disasters and plagues do not spare the lives of children, the Greek gods were capable of killing without mercy or remorse. If a human being were diagnosed with these behaviors, we would call that person a psychopath.

Although my other books offer abundant evidence showing that human beings are not naturally violent, for many years I wondered, "If human beings are not naturally violent, why did so many of our early ancestors worship gods capable of psychotic wrath?" An obvious answer is that when people personify nature in their quest to understand the underlying causes of natural disasters and plague, nature seems to have psychotic tendencies. Later in this book we will explore various religious systems, including the violent rituals of the Aztecs, to further show how psychotic nature can seem when we imagine it has a human personality.

A natural disaster can slaughter your family, but it can also save your family. After the Mongols conquered China and Korea, they attempted to conquer Japan. In the book *Divine Wind: The History and Science of Hurricanes*, Kerry Emanuel describes how Japan was saved from two Mongol invasions by typhoons. Like the ancient Greeks and countless populations throughout history, the Japanese personified nature and saw the typhoons as acts of divine intervention. Emanuel explains:

> In the year 1259, Kublai Khan, the grandson of Genghis Khan, became emperor of Mongolia . . . Thus it came to pass that Kublai mounted an invasion to conquer Japan . . . On October 29, 1274, the invasion began. Some 40,000 men, including about 25,000 Mongolians and Chinese, 8,000 Korean troops, and 7,000 Chinese and Korean seamen, set sail from Korea in about 900 ships . . . The Japanese defenders were horrified by the Mongol cavalry charging off the beaches, steeped as they were in the tradition of hand-to-hand combat between knightly warriors. With fewer troops and inferior weapons, the Japanese were rapidly pushed back into the interior. But by nightfall, the Korean pilots sensed an approaching storm and begged their reluctant Mongol commanders to put the invasion force back to sea lest it be trapped on the coast and its ships destroyed at anchor . . . The ships of the time were no match for the tempest, and many foundered or were dashed to bits on the rocky coast. Nearly 13,000 men perished, mostly by drowning. The Mongols had been routed by a typhoon . . .
>
> The second Mongol invasion of Japan assumed staggering proportions. One armada consisting of 40,000 Mongols, Koreans, and north Chinese was to sail from Korea, while a second, larger force of some 100,000 men was to set out from various ports in south China. To gauge the size of this expeditionary force, consider that the Norman conquest of Britain in 1066 engaged 5,000 men . . .
>
> On the fifteenth and sixteenth of August [1281], history repeated itself. Once again, the Korean and south Chinese mariners sensed the approach of a typhoon and attempted to put to sea. But the fleet was so unwieldy and

poorly coordinated that many of the ships collided at the
entrance of Imari Bay and were smashed by the typhoon,
as were most of those that made it to the open ocean . . .
The wreckage and loss of life was staggering. Once again,
Kublai Khan's designs on Japan were defeated by a
typhoon, and never again did he attempt such an invasion.
As a direct result of these famous routs, the Japanese came
to think of the typhoon as a "divine wind," or *kamikaze*,
sent by their gods to deliver their land from invaders.[16]

When our ancestors lacked the scientific means to explain the underlying causes of natural disasters, they often personified nature. To understand
how the personification of nature affected the behavior of our ancestors, we
can look at the Spartans. Today pop culture and action movies have glorified
the Spartans as the bravest and fiercest warriors who ever lived, but when I
studied military history at West Point, the reality of the Spartans surprised
me.

Most people today don't realize how extremely superstitious the Spartans
were. Their superstitious rituals can seem very odd to us today, but their
behavior makes sense when we recognize their lack of scientific explanations
for natural disasters and their belief in fickle gods capable of psychotic behavior. Historian Alfred Bradford describes how the superstitious beliefs of the
Spartans caused them to sacrifice animals to the gods, look for omens in the
organs of these sacrificial animals, and change their military plans if they
believed the gods were upset:

> The [Spartan] kings' most important sacred duty was
> to determine the will of the gods and, in particular, the
> will of the king of the gods, Zeus, their ultimate progeni-
> tor, before they led the army out of Sparta and out of
> Laconia [the Spartan territory]. The kings conducted sac-
> rifices in Sparta to Zeus the Leader and to Athena and the
> other gods associated with Zeus. They observed the sooth-
> sayer as he conducted the sacrifice and examined the liver

[of the sacrificial animal], its general shape, its texture, and its lobes; then they would determine if the omens were favorable. If they were, the kings instructed a Spartan known as the "Fire-Bearer" to light a torch at the altar and lead the army to the border of Laconia: at the border the kings again would conduct sacrifices to Zeus and Athena. If they determined that the omens were still favorable, then, and only then, would they lead their army across the border.

The kings stood between their people and the gods— to recognize and avert, or circumvent, divine displeasure and to curry divine favor. If the resident god of a river forbad them to cross, could they go around without risking divine retribution? If the enemy declared a certain month sacred, only to prevent an attack by the Spartans, could the Spartans ignore the declaration? If they were shaken by an earthquake while they were on campaign, was the earthquake a warning to the Spartans or an ill omen for their enemies?

On the day the kings expected to fight, if they had detected no cautionary signs, they initiated the religious ceremonies preparatory to a battle—they sacrificed to the Muses (to invite them to witness the courage of the Spartans and to inspire poets to write about their heroic deeds); and they sacrificed a goat, not to examine its liver, but simply to offer it to the gods as a treat. After they had completed these preliminaries, they ordered the Spartans to form their phalanx, and, at the first sight of the enemy phalanx, they instructed their men to put wreaths on their heads (as portents of victory), and they told the flute-players to play the royal battle song, "The Song of Castor," and they sang it, too.[17]

The Spartans were so superstitious that when the Persians invaded Greece in 490 BC, the Spartans did not join Athens in the Battle of Marathon because they thought fighting before the full moon would upset the gods. Historian Peter Krentz describes how Philippides, the runner who inspired the race that became known as the "marathon," tried unsuccessfully to enlist the help of the Spartans:

> Before they left Athens, the generals sent Philippides, a professional distance runner, to Sparta. Probably running barefoot, Philippides reached Sparta the day after he left Athens—that is, he covered roughly 150 miles (on the most likely route) in not more than about 36 hours. If the story once seemed incredible, it does no longer. In 1982, two RAF [Royal Air Force] officers ran from Athens to Sparta in 34 and 35.5 hours, demonstrating that Philippides could have done what Herodotus says he did . . .
>
> When he reached Sparta, Philippides asked for help. "Spartans," Herodotus reports that he said, "the Athenians beg you to rush to their defense and not look on passively as the most ancient city in Greece falls into slavery imposed by barbarians. For in fact Eretria has already been enslaved, and thus Greece has become weaker by one important city." In reply, the Spartans expressed their willingness to help, but said that they could not act yet. It was the ninth of the month, and a law prevented them from marching until the moon was full. The law in question probably applied only to the month of Karneia, during which the Spartans celebrated the festival of [the god] Apollo that gave its name to the month. Scholars of an earlier generation tended to dismiss Spartan religious qualms as specious excuses for inaction, but today it is generally recognized that the Spartans paid particular attention to the gods in their military life.[18]

Wanting to protect Greece from a Persian invasion, and looking for military victory and glory, the Spartans departed after the full moon to help Athens, but when they arrived the Athenians had already won the Battle of Marathon. The Spartans, who wished to be celebrated by future generations as brave warriors who fought in famous battles, had missed an opportunity to fight in one of the most famous battles in history—because of the moon. Greek historian Herodotus said, "After the full moon, 2,000 Spartans marched to Athens in such great haste that they arrived in Attica [the Athenian homeland] on the third day out of Sparta. They were too late to engage in battle."[19]

West Point never taught me that winning a military campaign had anything to do with sacrificing animals in a religious ceremony, finding omens in a goat's liver, or fighting battles on days that will please rather than anger the gods. When I studied the reality of the Spartans that differed from the pop culture glorification of the Spartans, I could not help but think, "The Spartans were really weird." I am not trying to make fun of the Spartans, but to show how much warfare has changed due to our greater scientific understanding of the natural world.

Could you imagine General Dwight Eisenhower—Supreme Allied Commander during World War II—not invading the beaches of Normandy because a soothsayer saw bad omens in the bloody liver of a sacrificial goat, or not fighting a battle on a particular day because it might offend the gods? Nobody at West Point ever explained to me why the Spartans were so superstitious, but my journey to unlock the mysteries of the human condition has increased my understanding and empathy for the Spartans and all human beings.

Many American soldiers find comfort in prayer, but the modern American army does not practice animal sacrifice to appease the gods, which was common in the ancient Greek and Roman armies. Describing the Persian invasion of Greece, the Athenian general Xenophon discussed the use of animal sacrifice to win divine favor: "The Persians and their friends came with an enormous army, thinking that they would wipe Athens off the face of the earth; but the Athenians had the courage to stand up to them by themselves, and they defeated them. On that occasion they had made a vow to [the goddess] Artemis that they would sacrifice to her a goat for every one of their enemies whom they killed, but, since they could not get hold of enough goats, they decided to sacrifice five hundred every year, and they are still sacrificing them today."[20]

Although animal sacrifice to appease the gods is not as common today, the modern world is still filled with superstitious rituals. What is the underlying cause of this superstition? I have heard people say, "Human beings are superstitious because they are stupid," but science shows that an underlying cause of superstition is not stupidity, but lack of control. One of the most disturbing experiences we can have as human beings is feeling helpless in a stressful situation.

Superstitious rituals give people the illusion of control, and conspiracy theories give people a "personified evil" where they can direct their anger over feeling helpless. In an article in the *Chicago Tribune*, Jeremy Manier discusses how lack of control is an underlying cause of superstition in baseball and many other areas of life:

> Baseball may be the most superstition-filled sport, with bizarre traditions that range from players who insist on chewing the same gum each day during a hitting streak to the Chicago Cubs' yearly reminder of the infamous billy goat curse. Now a new study by Northwestern University researchers has found that all such superstitions may have a common source: the feeling of a lack of control, which spurs people to concoct false patterns and meaning from the noise of life's chance events.
>
> The Chicago group found that making experimental subjects remember a time when they lacked control actually changed the way they viewed the world, and created a temporary need to see patterns where none existed.
>
> The study in Friday's edition of the journal Science represents the first experimental confirmation of a link that psychologists long suspected was behind superstitions, conspiracy theories, rituals and even some aspects of

religious belief . . . "Most of the time the groups you see with vast conspiratorial theories are those that don't have much control over the outcome of something," said [Jennifer] Whitson, now an assistant professor at the University of Texas' department of management . . .

In baseball, experts believe superstition and ritual pop up most often around tasks where players have the least control. Batters and pitchers often develop elaborate preparation routines, in part because their success often depends on random factors such as where a fly ball lands or whether the batter anticipates a pitch correctly. Anthropologist George Gmelch once wrote of a pitcher who insisted on washing his hands after every inning in which he gave up a run.

Fielders, by contrast, maintain few rituals—perhaps because a pro player's success in fielding a ball is so high. "Unlike hitting and pitching, a fielder has almost complete control over the outcome of his performance," Gmelch wrote in a 2000 article called "Baseball Magic." "He knows that, in better than 9.7 times out of 10, he will execute his task flawlessly. With odds like that there is little need for ritual."

Gmelch said in an interview that he grasped the possible link between religious rituals and the ingrained routines of ballplayers during college, when he also was a minor league baseball player. "In both cases you're looking for confidence, some sense that you have control over things," said Gmelch, professor of anthropology at the University of San Francisco . . . Baseball rituals can be calming even if they're irrational, Gmelch pointed out.[21]

What do the superstitious rituals in war and baseball have in common? They both result from humanity's craving to understand underlying causes, along with the discomfort we feel when lacking control in stressful situations.

Our craving to understand underlying causes gives us a powerful survival advantage when we discover the actual causes of our problems (such as the discovery that plagues are caused by microorganisms rather than angry deities). But when we are unable to discover these underlying causes, we may invent one in the form of a superstitious ritual. For example, if the Spartans could not figure out why they lost a battle, it was easy to invent a cause. A Spartan could reason, "The underlying cause of losing the battle was angering the gods, and to prevent the gods from being angry at us in the future we must conduct more animal sacrifice."

Another feature war and baseball have in common is they both involve a lot of luck. Carl von Clausewitz, arguably the most influential military strategist of all time, said, "There is no human affair which stands so constantly and so generally in close connection with chance as War. But together with chance, the accidental, and along with it good luck, occupy a great place in War."[22]

Thucydides was an ancient Greek who thought differently from most Greeks of his era, because he attributed unforeseen disasters in war to luck rather than the Greek gods. Born in the fifth century BC, Thucydides was a general, historian, and veteran of the Peloponnesian War. He tells us that during the Peloponnesian War, an Athenian tried to discourage the Spartans from invading Athens by saying, "Think, too, of the great part that is played by the unpredictable in war: think of it now, before you are actually committed to war. The longer a war lasts, the more things tend to depend on accidents."[23]

When Thucydides wrote about the Spartan army surrendering to the Athenians at the Battle of Sphacteria in 425 BC, he discussed how being killed by an arrow had less to do with one's amount of bravery and more to do with luck. Thucydides explained:

> The general impression had been that Spartans would
> never surrender their arms whether because of hunger or
> any other form of compulsion; instead they would keep
> them to the last and die fighting as best they could. It was
> hard to believe that those who had surrendered were the

same sort of people as those who had fallen [in battle]. Indeed, there was an occasion afterwards when an Athenian ally in order to insult one of the [Spartan] prisoners from the island asked him whether it was the ones who had fallen who were the real Spartans. The reply was that "spindles (by which he meant arrows) would be worth a great deal if they could pick out brave men from cowards," a remark which was intended to show that the ones who died were simply the ones who came in the way of the stones and the arrows.[24]

Most action movies make it seem like the strongest and bravest soldiers survive in combat, but many military strategists and veterans know that war has more in common with Russian roulette than a Hollywood film. Vietnam veteran Gene Dark said, "I arrived in Da Nang, with thirty-five marines. Only four of us were left, and all but one had a Purple Heart. I was so fortunate to be alive. Why had I survived? Was I faster, smarter, or tougher than the other marines? Of course not; in fact, the opposite was probably true. Was it just fate? I felt guilty that so many braver men than me had died. Every marine who ever fought a war feels the same way. Ask him and he will tell you about the guilt that he carries deep down inside for surviving when so many others died."[25]

When people lack control in war, baseball, or any situation in life, superstitious rituals can create the illusion of control. Superstitious rituals exist in many shapes and sizes, from harmless baseball traditions to bloody Aztec ceremonies that involved human sacrifice (I discuss human sacrifice in a later chapter). Also, people's reactions can vary when they do not know an underlying cause. Some people may be more prone to settling for easy answers, and others may be more willing to follow the truth, no matter where it takes them.

The reason our reactions to the unknown can vary is because we have different personalities and life experiences. Despite our differences, however, we all share a craving to understand the world around us. Without a "worldview," we would not be able to function. For some the craving is small and for others it is large, but it is a human craving that helped give birth to philosophy, religion, science, and the most fanatical ideologies in the world.

Our craving to understand underlying causes is embodied in the question "why"—a word used by children to find out why it rains, by adults to make sense of their lives, by scientists to explore the mysteries of the universe, and by theologians to question the nature of existence. New paradigms emerge when someone asks "why" to the questions so many others take for granted. "Why" is one of humanity's most powerful ideas, an idea that can liberate us, empower us, or ruin us.

It is important to increase our understanding of the human condition, because the less we know about our humanity and the many ways our human vulnerabilities can be exploited, the easier we are to manipulate. Since the question "why" can create such a strong craving to know, we will often settle for answers that are easy, oversimplistic, convenient, inaccurate, and even made up. Knowing this about our humanity, we must be vigilant by not allowing our craving to overpower our reason. When our country encounters a tragedy or serious problem, for example, our craving to find a cause is especially strong, which gives people in power an opportunity to manipulate us with propaganda.

If you ever doubt that human beings have a craving to understand the causes of events, look at how people react when a terrorist attack happens. Virtually everyone wants to identify a cause (even if the cause is as general as "evil"), which gives those in power an opportunity to spread misleading explanations. When a mass shooting happens in the United States, people debate whether it was caused by an evil gene, mental illness, not enough gun control, too much gun control, violent media, bad parenting, bullying, a "false flag operation" (a conspiracy where our own government orchestrated the shooting), or a combination of factors. When our economy descends into a recession, there is always an intense debate to identify the underlying causes.

In our quest to understand the world around us, our desire for certainty can overpower our curiosity. In *The End of War* and *Peaceful Revolution* I discuss how children are naturally curious, but their curiosity is often repressed. Healthy curiosity and critical thinking are necessary to overcome manipulation. The Plato's Cave allegory in my book *The End of War* shows how our craving to understand the world allows people to manipulate us with deceptive *shadow images*. These images can also hypnotize us with distractions that suppress our minds, like a lullaby putting us to sleep during a time when the survival of humanity requires us to be awake.

If human beings could move away from harmful superstitions such as animal and human sacrifice to appease the gods, can we move away from other harmful superstitions? Can we understand the underlying causes of problems such as war, injustice, oppression, racism, sexism, trauma, and environmental destruction? Can we use our heightened human awareness to work together to solve these problems? Can we make the arms of science and religion cooperate in a way that better serves humanity and our planet? And can we achieve a higher bliss than ignorance? Humanity can achieve all of this if we increase our understanding of the human condition, learn the art of waging peace, and recognize nature's cruel kiss.

## The Cruel Kiss of Mother Earth

When we search for the underlying causes of problems and arrive at inaccurate answers, it can silence our empathy. For example, if you believe a baby girl is born with a disability because she is cursed by the gods or paying back bad karma from a past life, it can reduce your empathy not only for her, but also her family. Some people have an extreme view of reincarnation and karma, causing them to believe that all our pain in this life results from evil acts we committed during past lives. I have met people who told me that when women are raped and children are molested, it is punishment for evil acts they committed during their past lives.

In 2013 I had a conversation with a woman who told me, "Everything bad that happens to children is a result of evil they committed during their previous lives." I responded, "I recently read a news story about a mother who sent text messages to her boyfriend, inviting him to rape her four-month-old daughter. The rape led to the infant's death. Did the four-month-old girl do something to deserve that?"[26] The woman replied, "Yes, that must have been punishment for her bad karma from a past life."

That is one example of how our human craving to understand underlying causes can result in inaccurate answers. Someone might respond, "But you cannot prove that the four-month-old girl did not cause her own rape and murder by committing evil in a past life." However, the *burden of proof* always rests on the person making a claim. If I said to you, "My real name is not Paul. My name is actually Zeus, and I am king of the Greek gods. I have been disguising myself as the person you call Paul so that I can observe your human activities up close," how would you respond?

If you responded, "I don't believe you," and I replied, "But you can't prove that I am not Zeus," you could say, "But you have the burden of proof, so you must offer evidence that you are Zeus. Until you can provide evidence that you are an immortal Greek god, I shouldn't accept your claim as true." In a similar way, if a person cannot provide evidence that a child was raped and murdered because of evil acts she committed during a past life, we should not accept the person's claim as true.

But what kind of evidence should we require from people who make outrageous claims? If I handed you a fake driver's license with the name ZEUS printed on it, would you suddenly believe I am an immortal Greek god and apologize for doubting my divine identity, or would you require more convincing evidence from me? The more a person's claim contradicts what we know about reality, the heavier their burden of proof becomes. As Carl Sagan said, "Extraordinary claims require extraordinary evidence."[27]

During an era when people believed the sun revolved around the earth, Galileo made outrageous claims that contradicted what people knew about reality, when he said the earth actually revolves around the sun. But unlike a person claiming to be an immortal Greek god, Galileo fulfilled the burden of proof by backing up his claim with strong evidence.

At West Point during my spare time, I studied hypnosis and magic tricks, becoming quite adept at these skills. Hypnosis and magic tricks showed me many ways to deceive people's perception, allowing me to better detect when someone is trying to fool me. Cult leaders and con artists use some of these deceptive methods to manipulate others, and they also tend to prey on vulnerable people searching for answers.

When people arrive at inaccurate answers to life's mysteries, like those who believed Poseidon caused earthquakes by shaking the world with his trident, we should not lose our empathy for them. We should not look down on the ancient Greeks or any past society that held superstitious beliefs, because as we strive to understand the underlying causes of our problems, many of us in the modern world have also arrived at inaccurate answers that silence our empathy.

In Rhonda Byrne's bestselling book *The Secret*, she promotes a concept called the "law of attraction," which suggests that we attract everything good and bad that happens to us through our positive and negative thoughts. According to the law of attraction, the cause of my father attacking me when I was four years old was not his war trauma, but my failure to think positive thoughts. Based on Byrne's view, because I had thoughts on a negative frequency I made him attack me, attracting these traumatic events to myself. Her belief system suggests that the American slavery system and the Holocaust were caused by the victims thinking on a negative frequency. If those harmed by slavery and the Holocaust had known the secret of positive thinking discussed in her book, their tragedies would not have happened. Journalist Victoria Moore explains:

> Summoning good things into your life—a new job, a five-bedroom house with garden or even a parking place—is, according to Byrne, simple. All you have to do is visualize what you want, focus on it and it will come—"exactly like placing an order from a catalogue."
>
> There are some refinements to the process. The innermost secret of *The Secret* is that you have to phrase your requests in the right way. This is apparently where many people go wrong. It is essential to be detailed in every particular. Byrne writes of a woman desperate for a boyfriend. She had visualized him—but he still failed to materialize. Byrne explains that he did not turn up because she had not made sufficient physical space for a man in her life. So she went to the garage and moved the car from the

middle so as to leave room for her imaginary partner's, then cleared out half her wardrobe and began sleeping on one side of her double bed. And, hey presto, the right man soon came along.

The other mistake people apparently make when ordering from the catalogue of life is not thinking positively enough . . . When you hit the shops with an up-to-the-limit credit card and a bank balance deep into overdraft territory, instead of saying you can't afford something, you must tell yourself: "I *can* afford that! I *can* buy that." I fear this may be how shopaholism begins, but Byrne insists that not only does such thinking make you feel better, it also creates material wealth . . .

It seems unusual that a self-help book should take such an extreme hedonistic and self-centered view, but, according to Byrne, true happiness comes from putting yourself before others. She also assuages any concerns you might have about overt materialism with an unusual interpretation of the Bible—saying that Abraham, Isaac, Jacob, Joseph, Moses and Jesus were all millionaires, "with more affluent lifestyles than many present-day millionaires could conceive of." . . .

We are all, she states, "human transmission towers," emitting thoughts on a particular frequency and attracting "all like things that are on the same frequency." This is why, she says, if you think negative thoughts, then bad things will happen. The trouble is that if you extend this to its logical conclusion, then you not only have to believe that good things come to positive thinkers, but also that anyone who suffers only has themselves to blame. So, if someone is fat, is that their fault for thinking fat thoughts? Surely Byrne cannot believe so. Yes, she does. "A person cannot think thin thoughts and be fat."

Byrne believes that if someone has cancer, they can

cure themselves by laughing—which implies that the converse is also true; that their cancer has been caused by negative thinking. Astonishingly, she even says this outright: "Illness cannot exist in a body that has harmonious thoughts." So what about those caught up in wars, acts of terrorism and natural disasters? The hundreds of thousands killed in the Asian tsunami, the thousands who died on 9/11, the millions put to death in the Holocaust? Are we simply to assume it was all their own fault? Byrne sounds rather weary as she skirts round this subject in her book but, basically, her answer is an extraordinary yes. "By the law of attraction, they had to be on the same frequency as the event," she says, allowing only a small concession: "It doesn't necessarily mean they thought of that event."[28]

When we believe that people suffer a personal tragedy because they thought on a negative frequency, were evil in a past life, or are being punished by the gods, it can silence our empathy. However, in the fifth century BC, a Greek named Hippocrates had a more empathetic view of human tragedies such as illness. Hippocrates is widely regarded as the father of modern medicine. The Hippocratic oath, which requires doctors to compassionately serve their patients, still guides the actions of many medical practitioners today.

Instead of viewing plague, epilepsy, and other illnesses as punishments from the gods, Hippocrates had a more compassionate view of those who suffered from sickness. Nearly twenty-five hundred years ago, he wrote the following about epilepsy: "I am about to discuss the disease called 'sacred.' It is not, in my opinion, any more divine or more sacred than other diseases, but has a natural cause, and its supposed divine origin is due to men's inexperience, and to their wonder at its peculiar character."[29]

Because the world has changed since ancient Greece, modern versions of the Hippocratic oath keep the spirit of compassion alive while adjusting the oath to deal with modern issues. The original Hippocratic oath explains how doctors should protect their patients from harm and injustice, not take sexual advantage of vulnerable people, and respect patient privacy by not gossiping or spreading rumors. Hippocrates had the revolutionary idea that illnesses are not punishments from the Greek gods but instead have natural causes,* and the following excerpt from the original Hippocratic oath shows how a more accurate understanding of the causes of illness can summon rather than silence our empathy:

> I will keep them [the sick] from harm and injustice
> . . . Whatever houses I may visit, I will come for the benefit
> of the sick, remaining free of all intentional injustice, of
> all mischief and in particular of sexual relations with both
> female and male persons, be they free or slaves. What I
> may see or hear in the course of the treatment or even out-
> side of the treatment in regard to the life of men, which
> on no account one must spread abroad, I will keep to
> myself, holding such things shameful to be spoken
> about.[30]

Gandhi said people can have a piece of the truth,[31] and Rhonda Byrne expresses a piece of the truth about the value of having a positive outlook. My other books discuss how a positive attitude based on hope, empathy, and appreciation can improve our quality of life and strengthen our ability to wage peace. Also, science shows that harboring negative feelings such as anger over a long period of time can weaken our immune system, and positive feelings such as hope, empathy, and appreciation can boost our immune system.

But does thinking negative thoughts cause all cancer, epilepsy, multiple sclerosis, Lou Gehrig's disease, HIV, Alzheimer's disease, malaria, polio, food poisoning, staph infection, glaucoma, cataracts, hearing loss, hepatitis, diabetes, and Parkinson's disease? Overwhelming evidence shows that

---

* Although Hippocrates, like some living before him, took the revolutionary step of separating the causes of illness from the Greek gods, his natural explanations of illness tended to be very inaccurate (similar to the ancient Greek philosophers I cited earlier who tried to explain the natural causes of earthquakes). I say that Hippocrates's natural explanations were "more accurate" than divine explanations, because he took a step in the right direction and helped lead humanity toward the path of scientific inquiry. The name Hippocrates also symbolizes a school of thought, since many writings along with the Hippocratic oath are attributed to him.

Rhonda Byrne's approach to positive thinking cannot prevent or cure all of these illnesses.

Byrne expresses a half-truth, because our attitude can in fact influence our physical health and the conditions of our surroundings, but not to the extent she claims. In my book *Peaceful Revolution*, I explain how a half-truth can be more dangerous than an outright lie.

I have met many compassionate people who believe in a more humane version of reincarnation and karma that does not blame rape victims for being raped, and I have also spoken with kind people who believe in parts of Byrne's teachings while rejecting the view that victims of natural disasters caused the disaster by thinking on a negative frequency. Nevertheless, activist Barbara Ehrenreich describes how these views, if we are not careful, can silence our empathy and cause harm:

> The other thing I find very, very disturbing about [the beliefs of Rhonda Byrne and others] is I just think it's cruel. It's cruel to take people who are having great difficulties in their lives and tell them it's all in their head, and they only have to change their attitude. My favorite example of this moral callousness is from [Rhonda Byrne] the author of *The Secret*, that was a bestseller . . . the book on how you can have anything you want, attract anything to yourself by thinking. And she was asked about the [Asian] tsunami of '06 and how could this happen, and she said, paraphrasing it, those people, the victims of it, must have been sending out tsunami-like vibrations into the universe to attract that to themselves, because nothing happens to us that we don't attract. And I think that's beyond amorality. I don't even know where to locate that.
>
> I'm not advocating gloom and pessimism or negativity or depression. Those can also be delusional. You can go around making up a story to yourself that everything you undertake is going to fail, and there's no reason to think that. My very radical suggestion is *realism*, just trying

to figure out what is actually happening in the world, and seeing what we can do about those parts of it that are threatening or hurtful . . .

What could be cleverer as a way of quelling dissent than to tell people who are in some kind of trouble, poverty, unemployment, etc. that it's all their attitude, that's all that has to change, that they should just get with the program, smile, no complaining. It's a brilliant form of social control, which by the way was practiced in the Soviet Union. One of the principles of Soviet Communism was optimism, so it's a form of social control by the way that has been widespread in totalitarian types of societies. But I think it has worked very well in America. Take the issue of class inequality. How could that be a problem if anyone can become rich by thinking about it?[32]

When I discuss our amazing human ability to arrive at "accurate answers" for the causes of our problems, I have met people who say, "All truth is relative. We cannot really know what is true and what is untrue, because there is no such thing as truth." *But there is such a thing as truth.* For example, it is a scientific fact that African Americans are not subhuman. It is a scientific fact that women are not intellectually inferior to men. And it is a scientific fact that the earth and other planets in our solar system revolve around the sun. Not long ago, people were imprisoned, beaten, and even killed for promoting these truths.

Many people used to believe the underlying cause of slavery in the United States was that black people were subhuman, and that God had made them to be slaves. But that was an inaccurate answer for the cause of slavery. Frederick Douglass explains how asking "why" as a child, along with his critical thinking ability, eventually led him to a more accurate answer for the cause of slavery:

[As a child I wondered] why am I a slave? Why are some people slaves and others masters? These were perplexing questions and very troublesome to my childhood. I was very early told by some one that *"God up in the sky"* had made all things, and had made black people to be slaves and white people to be masters . . . I could not tell how anybody could know that God made black people to be slaves. Then I found, too, that there were puzzling exceptions to this theory of slavery, in the fact that all black people were not slaves, and all white people were not masters . . .

I have met, at the South, many good, religious colored people who were under the delusion that God required them to submit to slavery and to wear their chains with meekness and humility. I could entertain no such nonsense as this . . . I saw that slaveholders would have gladly made me believe that, in making a slave of me and in making slaves of others, they were merely acting under the authority of God, and I felt to them as to robbers and deceivers.[33]

When we realize slavery does not result from God creating certain people to be slaves, but is instead caused by an unjust system, we gain a more accurate (and empathetic) understanding of those living under slavery. Although countless Christians throughout history supported slavery, during the nineteenth century many white Christians such as William Lloyd Garrison and John Brown saw slavery as a sacrilege against the core teachings of Jesus, and they risked their lives to end slavery. Garrison was almost killed by a mob, and Brown was executed for attempting to start a slave rebellion.

George Thompson, a white British citizen who advocated the end of slavery, told his fellow Christians: "Christian Ministers! I call first upon you; ye are ambassadors for God—your God is a God of love, your mission a mission of mercy, your message a message of salvation . . . In the name of the gospel, whose precepts and provisions are by slavery and its abettors despised and rejected . . . I call upon you to denounce this evil, to lift up your voice against it, to cry aloud and spare not until it ceases to 'make merchandise of the bodies and the souls of men.'"[34]

The intellectual equality of the races has been proven by geneticists to be a scientific fact. When we believe that racial inferiority is the underlying cause of a population's enslavement, it can silence our empathy for them, but the scientific understanding that injustice causes slavery offers us a more accurate (and empathetic) attitude toward those harmed by slavery. In what other ways can inaccurate beliefs silence our empathy?

When we believe that divine punishment is the underlying cause of earthquakes, it can also silence our empathy, but the scientific understanding that plate tectonics causes earthquakes offers us a more accurate (and empathetic) attitude toward those harmed by earthquakes. And when we believe that evil deeds from a past life, divine punishment, or thinking on a negative frequency are the underlying cause of cancer, it can silence our empathy, but the scientific understanding that cancer has genetic and environmental causes offers us a more accurate (and empathetic) attitude toward those who suffer from cancer.

Having accurate information about how our world works can increase our empathy in many ways. To offer another example of how truth can promote empathy, when we believe that humanity is born evil, naturally violent, and destined to forever wage war, it can silence our empathy, but the scientific understanding that violence is instead caused by trauma and other preventable factors offers us a more accurate (and empathetic) understanding of human beings. A quote from medical doctor Gary Slutkin that I shared earlier in this book stated: "Violence is like the great infectious diseases of all history. *We used to look at people with plague, leprosy, TB, as bad and evil people* [emphasis added] . . . What perpetuates violence can be as invisible today as the microorganisms of the past were."[35]

People alive today might see the Greek myth of Poseidon as silly, but Greek mythology is filled with powerful metaphorical truths. In my book *The Art of Waging Peace*, the chapters "The Labyrinth of Trauma" and "The Siren Song of Rage" show that Greek mythology can teach us a lot about our humanity when we know how to translate the language of symbols and metaphors.

I have met people who reject the possibility that the Bible contains any metaphorical truth. But a person who believes the Bible is literally true can also explore the metaphorical truth of the Garden of Eden (where in the Bible does it say a story cannot have more than one meaning?), and even an atheist can find wisdom in a biblical metaphor if it helps us better navigate the problem of human existence. By revealing our shared human vulnerabilities, the metaphorical truth of the Garden of Eden has increased my empathy for all people, and we can all meditate on this metaphor to strengthen our muscle of empathy.

Because my journey to understand the human condition has taught me that people have a craving to understand underlying causes, and their yearning to make sense of the world can lead them to inaccurate answers, I have more empathy for humanity. I see our *craving for explanations* as a feature on the landscape of our shared humanity, and I wage peace to spread the message of empathy and resolve the true underlying causes of war, injustice, racism, sexism, and environmental destruction. How do I know that my approach to creating solutions is not as inaccurate as the view that innocent people suffer from rape, war, and injustice because of their negative thought frequencies? Because I offer strong evidence in the books I write and courses I teach to support what I say.

For example, someone might say we can solve all the world's problems by just thinking positive thoughts or simply praying for divine intervention, but the civil and women's rights movements serve as evidence that solving serious problems requires *hard work*. If we want to find evidence that hard work is necessary to create significant change in the world, we can look at *all of human history.*

In *The Secret* Rhonda Byrne says Socrates knew "the secret," yet she does not mention that he criticized injustice, experienced great adversity as he tried to create positive change, and was executed by the Athenian government. If Socrates knew "the secret," why did he live in poverty, why was he ridiculed by his fellow citizens, and why did the Athenian government make him swallow poison? As I discussed earlier in this book, Frederick Douglass tells us:

> If there is no struggle, there is no progress. Those who
> profess to favor freedom, and yet depreciate agitation, are

men who want crops without plowing up the ground. They want rain without thunder and lightning. They want the ocean without the awful roar of its many waters. This struggle may be a moral one; or it may be a physical one; or it may be both moral and physical; but it must be a struggle. Power concedes nothing without a demand. It never did, and it never will.[36]

If we want to find evidence that supports what Frederick Douglass said, we can again look at *all of human history*. During the civil rights movement, people prayed not only with words but also with action by marching, boy-cotting, and protesting. They prayed not just on their knees, but also on their feet. Rabbi Abraham Heschel, who marched with King during the civil rights movement, said: "For many of us the march from Selma to Mont-gomery was about protest and prayer. Legs are not lips and walking is not kneeling. And yet our legs uttered songs. Even without words, our march was worship. I felt my legs were praying."[37]

People such as Rabbi Abraham Heschel, Martin Luther King Jr., and many others saw action as the highest form of prayer. Helplessness is a major cause of inaction, and when people do not take action because they feel help-less, they are more likely to arrive at inaccurate answers to their problems. When we don't know how to take effective action to defeat injustice, we are more likely to believe that "the law of attraction" or divine intervention are our only options. When we feel helpless and don't know the art of waging peace, we are also more likely to believe that a messianic president will solve all our problems for us. Positive change is most likely to happen on a large scale when people organize themselves and demand change. If we want to find evidence that supports this claim, once again we can look at *all of human history*.

To understand why our ancient ancestors felt helpless, we must explore the reality of nature, not the sanitized view of nature that has been handed to us in the twenty-first century. Many people today look down on our ancient ancestors as being primitive, cruel, violent, and stupid. I have heard people say, "Why were human beings in the past so superstitious? Why did they wage so much war? Humanity must be naturally violent, and also naturally stupid." When we study the reality of nature, however, the behavior of our ancient ancestors makes a lot of sense.

First of all, it was easier for a nomadic tribe from long ago to see nature as generous and benevolent, because when there was a drought, flood, or lack of food, they could simply move to another area. If you were living in a nomadic tribe that had survived for thousands of years, then your people's experience of nature would have been as follows: there is no water, so you go somewhere else and find water; there is no food, so you go somewhere else and find food. Nature seems to always generously provide what the tribe needs, and if nature had not provided food and water for a single generation, then the tribe would have died out.

If you were living in a nomadic tribe thousands of years ago, you would tend to see nature as generous and benevolent, and your deities might be depicted as kind spirits offering blessings and gifts. But nature tended to seem more hostile for people living in ancient agricultural societies, because when there was a drought, flood, or lack of food, they could not easily migrate like a nomadic tribe. They often felt stuck.

Imagine living in an agricultural society three thousand years ago, where people have lost the knowledge needed to survive as nomadic hunter-gatherers.* What happens if a drought lasting for several years wipes out your city's crops? Many of the people in your city, including your friends and family, might starve to death. What happens if there is a plague? It might cause half of the people you know, including your children, to die a horrific and agonizing death. Historian Joseph Patrick Byrne discusses how the plague known as the "Black Death" killed about half of Europe's population:

---

* There have been many examples in history where large groups migrated, but the larger and more dependent a society was on agriculture (rather than foraging or pastoralism), the more difficult it was to move. In his book *The Agricultural Revolution in Prehistory*, Graeme Barker discusses how nomadic and sedentary cultures existed as a wide spectrum. Numerous Bronze Age sedentary cultures were toward one end of the spectrum (heavy reliance on agriculture), while our earliest nomadic ancestors were on the other end of the spectrum (heavy reliance on hunting-gathering).

[William] Naphy and [Andrew] Spicer posit a population of western Europe in 1290 of 75 to 80 million, and
a mid-Plague estimate in 1430 of 20 to 40 million, for a
maximum population drop of 75 percent. Of course the
pestilence by no means accounts for this entire drop—
famine, war, and other diseases did their dirty jobs—but
if their estimates are anywhere near accurate, the demo-
graphic effect was horrendous. One trend is clear in recent
scholarship: no one is reducing the generic percentage loss.
Several decades ago it was "a quarter to a third" of the population [was killed by the plague]; more recently "a third
to a half"'; for England, historian John Aberth suggests 40
to 60 percent is warranted by local studies. In 2002 historian Christopher Dyer summed up the view of many: "it
would be reasonable to estimate the death rate in 1348–
1349 at about half of the English population. Its effects
were universal, and no village, town nor region for which
records exist escaped. If the total population stood at about
5 or 6 million, there were 2.5 or 3 million casualties . . ."
    The medieval Christian believed that all people sin
and that all sinful people are unworthy of any gift from
God. Rather, because of sin and disobedience, they are
justly deserving of any punishment God deems appropri-
ate, including the Black Death.[38]

Imagine not knowing what is causing so many people around you to
die from the Black Death—an illness that inflicted terrible suffering on people as dark spots caused by rupturing blood vessels appeared beneath the
skin, pus-filled blisters that burn like hot coals appeared all over the body,
and swellings as large as apples appeared around the neck, groin, and armpits.
The Black Death also caused people to vomit blood.[39]
    Italian writer Giovanni Boccaccio, who lived during the Black Death,
described how the streets would fill with rotting corpses: "And many of them
fell dead in the public streets, by day and night, with many others dying in

their own homes. With regard to the latter, it was generally only the stench of their rotting bodies which signaled to neighbors that they had died. With these, and with all the others who were dying throughout the city, bodies were everywhere . . . The whole atmosphere seemed to be filled and polluted by the stench of dead bodies." [40]

The painful blisters and large swellings caused by the Black Death, along with the corpses filling the city and the constant stench of rotting flesh, sound worse than anything I ever saw in the horror movies that were popular when I was growing up. Unlike a horror movie, the monsters causing the Black Death could not be seen or heard. When we cannot see or hear what is killing us, we can easily arrive at inaccurate explanations for the causes of our problems. Since viruses and bacteria are invisible to the naked eye, it is understandable how people living during the time of the Black Death could believe the plague was an act of divine wrath.

Today it has become trendy to trash-talk humanity, to say human beings are inherently crazy and stupid, and to make fun of those who lived before us. I have heard people say, "The Christians living in the Middle Ages were a bunch of barbaric idiots who believed in superstition." But what would you have most likely believed if you lived back then? Without a microscope or formal education in medical science, a person living at that time could not miraculously discover the cause and cure for the Black Death, since human beings did not develop a deep understanding of "germs" until about five hundred years later.

When I think of the people who watched helplessly as their friends, spouses, parents, and children died from the Black Death, I feel immense compassion for these fragile and vulnerable human beings who struggled as best they could, craving to understand underlying causes, grasping desperately for some kind of explanation, unable to see the microscopic killers massacring their families. As you read the following quote from Joseph Patrick Byrne, try to imagine the panic, confusion, and helplessness these people must have felt while witnessing the horrendous suffering and death around them:

Sicilian Michele da Piazza in Messina attributed the epidemic to "God's vengeance." People vainly hoped a cult statue of Mary "would drive the demons from the city and deliver it from the mortality." Presumably, the demons were inducing the sinful behavior that provoked God's ire rather than causing the disease directly . . . Like Allah, the Christian God was sometimes believed to use demons as agents of his wrath, and some plague images display demonic archers delivering pestilence . . . Pestilence was almost unanimously attributed to an angry God, however, rather than Satan or the Devil, during the Pandemic's first two centuries.

In a rare case, 16th-century theologian Martin Luther attributed the plague of 1527 to "Satan's fury," expressing his faith that God would save their souls even if Satan "should devour our bodies." Early Stuart physician and astrologer Simon Forman in his plague essay (1607) noted that there were natural plagues brought on by the stars (planets), divine plagues prompted by human sin and wickedness, and devil-induced plagues.[41]

As these people tried to understand the cause of the mysterious Black Death without the help of a microscope, they came up with many different answers. According to the previous quote, some believed the plague was caused by God's vengeance, others believed malicious demons were the cause, some believed God had sent the demons, and others blamed Satan. Some people thought like Hippocrates and saw the plague as having a natural rather than divine origin, but they were probably in the minority, and their natural explanations were also inaccurate (such as the medieval belief that the plague was caused by the planets). Like children who blame themselves for their parents' divorce, or children who believe they must have done something wrong to deserve being physically abused, our ancestors tended to blame themselves for plagues and natural disasters.

Understanding the struggles of our ancestors has greatly increased my compassion for humanity, because when we increase our respect and empathy for the human beings who lived before us, we can also increase our respect and empathy for ourselves. Geneticist Spencer Wells gives us information that can increase our compassion for the ancient humans who formed the first agricultural societies:

> Early agriculturalists were taking on a new set of risks when they committed themselves to a settled existence. The most important was a decrease in the breadth of their resource base. By focusing cultivation on a few species, they were reducing their choices in the event of a climatic shift. Droughts, intense periods of cooling (such as the Dryas periods at the end of the last ice age) and shifts in watercourses were all very easy to deal with for Palaeolithic hunter-gatherers. Their response to any of these changes was to move into another area with better resources . . . Once humans adopted agriculture, though, they were loath to move. This led to occasional famines, such as those seen today in many parts of the developing world. In the early days of agriculture, during the turbulent climatic conditions of the early postglacial period, famine episodes would have been even more likely.
>
> The second main worry for our Neolithic agriculturalists was the increase in disease . . . Most diseases can exist only in large populations, where a threshold number of people remain infected, allowing the disease to remain in the population. These are so-called endemic diseases, such as smallpox or typhoid . . . Historian William McNeill has suggested that many of the plagues described in the Bible may have had their origin in the outbreaks of epidemic disease during the early days of the agricultural transition in Eurasia.
>
> The final negative aspect of a sedentary lifestyle was the growing stratification of society. In general, hunter-gatherers are remarkably egalitarian, having few social divisions. Typically, taking modern-day populations such

as that of the San or Australian Aborigines as a model, there is a group leader who sits in judgment over some aspects of group life, but no formalized set of social divisions such as the ones that exist in settled societies. Perhaps because there is simply less to fight for (in terms of accumulated wealth), large-scale warfare is rare in hunter-gatherer societies . . . The massive growth in population during the Neolithic created conditions in which some form of social stratification was inevitable. Once this occurred, the seizure of power and the growth of empires was not far behind, which led to war on a scale that had never been seen in the Palaeolithic. And while warfare was bad enough on its own, it also had a knock-on effect on other aspects of Neolithic life. The high mortality associated with large-scale warfare was probably exacerbated by the spread of disease and the destruction of cropland during the hostilities, leading to a vicious chain reaction of mortality.

Given all of the negative aspects of the Neolithic [agricultural] revolution, why did our ancestors still embrace their new lifestyle? Not everyone did, in fact—small pockets of hunter-gatherers existed in almost every region of the world until quite recently. Their reasons for maintaining an ancient lifestyle probably had something to do with the environment (for instance the San and the Australian Aborigines live in marginal, arid environments that are difficult for agriculture), as well as a conscious decision to remain hunter-gatherers. For the rest of the world's population, though, there was no turning back. It is possible that the shift in thinking that allowed humans to accept agriculture, in spite of all its negative aspects, could have occurred in a few generations. Once the collective memory of hunting and gathering was replaced by one involving food production, it would have been virtually unthinkable to return to the old ways.[42]

The myth of Poseidon's wrath, if we interpret it literally as a large man living in the ocean who shakes the earth with his trident, can seem silly. But if we understand this myth metaphorically, it reveals a disturbing yet important truth about the destructive power of nature. Science tells us that nature has eradicated most of the species that ever existed, and it has come close to wiping us out as well. As I mentioned in the previous chapter, within the past two hundred thousand years, humanity almost went extinct. Because so few people were left alive on the planet, every person living today is related, and genetic evidence proves we are all very distant cousins.

The *cruel kiss of mother earth* is a metaphor for the paradox of nature. One person can see nature as benevolent and nurturing, while another person can see nature as cruel and destructive, but who is right? When we observe nature on a global scale, we can understand how both of their perceptions contain a piece of the truth.

To some nature can seem like a cruel and psychotic Greek god, and to others nature can seem like a loving goddess whose kisses take the form of abundant food and fresh water. We can find a piece of the truth in both perspectives, because although nature sustains our existence, it can also harm us with earthquakes, volcanic eruptions, tornadoes, hurricanes, forest fires, tsunamis, plagues, droughts, floods, parasites, poisonous insects and snakes, harsh winters, scorching summers, and swarms of locusts that consume essential crops.

This paradox is embodied in Christianity, because the New Testament often describes God as loving, yet the Old Testament clearly depicts the harsh reality of nature. According to the book of Genesis, when God banishes Adam and Eve from the Garden of Eden, he tells them about the painful struggle of agricultural life that awaits them: "Cursed is the ground because of you; through painful toil you will eat food from it all the days of your life. It will produce thorns and thistles for you, and you will eat the plants of the field. By the sweat of your brow you will eat your food until you return to the ground, since from it you were taken; for dust you are and to dust you will return."[43]

The paradox of nature's simultaneous benevolence and wrath is also embodied in the Hindu gods Shiva and Vishnu. Vishnu compassionately intervenes to help humanity, while Shiva is often portrayed as a destroyer. Kali, a wife of Shiva, is a metaphor for the inevitability of time, old age, and death. Her psychotic wrath can make Poseidon's wrath seem relatively mild. Anthropologist Wolf-Dieter Storl explains:

> None of the black goddesses, however, is as terror inspiring as Kali, Shiva's most awesome Shakti [wife]. Kali Ma, "the black mother," is bloodthirsty and cruel like a man-eating tigress. She is [a metaphor for] time (kala) that mercilessly devours everything that dared manifest itself in the world of existence. She absorbs all, destroys all. For is it not true that every moment is immediately destroyed by time, every present becomes in an instant the past? Her ravishing hunger devours each second. Who can withstand her? Truly, she is sheerest evil for the ego, that sense of personal identity that longs to build itself a monument, give itself some hold, some sort of permanence.
>
> How desperately humanity has tried to escape her clutches! Egyptians mummified their bodies, alchemists searched tirelessly for the "elixir of life," Hernando de Soto looked for the "fountain of eternal youth" in far-off Florida. And even now, laboratory chemists are trying to synthesize "the pill" that would extend life indefinitely, while gene-technologists place their hopes in the miracle of genetic engineering. In California, those who can afford it let themselves be quick-frozen in dry ice at the moment of death, in the hope that future scientists will be able to raise them from the dead . . . In every case, it is the ego that wants to remain, that struggles heroically against all odds. Yet the struggle is hopeless. Like a vampire, black Kali sucks life's blood and devours the corpses.
>
> A common icon shows Kali drunk on blood and gore, dancing madly in the midst of a battle and doomsday fire over the bodies of the slain. There is no one to stop her!

Even Shiva lies as a pale, bloodless corpse under her feet. With one of her four arms she is swinging the severed head of her opponent, and another hand is twirling a blood-stained scimitar. Except for a girdle of hacked-off arms, a necklace of fifty skulls, and earrings made from the corpses of children, she is stark naked. Wild, disheveled hair swirls around her head, while her three bulging, bloodshot eyes roll about in lunatic frenzy. A long, lolling red tongue, eager to lap up blood, hangs down her chin . . .

Kali stands [as a metaphor] for the dark mystery out of which all arises and into which it disappears again . . . Since there is no resisting the power of such a goddess, one can but submit to her will and soothe her with sacrifices. In the *Kalika Purana*, Shiva tells his sons, the bhairavas, that Mother Kali can be pleased for five hundred years with the blood of a gazelle or of a rhinoceros, but the blood of a human being satisfies her for a thousand years.[44]

Classics scholar M. I. Finley describes how the Greek historian Thucydides, who lived in the fifth century BC, saw nature as neither cruel nor benevolent, but indifferent to human suffering: "[Thucydides] was not tempted to muse about divine intervention or the like, not even in his account of the plague. That was the most shattering and influential 'accident' of the whole war; it moved Thucydides to an unsurpassed piece of dramatic and emotional writing . . . He made the point, with equal explicitness, that, 'as for the gods, it seemed to be the same thing whether one worshipped them or not, when one saw the good and the bad dying indiscriminately.'"[45]

Lao-tzu, an ancient Chinese philosopher who became the founder of the spiritual tradition known as Taoism, also saw nature as indifferent to our suffering. He said nature destroys living creatures just as mercilessly as human beings destroy sacrificial objects known as straw dogs. Lao-tzu said, "Heaven and Earth are heartless, treating creatures like straw dogs."[46]

Chinese writer Su Ch'e, who was born in AD 1039, explained what Lao-tzu meant: "Heaven and Earth aren't partial. They don't kill living things out of cruelty or give them birth out of kindness. We do the same when we make straw dogs to use in sacrifices. We dress them up and put them on the altar, but not because we love them. And when the ceremony is over, we throw them into the street, but not because we hate them."[47]

Ultimately, when we describe nature as benevolent, cruel, or even indifferent, these are projections of human characteristics onto the great mystery we call the universe, which reveals itself to us while also transcending our understanding. As I explain later in this book, science can increase our understanding, leading us to more accurate answers to our problems, but every scientific discovery also leads to deeper mystery.

Although we can learn so much about nature and the universe, Albert Einstein realized the human mind cannot fully comprehend the ultimate mystery of the universe. Many theologians and atheists agree with Einstein, and I will offer evidence in a later chapter to support his claim. I will also discuss how we can perceive the beauty of the eternal mystery that not only surrounds us, but shines like the sun deep within us.

To find light in darkness, I have had to increase my understanding so that I not only have more empathy for all human beings alive today, but also our ancestors who made our existence possible. As I mentioned in the previous chapter, empathy gives us the deepest form of understanding into other human beings. A deep understanding of those who lived before us is necessary to realize how and why we inherited our modern problems.

I have heard people say, "How could our cruel ancestors ever want to conquer something as beautiful as nature?" This is easy to say when so many people today see nature as harmless flowers, birds, and trees, but nature was often dangerous to our ancestors. Humanity's conquest of nature began with the creation of stone tools and the transformation of fire—one of nature's most destructive forces—into a powerful servant. If we enjoy the benefits of agriculture and electricity, these luxuries were made possible because our ancestors tamed nature by conquering many facets of it.

Humanity has transformed nature from a metaphorical wolf into a lapdog by creating parks, flowerbeds, and gardens. Today most people don't worry about predators eating their families alive, or having to give birth on a dark night in the cold wilderness with no civilization for thousands of miles around. As a result, when many people hear the word "nature" today they tend to think of pleasant experiences like sitting on a beach while watching the ocean, walking through a park filled with trees, hiking in the mountains, and camping in the woods, but they don't think of time, decay, old age, and death, which are fundamental laws of nature. They don't think of plague and infant mortality, which are aspects of nature that have killed countless human beings. For many animal species living in the wild, most of their young do not survive until adulthood.

According to Kenneth Hill, a professor at Johns Hopkins University, today the infant mortality rate in America and most developed countries is less than 10 out of every 1,000 babies dying before their first birthday (less than 1 percent), but before 1900 the infant mortality rate was around 200 out of every 1,000 babies dying before their first birthday (20 percent).[48] After 1900 infant mortality rates dropped so dramatically due to better sanitation, the invention of antibiotics, and other improvements in medical technology. The woman who raised my grandfather was not his mother, but his grandmother—Francis Chappell. Born in 1842 as a slave in Virginia, she had given birth to fourteen children, but by the time she was sixty-four years old, eight of her children had died. During that era, her tragedy was not unusual.

Not even children of the rich were protected from an early death. According to historian Jonathan Dewald: "Everyone faced the likelihood that children would die in infancy and childhood, and wealth offered scant protection against early modern diseases. In the seventeenth and eighteenth centuries, when living conditions had improved substantially, child mortality remained high among even the richest European nobles. One-third of the children of the English peerage died before the age of twenty, and a slightly higher percentage of the German nobles' children did so."[49]

Furthermore, by calculating the slow rate of population expansion before agricultural societies emerged, Professor Kenneth Hill says that when we apply statistical models to nomadic tribes living before recorded history, around half of their children probably died before age five. He explains: "Thus the requirements of population dynamics indicate that, over the long haul of prehistory, the probability of dying by age five for females was probably no lower than 440 per thousand live births [44 percent], and was probably no higher than 600 [60 percent]."[50]

The reason I am discussing the enormous challenges our ancestors overcame is because we must strengthen our respect, empathy, and appreciation for human beings and stop viewing ourselves as a cancer or virus upon the earth. In the film *The Matrix*, the villain Agent Smith is a sentient computer program who despises humanity. He says: "When I tried to classify your species, I realized that you're not actually mammals. Every mammal on this planet instinctively develops a natural equilibrium with the surrounding environment, but you humans do not. You move to an area and you multiply, and multiply until every natural resource is consumed. And the only way you can survive is to spread to another area. There is another organism on this planet that follows the same pattern. Do you know what it is? A virus. Human beings are a disease, a cancer of this planet. You are a plague. And we are the cure."[51]

I think *The Matrix* is a brilliant science-fiction movie filled with powerful metaphorical truth, but I have met people who take that speech literally. Although the speech oversimplifies why we are destroying our environment, I have met many people who use the metaphor of a virus or cancer to describe human beings. However, comparing humanity to a cancer upon the earth does not acknowledge the millions of activists working hard to save our environment. The human population has activists who are struggling and sacrificing to create a better world, but a cancerous tumor lacks "activist cancer cells" working hard to save the body it inhabits. Because the speech reflects growing cynicism about humanity, I have also met people who call human beings a plague, yet have never seen *The Matrix*.

An environmental movement that cynically trash-talks humanity as being the scum of the earth will ultimately fail, because the most effective movements in history consist of an expansion of empathy, rather than its reduction. I have met some environmental activists who love humanity, and one purpose of this book is to further increase our respect, empathy, and appreciation for human beings, along with the other creatures who share this planet with us.

The more I learn about nature's tendency to drive organisms into extinction, the more compassion and appreciation I have for our ancestors who survived against all odds so we can be here today. The more I learn about nature's metaphorical wrath, the more empathy I have for other creatures struggling to survive in the wild. By growing our muscle of empathy, we can strengthen our ability to solve problems such as environmental destruction, nuclear weapons, and war, which threaten human survival.

In the Bible, the book of Deuteronomy states: "I call heaven and earth to witness against you today, that I have set before you life and death, blessing and curse. Therefore choose life, that you and your offspring may live."[52] This passage from the Bible reveals that human beings are freaks of the universe in another interesting way. We are the only organism on the planet capable of making a remarkable choice. Because of our technological ability to destroy ourselves, we can *choose* to drive ourselves extinct, or we can *choose* to use our heightened human awareness to prevent our extinction.

We have become our own greatest threat to our survival, which is an alarming yet incredible fact. Despite my childhood trauma and the lingering scars it left in my mind, I have chosen to work with many other people to end war, abolish nuclear weapons, stop environmental destruction, and save humanity from itself. What will you choose?

# CHAPTER 3

# Tools Made of Flesh, Blood, and Bones

## *When Tools Begin to Scream*

All of my books discuss paradoxes. What is a paradox? According to the *Random House Dictionary*, a paradox is "a statement or proposition that seems self-contradictory or absurd but in reality expresses a possible truth."[1] In the previous chapter, we explored a paradox I call *the cruel kiss of mother earth*. At first glance the metaphor of a *cruel kiss* seems like a paradox—a seemingly absurd contradiction—but looking closer reveals how this metaphor accurately symbolizes the ways nature can benefit or harm us.

Throughout this book I will share more paradoxes. A paradox we will discuss in this chapter is that *many other animals can teach us how to be human*. At first this sounds like an absurd contradiction, because how can a creature other than a human being teach us how to be human? However, I will share a story from my childhood that reveals the truth of this paradox. It is the story of how I was raised by wolves.

My father met my Korean mother while he was stationed in Korea as a soldier. After they married in 1975, they moved to the United States. Stationed at Aberdeen Proving Ground in Maryland during the late 1970s, my father was ending his long military career, and my mother was getting adjusted to living in a foreign country. One day my father brought home a male Chihuahua for my mother, to keep her company while he was at work.

In 1979, a year before my birth, my father also adopted a sick puppy, a female Chihuahua who was going to be euthanized. She was ill and nobody else wanted her, but he gave her a home and paid for the medical treatment to restore her health. He told my mother, "I couldn't stand to see the poor little thing suffer." The female Chihuahua became very protective of me. One day when I fell down and hurt myself as a toddler, she started barking, alerting my mother that I was in trouble. My mother came to help me, and told me the story when I became older.

As a child I noticed that my father had a profound compassion for animals. Even as his war trauma tormented him to the point of madness, he found a small amount of comfort by feeding the birds in our backyard. My mother told me that during his last year in the army—the year I was born— he came home from work upset, because someone had destroyed a bird's nest outside of his office, knocking the nest on the ground and smashing the eggs. This senseless act of cruelty angered him, but he was unable to discover who did it.

Shortly before my first birthday, the male and female Chihuahuas my parents adopted had a litter of three puppies: two females and one male. My parents kept the two females, and gave the male to another family. That is how I grew up with four dogs. Without them, I would have never written this book, and I would not be the person I am today.

One day when I was around seven years old and my father was viciously beating me, I had a fantasy that those four little Chihuahuas transformed into large wolves, ran to my rescue, and protected me from my father's rage. I started having this fantasy often, not only when my father beat me, but also when other children bullied me. As a child I was desperate for a protector—a parent or older sibling who would defend me—but much to my disappointment, I was an only child living in a house with a traumatized war veteran, and those four dogs were too small to intervene when I felt my life was in danger. I knew they would never become large wolves capable of defending me from violence. I did not realize at the time, however, that they had been protecting me all along.

If I had not grown up with those dogs, I would have become an adult who is far more psychotic than the man I am today. Those dogs did in fact protect me in a very important way—by keeping my capacity for empathy alive. Neuroscience has shown that the affection and love we receive as children stimulates important neural connections in our brain, creating our ability to feel empathy. By giving me affection and unconditional love in a house filled with terror and unpredictable violence, those dogs protected my ability to feel empathy. They were too small to defend my physical body from pain, but they were loving enough to protect the neural connections in my brain responsible for empathy. As a result, they guarded the core of my humanity.

Those dogs taught me vital lessons about unconditional love and loyalty, and if they had not helped anchor me to my humanity as I journeyed through the storm of trauma, I have no doubt that I would have self-destructed before the age of twenty. In this way, I was raised not only by my parents, but also by four little dogs—descendants of wolves. In fact, new scientific evidence reveals that wolves and dogs can be classified as the same species. Anthropologist Darcy Morey explains:

> [In 1993 biologist Robert K. Wayne wrote] "The domestic dog is an extremely close relative of the gray wolf, differing from it by at most 0.2% of mtDNA sequence. In comparison, the gray wolf differs from its closest wild relative, the coyote, by about 4% of mitochondrial DNA sequence . . ." Thus, the wolf was established as the basic ancestor of the dog. In fact, in the same year that Wayne's influential publications came out the Smithsonian Institution, in conjunction with the American Society of Mammalogists, formally reclassified the dog to recognize it as a mere variety of the wolf. One startling implication of this new standard is that one's toy poodle, or Chihuahua, or what have you, is now a mere variety of the wolf, *Canis lupus*. That is, dogs and wolves can now be regarded as the same species.[2]

Indeed, human beings are the most unusual creatures on the planet. What other species can grow up viewing its own father as a dangerous predator, yet have its empathy strengthened because four descendants of predatory wolves lived in its childhood home? What other organism can see itself as an outcast raised partly by wolves? My statement is not metaphorical, because when we realize that dogs and wolves can be classified as the same species, and that a healthy human upbringing involves the stimulation of empathetic connections in our brain, my description of being raised partly by wolves is literally true from a scientific perspective.

One of the great paradoxes of learning what it means to be human is that animals can help us unlock our full human potential. In the book *Exploring Native American Wisdom*, Fran Dancing Feather and Rita Robinson tell us:

> Because indigenous people throughout the world spend a great deal of time outdoors, this is where their best education takes place. If we live outside, it is imperative for our survival to understand the behavior of animals. They teach us.
>
> Part of trusting Creation is to seek the instinctual wisdom of the animals. Animals did not create the earth, but they have developed the necessary instincts to survive in it. Their instincts are incorrupt, unlike those of humans. If we want to know ourselves and our Creator better, we learn an incredible amount from observing animals in their natural environment . . .
>
> [The behavior of dogs teaches us the following:] "I am the most loyal animal. If you take me into your heart when I am very young, I will stand by you until the day I die. I will always let you know when there is danger nearby with the racket I will make. When everyone else has let you down, I will still be your best friend. I truly care about everything that happens to you. We are related to the great wolf. He was our first grandfather and teacher. You can see a bit of Wolf in me. My teeth are similar to those of Grandfather Wolf. I still have many of his hunting skills with my sharp hearing and keen sense of smell. But the look in our eyes is different. I possess far greater skill at tail wagging and bonding with humans. If I live in your house, I will always be there waiting when you come

home. Don't forget that you hold the highest place of honor in my life . . . We are helpful animals. I am letting you know about honor and respect, which are the great gifts given to us by the Creator of all things. Try treating others with a more loyal attitude. Stand behind those you love and there will always be plenty of food, love, and shelter in your life. Be an example of love and loyalty to others, and to the Mother Earth."[3]

One of our most amazing human strengths is our ability to learn from many kinds of teachers. I have learned so much from Gandhi and Martin Luther King Jr., but my teachers have also been trauma and adversity. I have learned a lot from Susan B. Anthony and Wangari Maathai, but my teachers have also been sadness and loss. My professors have been empathy and hope, along with rage and despair. I have been taught not only by the soaring intelligence of human beings, but also by the silent wisdom of dogs.

Earlier in this book I discussed how we can learn about posturing (also known as warning aggression) by observing the behavior of various animals. This allows us to better understand human aggression. Understanding our humanity is essential for walking the road to peace, and why limit our sources of understanding? Why not learn from both Eastern and Western philosophies? Why not learn from Native American wisdom? Why not learn from the struggle and adversity in our lives? Why not learn from our defeats as well as our victories? Why not learn from other human beings, regardless of their skin tone, gender, or age? Why not learn from the other creatures that share this planet with us?

Four dogs taught me valuable life lessons about unconditional love and loyalty. Although they all died before I was fourteen years old, they live on through my work to wage peace. How did those dogs end up in my parents' home as protectors of my empathy and humanity? As a child I did not realize those dogs and my slave ancestors originated from the same source—a part of our brain that makes tools not only from sticks and stones, but also from flesh, blood, and bones.

To explain how dogs and slaves emerged from the same part of our primordial human mind, we must first recognize a basic fact about the human condition: human beings are toolmakers. Some other species, such as chimpanzees, make simple tools out of sticks. But human beings are extremely unusual because we try to turn *everything* into a tool.

A tool is an object created out of one or more things to serve a function.* Our nomadic ancestors began by turning sticks and stones into tools. They then turned fire into a tool.** They even turned animal skins into clothes— a tool for keeping ourselves warm and protecting our bodies from the elements. A house is a tool that provides shelter, and our early ancestors created many kinds of simple homes to aid their survival.

But our ancestors did not stop there. After turning sticks, stones, and other inanimate objects into tools, they turned living organisms into tools. When our ancestors transformed wild plants into cultivated crops, they made a new kind of tool. Crops are food-producing tools. Their function is to fill the bellies of human beings.

And our ancestors did not stop there. In addition to turning plants into tools, they also turned animals into tools. The domesticated dog is not a wild animal, but was created by human beings to serve as a tool. Because the temperament of dogs is different from wolves, a wolf pup raised in a human home will not act like a dog. Wolves are unable to read human behavior the way dogs can, and do not bond with human beings the way dogs do. Our ancient ancestors created various breeds of dogs to provide protection, assist with hunting, guard livestock, and serve other functions.

Human beings transformed wild horses into transportation tools that serve the same function as a car. Horses and other "beasts of burden" also serve the function of hauling heavy weight. Human beings bred wild animals into domesticated sheep, which serve the function of providing material (wool) for clothes. And our ancestors bred wild animals into domesticated cows and pigs—tools that serve the same food-producing function as crops.

Nor did our ancestors stop there. Not only did they turn wolves, horses, and many other animals into tools, but they also turned other human beings

---

* Toolmaking is widely considered to involve learned rather than instinctual behavior, so most scientists would not consider spiderwebs as an example of toolmaking behavior
** To be more specific, fire is an object or form of matter undergoing a chemical reaction.

into tools. This is where slaves came from. Because we try to turn everything into a tool, slavery is an inevitable result of our relentless toolmaking impulse. Because our toolmaking impulse has no limits, we have even turned the sun and wind into tools. We turned the sun into an electricity-producing tool through the invention of solar panels, and we transformed wind into an electricity-producing tool through the creation of wind turbines.

If you try to count the number of tools in your home, it can be difficult because there are so many. Toothbrushes, dental floss, and toothpicks are tools for cleaning our teeth. Combs, shampoos, and conditioners are tools for cleaning and grooming our hair. Beds, blankets, and pillows are tools that help us sleep more comfortably at night. Curtains, windows, and doors are tools that allow us to control the flow of light, air, and people entering our homes.

Many tools people use every day are rarely thought of as tools, such as soap (a body-cleaning tool) and deodorant (a sweat prevention tool). Other examples of household tools include pens, paper, refrigerators, computers, toilets, toilet paper, showers, bath towels, clothes hangers, shoes, silverware, pots and pans, dressers, nightstands, lightbulbs, batteries, brooms, kitchen cabinets, nail clippers, scissors, books, keys, wallets, and phones. I could easily list a hundred more examples of common tools used in homes, which does not include the countless tools found outside of homes.

Because human beings create and use so many tools, people around the world constantly pile their discarded tools in garbage cans and landfills. Human garbage consists of two things: uneaten food and discarded tools. To list a few examples of the many kinds of discarded tools that end up as garbage, a typical landfill contains plastic bottles (tools for storing liquid), plastic bags (tools for carrying objects), and old electronics (tools that provide a wide variety of functions).

We are the only species on the planet being threatened not only by the tools we currently have (such as bombs and nuclear weapons), but also by the tools we throw away. Today many people are harnessing their ingenuity to reduce the enormous flow of discarded tools that threaten our environment and health. To create a sustainable human future and a more peaceful and just world, we must transform how we see all our tools—the ones made of sticks and stones along with the ones made of flesh, blood, and bones. This chapter will reveal some essential ideas that can help us with that transformation.

Of all the tools humanity ever created, our ancient ancestors found slaves to be one of the most useful. A slave is a tool that can tend to crops in the hottest weather, allowing you to relax in the shade. A slave is a tool that can walk long distances to retrieve water from a well, performing the most monotonous and difficult forms of manual labor while you focus on more pleasant tasks. In many ways a slave is the ultimate tool, and the most versatile tool we ever created is, surprisingly, each other.*

Since my childhood, I have wondered why slavery originated. I often heard people say slavery originated because humanity is naturally greedy and violent. Greed and violence have certainly enabled slavery, but I discovered a deeper explanation for the origin of slavery. Everything humanity has ever come in contact with, we have tried to turn into a tool at some point in our history. This includes inanimate objects, plants, animals, and human beings.

In many cases, the process of transforming something into a tool can be harmless. By using the stars to navigate, for example, our ancestors harmlessly used the night sky as a tool.** By molding clay into shaped containers, our ancestors harmlessly created pots as storage and cooking tools. However, the process of transforming something into a tool can also cause harm. Tragically, people have killed elephants to shape their ivory into tools (and art), and today some people have the inaccurate belief that rhinoceros horns can cure cancer. Endangered rhinoceroses are being hunted to extinction because people mistakenly believe their horns can be used as medicine. Medicine, of course, is an illness-curing tool.

---

* Many people today are trying to create tools that are more versatile than human beings, in the form of computers with advanced artificial intelligence. Artificial intelligence may be the future of human toolmaking, with its own set of potential risks. Emerging evidence shows that the greatest threat smarter computers could pose to human beings in the near future is not waging war against us (as is so often depicted in science fiction films), but taking our jobs.
** Other animals have a natural ability to navigate by using the sun, moon, earth's magnetic field, etc. But using the night sky to navigate is not a natural human ability. Our ancestors transformed the night sky into a map—a tool. Of course, some forces of nature such as tornadoes or black holes (if we ever come near one) may be so powerful and dangerous that we will never be able to transform them into useful tools. But if humans could, we probably would.

Since humanity has tried to turn everything we have come into contact with into a tool, including things as diverse as the night sky and rhinoceros horns, turning people into tools was inevitable. The toolmaking impulse of our ancestors was so powerful that it did not exclude human beings.

But there is a big problem with slavery: human beings don't like being treated as tools. This is why white slave owners manufactured propaganda, which said God created Africans as inferior subhumans born to be slaves. In order to oppress a large group of people, you must first oppress their minds. This was accomplished by making it illegal to teach slaves to read, and spreading propaganda that eased the conscience of slave owners while making slaves believe in their own inferiority. When slaves did not believe this propaganda and tried to escape or rebel, they were violently attacked.

Dogs and slaves have been used as tools by civilizations around the world, but dogs are different from slaves in a key way. By breeding wolves and their descendants, humanity created the domesticated dogs we call "man's best friend." Because they were bred to interact peacefully with us, modern dogs are happy when they have a kind human companion, and living around loving human beings is beneficial to a dog's mental well-being. When dogs are treated well while performing services such as herding sheep or guiding the blind, this does not cause them mental anguish.

Unlike dogs, wild animals such as wolves, chimpanzees, and dolphins do not belong in captivity. They have not been bred for many generations to live in human communities.* Their natural environment is in the wild, and they belong with their own species in the wild rather than in proximity with people. Because human beings were not designed to be slaves, and the enslavement of human populations for many generations has not been able to alter the human condition, cruel and brutal measures must be used to enslave us.

During his experiences as a slave, Frederick Douglass had an ingenious revelation about the slave owners who held others in captivity. He realized slavery was harmful not only to slaves, but also to slave owners, because it

---

* The process of domesticating dogs so they could live peacefully in human communities is very different from keeping generation after generation of wild animals in zoos, where they are kept apart from both their natural environment and human communities.

silenced their empathy. Douglass said, "The slaveholder, as well as the slave, was the victim of the slave system. Under the whole heavens there could be no relation more unfavorable to the development of honorable character than that sustained by the slaveholder to the slave."[4]

As a child living as a slave in Maryland, Douglass saw how the very act of owning a slave required people to silence their empathy, because they had to be heartless and even cruel to deny humanity's natural craving for freedom and fairness. He explains how Sophia Auld, the wife of his master Hugh Auld, had never owned slaves. But owning her first slave—a nine-year-old Frederick Douglass—transformed her from an angel into a demon:

> Mrs. Sophia was naturally of an excellent disposition—kind, gentle, and cheerful. The supercilious contempt for the rights and feelings of others, and the petulance and bad humor which generally characterized slaveholding ladies, were all quite absent from her manner and bearing toward me. She had never been a slaveholder . . . but had depended almost entirely upon her own industry for a living. To this fact the dear lady no doubt owed the excellent preservation of her natural goodness of heart, for slavery could change a saint into a sinner, and an angel into a demon . . . So far from deeming it impudent in a slave to look her straight in the face, she seemed ever to say, "Look up, child; don't be afraid."
>
> The sailors belonging to the sloop esteemed it a great privilege to be the bearers of parcels or messages for her, for whenever they came, they were sure of a most kind and pleasant reception. If little Thomas was her son, and her most dearly loved child, she made me something like his half-brother in her affections . . . Nor did the slave-boy lack the caressing strokes of her gentle hand, soothing him into the consciousness that, though motherless, he was not friendless . . .

> Mr. Hugh [Auld] was altogether a different character
> . . . I was of course of very little consequence to him, and
> when he smiled upon me, as he sometimes did, the smile
> was borrowed from his lovely wife, and like borrowed light,
> was transient, and vanished with the source whence it was
> derived . . . So for a time everything went well . . . [Mrs.
> Sophia] at first regarded me as a child, like any other. This
> was the natural and spontaneous thought; afterwards, when
> she came to consider me as property, our relations to each
> other were changed, but a nature so noble as hers could
> not instantly become perverted, and it took several years
> before the sweetness of her temper[ment] was wholly lost.[5]

When we view living creatures merely as objects, it can harm us by silencing our empathy. This harm is represented metaphorically by King Midas in Greek mythology. Midas is the mythological figure who had the power to transform everything he touched into gold, but how did Midas obtain the "golden touch" in the first place? He received it as a reward for an act of kindness.

According to Greek mythology, Seilenus was an elderly friend of Dionysus, the Greek god of wine and festivals. *The Dictionary of Greek and Roman Biography and Mythology* describes how Midas treated Seilenus with kindness: "During the expedition of Dionysus from Thrace to Phrygia, Seilenus in a state of intoxication had gone astray, and was caught by country people in the rose gardens of [King] Midas. He was bound in wreaths of flowers and led before the king . . . Midas received Seilenus kindly, conversed with him, and after having treated him hospitably for ten days, he led him back to his divine pupil, Dionysus, who in his gratitude requested Midas to ask a favour. Midas in his folly desired that all things which he touched should be changed into gold."[6]

The Roman poet Ovid describes how King Midas's "golden touch" became a curse:

Doubtful himself of his new power, he pulled a twig down from a holm-oak, growing on a low hung branch. The twig was turned to gold. He lifted up a dark stone from the ground and it turned pale with gold. He touched a clod [of dirt] and by his potent touch the clod became a mass of shining gold. He plucked some ripe, dry spears of grain, and all that wheat he touched was golden. Then he held an apple which he gathered from a tree, and you would think that the [magical race of nymphs] Hesperides had given it. If he but touched a lofty door, at once each door-post seemed to glisten. When he washed his hands in liquid streams, the lustrous drops upon his hands might have been those which once astonished [Princess] Danae.

He could not now conceive his large hopes in his grasping mind, as he imagined everything of gold. And, while he was rejoicing in great wealth, his servants set a table for his meal . . . with needful bread: but when he touched the gift [of bread given to him by] Ceres with his right hand, instantly the gift of Ceres stiffened to gold; or if he tried to bite with hungry teeth a tender bit of meat . . . as his teeth but touched it, shone at once with yellow shreds and flakes of gold. And wine, another gift of Bacchus, when he mixed it in pure water, can be seen in his astonished mouth as liquid gold. Confounded by his strange misfortune—rich and wretched—he was anxious to escape from his unhappy wealth. He hated all he had so lately longed for. Plenty could not lessen hunger and no remedy relieved his dry, parched throat. The hated gold tormented him no more than he deserved.[7]

King Midas's "golden touch" is a metaphor for the mindset that sees everything as an object, tool, or dollar sign. This attitude perceives human beings and other creatures not as living beings, but merely as objects to be exploited. To offer one example, the mindset of the golden touch can cause us to see a human being as a sex object whose only function is to serve as a tool for satisfying our lust. The mindset of the golden touch does not view human beings with an attitude of empathy, love, and responsibility, but exploitation.

Writer Herman Hesse, who received the Nobel Prize in Literature in 1946, described how seeing living creatures merely as objects, tools, or dollar signs hurts us by robbing us of the blissful experience of unconditional love. When the golden touch causes Midas to suffer from thirst and hunger, this is a metaphor for the psychological thirst and hunger we experience when greed alienates us from our humanity and the living creatures around us. Hesse explains:

> If I inspect a forest with the intention of buying it, renting it, cutting it down, going hunting in it, or mortgaging it, then I do not see the forest but only its relation to my desires, plans, and concerns, to my purse. Then it consists of wood, it is young or old, healthy or diseased. But if I want nothing from it but to gaze, "thoughtlessly," into its green depths, then it becomes a forest, nature, a growing thing; only then is it beautiful.
>
> So it is with people, and with people's faces too. The man whom I look at with dread or hope, with greed, designs, or demands, is not a man but a cloudy mirror of my own desire. Whether I am aware of it or not, I regard him in the light of questions that limit and falsify: Is he approachable, or arrogant? Does he respect me? Is he a good prospect for a loan? Does he understand anything about art? A thousand such questions are in our minds as we look at most people we have to deal with, and we are considered expert psychologists if we succeed in detecting in their appearance, manner, and behavior whatever it is that will abet or hinder our plans. But this attitude is a shabby one . . .
>
> At the moment when desire ceases and contempla-

tion, pure seeing, and self-surrender begin, everything changes. Man ceases to be useful or dangerous, interesting or boring, genial or rude, strong or weak. He becomes nature, he becomes beautiful and remarkable as does everything that is an object of clear contemplation. For indeed contemplation is not scrutiny or criticism, it is nothing but love. It is the highest and most desirable state of our souls: unconditional love.

If we have once achieved this state, be it for minutes, hours, or days (to sustain it permanently would be perfect bliss), then people no longer appear as they used to. They are not mirrors or caricatures of our desire, they become nature once more. Beautiful and ugly, old and young, cordial and offensive, open and taciturn, harsh and mild are no longer opposites, nor are they standards of judgment. All are beautiful, all are remarkable, no one can any longer be despised, hated, misunderstood.[8]

Unconditional love is a higher expression of empathy, and Herman Hesse describes unconditional love as "bliss" and "pure seeing." By empowering us to see beneath the shallow surface, the mindset of unconditional love improves our ability to think and understand. As I explained in chapter 1, since unconditional love gives us the deepest insight into another human being, when Sun Tzu said, "Know your enemy" and Jesus said, "Love your enemy" they were essentially saying the same thing. The deepest way to know another human being is through the unconditional love that Jesus, Gandhi, Martin Luther King Jr., and many other spiritual teachers taught us to embrace.

The mindset of unconditional love gives us calm, deep understanding, a yearning to serve our community, and a fulfilling sense of connection with others. When our thinking is built on this strong foundation of calm, understanding, service, and connection, we behave much differently than a person whose thoughts are built on the shaky ground of greed and selfishness. The mindset of unconditional love is the opposite of the mindset of the golden touch, and most people live somewhere between these two extremes. As we move closer and closer to love, we strengthen our ability to wage peace, and we begin to attain a *higher bliss* than ignorance.

The Bible says that seeing the world with the mindset of unconditional love, which Jesus embodied, is greater than having faith in God. According to the Bible, God *is* love. The book of 1 John states: "Whoever does not love does not know God, because God is love . . . No one has ever seen God; but if we love one another, God lives in us and his love is made complete in us . . . Whoever lives in love lives in God, and God in them."[9]

The book of 1 Corinthians further describes the importance of seeing with the mindset of unconditional love:

> If I speak in the tongues of men or of angels, but do not have love, I am only a resounding gong or a clanging cymbal . . . If I have a faith that can move mountains, but do not have love, I am nothing . . . Love is patient, love is kind. It does not envy, it does not boast, it is not proud. It does not dishonor others, it is not self-seeking, it is not easily angered, it keeps no record of wrongs. Love does not delight in evil but rejoices with the truth. It always protects, always trusts, always hopes, always perseveres . . . And now these three remain: faith, hope and love. But the greatest of these is love.[10]

As I will explain later in this chapter, the mindset of unconditional love gives us the strength to solve problems such as war, oppression, injustice, racism, sexism, trauma, poverty, and environmental destruction. Although human beings are the most unusual species on the planet, other creatures are certainly capable of feeling panic, agony, and many other painful experiences we would not wish upon ourselves. What does the mindset of unconditional love tell us to do when our tools begin to scream? How does the mindset of unconditional love tell us to treat our fellow human beings?

To answer these questions, we must first ask ourselves if this mindset is even practical in the modern world. To understand why the mindset of unconditional love is in fact the most practical and powerful force on earth, I will discuss a secret that all oppressors know, but many of the oppressed do not.

## *This Is the Thing to Bomb*

Human beings are not the only species capable of making tools. To mention just a couple of examples, crows can use twigs to extract insects from wood,[11] and the PBS documentary *Ape Genius* shows that chimpanzees are capable of sharpening sticks, which they use to hunt small animals. But human beings are the most unusual toolmaker, because we are the only creatures on the planet who worry about our tools murdering us. As far as we know, crows don't worry about their twigs coming to life and strangling them to death, and chimpanzees don't have nightmares about their sharpened sticks starting a violent rebellion against their creators. But human beings have not only dreamed such nightmares. We have also lived them.

Our fear of being killed by our tools is depicted in what Joseph Campbell called our modern mythology: science fiction. In the novel *Frankenstein*, written by Mary Shelley in the nineteenth century, Frankenstein is not the name of the monster. It is the name of the monster's creator. Victor Frankenstein was a scientist intent on creating life. Piecing together a "man" from the body parts of corpses, he brought his creation to life through his technological brilliance. But when the monster awoke, Frankenstein was so horrified by his creation that he ran away and abandoned him. The monster was left to wander afraid and alone. Eventually, the monster's sense of loneliness, abandonment, betrayal, and alienation caused him to seek revenge against his creator.

Victor Frankenstein's life was destroyed by his creation, and modern science-fiction films offer many metaphors of technology turning against humanity. In the *Terminator* and *Matrix* films, the robots humanity created are waging war against their makers. In the film *Blade Runner*, an artificial life-form kills the man who engineered him by gouging out his eyes. In the film *2001: A Space Odyssey*, a computer attempts to kill the human beings on its ship. And in the *Battlestar Galactica* television series that debuted in 2004, humanity is being hunted to extinction by their creations, a race of robots known as the Cylons.

Martin Luther King Jr. described how the tension between human beings and their tools dates back thousands of years, when the Egyptian pharaohs used slaves as tools for building the pyramids. Because potential slave revolts are a threat to slave owners, the pharaohs developed effective strategies for keeping their tools under control. King explained: "The Pharaohs had a favorite and effective strategy to keep their slaves in bondage: keep them fighting among themselves. The divide-and-conquer technique has been a potent weapon in the arsenal of oppression. But when slaves unite, the Red Seas of history open and the Egypts of slavery crumble."[12]

The greatest threat to an oppressive system is empathy. The tools oppressors fear most are not guns or tanks, but tools that empathize with each other. This is why slavery, European colonialism, and every other oppressive system protects itself by turning the oppressed against each other. To quote the old adage from warfare, "Divide and conquer."

In his novel *The Grapes of Wrath*, John Steinbeck explains how empathy threatens oppressive systems, because it allows the oppressed to move from the isolated sense of "I" to the connected perception of "we." Steinbeck reveals the power of empathy by describing oppressed farmers who move from a sense of mistrust and alienation toward a perception of love and solidarity:

> One man, one family driven from the land; this rusty car creaking along the highway to the west. I lost my land, a single tractor took my land. I am alone and I am bewildered. And in the night one family camps in a ditch and another family pulls in and the tents come out. The two men squat on their hams and the women and children listen. Here is the node, you who hate change and fear revolution. Keep these two squatting men apart; make them hate, fear, suspect each other. Here is the anlage of the thing you fear. This is the zygote. For here "I lost my land"

is changed; a cell is split and from its splitting grows the thing you hate—"We lost *our* land." The danger is here, for two men are not as lonely and perplexed as one. And from this first "we" there grows a still more dangerous thing: "I have a little food" plus "I have none." If from this problem the sum is "We have a little food," the thing is on its way, the movement has direction. Only a little multiplication now, and this land, this tractor are ours. The two men squatting in a ditch, the little fire, the side-meat stewing in a single pot, the silent, stone-eyed women; behind, the children listening with their souls to words their minds do not understand. The night draws down. The baby has a cold. Here, take this blanket. It's wool. It was my mother's blanket—take it for the baby. *This is the thing to bomb* [emphasis added]. This is the beginning— from "I" to "we."[13]

When John Steinbeck said, "This is the thing to bomb," he expressed a simple yet profound truth. An oppressive system defends itself by bombing people's empathy. Steinbeck used the word "bomb" as a metaphor, because the most effective way to bomb people's empathy is not with explosives cased in metal, but with propaganda techniques that fill their minds with fear, mistrust, and hatred. If you can divide people with fear, they are much easier to conquer and control.

Every slave system and empire in recorded history has used the technique of dividing and conquering. Historian John Wacher tells us, "But winning and holding an empire was not achieved solely by developing highly trained and well-equipped forces. Greek history, with which the Romans were well acquainted, and their own involvement with the Greeks of both southern Italy and Greece, taught the Romans the invaluable lesson of divide and conquer. Rome rejected loose alliances, associations of equals, and federal solutions to political problems . . . she imposed her rule directly over an ever-growing area, and she often did so by encouraging dissension amongst her opponents."[14]

International relations professor Micheline Ishay also tells us, "Coloniz-ing states often used preferential treatment to pit one group or one tribe against another, enabling the colonizers to divide and conquer. For instance, Belgium kept control of Rwanda by privileging Tutsis over Hutus, and the British conveniently maintained tensions between Muslims, Sikhs, and Hin-dus in India, as well as strife between the Malays and the Chinese in the Malayan territories. European 'divide and rule' and co-optation methods retarded and blocked national awareness and unity that might have threat-ened their colonial rule."[15]

I have often heard people describe empathy as a naive and wimpy moral ideal. But since empathy is dangerous to all forms of injustice, it is far from naive and wimpy. Jeremy Rifkin explains how discoveries in neuroscience reveal that empathy is not a naive and wimpy moral ideal, but an essential part of being human:

> The point that [neuroscientist Dr. Marco] Iacoboni and other scientists are making is that we are wired for empathy—it is our nature and what makes us social beings. The growing body of experimental research into the role mirror neurons play in empathic development is impressive and is already rewriting the script on the evo-lution of human development.
>
> While scientists have noted that visual gestures and expressions, as well as auditory resonances, activate mirror neurons, they are also finding that touch does so as well, creating still another sensory path for empathic extension. We've all had the experience of watching a spider or snake crawling up on another person and feeling the same shiver of repulsion as if it were crawling on us . . . Likewise, when we say "I feel your pain," the reality is that specific mirror neurons allow us to do just that.[16]

The nature of empathy is still mysterious to neuroscientists, and it may be that empathy is so complex that it cannot be explained simply by "mirror neurons." It could be many years before scientists unlock the puzzling neuroscience of empathy, meaning, and understanding. Journalist Ben Thomas explains: "In the final analysis, the one conclusion that's emerged loud and clear from all these debates is that mirror neurons aren't the end-all of understanding, empathy, autism, or any other brain function . . . It may very well turn out that 'meaning' and 'understanding' aren't single processes at all, but tangled webs of processes involving motor emulation, abstract cognition, and other emotional and instinctual components whose roles we're only beginning to guess."[17]

Fortunately, we do not have to wait on neuroscience to completely figure out empathy, because we know enough about empathy to start applying its practical power to our lives right now. Not only can we start today, but the world demands that we begin as soon as possible. What science is just now discovering about the power of empathy, great spiritual teachers such as Buddha and Jesus knew in the ancient past.

Herman Hesse described how Siddhartha Gautama, who became known as the Buddha in the sixth century BC, was motivated by unconditional love to help others: "How, indeed, could he [Siddhartha Gautama] not know love, he who has recognized all humanity's vanity and transitoriness, yet loves humanity so much that he has devoted a long life solely to help and teach people? Also with this great teacher . . . his deeds and life are more important to me than his talk . . . Not in speech or thought do I regard him as a great man, but in his deeds and life."[18]

Although unconditional love is a higher expression of empathy, in *Peaceful Revolution* I explain why solidarity is the highest expression of empathy. In the Bible, the book of Ecclesiastes expresses the power of solidarity: "Two are better than one . . . If one falls down, his friend can help him up. But pity the man who falls and has no one to help him up! Though one may be overpowered, two can defend themselves. A cord of three strands is not quickly broken."[19]

When the song of empathy is silent, there can be no music of unconditional love and solidarity. But how can we protect our empathy from being silenced? How can we expand our empathy so that we perceive our shared humanity in all people? By exploring how a dangerous controversy split the

American women's rights movement, we will learn one of the most important lessons for maintaining empathy and overcoming division.

In the early nineteenth century, American women could not vote, own property, or graduate from college. In fact, they were treated as property. One of the most prominent women's rights activists during the nineteenth century was Frederick Douglass, an escaped slave. Although American women were not guaranteed the right to vote until the Nineteenth Amendment was ratified in 1920, Douglass supported their right to vote in the 1840s. He said, "When I ran away from slavery, it was for myself; when I advocated emancipation, it was for my people; but when I stood up for the rights of woman, self was out of the question, and I found a little nobility in the act."[20]

The first women's rights convention was held at Seneca Falls, New York, in 1848. Approximately three hundred people attended the convention, including Frederick Douglass, the only African American participant.[21] Women's rights activist Elizabeth Cady Stanton wrote a revolutionary document, the Declaration of Rights and Sentiments, which she hoped the convention participants would support. In the declaration, Stanton listed many grievances women had against men, a few of which are quoted here: "He has taken from her all right in property, even to the wages she earns . . . As a teacher of theology, medicine, or law, she is not known. He has denied her the facilities for obtaining a thorough education—all colleges being closed against her."[22]

In addition, women were seen as not intelligent enough to serve on a jury, and most were considered too incompetent to testify in court. Historian Elisabeth Griffith tells us, "You had no rights . . . No right to property, no right to sign contracts, no right to your children, no right to the clothes on your back. If you were so bold as to escape a dreadful marriage, you took one outfit with you, not your children, not your suitcase. You got nothing."[23]

The Declaration of Rights and Sentiments also asserted that women had the right to vote just as men did, but this was so controversial that many of the participants at the Seneca Falls Convention opposed it. When the resolution proclaiming women's right to vote seemed unlikely to pass, Elizabeth Cady Stanton asked Frederick Douglass for help. At this moment Stanton and Douglass formed one of the most important alliances in American history, and because of their combined efforts the movement to gain women the right to vote was born. In his excellent book *Frederick Douglass on Women's Rights*, historian Philip Foner tells us:

> Even before the convention opened, Elizabeth Cady Stanton had been warned that the proposed resolution [for women's right to vote] was too radical a step. [Women's rights activist] Lucretia Mott felt that the demand for the vote was too advanced for the times. "This will make us ridiculous," she cautioned. "We must go slowly."
>
> But Stanton was determined to press the issue, and she looked about the convention for an ally. "I knew Frederick, from personal experience, was just the man for the work," she told an audience of suffragists years later. Hurrying to Douglass's side, Stanton read him the resolution, and, having been reassured that he would take the floor in her support, she determined to hold to her purpose.
>
> When she introduced her daring proposal, the general sentiment appeared to be moving against the resolution, and it seemed that it would go down to defeat. It was at this critical juncture that Douglass asked for the floor and delivered an eloquent plea in behalf of woman's right to the elective franchise. The resolution was then put to a vote and carried by a small margin.[24]

The Declaration of Rights and Sentiments was so controversial that only one hundred of the three hundred convention participants signed it. Describing the regret many of the signers felt over supporting the declaration, Elizabeth Cady Stanton said, "So pronounced was the popular voice against us, in the parlor, press, and pulpit that most of the ladies who had attended the convention and signed the declaration, one by one, withdrew their names and influence and joined our persecutors. Our friends gave us the cold shoulder and felt themselves disgraced by the whole proceeding."[25]

Nevertheless, the Seneca Falls Convention marked a turning point in American history. Stanton's revolutionary declaration became the founding document of the women's rights movement, serving as a demand for justice and call to action.

However, the movement encountered new problems when the alliance between Stanton and Douglass fell apart because of a controversy surrounding the Fifteenth Amendment. After the American Civil War ended in 1865, the Fifteenth Amendment granting black men the right to vote was proposed in 1869. White women such as Elizabeth Cady Stanton and Susan B. Anthony had been dedicated anti-slavery activists, and they felt betrayed because the amendment did not also grant women the right to vote.

The Fifteenth Amendment split the women's rights movement. Stanton, Anthony, and their followers said the movement should oppose the amendment's ratification since it did not include voting rights for women. Other women's rights activists said women should do everything they could to support the amendment, because black people in the South were being massacred after the Civil War and the right to vote could offer them some protection.

In the late 1860s, women's right to vote was far more controversial than giving black men the right to vote, and neither African Americans nor women had the political power needed to rewrite the Fifteenth Amendment. The broad public support required to create a constitutional amendment for female voting rights would not exist until fifty years later, after Douglass, Stanton, and Anthony had all died. In the meantime, the oppressive system forced them to choose between voting rights for black men, or nothing.

During the nineteenth century, many white women had worked not only for women's rights, but also the abolition of slavery. Slave owners had tried to split white women from the anti-slavery movement, and the Fifteenth Amendment gave the opponents of racial equality an opportunity to create new and dangerous divisions among the oppressed. Henry B. Blackwell, husband of women's rights and anti-slavery activist Lucy Stone, allied himself with former slave owners and used his influence to turn white women against black men. And Susan B. Anthony began to praise people who had wanted oppressed women and oppressed black men to fight each other. Philip Foner explains:

Douglass also objected to [Susan B.] Anthony's praise of James Brooks, who was then championing woman suffrage in Congress. Douglass pointed out that it was simply "the trick of the enemy to assail and endanger the right of black men." Brooks, former editor of the *New York Express*, a viciously anti-Negro, pro-slavery paper, was playing up to the leaders of the woman's rights movement in order to secure their support in opposing Negro suffrage. Douglass warned that if the women did not see through these devices of the former slave owners and their allies, "there would be trouble in our family . . ."

[Douglass] joined Lucretia Mott, Susan B. Anthony, Elizabeth Cady Stanton, and Lucy Stone in petitioning the New York Constitutional Convention to amend the state constitution so "as to secure the right of suffrage to all citizens, without distinction of race or sex . . ." Many of the women in the [Equal Rights] association, led by Stanton and Anthony, were incensed by the Republican party's* indifference to their demands for woman suffrage and attributed it to the influence of a number of former abolitionists. In their anger—an anger not too difficult to understand in view of the historic discrimination against women—they not only began to claim priority for woman suffrage, but announced that they were ready to make common cause with any group, even those opposed to Negro suffrage . . .

Henry B. Blackwell, Lucy Stone's husband and a contributor to *The Revolution*, even dispatched an open letter to southern legislatures in which he set out to prove that, by granting suffrage to women, the combined white vote would be increased sufficiently to defeat the combined

---

* The Republican Party was considered the most progressive major political party during that era. The Republican Party had been against slavery.

black vote; thus, "the Negro question would be forever removed from the political arena . . ."

[The situation was desperate because] Negroes who dared to protest [unjust treatment] were being lynched by the Ku Klux Klan and other extralegal organizations and . . . hundreds of blacks were being massacred in anti-Negro riots in Memphis, New Orleans, and other southern cities. These tragic events, which threatened to wipe out the gains of the Emancipation Proclamation and the Thirteenth Amendment, had led even moderates in the North to see the critical necessity of the Negro vote to safeguard the legal freedom the ex-slaves had secured during the Civil War . . .

A heated controversy arose between Douglass and the feminists at the annual meeting of the Equal Rights Association in New York early in May 1869. Douglass argued earnestly that white women were entitled to the ballot and expressed his regret that they had not been included in the amendment. But he insisted that they must understand that his people were confronted by special problems. "When women," he said, "because they are women, are dragged from their houses and hung upon lamp-posts; when their children are torn from their arms, and their brains dashed upon the pavement; when they are objects of insult and outrage at every turn; when they are in danger of having their homes burnt down over their heads; when their children are not allowed to enter schools; then they will have an urgency to obtain the ballot equal to our own." When someone in the audience shouted, "Is that not all true about black women?" Douglass replied: "Yes, yes, yes; it is true of the black woman, but not because she is a woman, but because she is black." Women, he said, had many ways to redress their grievances; the Negro had only one.

The answering arguments by Susan B. Anthony and Lucy Stone revealed that they were by now fully convinced that the task of implementing the freedom of the Negro in the South had to be subordinated to the cause of white women. Anthony argued that "if intelligence, justice, and morality are to have precedence in the government, then let the question of women be brought up first and that of the Negro last." Stone insisted that woman suffrage was more imperative than voting rights of Negroes. She spoke of the "Ku-Kluxes here in the North in the shape of men who take away the children from the mother and separate them as completely as if done on the block of the auctioneer."* Still, she was willing to favor passage of the amendment if it could not be changed to include women: "I will be thankful in my soul if *any* body can get out of the terrible pit."

However, in the case of Anthony, Stanton, and the vast majority of the white women delegates there could be no compromise . . . They and their supporters did not hesitate to raise a barrage of derogatory epithets against black men, referring to them as "Sambos" and "ignorant barbarians" who were a menace to black as well as white women and would become more so if enfranchised.

While Douglass replied sharply to the slurs cast upon black men, he still tried to prevent the breach from becoming worse. He introduced a resolution . . . [and] read with special emphasis that section of his resolution which spoke of the amendment as the "culmination of one-half of our

---

* A friend of mine, who is a white mother, responded as follows to Lucy Stone's comparison that white children separated from their mothers through divorce is as bad as black children separated from their mothers by being sold into slavery: "Only a woman who hasn't had her child actually auctioned [into slavery] could say something like this. Losing custody of your children would be an agony, but having your child sold as a thing would have to be worse because you'd know how little value was attached to what is so precious to you."

demands" and called for the redoubling "of our energy to secure the further amendment guaranteeing the same sacred rights without limitation to sex." But the majority of the women were not impressed . . .

[Some women's rights activists did support the Fifteenth Amendment such as] Julia Ward Howe, author of the "Battle Hymn of the Republic," Lydia Maria Child, an outstanding abolitionist leader, Mary Ashton Livermore, woman's rights leader in Illinois, Frances Dana Gage, Ohio abolitionist, and Lucy Stone. Stone broke with her husband, Henry B. Blackwell, who strongly opposed ratification of the Fifteenth Amendment. Lydia Maria Child publicly rebuked Stanton and her colleagues for denouncing the Negro's right to vote in "the sneering tone habitually assumed by slaveholders and their copperhead allies . . . "

Mary Ashton Livermore refused to publish articles by Anthony and Stanton on the Fifteenth Amendment in her paper, *The Agitator*, because they called upon women to oppose the amendment and demeaned the Negro male's right to suffrage. She assured black Americans that "the Western women moving for woman's enfranchisement, do not oppose the Fifteenth Amendment. We have never heard it opposed at a Western women's meeting, in a single instance. Western women comprehend that humanity is one—that the colored man cannot be elevated without, at the same time, uplifting the colored woman—and they see clearly that through the gap in the fence made by the colored man, as he passes over into citizenship, all American women will pass to the same destination . . ."

[Lucy Stone said] "Negro men, and all women, suffer a grievous, common wrong, and are glad when either class, or individuals of either class, can escape from it. Let the friends of both causes cheerfully give each other credit for real facts. Each bitterly needs all the help of the other."

Writing in *The Woman's Advocate*, Frances Dana Gage announced her disagreement with Stanton and Anthony, with whom she had collaborated for years: "Could I with breath defeat the Fifteenth Amendment, I would not do it. That Amendment will let the colored men enter the wide portals of human rights. Keeping them out, suffering as now, would not let me in all the sooner, then in God's name why stand in their way? It is my earnest wish that the Fifteenth Amendment may be ratified. Let us apply the Golden Rule now and forever . . ."

All this made no impression on Stanton, Anthony, and their followers. Women, wrote Stanton, had "too much pride, self-respect, and womanly dignity" to rejoice in the adoption of the Fifteenth Amendment . . . [Stanton] was particularly bitter over Douglass's retreat from the position he had espoused in the early stages of the American Equal Rights Association, especially since he had been the first among the "woman's rights men" to advocate woman's right to the ballot. Stanton made this clear when she wrote that "common-sense women . . . felt towards the Fifteenth Amendment, which places all women under the heels of all men, precisely as Mr. Douglass would have felt had it proposed to enfranchise the men of all races but his own."

Douglass viewed this attack as proof that women like Elizabeth Cady Stanton simply did not understand the special problems facing black Americans in the crucial years immediately following the Civil War. He regretted that he had to part company with many women who were his personal friends and with whom he had worked so closely for thirty years. But he was comforted by the knowledge that the Fifteenth Amendment was being ratified by state after state and that especially in the West, women active in the woman's cause had been involved in petitioning the state legislatures, urging ratification.

In a speech in Boston on December 25, 1869, Douglass expressed his gratitude to these women. Then, describing his elation at the victories gained by the antislavery cause, he went on to remind the men and women present that the battle was not over, for women had yet to gain the vote. "Women are entitled to the ballot, alike by right . . ." he declared. To thunderous applause, he vowed that once the Fifteenth Amendment became part of the law of the land, he would devote himself to the struggle to gain the vote for women.

On March 30, 1870, President Ulysses S. Grant proclaimed the adoption of the Fifteenth Amendment. Celebrations were the order of the day. Amid the rejoicing, Douglass did not forget his pledge to the women of America. He called for the immediate organization of a campaign for a new amendment to the Constitution, granting woman suffrage . . . Eager to show women that they had not lost a champion, he devoted special attention to their cause in his new paper . . .

Peace was restored at the 1876 convention of the National Woman Suffrage Association. Douglass had been invited to attend, and he came. While neither Stanton nor Anthony expressed any regret over their criticism of their former friend and ally, they made it clear that they needed his help in the continuing campaign for woman's rights. Douglass responded briefly and indicated that he still smarted from the way in which some woman's rights leaders had referred to black men as "ignorant, besotted creatures" during the heated battle over the Fifteenth Amendment. Nevertheless, he announced that he was "willing to be part of the bridge over which women should march to the full enjoyment of their rights." Once the reconciliation had taken place, Douglass was again a familiar figure at women's rights conventions . . .

He brushed aside all arguments against woman's ability to use the vote intelligently, insisting: "I know of no class better equipped to manage the ballot than American women . . ." Even more, he told the women at these meetings that he regarded their movement to be more important than the movement to end slavery, significant though that had been, because their struggle "comprehends the liberation and elevation of one-half of the whole human family," and "if successful, it will be the most stupendous revolution the world has ever witnessed."

Not all who were associated with the woman's movement were happy over Douglass's return to their ranks and over the publicity his appearances received in the press. Southern suffragists had begun to organize in the 1880s, and they grew increasingly annoyed with the northern suffragists for extending so warm a welcome to a black man. Southern politicians, they were convinced, would never enfranchise women if a Negro was too prominent in the cause . . .

Douglass was never invited to attend a meeting of a southern suffrage association, but he remained a welcome visitor to meetings of the leading women's organizations in every other part of the country. On every occasion, as speaker and writer, he paid tribute to the contributions of women to the struggle for a more democratic America. Shortly before his death, he listed the departed veterans of the woman's rights movement—Lucretia Mott, Ernestine L. Rose, Angelina Grimké, Lucy Stone, and others—as among "the best of mankind," and said: "No good cause can fail when supported by such women." In nearly every speech he delivered, in every article he wrote for a magazine or newspaper, in every one of his three autobiographies, he included a tribute to women, black and white . . .

[When he died in 1895 from a heart attack] news-
papers in the United States and Europe carried the news
of Douglass's death on their front pages. While many
headlined the news with statements such as "Greatest
Negro Leader Dead," some featured the report under the
headline, "Friend and Champion of Women Dies." Not
a few carried the statement Elizabeth Cady Stanton made
in a letter to Susan B. Anthony which was to be read at
memorial services for Douglass: "He was the only man I
ever saw who understood the degradation of the disen-
franchisement of women. Through all the long years of
our struggle he has been a familiar figure on our platform
with always an inspiring word to say. In the very first convention, he helped me to carry the resolution I had
penned demanding woman suffrage. Frederick Douglass
is not dead. His grand character will long be an object
lesson in our National history. His lofty sentiments of liberty, justice and equality, echoed on every platform over
our broad land, must influence and inspire many coming
generations."[26]

To be fair to Elizabeth Cady Stanton and Susan B. Anthony, they saw
the Fifteenth Amendment as consolidating even more power for men, which
they believed would increase women's oppression. One way oppressive systems turn oppressed people against each other is by placing them in desperate
situations that require difficult choices, and a life-changing lesson we can
learn from Frederick Douglass's behavior during the Fifteenth Amendment
controversy is *the importance of not being petty when conflicts arise.* Not being
petty means being respectful during disagreements, not taking everything
personally, giving people the benefit of the doubt, and not holding a grudge.

A story I heard from a friend illustrates what it means to take everything
personally. My friend told me that when he would ride in his father's car as
a child, if his father was in a hurry he would scream and curse at every red
light, as if the stoplights had a personal grudge against him. His father had

taken the red lights personally, rather than realizing it was not personal. Because Douglass did not take everything personally, he realized Stanton's anger was largely caused by the difficult circumstances affecting American women. This allowed him to treat her with respect and empathy.

When a conflict was in fact personal, Douglass realized the most effective way to resolve it was also with the power of respect and empathy. In *The Art of Waging Peace* I discuss how conveying respect makes us much more effective at resolving conflict. Douglass explained how disrespect could damage the women's rights movement or any cause in two ways: "A cause may be damaged in two ways . . . One is by evincing too little respect for the opinions of those who happen to differ from us, and the other is too little respect for those who agree with us."[27]

The army has a motto "One team, one fight," which means we may experience disagreements and conflicts as fellow soldiers, but at the end of the day we are all on the same team. Every social movement has petty conflicts caused by envy, misunderstanding, miscommunication, and people disrespecting each other. I have seen activists demonize each other over small disagreements within their movement, seeming to forget they are all on one team, and their one fight should be against injustice, not each other.

The opposite of being petty is being gracious. Graciousness is a vein in the muscle of empathy. Like the veins in an athlete's arm, which become more visible when the athlete's biceps flex and grow, the stronger the muscle of empathy becomes, the more prominent the vein of graciousness will be. When people in any stressful situation are verbally attacking each other, we can use gracious words and behavior to calm and soothe the tensions around us. In the Bible, the book of Proverbs says, "Gracious words are a honeycomb, sweet to the soul and healing to the bones."[28] Because graciousness is so practical and powerful, just one person choosing to be gracious during a conflict can make a significant positive difference.

Human beings are indeed unusual creatures, because the power of our actions depends less on our instincts and more on the depth and breadth of our understanding. One reason this book explores empathy, graciousness, ancient history, the human condition, trauma, oppression, and so many other subjects is because to effectively wage peace we must strive to increase the quality and quantity of our understanding, just as generals who wage war strive to increase the quality and quantity of their soldiers. As philosopher Francis Bacon told us, "Knowledge is power."[29]

The science-fiction film *Blade Runner* (the final-cut version) can help us better understand the methods used by oppressive systems and the path to liberation. *Blade Runner* takes place in a futuristic world where humanity has created artificial life forms called "replicants." Replicants look like adult humans and do the jobs people no longer want to do. Replicants fight in wars, work as sex slaves, and perform dangerous manual labor. They are basically slaves. Replicants are stronger than and at least as smart as human beings, but they are given only a four-year lifespan. This reduces their capacity to organize themselves and rebel against their human masters.

In the film four replicants escape from slavery and hide in Los Angeles. They are looking for their creator, a rich and eccentric scientific genius, whom they hope will be able to extend their lifespan. The main character, Rick Deckard, is an agent in the Los Angeles police department who is assigned to hunt and kill the replicants. In this futuristic world the euphemism "retire" is used to describe the act of killing a replicant.

Deckard does not realize he is also a replicant, who has been given artificial memories to make him believe he is human. The film never directly states he is a replicant, and it is easy to watch the entire movie and miss the few clues that reveal this hidden part of the story. One of the clues is a memory Deckard has of a unicorn running toward him, which was implanted in his mind by his eccentric creator (the unicorn scene is in the final-cut version of the film, but not the original version).

*Blade Runner* metaphorically illustrates how oppressive systems get the oppressed to not only fear, mistrust, and hate each other, but also oppress, hurt, and kill each other.* Just as human beings use Deckard against his fellow replicants, exploitive systems such as slavery and colonialism have used the oppressed against the oppressed.

Oppressive systems are certainly not the cause of every conflict. Conflicts in a human community are normal, but they do not have to be destruc-

---

* The "kissing scene" in the film shows Deckard, who does not yet realize he is a replicant, aggressively treating a female replicant as a sex object.

tive. Just as burning embers are an inevitable consequence of campfires, conflicts are an inevitable consequence of living in a human community. If burning embers are not extinguished properly, they can spread fire and destroy an entire forest. In a similar way, if conflicts are not resolved properly, they can spread strife and destroy an entire community. All of us can learn to douse the embers of conflict with the water of effective conflict resolution. When conflicts are resolved effectively, they give people an opportunity to clear up misunderstandings, better understand each other, and strengthen their bonds of solidarity.

Although oppressive systems are not the cause of every conflict, they have mastered the art of throwing gasoline on the conflicts that do arise. They can also behave like arsonists by starting new fires. It can be challenging to maintain empathy for someone who passionately disagrees with you, and it does not help when an oppressive system is bombing the empathy you have for that person.

From the perspective of an oppressive system, there are four methods for bombing the empathy people have for each other. First, encourage them to fear, mistrust, and hate each other. Second, make them compete for food and other basic necessities. Third, put them in stressful and even desperate situations that cause them to seek favors from their oppressors.* And fourth, condition them to identify more with their oppressors than each other. Propaganda is a metaphorical plane capable of bombing empathy in these four ways.

---

* The temptation of receiving favors from an oppressive system makes it more likely that the oppressed will betray each other. If you were a slave living in desperate conditions who would be rewarded for telling your master about a slave who planned to run away, the temptation to betray your fellow slave could increase. This is yet another reason why empathy and solidarity among the oppressed is so important.

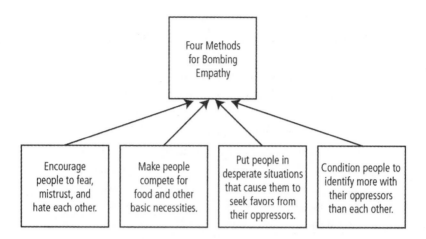

Figure 3.1: Four Methods for Bombing Empathy

Gandhi and Martin Luther King Jr. showed that we are most effective at overcoming oppression when we empathize with all human beings, including those viewed as oppressors. However, propaganda creates a sense of identification with those in power based not on genuine empathy, but on submissive idol worship. This leads to what I call *idolatrous identification* (which can be seen in cults, fascist ideologies, and cultures of celebrity worship) rather than *empathetic identification*. Malcolm X described how submissive idol worship, which is very different from genuine empathy, caused some slaves to identify more with their masters than other slaves:

> [During slavery] there were two kinds of slaves, the house Negro and the field Negro. The house Negroes—they lived in the house with master, they dressed pretty good, they ate good because they ate his food—what he left. They lived in the attic or the basement, but still they lived near the master; and they loved the master more than the master loved himself. They would give their life to save the master's house—quicker than the master would. If the master said, "We got a good house here," the house Negro

would say, "Yeah, we got a good house here." Whenever the master said "we," he said "we." That's how you can tell a house Negro.

If the master's house caught on fire, the house Negro would fight harder to put the blaze out than the master would. If the master got sick, the house Negro would say, "What's the matter, boss, *we* sick?" *We* sick! He identified himself with his master, more than his master identified with himself. And if you came to the house Negro and said, "Let's run away, let's escape, let's separate," the house Negro would look at you and say, "Man, you crazy. What you mean, separate? Where is there a better house than this? Where can I wear better clothes than this? Where can I eat better food than this?" That was that house Negro . . .

On that same plantation, there was the field Negro. The field Negroes—those were the masses. There were always more Negroes in the field than there were Negroes in the house . . . That house Negro loved his master, but that field Negro—remember, they were in the majority, and they hated the master. When the house caught on fire, he didn't try to put it out; that field Negro prayed for a wind, for a breeze. When the master got sick, the field Negro prayed that he'd die.[30]

Malcolm X expresses a piece of the truth, but he is exaggerating the behavior of most house slaves for dramatic effect and oversimplifying the complexity of slave life. Although many slaves submissively viewed their masters as idols, our human tendency to rebel when we see clear signs of injustice was more common than Malcolm X acknowledged.

Historian Henry Louis Gates gives us more insight into the reality of slave life, and explains how education in the form of literacy was the most powerful force against slavery. This is why it was illegal to teach slaves to read. Indeed, knowledge *truly* is power. Gates tells us:

And was Malcolm X right about in his black-and-white depiction of the "politics," as it were, between house and field [slaves]? With all due respect to Malcolm, the answer is: not really, though there are always exceptions. In the first place, it is important to remember that the historical record is full of masters expressing their fears that their house servants were trying to poison them! As Robin Kelley and Earl Lewis explain in *To Make Our World Anew: Vol. 1: A History of African Americans to 1880*, "As early as 1755 a Charleston slave woman was burned at the stake for poisoning her master, and in 1769 a special issue of the *South Carolina Gazette* carried the story of a slave woman who had poisoned her master's infant child." And there were many other cases of poisoning and allegations of poisoning . . .

In addition, historically, as Frederick Douglass eloquently points out, the slave who had access to literacy—far more likely to have been a house slave, to use Malcolm's formulation, than a field slave—found the urge to achieve *physical* freedom, to run away, well-nigh irresistible. Once they were literate, they understood even more fundamentally than when illiterate that they were intellectual equals, by *nature*, with their masters, and that the deprivation of the right to learn to read and write was another form of slavery—*metaphysical slavery*. And so, these literate slaves (whether living in the house or in the field, and in the house *and* then the field, like Douglass did) spent a lot of time plotting their escape. Few slaves—whether literate or not, whether working in the house or the field—really wanted to remain slaves, and we can see this clearly by their behavior during the Civil War.[31]

In his third autobiography, Frederick Douglass discussed a slave named Aunt Katy who beat and starved him when he was a small child. Because slave owners often did not give slaves sufficient amounts of food, Aunt Katy took food from children such as Douglass in order to feed her own children. Her behavior is an example of how the oppressed can fight over basic necessities and seek favors from their oppressors. Douglass described how Aunt Katy deprived him of food when he was around five years old:

> I, without any fault of my own, was born [in slavery] . . . The practice of separating mothers from their children and hiring them out at distances too great to admit of their meeting, save at long intervals, was a marked feature of the cruelty and barbarity of the slave system; but it was in harmony with the grand aim of that system, which always and everywhere sought to reduce man to a level with the brute. It had no interest in recognizing or preserving any of the ties that bind families together or to their homes . . . My only recollections of my own mother are of a few hasty visits made in the night on foot [a 24 mile roundtrip], after the daily tasks were over, and when she was under the necessity of returning in time to respond to the driver's call to the field in the early morning . . .
>
> Ambitious of old master's favor, ill-tempered and cruel by nature . . . [Aunt Katy] had a strong hold upon old master, for she was a first-rate cook, and very industrious. She was therefore greatly favored by him—and as one mark of his favor she was the only mother who was permitted to retain her children around her, and even to these, her own children, she was often fiendish in her brutality. Cruel, however, as she sometimes was to her own children, she was not destitute of maternal feeling, and in her instinct to satisfy their demands for food she was often guilty of starving me and the other children. Want of food was my chief trouble during my first summer here . . . I have often been so pinched with hunger as to dispute with old "Nep," the dog, for the crumbs which fell

from the kitchen table. Many times have I followed, with eager step, the waiting-girl when she shook the tablecloth, to get the crumbs and small bones flung out for the dogs and cats . . .

[One day] I found it quite impossible to do so [without food] any longer. Sundown came, but no bread; and in its stead came the threat from Aunt Katy, with a scowl well-suited to its terrible import, that she would starve the life out of me. Brandishing her knife, she chopped off the heavy slices of bread for the other children, and put the loaf away, muttering all the while her savage designs upon myself. Against this disappointment, for I was expecting that her heart would relent at last, I made an extra effort to maintain my dignity, but when I saw the other children around me with satisfied faces, I could stand it no longer. I went out behind the kitchen wall and cried like a fine fellow. When wearied with this, I returned to the kitchen, sat by the fire and brooded over my hard lot. I was too hungry to sleep. While I sat in the corner, I caught sight of an ear of Indian corn upon an upper shelf. I watched my chance and got it, and shelling off a few grains, I put it back again. These grains I quickly put into the hot ashes to roast. I did this at the risk of getting a brutal thumping, for Aunt Katy could beat as well as starve me. My corn was not long in roasting, and I eagerly pulled it from the ashes, and placed it upon a stool in a clever little pile. I began to help myself, when who but my own dear mother should come in.

The scene which followed is beyond my power to describe. The friendless and hungry boy, in his extremest need, found himself in the strong, protecting arms of his mother. I have before spoken of my mother's dignified and impressive manner. I shall never forget the indescribable expression of her countenance when I told her that Aunt

Katy had said she would starve the life out of me. There was deep and tender pity in her glance at me, and, at the same moment, a fiery indignation at Aunt Katy, and while she took the corn from me, and gave in its stead a large ginger-cake, she read Aunt Katy a lecture which was never forgotten. That night I learned as I had never learned before, that I was not only a child, but somebody's child. I was grander upon my mother's knee than a king upon his throne. But my triumph was short. I dropped off to sleep, and waked in the morning to find my mother gone and myself at the mercy again of the virago in my master's kitchen, whose fiery wrath was my constant dread.

My mother had walked twelve miles to see me, and had the same distance to travel over again before the morning sunrise. I do not remember ever seeing her again. Her death soon ended the little communication that had existed between us, and with it, I believe, a life full of weariness and heartfelt sorrow. To me it has ever been a grief that I knew my mother so little, and have so few of her words treasured in my remembrance. I have since learned that she was the only one of all the colored people of Tuckahoe who could read. How she acquired this knowledge I know not . . . I can therefore fondly and proudly ascribe to her an earnest love of knowledge. That in any slave state a field-hand should learn to read is remarkable, but the achievement of my mother, considering the place and circumstances, was very extraordinary. In view of this fact, I am happy to attribute any love of letters I may have, not to my presumed Anglo-Saxon paternity, but to the native genius of my sable, unprotected, and uncultivated mother—a woman who belonged to a race whose mental endowments are still disparaged and despised.[32]

Slavery was so common throughout recorded history that people of all races have been slaves, including countless white people. State-sanctioned slavery no longer exists today due to the courageous efforts of the abolitionist movement (I discuss the current problem of illegal slavery in *The Art of Waging Peace*), but oppressive systems come in many shapes and sizes. All oppressive systems use at least one of the four methods to bomb empathy. Because oppressive systems drop bombs from the plane of propaganda, we must strengthen our muscle of reason and increase our understanding so that we can see through the illusions of propaganda. We must also make our muscle of empathy so strong that it can withstand any bomb.

What will humanity's future look like if we no longer exploit people as tools? Will people no longer be employed by companies, and will nobody ever work hard again? Certainly not, because from now until the end of time, great achievements will always require hard work. Treating people as human beings rather than tools simply means a change in our current priorities. A world where people are no longer exploited as tools will still allow companies to make a profit, but the priority will be people over profit, rather than profit over people.

Martin Luther King Jr. said, "We as a nation must undergo a radical revolution of values. We must rapidly begin the shift from a thing-oriented society to a person-oriented society. When machines and computers, profit motives and property rights, are considered more important than people, the giant triplets of racism, extreme materialism, and militarism are incapable of being conquered."[33]

When people are treated not as human beings who feel pain, but as hammers without hearts, they become tools. But when the value of human life gains a higher priority than profit, then people cease to be tools. Many of the problems people face today are due to our society's priorities being arranged in a way that promotes what King called "extreme materialism." As the civil and women's rights movements demonstrated, waging peace is an effective method for rearranging our society's priorities, but an oppressive system will fight ferociously to prevent itself from being rearranged.

History teaches us that liberating ourselves from oppression requires us to first liberate our minds from ignorance. By discussing state-sanctioned slavery as an example, I have revealed the four methods used to bomb empathy so that we can better protect ourselves from propaganda and division. As we increase our understanding about the human condition and the anatomy of oppression, we can strengthen our empathy and learn to wage peace in a world where bombs continue to fall.

## *Cruelty and Brutality*

As I explained at the beginning of this chapter, human beings are the most unusual toolmakers in the world because we try to transform everything into a tool, including inanimate objects, plants, animals, and our fellow human beings. And as we just discussed, human beings are the only creatures, as far as we know, who worry about our tools murdering us. However, another feature of our toolmaking behavior makes us even more unusual. To understand the most unusual and puzzling feature of our toolmaking behavior, we must talk about Alexander the Great and his horse.

Living in the fourth century BC, Alexander the Great was a Macedonian king and general who created the largest empire on earth up until that time. He used his horse as a tool for transportation, just as we use a car. He also used his horse as a tool for fighting in combat, just as modern American soldiers use armored vehicles. But did Alexander treat his horse like a piece of military equipment? Historian Norman Cantor recounts an ancient story that describes how Alexander became the owner of the horse that helped him conquer nations:

> [King of Macedonia and Alexander's father] Philip and his grooms could not break the horse . . . Philip and his grooms were about to give up on the Balkan horse as incapable of ever being broken in when Alexander, who was there, remarked that they were losing a wonderful horse simply because they were too inexperienced and too spineless to handle him. Initially Philip remained silent, but after Alexander repeated his comment and became visibly upset,

Philip asked Alexander if his criticism of his elders was due
to his knowing more than his elders, to which Alexander
replied that he could at least handle *this* horse better than
they. His father then asked his son what the consequence
of his impulsiveness would be, were he to not succeed in
handling the horse. His answer, which was the promise to
pay the price of the horse, resulted in much laughter.

After the financial terms between father and son were
settled, Alexander quickly ran toward the horse. He did
not immediately mount the horse. Earlier, he had noticed
that the horse was greatly bothered by the sight of its own
shadow, and so after he took the reins, he turned the horse
toward the sun. For a short while, he ran beside it, and
patted it in order to calm its panting. Then, after gently
setting aside his cloak, he quickly and firmly mounted the
horse, using the reins to put pressure on the bit without
hurting its mouth. Once Alexander felt comfortable that
the horse had dropped its menacing demeanor and was
eager to gallop, he gave it some rein and urged it on, using
a firmer voice and kick of his foot.

Silence fell over the crowd. But when Alexander
returned truly pleased with himself, he was welcomed with
cheers and applause. Philip was said to have burst into tears
of joy. After Alexander dismounted, Philip kissed his head
and said to him, "Son, look for a kingdom that matches
your size. Macedonia has not enough space for you."
Alexander was about twelve years old when this occurred.

So the oft-told story goes. Alexander called the horse
Bucephalus, and the two were devoted to each other. *He
loved that horse* [emphasis added] and for twenty years,
until Bucephalus died on the border between Afghanistan
and Pakistan, Alexander rode Bucephalus into battle and
would ride no other until the aged steed died. *For Alexander the horse was much more than an instrument* [emphasis

added]. After Bucephalus's death, Alexander founded a
city on the Hydraspes River and called it Bucephala in
honor of his loyal mount.[34]

Alexander the Great was a violent conqueror who treated his horse better
than many people treat their fellow human beings. Since my childhood I
have found it strange and puzzling that human beings treat living creatures,
whether we use them as tools or not, in such extremely different ways. One
person can treat a horse as a living creature worthy of respect and empathy,
while another person can abuse a horse as if it is worthless, like an object to
be used and thrown away.

For example, philosopher Friedrich Nietzsche suffered from a psychological collapse that he never recovered from, but his last action before his
collapse was trying to protect a horse being beaten by its owner. Nietzsche's
final act before his mental breakdown illustrates our unusual nature as toolmakers, because while one man can beat his horse ruthlessly, another man
can try to protect the animal with his own body. According to philosopher
Rüdiger Safranski: "On January 3, 1889, just after Nietzsche left his apart-
ment, he caught sight of a carriage driver beating his horse on the Piazza
Carlo Alberto. Nietzsche, weeping, threw himself around the horse's neck
to protect it. He collapsed in compassion with the horse."[35]

Many people revere dogs as "man's best friend," but people are also capable of torturing dogs in horrific ways. What makes us so unusual as toolmakers is our capacity for extreme compassion or extreme cruelty—our
ability to use a hammer to build a hospital or shatter someone's skull, our
ability to treat a dog as a family member or a piece of trash. No other organism on the planet is capable of slaughtering large numbers of living creatures
not for food or survival, but simply for pleasure. No other organism creates
animal shelters to help abused and abandoned pets, or tries to protect endangered species from going extinct.

As human beings we have all wondered about the nature of cruelty at
least once in our lives. None of us want to be treated cruelly, and whenever
the media reports a mass shooting, I always hear some people say with shock
and horror in their voices, "How could anyone do something like that?" As

a small boy I wanted to know where cruelty comes from. What makes one person cruel and another person compassionate? Is cruelty as natural to being human as our heartbeat, or is cruelty more like a chronic illness, a result of something that has gone wrong? If we want to make our world safer and more peaceful, understanding the causes and cures for cruelty is essential. Much to my disappointment, I was never taught any of this in school.

As I journeyed to understand the causes and cures for cruelty, I had a surprising realization. Cruel actions, if we define them as *inflicting, watching, and enjoying the suffering of a living creature (without that creature's consent)*, are relatively rare in the world. Most of the behavior we perceive to be cruel is not actually cruel. Even more surprising, I learned that a human behavior exists that is more dangerous than cruelty, yet few people have ever heard of it.

To describe the behavior more dangerous than cruelty, I must first tell a quick story. After graduating from West Point at the age of twenty-two, I served in the army for seven years until I was twenty-nine. When I was twenty-five the army assigned me to Washington, DC. As I was flying to Washington, DC to begin my assignment, I sat next to a kind young woman on the plane who was about my age.

She asked me, "What do you do?"

"I'm in the army," I replied.

After she asked me several follow-up questions, I asked her, "What do you do?"

She said, "I'm Karl Rove's aide."

"That's very interesting," I said, pausing for a moment and thinking to myself. I had read articles where some peace activists and liberals had described Karl Rove as one of the worst human beings on the planet. According to them, he was the cruel monster behind President George W. Bush, the Iraq War, and many of our nation's other problems. Because I was suspicious of stereotypes, I asked her, "You are certainly aware that some people have a bad perception of Karl Rove. I would like to hear your thoughts on that. Is there any truth to their perception?"

She answered, "Karl Rove is one of the nicest people I have ever met, and he is a great person to work for." She gave me specific examples of Karl

Rove's kindness, and because I am not naive, I kept in mind that she might be biased. But when I thought about her words critically, I realized there could be some truth to what she was saying. Putting my preconceptions aside, I started to think about politics and violence in new ways.

I wondered how violent Karl Rove, George W. Bush, and Dick Cheney really were. There is no evidence that they have ever assaulted their wives or children. And when the Vietnam War occurred, none of them volunteered to deploy. They did not seem eager to fight in a war, to kill, or be killed. You would probably be terrified if I put you and a violent serial killer in a small room together and locked the door, but you would probably not be scared at all if I locked you in a room with Karl Rove, George W. Bush, or Dick Cheney.

Yet a riddle remained: how could people so nonthreatening in a personal setting be capable of starting the ultimate act of violence that is war? Several years later one of my peace activist friends told me, "Many of the world's most dangerous serial killers don't ever get caught or go to jail. They end up in Washington, DC, running our nation's government."

But this comment is an oversimplification, because there is a key difference between most serial killers and most people who work in Washington, DC. If we do not understand this difference, we cannot understand the root causes of war. To explain why most serial killers and most politicians differ in their behavior, we must explore kindness, violence, and the human condition.

In all of human history, there has never been a recorded instance of a human being becoming traumatized from receiving a genuine act of kindness.* However, receiving an act of violence against our will is one of the most traumatic events we can experience.

Not only can receiving violence cause trauma, but so can inflicting violence. In all of human history, there has never been a recorded instance of a human being becoming traumatized from inflicting a genuine act of kindness.** But inflicting violence can create trauma so severe that people never

---

* People suffering from trauma can misinterpret acts of kindness in a way that reopens their old psychological wounds, but the act of kindness itself does not cause trauma.

** When I use the word "genuine," I am referring to acts of kindness where we do not look for anything in return. Being kind can sometimes have negative consequences if the recipient misinterprets or does not appreciate your kindness and reacts badly, but being kind in and of itself does not cause trauma in a person who is kind.

recover from it. To understand why inflicting violence can be so traumatizing, consider the following thought experiment.

A thought experiment is a scientific technique that is very useful when an experiment cannot be performed in a laboratory. Thought experiments greatly helped Albert Einstein with his scientific work, and they are helpful to our cause because we can use them to explore scenarios too unethical to perform in a laboratory.

Although many people will find this thought experiment and the examples I provide afterward disturbing to read, exploring this darkness is necessary to find hidden sources of light. By journeying into darkness, we will find more evidence that human beings are not naturally violent, and we will uncover a root cause of all war and injustice that remains hidden to most people today. This light gives me the kind of hope that increases my empathy and motivates me to wage peace.

To conduct our thought experiment, imagine if I asked you to spend an entire afternoon with a five-year-old girl. During this afternoon your priority is to get to know this child as well as possible. Find out what she wants to be when she grows up, how many siblings she has, if she has any pets, what her favorite game is, and what kind of food she likes. Go to the park with this little girl, play her favorite game with her, eat a delicious meal together, and get to know her as well as possible. Then at the end of this afternoon, I want you to take a hammer, look the little girl in the eyes, and without looking away or blinking, I want you to kill her by hitting her in the forehead with the hammer as hard as you can.*

According to military studies, around 98 percent of human beings would be traumatized from inflicting this intimate act of violence on a small child at close range.** But let's consider another scenario. What if you don't

---

* Of course, in this thought experiment the person does not know at the beginning of the afternoon that he or she will have to murder the little girl. If a person knew this at the beginning of the afternoon, he or she would probably maintain emotional distance and not get to know the little girl very well.

** I have derived the 98 percent figure (which refers to people who are not psychotic) from research into PTSD and the Swank and Marchand study, which I discuss later in this chapter. However, when we consider the new research being done on serial killers, we can deduce that the percentage of people traumatized from the act I describe in the thought experiment would probably be *at least* 98 percent, if not higher.

spend an afternoon with the little girl? What if she is a complete stranger to you when you kill her with a hammer? The percentage of people traumatized by committing this violent act will decrease a little below 98 percent.

Furthermore, what if instead of looking her in the eyes when you kill her, you hit her in the back of the head with a hammer? What if you never see her face? Again, the percentage of people traumatized will decrease slightly.

In addition, what if you don't use a hammer at all, but shoot her with a rifle at a much farther distance? And what if you believe this child is subhuman and dangerous? What if you believe she is part of an evil group of people determined to kill your family? Yet again, the percentage of people traumatized by killing the little girl will decrease even more.

Finally, what if instead of using a hammer or rifle, you drop bombs on this child from far away? If one hundred people look children they know in the eyes and murder them with hammers, around 98 percent of the killers will suffer from psychological trauma. But if one hundred people bomb children they have no empathy for from far away, only a few of the bombers will suffer from trauma.

Our thought experiment reveals that psychological, emotional, and physical distance make it much easier to hurt and kill human beings, and this insight is backed up by all the evidence from military history. This insight is actually a fact about the human condition, which the military already knows. The military knows that increasing the amount of psychological, emotional, and physical distance between soldiers and the people they kill will decrease the percentage of soldiers who suffer from psychological trauma. In his groundbreaking book, *On Killing*, Lieutenant Colonel Dave Grossman says:

> It has long been understood that there is a direct relationship between the empathic and physical proximity of the victim, and the resultant difficulty and trauma of the kill . . . At the far end of the spectrum are bombing and artillery, which are often used to illustrate the relative ease of long-range killing. As we draw toward the near end of the spectrum, we begin to realize that the resistance to

killing becomes increasingly more intense . . .

[Glenn] Gray states the matter clearly: "Many a pilot or artilleryman who has destroyed untold numbers of terrified noncombatants has never felt any need for repentance or regret." And [Gwynne] Dyer echoes and reinforces Gray when he notes that there has never been any difficulty in getting artillerymen, bomber crews, or naval personnel to kill . . .

Artillery crews, bomber crews, naval gunners, and missile crews—at sea and on the ground—are all protected by the same powerful combination of group absolution, mechanical distance, and, most pertinent to our current discussion, physical distance.

In years of research and reading on the subject of killing in combat I have not found one single instance of individuals who have refused to kill the enemy under these circumstances, nor have I found a single instance of psychiatric trauma associated with this type of killing. Even in the case of the individuals who dropped the atomic bombs on Hiroshima and Nagasaki, contrary to popular myth, there are no indications of psychological problems. Historical accounts indicate that the pilot of the aircraft that made the weather reconnaissance for the *Enola Gay* had a series of disciplinary and criminal problems before the bombing, and it was his continued problems after leaving the service that formed the sole basis of the popular myth of suicide and mental problems among these crews.[36]

Recently, some American drone pilots have experienced trauma from killing people at long range (partly because they can see their victims die on a video screen), but they comprise a small percentage of the total drone pilots. Also, some people serving in bomber crews have felt regret over the people they killed, but only after recognizing the humanity of their victims. How does the human mind react when we are so close to those we kill that our faces get splattered with chunks of flesh, warm blood, and splintered bones from our victims?

During the Nazi Holocaust, policemen in Police Battalion 101 were ordered to execute large numbers of Jews at close range. To reduce the percentage of policemen who would suffer from psychological trauma, the Nazis dehumanized the Jews as being subhuman and evil. Also, the policemen were ordered to shoot the Jews in the back of the head, so they would not have to look their victims in the face.

However, shooting people in the back of the head still caused incidents the policemen found traumatizing. One policeman said, "At first we shot freehand. When one aimed too high, the entire skull exploded. As a consequence, brains and bones flew everywhere. Thus, we were instructed to place the bayonet point on the [back of] the neck."[37]

Another policeman explained why using bayonets to aim did not remove the gruesome aspects of killing: "Through the point-blank shot that was thus required, the bullet [still] struck the head of the victim at such a trajectory that often the entire skull or at least the entire rear skullcap was torn off, and blood, bone splinters, and brains sprayed everywhere and besmirched the shooters."[38]

In his book *Ordinary Men*, Christopher Browning describes how some of the policemen in Police Battalion 101, many of whom had been "ordinary men" rather than experienced killers prior to World War II, reacted to killing at close range:

> For his first victim August Zorn was given a very old man. Zorn recalled that his elderly victim "could not or would not keep up with his countrymen, because he repeatedly fell and then simply lay there . . . Because I was already very upset from the cruel treatment of the Jews during the clearing of the town and was completely in turmoil, I shot too high. The entire back of the skull of my Jew was torn off and the brain exposed. Parts of the skull flew into Sergeant Steinmetz's face. This was grounds for me, after returning to the truck, to go to the first sergeant

and ask for my release. I had become so sick that I simply couldn't anymore. I was then relieved by the first sergeant."

Georg Kageler, a thirty-seven-year-old tailor, made it through the first round [of executions] before encountering difficulty. "After I had carried out the first shooting and at the unloading point was allotted a mother with daughter as victims for the next shooting, I began a conversation with them and learned that they were Germans from Kassel, and I took the decision not to participate further in the executions. The entire business was now so repugnant to me that I returned to my platoon leader and told him that I was still sick and asked for my release . . ."

[Franz Kastenbaum said] "The shooting of the men was so repugnant to me that I missed the fourth man [that I was assigned to shoot] . . . It was not that I could no longer aim accurately, rather that the fourth time I intentionally missed. I then ran into the woods, vomited, and sat down against a tree. To make sure that no one was nearby, I called loudly into the woods, because I wanted to be alone. Today I can say that my nerves were totally finished. I think that I remained alone in the woods for some two to three hours . . ."

Most of those who found the shooting impossible to bear quit very early. But not always. The men in one squad had already shot ten to twenty Jews each when they finally asked to be relieved. As one of them explained, "I especially asked to be relieved because the man next to me shot so impossibly. Apparently he always aimed his gun too high, producing terrible wounds in his victims. In many cases the entire backs of victims' heads were torn off, so that the brains sprayed all over. I simply couldn't watch it any longer." At the unloading point, Sergeant Bentheim watched men emerge from the woods covered with blood and brains, morale shaken and nerves finished . . .

> As with First Company, alcohol was made available to the policemen under Drucker and Steinmetz who stayed in the forest and continued shooting . . . When the men arrived at the barracks [after executing the Jews], they were depressed, angered, embittered, and shaken. They ate little but drank heavily. Generous quantities of alcohol were provided, and many of the policemen got quite drunk. Major Trapp made the rounds, trying to console and reassure them, and again placing the responsibility on higher authorities. But neither the drink nor Trapp's consolation could wash away the sense of shame and horror that pervaded the barracks.[39]

Despite the difficulties of killing at close range, only about 10 to 20 percent of the policemen in Police Battalion 101 refused to kill,[40] because the Nazi government had put an extraordinary amount of effort into dehumanizing the Jews.* In *Ordinary Men*, Christopher Browning describes how police commander Major Trapp encouraged his men to participate in the executions: "The Jews stood outside their circle of human obligation and responsibility. Such a polarization between 'us' and 'them,' between one's comrades and the enemy, is of course standard in war . . . Major Trapp appealed to this generalized notion of the Jews as part of the enemy in his early-morning speech. *The men should remember, when shooting Jewish women and children, that the enemy was killing German women and children by bombing Germany* [emphasis added]."[41]

The Nazi government implemented additional distancing techniques to protect the executioners from the trauma of killing at close range. The most infamous distancing technique was the gas chamber, which allowed people

---

* The book *Ordinary Men* does not spend much time discussing the essential role dehumanization played in the massacres, and Browning mentions that many of the personal testimonies left out the influence of dehumanization due to "stark legal consideration [because] according to German law, among the criteria for defining homicide as murder is the presence of a 'base motive,' such as racial hatred. Any member of the battalion who openly confessed to anti-Semitism would have seriously compromised his legal position" (*Ordinary Men*, 150). Dehumanization played a crucial role in the massacres by making people more willing to kill and less likely to experience trauma.

to kill without having to see their victims die. Historian Richard Breitman describes why General Erich von dem Bach-Zelewski and SS Commander Heinrich Himmler wanted to switch from firing squads to poison gas: "[Bach-Zelewski asked] Himmler to spare not the victims but the policemen. Pointing out how shaken the executioners were, he complained that these men were now finished for the rest of their lives: they would either be neurotics or savages . . . Himmler had wanted a neater, cleaner, less upsetting way of killing large numbers of people, and poison gas was the obvious solution."[42]

When soldiers kill at close range for a long time, their minds can become desensitized, numb, and even insane. Adolf Eichmann, one of the most notorious war criminals of the twentieth century, helped organize the Holocaust and was later executed for war crimes. Yet he became upset when he saw German soldiers killing Jews at close range, not because he cared about the Jewish victims, but because he was concerned about the well-being of the German executioners.

Despite his strong support of the Holocaust, Eichmann could not stand the sight of bloody wounds, nor would he seem intimidating if you and he were locked in a small room together. In her book, *Eichmann in Jerusalem*, Hannah Arendt tells us:

> [Eichmann said] "If today I am shown a gaping wound, I can't possibly look at it. I am that type of person, so that very often I was told that I couldn't have become a doctor. I still remember how I pictured the thing to myself, and then I became physically weak, as though I had lived through some great agitation. Such things happen to everybody, and it left behind a certain inner trembling . . ."
>
> [Describing an experience near one of the concentration camps, Eichmann said] "I saw the most horrible sight I had thus far seen in my life. The truck was making for an open ditch, the doors were opened, and the corpses were thrown out, as though they were still alive, so smooth were their limbs. They were hurled into the ditch, and I

can still see a civilian extracting the teeth with tooth pliers. And then I was off—jumped into my car and did not open my mouth any more. After that time, I could sit for hours beside my driver without exchanging a word with him. There I got enough. I was finished. I only remember that a physician in white overalls told me to look through a hole into the truck while they were still in it. I refused to do that. I could not. I had to disappear . . ."

[When Eichmann visited the city of Lwów and witnessed executions, he] went to see the local S. S. commander, and told him: "Well, it is horrible what is being done around here; I said young people are being made into sadists. How can one do that? Simply bang away at women and children? That is impossible. Our people will go mad or become insane, our own people."[43]

Like Eichmann, General Bach-Zelewski was another Nazi war criminal who did not like seeing killing at close range. In *Ordinary Men*, Browning tells us, "This psychological burden [of seeing mass murder at close range] was serious and extended even to Bach-Zelewski himself. Himmler's SS doctor, reporting to the Reichsführer on Bach-Zelewski's incapacitating illness in the spring of 1942, noted that the SS leader was suffering 'especially from visions in connection with the shootings of Jews that he himself had led, and from other difficult experiences in the east.'"[44]

What does all of this reveal about the human condition? It shows that if we want to kill without experiencing guilt, remorse, or trauma, we must silence our empathy either through cruelty or something I call brutality. What is brutality? It is a form of psychological blindness. It is the ability to kill or support the act of killing because we are psychologically blind to the suffering we are causing. Two factors that cause the blindness of brutality are dehumanization and physical distance from someone's suffering.

The blindness of brutality allows politicians to start a war, even if they love their families, are kind to their neighbors, and would be terrified of fighting in a war themselves. These politicians do not have to see the victims of war suffer and die. They do not have to kill people while looking them in the eyes, or risk being killed.

The blindness of brutality differs from cruelty, because cruelty occurs when we inflict, watch, and enjoy the suffering of a living creature. When cruelty occupies our mind we want to revel in the suffering of others, but when brutality occupies our mind we do not want to watch people suffer where we are close enough to smell their sweat. Brutality makes us blind to the pain of others by encouraging us to look away, deny what is really happening in the world, or rationalize atrocities as being "necessary for the greater good."

If we want to overcome the root causes of war and injustice, we must understand that brutality is much more dangerous than cruelty. The blindness of brutality causes far more suffering around the world than the small minority of people who are capable of truly psychotic acts of cruelty. Brutality enables cruelty, just as cold temperatures enable ice. If we really want to fight cruelty, which takes many shapes and sizes around the world, we must also fight the brutality that enables cruelty.

Martin Luther King Jr. also realized that brutality is more dangerous than cruelty. In *The End of War* the word I use for brutality is "apathy." King realized the opposite of good is not evil. The opposite of good is apathy. He said, "History will have to record that the greatest tragedy of this period of social transition was not the vitriolic words and the violent actions of the bad people, but the appalling silence and indifference of the good people. Our generation will have to repent not only for the words and acts of the children of darkness, but also for the fears and apathy of the children of light."[45]

In schools bullying is sustained not just by the bullies, but the students who look the other way, ignore the problem, or are afraid of also being bullied. Holocaust survivor Elie Wiesel said this kind of neutrality, which is also an aspect of brutality, enables the worst atrocities in the world to occur. He said, "We must always take sides. Neutrality helps the oppressor, never the victim. Silence encourages the tormentor, never the tormented."[46]

This subject matter may seem dark, but if we look closer we will find light in the darkness. Exploring the blindness of brutality reveals that the vast majority of human beings cannot commit intimate acts of violence at close range without experiencing guilt, remorse, or trauma. This counters the myth that human beings are naturally violent. This also gives me realistic hope that humanity can create a more peaceful world if we work to overcome brutality and the other root causes of war and injustice, rather than dealing merely with symptoms. I discuss these other root causes in *The End of War*, and I offer techniques for defeating apathy in my other books.

If human beings were to experience *pure war*, even for a short amount of time, almost everyone would become traumatized. What is pure war? It is war stripped of all the psychological and physical distancing techniques used by militaries, politicians, and governments to make war seem less repulsive. It is war where there is no propaganda that dehumanizes the enemy, where you empathize with the people you are massacring, where there is no authority figure who helps you rationalize the use of violence, where there is no training to desensitize you to the act of killing, and where all the violence is inflicted at close range. Because a pure war would be so horrific to most soldiers and so impractical as a way of waging war, it has never happened in human history.

As I mentioned earlier, around 98 percent of people will experience psychological trauma in extreme killing situations. But if this is true, it means around 2 percent of people can kill in the most intimate circumstances without becoming traumatized. Why does this 2 percent seem immune to trauma? To understand this, we can look at World War II, which was horrific yet still far removed from pure war. Roy Swank and Walter Marchand, who both served as medical doctors in the U.S. military during World War II, conducted a study during the war that concluded 98 percent of soldiers became psychological casualties after sixty days of sustained day and night combat.

But why were 2 percent of soldiers immune to psychological trauma and not driven insane by war? According to their study on combat trauma, that 2 percent seems to have already been insane. Swank and Marchand said, "All normal men eventually suffer combat exhaustion [also known as post traumatic stress disorder] in prolonged continuous and severe combat. The exceptions to this rule are psychotic soldiers, and a number of examples of this have been observed."[47]

Why do I use the word "brutality" to describe the psychological blindness that enables killing? To solve a large-scale problem we must first give it a name, just as people in the past could not fight polio unless they first named the illness they were trying to study, understand, and cure. As far as I know, there is no word in the English language that captures the problem I am describing as brutality. If we want to create a more peaceful and just world, we must study, understand, and cure the blindness of brutality.

A problem with the English language is that we often use one word to mean too many things. For example, love can refer to a wide range of experiences that vary greatly in intensity and depth. People can use the word "love" to say, "I love my children. I love chocolate. I love watching television. I love my country. I love shopping. I love God. I love playing baseball. I love peace and justice."

Also, love can refer to sex, romance, friendships, and various family relationships. When we use one word to mean so many things, it often creates miscommunication and misunderstanding. This is why in *Peaceful Revolution* I use words such as "empathy," "unconditional love," and "solidarity" to describe specific features on the landscape of love.

To cure the blindness of brutality that creates the conditions for war and injustice, we must have a precise word to describe it. Like the word "love," the word "apathy" also encompasses a broad range of behaviors. A person can say, "I am apathetic about what we eat for dinner tonight. I don't care if we have pizza or tacos." Of course, this example of apathy is very different from the apathy of Adolf Eichmann, who was indifferent to the suffering of his murdered victims.

Brutality is the deadliest form of apathy. Although I explain the dangers of apathy in *The End of War*, this discussion of brutality gives us a deeper understanding of apathy's most deadly form. Humanity needs a word to represent the psychological blindness that enables violence and injustice if we are going to move forward as a species. Instead of inventing a word people have never heard of, I think it is more effective to use a word such as "brutality" that already evokes a negative connotation.

The meaning of words changes over time. To offer one example, the word "gay" used to mean "happy," and now it refers to someone who is homosexual. To create a more peaceful and just world, we must work together to cure the dangerous psychological blindness that enables so many of our problems, and we must give it a name so that it can no longer hide.

Cruelty and brutality are partners in crime. War, slavery, and all unjust systems are enabled not only by cruelty, but also brutality. Exploring the blindness of brutality even reveals how animals can be mistreated in gruesome ways. Feeling empathy for animals is as natural to human beings as feeling empathy for people. To offer evidence to support this claim, every nomadic tribe of hunter-gatherers we know about performs rituals to express empathy, appreciation, respect, and reverence for the animals they kill.

As I mentioned in chapter 1, when journalist Bill Moyers asked mythologist Joseph Campbell, "Do you think [hunting] troubled early man?" Campbell replied, "Absolutely, that's why you have the rites, because it did trouble him . . . [These rites included] rituals of appeasement to the animal, of thanks to the animal . . . And some kind of respect for the animal that was killed . . . And more than respect . . . [The buffalo] was the sacred animal for the [American] Indians."[48]

Psychologist Erich Fromm explains how brutality not only enables us to hurt human beings, but also animals:

> That the element of familiarity and empathy plays a role in the generation of inhibitions against killing animals can easily be detected from reactions to be observed in everyday life. Many people show a definite aversion to killing and eating an animal with which they are familiar or one they have kept as a pet [such as a dog or cat in America]. There are a large number of people who would not kill such an animal and to whom the idea of eating it is plainly repulsive. The same people usually have no hesitation in eating a similar animal where this element of empathy is lacking.
>
> But there is not only an inhibition against killing with regard to animals that are individually known, but also inasmuch as a sense of identity is felt with the animal as

another living being. There might be a conscious or unconscious feeling of guilt related to the destruction of life, especially when there is a certain empathy. This sense of closeness to the animal and need to reconcile oneself to killing it is quite dramatically manifested in the rituals of the bear cult of Paleolithic hunters [who performed rituals to show respect and appreciation to the animals they killed, and atone for the guilt that could arise from killing].

The sense of identity with all living beings that share with man the quality of *life* has been made explicit as an important moral tenet in Indian thinking and has led to the prohibition against killing any animal in Hinduism . . . Whenever another being is not experienced as human, the act of destructiveness and cruelty assumes a different quality. A simple example will show this. If a Hindu or a Buddhist, for instance, provided he has a genuine and deep feeling of empathy with all living beings, were to see the average modern person kill a fly without the slightest hesitation, he might judge this act as an expression of considerable callousness and destructiveness; but he would be wrong in this judgment. The point is that for many people the fly is simply not experienced as a sentient being and hence is treated as any disturbing "thing" would be: it is not that such people are especially cruel, even though their experience of "living beings" is restricted.[49]

Although human beings are the most unusual creatures on the planet, indigenous people have known for a long time that we share many similarities with other forms of life. Recently, science has confirmed the knowledge of indigenous people by revealing that human beings and other animals share most of the same DNA. How should we treat these animals and other forms of life? How far should we extend our circle of empathy to the creatures around us? I cannot answer this question for you. To answer this question, you must consult the mindset of unconditional love that shines within you.

And to hear the wisdom of the mindset of unconditional love, you must strengthen your muscle of empathy.

Most of the people who worked to abolish slavery in the nineteenth century were committed Christians. They believed it was their Christian duty to end all slavery, yet there is not a single sentence in the Bible saying the entire institution of slavery is wrong. If the Bible does not contain a single sentence denouncing all slavery, why did they feel it was their Christian duty to go against the norm and put themselves at risk by opposing slavery? They listened to the mindset of unconditional love that shines within them—the mindset symbolized by the life of Jesus.

What science is just now revealing about the enormous power of empathy, great spiritual teachers knew long ago. St. Francis of Assisi, who lived centuries before the neuroscientists of the twenty-first century, understood the power of empathy when he had compassion for many forms of life, not just human life. Describing the empathy of Siddhartha Gautama, who became known as the Buddha, Gandhi wrote, "Look at Gautama's compassion! It was not confined to mankind, it was extended to all living beings."[50]

Philosopher, Christian theologian, and Nobel Peace Prize Laureate Albert Schweitzer used the phrase "Reverence for Life" to describe a strong muscle of empathy. In the following excerpt from his autobiography, he also reveals that apathy for life's well-being, which I call brutality, is a kind of *thoughtlessness*:

> The ethic of Reverence for Life is the ethic of love widened into universality. It is the ethic of Jesus, now recognized as a logical consequence of thought . . . Standing, as all living beings are, before this dilemma of the will to live, man is constantly forced to preserve his own life and life in general only at the cost of other life. If he has been touched by the ethic of Reverence for Life, he injures and destroys life only under a necessity he cannot avoid, and never from thoughtlessness . . .
>
> With its active ethic of love, and through its spirituality, the concept of the world that is based on respect for

life is in essence related to Christianity and to all religions that profess the ethic of love . . . If people can be found who revolt against the spirit of thoughtlessness and are sincere and profound enough to spread the ideals of ethical progress, we will witness the emergence of a new spiritual force strong enough to evoke a new spirit in mankind. Because I have confidence in the power of truth and of the spirit, I believe in the future of mankind.[51]

## Painting with Knives

Trauma is the soul's way of screaming. But what happens when people cannot hear you scream? The need to communicate is part of the human condition. All people share this need regardless of their skin color, political views, or religious beliefs, because the urge to express our emotions is a feature on the landscape of our shared humanity. If something wonderful happens in your life, you probably want to share the good news with a friend. If you have a bad day at work or a family member dies, it helps to have someone willing to listen to you.

In the ancient Greek epic the *Iliad*, written by Homer nearly three thousand years ago, our human urge to express our emotions is represented by Achilles, the most ferocious, skilled, and powerful warrior in the world. In the *Iliad*, Achilles became enraged at his commander King Agamemnon during the Trojan War. Achilles's mother, the sea goddess Thetis, heard her son's pain, consoled him near the battlefield, and reminded him that it is important to express how we feel:

> But Achilles wept, and slipping away from his companions, far apart, sat down on the beach of the heaving gray sea and scanned the endless ocean . . . So he wept and prayed and his noble mother heard him, seated near her father, the Old Man of the Sea in the salt green depths. Suddenly up she rose from the churning surf like mist and

> settling down beside him as he wept, stroked Achilles gen-
> tly, whispering his name, "My child—why in tears? What
> sorrow has touched your heart? Tell me, please. Don't har-
> bor it deep inside you. We must share it all."[52]

Because human beings share the need to communicate, we like to be listened to. Every culture views listening as respectful and not listening as disrespectful. In all of human history, I don't think anyone has ever seriously said, "I hate it when people listen to me!" I don't think anyone has ever complained, "My spouse and I need to go to marriage counseling, because my spouse listens to me all the time and I can't stand it anymore!"

When most people in our society are not taught the art of listening, it can seem rare to find someone who truly listens with empathy and depth. One of the most fulfilling forms of expression human beings can experience is a meaningful conversation with a friend, which can benefit both our psychological and physical well-being. Numerous scientific studies have shown that if we bottle up our agony, rather than express our pain in healthy ways, this repression can cause psychological problems and harm our physical health. When our early ancestors lived on the harsh African savannah, the human need to communicate aided their survival by increasing their capacity for cooperation, understanding, and solidarity. Communication also gives us a way to solve conflicts without resorting to violence.

Communication functions like an interstate highway by allowing thoughts and emotions to travel from one person to another. But just as a fully grown elephant cannot fit inside a car, massive trauma is too big to completely fit inside the confined vehicle of language. Extreme trauma is a creature so large that it cannot be entirely caged by words.

When I describe my trauma with metaphors and personal reflections, it is like showing you pictures of a monster. Although these pictures can be disturbing, they do not capture the full horror of *living* with the monster of trauma. In a similar way, a person reading the *Iliad* or watching an excellent war film such as *The Thin Red Line* can gain more empathy for soldiers and a better understanding of war trauma, but reading an epic as powerful as the *Iliad* or watching a brilliant war film can never truly convey the full horror of war.

In addition to the vehicle of language, vehicles of expression such as music, dance, painting, and rituals also give us ways to express our emotions. Some people even express their emotions through the way they dress. However, massive trauma is so big that it cannot completely fit inside any of these vehicles either. Composer Ludwig van Beethoven and countless others have used art as a way of exploring and expressing their trauma, and it is no coincidence that many great artists are also tortured souls. Musician and journalist Robert Kahn describes Beethoven's life:

> Beethoven had every reason to be depressed. It was a natural result of his life. As a child, Beethoven suffered years of randomly inflicted violence from an alcoholic father who drank himself into poverty and death . . . After Beethoven's mother died, his father slid deeper into alcoholism. Ludwig became de facto head of his family at age sixteen. Two years later, he had to intercede with the Bonn police to keep his drunken father out of jail . . . The tremendous effort it must have taken to recover from the suffering he endured almost certainly contributed to the depth of feeling of Beethoven's greatest music. But the suffering also cost him tremendously.[53]

Although neuroscience reveals that empathy allows us to feel the joy and pain of others, listening to Beethoven's music or reading about his life cannot fully communicate his lifetime of agony. However, there is a vehicle of expression more effective than language, music, dance, painting, or ritual for communicating what trauma truly feels like. This vehicle of expression can literally make other people feel our pain. What method of expression is the most effective way to communicate the experience of trauma? The answer is the *vehicle of violence*.

By doing to people what my father did to me, I could help them better understand my pain. If I used the vehicle of violence to inflict extreme trauma on people, I would no longer be showing them pictures of the monster of trauma. I would be showing them the real thing. The vehicle of violence is the only method of expression that allows people to see, hear, and feel the monster of trauma in all of its horrifying detail.

In the poem "Boy Breaking Glass" by Gwendolyn Brooks, a boy who commits acts of destruction says, "I shall create! If not a note, a hole. If not an overture, a desecration."[54] When people cannot communicate their suffering in productive ways, they will often choose destructive methods. Before I discovered the power of creative writing, I longed to become an artist of destruction. I wanted to paint with knives.

When we paint with knives, we use a weapon for a brush, and our canvas becomes living flesh. When I sank into the abyss of agony as a traumatized child, I wanted to paint the world with my pain. I wanted to use a knife to write my rage. Instead of writing for peace, what if I had focused all of my energy on dialoguing through destruction? In the dialogue of destruction one side speaks with violence, and the other side replies with screams and suffering.

My journey from trauma to peace has been a long and difficult struggle, and I could not have come so far without the help of angels. When I use the word "angels," I am not referring to winged creatures from the Bible, but everyday human beings, the unsung heroes of peace and justice, who do life-changing work yet often remain unrecognized and unseen. Before I can discuss the unsung heroes of peace and justice—the angels of empathy who walk among us—I must first debunk a widely believed myth about cruelty.

Many people in our society believe the myth that cruelty is a natural human urge. In reality, most cruel acts are distortions of *other* human urges, like a ray of light that becomes distorted as it passes through a warped piece of glass. For example, in *The Art of Waging Peace* I describe how the cruel behavior of berserker rage results from a *distortion of the urge to feel safe.* As I just explained in this chapter, many of the cruel impulses I felt growing up resulted from a *distortion of the urge to communicate.*

Since the causes of our violent impulses are hidden deep in our unconscious mind, like secrets buried deep underground, I spent most of my childhood not knowing why I fantasized about maiming and killing people. Years of introspection, meditation, and contemplation have allowed me to study, understand, and give a conscious voice to the unconscious causes of violence within me. I once wrote a statement to myself that described how my unconscious urge to communicate fueled my desire to assault people who had hurt me:

*You hurt me. Now I will hurt you, because I am a*
*sharing person who wants you to feel what I feel, too.*

Trauma is a lonely experience. Inflicting violence on others is a way to bridge the gap of isolation by allowing others to feel our pain. Like many children, I was never taught how to express my agony in healthy and productive ways. The method of expression my father taught me was violence. Descending deeper into trauma and social isolation as a teenager, my mind sought refuge in violent daydreams. I was often consumed by vivid fantasies where I imagined myself massacring people in a rampage.

During my sophomore year at West Point, several of my friends and I were doing manual labor as punishment for various offenses (I had missed a class). While we were on a break, one of my friends said, "This is really boring."

I replied, "Do you remember being in high school, being bored, and fantasizing about killing all of the kids in your class?"

My friends had shocked looks on their faces. One of them said, "I don't remember ever fantasizing about that in high school." Everyone else agreed.

Surprised by their reaction, I said, "Are you joking?" I thought everyone fantasized about killing the people around them, so I added, "Then what did you think about when you were bored in class?"

One of my friends responded, "Well, I didn't fantasize about murdering people! Hey man, you are starting to worry me. That isn't normal. How often would you think about killing everyone in your class?"

"I fantasized about it every day," I said, still thinking they were joking with me and not telling me the truth. I had a difficult time believing that everyone did not have those violent fantasies.

Another one of my friends asked, "So do you think about killing us?"

I replied, "Honestly, I can't say that I ever have. I guess I have changed since high school."

Several years later I spoke with one of my few friends from high school. I told him the story and said, "I still think they weren't telling me the truth. Doesn't everyone fantasize about killing the people around them?" He said with shock in his voice, "I honestly never thought about that in high school." Then he asked with hesitation, "In your fantasies would you kill me too?" I said, "Yes, but it was nothing personal. I wanted to kill everyone around me back then. I just didn't feel safe around human beings. It's a difficult experience to explain."

Empathy allows us to understand the deep pain beneath people's violent behavior. Only by confronting the root causes of this pain, rather than its surface symptoms, can we truly heal the virus of violence in our society. Boxer Mike Tyson had a very traumatic upbringing, which I discuss in *Peaceful Revolution* and *The Art of Waging Peace*. In an interview with several reporters, he said: "I wish one of your guys had children so I could kick them in their fucking head or stomp on their testicles so you could feel my pain, because that's the pain I have waking up every day."[55]

To help us better understand the various causes of cruelty and violence, forensic psychologist Katherine Ramsland describes how trauma can compel people to commit mass murder: "The psychology of a mass murderer is somebody who wants to at one big event to take out as many people as they can, has to do with a measure of their own pain, and they want as many people to pay for it as possible. Everyone now knows: I was in pain and you did nothing."[56]

My lifelong exploration of violence and human nature not only convinced me that human beings are not naturally violent, but it also left me with a puzzling question that I have spent many years studying. Why are people not *more* violent? Many people with traumatic upbringings do not become cruel. Many people who are severely abused as children do not repeat the pattern by inflicting their trauma on others. I know people who cry when they are in pain, which is a healthy and effective way to communicate their suffering. I am unable to cry when I am in pain, because I have been conditioned to respond with rage.

Although children can break things or slap someone when they are upset, this is mostly due to their lack of communication skills and inexperience at coping with difficult emotions such as frustration. When adults are upset they can also break things and hurt people, but their anger usually falls far short of the rage I have experienced. The tragic event most likely to make a psychologically healthy adult snap and erupt in homicidal violence is *betrayal*—the rupturing of trust—yet the majority of psychologically healthy adults who are betrayed don't go on murderous rampages.

In an interview in *Guernica* magazine, Katherine Rowland asked me: "I totally agree that [cruelty is] distorted. But how can we say that people who experienced horrible instances of violence default to a state of perpetuating that violence, and yet at the same time assert, as you do, that violence is not a natural human impulse?"

I replied:

> I think we have to see trauma as a wound, it's a psychological wound similar to a physical wound, it's a wounding of the mind. It can repair itself if the person does the right things, but like any other wound, it can become worse. The default setting of a physical wound is to heal. But if the physical wound is bad enough [such as a severe gunshot wound in the stomach], the default state is to get worse. If the psychological wound is extremely severe—just like if a physical wound is extremely severe—self-repair becomes far more difficult and without extraordinary methods to heal yourself the wound will likely get worse. Trauma is a very deep, severe form of psychological wound, which can exceed the mind's ability to naturally repair. And just as a severe physical wound that exceeds the body's ability to self-repair can lead into a downward spiral of infection and death, an unhealed psychological wound can lead into a downward spiral of rage and madness.[57]

One of the most dangerous causes of cruelty, which I am very fortunate not to experience, is the *distorted urge for sexual intimacy*. During puberty our brain is going through critical changes. Puberty is a fragile time for the development of the human brain, and sometimes things can go wrong during this delicate process (or earlier in life) and a person can begin to associate sexual intimacy with inflicting pain. Extensive scientific research shows that many strong emotions, not just love, can be channeled into our sexual impulse. Psychologist Erich Fromm explains:

> Sexual desire aims at fusion—and is by no means only a physical appetite, the relief of a painful tension. But sexual desire can be stimulated by the anxiety of aloneness, by the wish to conquer or be conquered, by vanity, by the wish to hurt and even to destroy, as much as it can be stimulated by love. It seems that sexual desire can easily blend with and be stimulated by any strong emotion, of which love is only one.[58]

Human beings are the only species on the planet that can use sex to harm and humiliate. We are the only species capable of using sex as a weapon. People have sex not only to reproduce or express love, but also to seek revenge and provoke envy. No other animal commits rape with the sole intention of inflicting harm, humiliation, and trauma.

Serial killers take this distortion of sex to its utmost extreme by harming, humiliating, and murdering their victims. Although the vast majority of people who associate sexual intimacy with inflicting pain are not serial killers,* many serial killers derive sexual pleasure from murdering women. Someone once told me, "Serial killers are just acting out humanity's naturally violent instinct to kill."

I replied, "But why would serial killers rape and then murder women? This completely contradicts the human impulse to reproduce, and if every man had an urge to rape and murder dozens of women, our species would quickly go extinct. Some serial killers even have sex with rotting corpses and

---

* "Sadomasochism" or "S&M" are terms commonly used to describe *consensual* sexual pleasure derived from inflicting and receiving pain. When not consensual, most people would consider this torture.

keep body parts as souvenirs. No other species on the planet does that. How can having sex with a corpse that has been rotting for days be human nature, especially if seeing this act up close would make many people vomit? Isn't it obvious that serial killers are an example of psychological illness—of something that has gone wrong—rather than human nature?"

Having sex with a corpse is an obvious distortion of the urge for sexual intimacy. In his book *Female Serial Killers*, Peter Vronsky says this distortion is not unusual among male sexual murderers: "In an FBI study of male sexual killers, rape had occurred in 42 percent *after* the death of the victim and in 56 percent before [and] in the other 2 percent there was no rape despite the sexual nature of the murder."[59]

Vronsky also reveals that male serial killers are often driven by sexual lust, while female serial killers are driven less by lust and more by other urges, including the desire to express themselves. Vronsky explains:

> Serial killing, whether perpetrated by male or female, has always stood in its own special corner of criminal depravity. Most of us can understand killing once—we can imagine a degree of jealousy, fear, desperation, rage, or even greed that could lead to taking a life. Most murderers do not know they are about to kill—it is not planned or intended. Many sincerely and deeply regret their act, make no attempt to evade justice, and rarely kill again. Serial killers, however, are opposite in every way from the common kind of murderer . . .
>
> There are some notable differences [between male and female serial killers]. Male serial killers frequently commit kidnapping, confinement, rape, and mutilation to express their rage and desire for control; female serial killers usually throw themselves straight into the kill—no stopping for mutilation or for a bite along the way. No polaroids or masturbation at the scene or sex with the corpse. The female serial killer is all business . . . and it's murder. In that sense she is infinitely deadlier than the fantasy-driven male predators.

Male serial killers can sometimes actually overlook killing some of their victims, because murder is not always a central part of their fantasy. Their fantasy could be to dominate their victim through physical and sexual assault without murder necessarily being a part of it. Once their assault is exhausted for the time being, the victim is of no further interest to the offender—dead or alive. If the victim survived the physical assault, the offender might kill to avoid having a witness to the assault or rape. The offender may kill the victim out of shame. Or not kill at all. A few might even trip-out on the power of granting mercy . . .

Female serial killers rarely, unless accompanied by a male partner, kidnap and rape their victims. Female serial killers rarely if ever kill to harvest the corpse or some body part of their victim for their own hedonistic lust. They almost never capture, bind, confine, and torture their victims before killing them. The female serial killer's gratification *begins* with the victim's death and often continues for days, weeks, and months afterwards. While for many serial killers death is only a conclusion to their fantasy or a function of it, females kill to kill. *It is their mode of expression* [emphasis added].

One frequent reason given by male serial killers as to why they did not kill a particular victim is because they learned something about them. This triggers a personalization of the victim in the offender's perception and misdirects their killing desire. This phenomenon reflects the proclivity of male serial killers to target strangers whom they objectify, imposing their own lethal fantasy upon them. Yet if they come to somehow see the victim for who they really are, the fantasy can be interrupted.

According to FBI behaviorists, the best way of surviving a serial killer's attack is to attempt to talk to them and let them get to know you as a person, to deflate the serial killer's fantasy construct of you as their victim. None of this is going to help the victim of a typical female serial killer . . . There are almost no accounts from survivors of female serial killers. Women killers do not change their minds once they make the decision to murder and they rarely go through any kind of fantasy torture ritual on the way there—they go straight for the kill . . .

We know that an overwhelming majority of serial killers experienced traumatic childhoods usually in the form of physical and sexual abuse. This applies to males as equally as females (with the exception of female partners of males). This observation is not intended to defend the serial killer—lots of children are abused and do not become serial killers. The point is that abused children can develop psychological states that facilitate the emergence of a serial killer—psychopathy . . . Brain injuries can cause violent behavioral patterns and many serial killers have a history of head injuries when they were children or recent injuries prior to the onset of killing. But again, this is not the *cause* alone of their murderous behavior—already other behavioral problems are frequently present. Most people who sustain head injuries do not become killers.[60]

The distortion of a human urge can make us cruel, but when people reach the most extreme end of cruelty by becoming serial killers, other factors have also caused something to go wrong in their brain. These other factors might include head injury, a biochemical imbalance, neglect during early childhood, extreme physical and sexual abuse, or other problems. Peter Vronsky says, "Social isolation—loneliness—might be arguably the *most* common characteristic of the childhood of serial killers."[61]

As I mentioned earlier in this book, when someone gets malaria, cancer, or HIV, I have never heard anyone say, "Oh, that's just human nature." We know these illnesses are not a necessary part of being human, but result from something that has gone wrong within the human body. However, if someone becomes violent, I often hear people say, "Oh, that's just human nature," even though violence, like an illness, results from something that has gone wrong. In all of my books I show that violence has causes we can understand and prevent—similar to an illness. According to Gary Slutkin, the medical doctor I quoted earlier: "Violence is like the great infectious diseases of all history . . . What perpetuates violence can be as invisible today as the microorganisms of the past were."[62]

Cruelty is a distortion of various human urges. It is a psychological sickness—a malfunctioning of the human mind. Many acts of cruelty are *corrupted communication*, but how do I know that cruelty is corrupted rather than natural communication? How do I know that human beings are not supposed to communicate through cruel acts?

The evidence that human beings react badly to cruelty is overwhelming. If we were supposed to communicate with cruelty, why would messages delivered in the form of extremely cruel acts produce so much trauma? If we were supposed to communicate with cruelty, why would people react so much better to *compassionate communication*?

Describing some of the cruel treatment he received as a prisoner in a Nazi concentration camp, Victor Frankl discussed how cruelty produces a naturally bad reaction in human beings:

> Beatings occurred on the slightest provocation, some-times for no reason at all. For example, bread was rationed out at our work site and we had to line up for it. Once, the man behind me stood off a little to one side and that lack of symmetry displeased the SS guard. I did not know what was going on in the line behind me, nor in the mind of the SS guard, but suddenly I received two sharp blows on my head. Only then did I spot the guard at my side who was using his stick. *At such a moment it is not the physical pain which hurts the most (and this applies to adults as much as to punished children); it is the mental agony caused by the injustice, the unreasonableness of it all* [emphasis added].[63]

In Mary Shelley's novel *Frankenstein*, the monster created by scientist Victor Frankenstein tells his creator, "I was benevolent and good; misery made me a fiend."[64] When I met playwright Ricardo Pitts-Wiley at a nonviolence workshop and asked him why he wrote a play about *Frankenstein*, he said, "I have always been interested in the art of monster making. What I mean by the art of monster making is the way societies transform human beings into monsters through trauma, abuse, alienation, despair, and other monster-making methods. In Mary Shelley's novel, the monster is not born bad. He just wants to be loved by the scientist who created him, who he sees as his father. But he is rejected by his father, and becomes alienated, confused, and alone. He is not born a monster. He becomes a monster."[65]

Buddha, Jesus, and other great spiritual teachers taught us the power of universal empathy. Jesus even said, "Love your enemies."[66] If we truly want to reduce violence in our society, we must understand the *root causes of violence.** We must understand the art of monster making. Our society does more to address the symptoms of violence rather than reduce the root causes. Since empathy gives us the deepest insight into other human beings, it is vital for reducing the root causes of violence and practicing the art of *unmaking* monsters.

## *Angels of Empathy*

A small percentage of violent people, such as serial killers, may never be able to function in a healthy and loving way, but most of us can *choose* compassion over cruelty. I became a peace activist instead of a murderer because I chose to pursue peace instead of violence. We have the power to choose, but our choices depend on our options. When I was fifteen years old, a high school English teacher gave me an option that saved my life.

---

* In *The End of War* I discuss the causes of wars between countries. In this chapter I discuss some common causes of interpersonal cruelty, and there are additional causes not discussed in this section. As I explain in *Peaceful Revolution*, when people's muscle of empathy and muscle of conscience are underdeveloped, this can also lead to cruel or brutal behavior. A person can suffer from several causes of cruelty at the same time.

When I was fifteen I wrote a short story for an English assignment. A few days later my teacher Janice Vaughn said, "I really liked your story. You should think about being a writer." Sometimes a few simple words can radically change our lives. I had never thought about being a writer before, because I had never liked reading books. But I pondered what she said and realized I had enjoyed writing that story. So I wrote another, and another, and another. I began writing obsessively, and at West Point I spent more time writing than doing my homework.

After writing fiction for about six years, I developed a preference for writing nonfiction when I was twenty-one, but the seed that sprouted into my love of nonfiction was planted much earlier. When I was sixteen, a year after being in Mrs. Vaughn's class, my English teacher Jean Arndt said, "Mrs. Vaughn told me you are a great writer." During the school year Mrs. Arndt also encouraged me to be a writer, saying, "You write excellent essays. Have you thought about writing nonfiction?"

Even today, I am still amazed that a little encouragement can dramatically alter the course of someone's life. Because Mrs. Vaughn and Mrs. Arndt planted those seeds of encouragement in me, I became more interested in writing with words than painting with knives.

When I was twenty-five I tried to publish a nonfiction book I had written about philosophy and peace called *Nature's Intent*. After sending book proposals to dozens of publishing companies, a publishing vice president named Jo Ann Deck called me to discuss her interest in publishing my book. I had never been published before, and by that point I had received hundreds of rejection letters for my previous books and stories, so getting a call from her was a joyous surprise.

During our first phone conversation, she explained why she was interested in my ideas, and how her father-in-law being a World War II veteran had further increased her interest in peace. At that time I never imagined that she would become the first real mentor I ever had, and an important counterbalancer to my childhood trauma (I discussed the topic of counterbalancers in the first chapter).

After Jo Ann's publishing company rejected *Nature's Intent* despite her wish that it be published, she worked with me to improve my skills as a writer. She even paid out of her own pocket for an editor who gave me additional help. She also convinced me to integrate personal stories into my nonfiction writing, which I had never done, because I don't like my personal information being available for public consumption. In fact, I had always wanted to use a pen name for my books, but Jo Ann persuaded me to use my real name.

Because she explained how my personal stories could help people in a variety of ways, I began experimenting with a more personal style of writing. Although I still prefer to keep my life private, I have taken the uncomfortable step of exposing my psychological wounds to the world, since these personal stories can serve the mission of peace by illustrating my ideas and helping readers more easily relate to the content.

I have benefitted greatly from reading people's autobiographies, but I remain a private person who prefers not to broadcast my personal issues to the world. One reason I am like this is because when I was in my early twenties, I realized people could not truly understand my trauma. If I wrote with the desire that people would understand me, I felt like it would be a dead-end path filled with frustration and disappointment. Instead of writing so people would understand me, I decided to write so I could better understand other people. Writing helped me explore the human condition, come to terms with my life experiences, know myself more deeply, and understand our shared humanity.

Like an explorer searching for hidden treasures, writing allowed me to journey into the darkest caverns of my mind and study the deepest mysteries of the universe. In this darkness and mystery I found light. Writing also became a weapon that empowered me to fight problems such as war, injustice, and trauma. I am thirty-three years old as I write this, and for the past eight years Jo Ann has been a vital ally, mentor, and guide who has made my peace work possible.

When I dedicated *The Art of Waging Peace* to Jo Ann, I called her a "goddess of compassion" and "strategic mastermind." I regret that I cannot spend the next hundred pages writing about all of the incredible ways she has helped me. Just as the Greek goddess Athena, who was called the "Hope of Soldiers,"[67] helped the warrior Odysseus on his journey in the Greek epic the *Odyssey*, Jo Ann has been a metaphorical goddess in my life.

I have met many unsung heroes of peace and justice such as Jo Ann, and I have been profoundly influenced by these angels of empathy who walk among us. Although these angels are human and not perfect, peace and progress could not exist without their compassion, dedication, and hard work. Historian Judith Wellman discusses the importance of the unsung heroes of peace and justice in the women's rights movement:

> The printed *Report* contained the names of the sixty-eight women who had signed the Declaration of [Rights and] Sentiments and the thirty-two men who had supported it. Forty years later, Frederick Douglass, himself one of the signers, would reflect on the composition of this group. "Then who were we," he asked, "for I count myself in, who did this thing? We were few in numbers, moderate in resources, and very little known in the world. The most that we had to commend us, was a firm conviction that we were in the right, and a firm faith that the right must ultimately prevail."
>
> Of these signers—only four—Douglass, Lucretia Mott, Martha Wright, and Stanton herself—would achieve national recognition. The others remained virtually unknown.[68]

Commenting on an anti-slavery convention, Frederick Douglass further discussed the importance of the unsung heroes of peace and justice in the movement to end slavery:

> We never feel more ashamed of our humble efforts in the cause of emancipation than when we contrast them with the silent, unobserved and unapplauded efforts of those women through whose constant and persevering endeavors this annual exhibition is given to the American public. Anti-slavery authors and orators may be said to

receive compensation for what they do, in the applause
which must, sooner or later, redound to them; but not so
with the thousands whose works of use and beauty adorn
this fair. It is for them to work, unnoticed and unknown,
and sometimes unenquired for, and many of them unable
to see the good that results from their efforts.[69]

Harriett Tubman was an unsung hero of peace and justice who remained
anonymous for many years, but became well-known after the American Civil
War ended. She had dedicated her life to the dangerous mission of rescuing
slaves and bringing them to safety on the "underground railroad." When she
asked Frederick Douglass to endorse a book being written about her life, he
replied:

> You ask for what you do not need when you call upon
> me for a word of commendation. I need such words from
> you far more than you can need them from me, especially
> where your superior labors and devotion to the cause of
> the lately enslaved of our land are known as I know them.
> The difference between us is very marked. Most that I
> have done and suffered in the service of our cause has been
> in public, and I have received much encouragement at
> every step of the way. You on the other hand have labored
> in a private way. I have wrought in the day—you in the
> night. I have had the applause of the crowd and the satis-
> faction that comes of being approved by the multitude,
> while the most that you have done has been witnessed by
> a few trembling, scarred, and foot-sore bondmen and
> women, whom you have led out of the house of bondage,
> and whose heartfelt "God bless you" has been your only
> reward. The midnight sky and the silent stars have been
> the witnesses of your devotion to freedom and of your
> heroism. Excepting John Brown—of sacred memory—I
> know of no one who has willingly encountered more perils

and hardships to serve our enslaved people than you have.[70]

The unsung heroes of peace and justice may not be widely known, but their good deeds are recorded as ripples in the cosmic ocean. These ripples can stir the stagnant waters of apathy, inspire other ripples of kindness to emerge, and reach across the planet and far into the future. Because Jo Ann had kind friends when she was in college, they created ripples that affected me, and I will create ripples that affect others.

I have never met Jo Ann's college friends. She lost touch with them over the years, yet they have impacted me by impacting her. Describing how they influenced her, Jo Ann told me, "They taught me that you can maintain your idealism in the world. You don't have to be like everybody else. This doesn't mean that you need to make anyone else feel bad because they are not like you, because you can be an example. You don't need to throw the fact that you maintain certain ideals in other people's faces, but when they ask you about it, you can explain without being condescending. People are doing the best they can with what they know, and we can inspire each other to stretch ourselves to do better."[71]

We can create ripples of peace and justice in the cosmic ocean, or ripples of cruelty. We can create ripples that help people strengthen their muscle of empathy and develop "Reverence for Life," or ripples that promote brutality. The full effects of these ripples will forever remain a mystery, because we cannot fathom the complete impact these ripples may have on those living in the world today, or on future generations. Even the smallest actions, such as a few encouraging words from Mrs. Vaughn and Mrs. Arndt, can create life-changing ripples. Even the smallest actions may eventually become a light to someone trapped in darkness.

CHAPTER 4

# Soldiers as Christ Figures

### *What* The Iliad *Teaches Us About War, West Point, and Being Human*

One of the most common questions people ask me is, "Why did you join the military?" Because people expect me to answer this question in less than thirty seconds, I usually give a short answer. However, the longer answer is far more surprising and useful, not because of what it reveals about me, but what it reveals about all human beings. By explaining in this chapter why I joined the military, you will learn something important about me, and you will learn something even more important about yourself.

Why people join the military is a fascinating question, because most human beings are terrified of combat. During my first semester at West Point, this fact of the human condition was explained to me when every male freshman had to take a mandatory boxing class. My boxing instructor said, "You have to take boxing for two reasons. The first reason is that you have to learn how to defend yourself. The second reason is that people are naturally afraid of fighting, and this class will help you overcome that fear."*

Mike Tyson, one of the greatest boxers who ever lived, said the following about himself and fellow boxing champion Evander Holyfield: "What myself and Evander did for a living is what people avoid their whole entire life. If somebody tells you they're not afraid when they go in the [boxing] ring, either they're lying or they're totally insane."[1]

---

* In societies throughout history, "proving one's manhood" has often been sought by overcoming a difficult challenge. These challenges can assume a variety of forms, depending on the culture. Since violence naturally frightens people and overcoming this fear can be such a significant challenge, being brave enough to face physical violence has been used as a way of proving one's manhood in many societies around the world. The bravery needed to face physical violence (nonviolently rather than violently) was even cited by Martin Luther King Jr. and other members of the civil rights movement as a characteristic worthy of admiration and emulation.

What do people find more frightening? Boxing or tennis? Boxing or golf? Boxing or baseball? Boxing or basketball? Certainly, people tend to be more afraid of boxing than these other sports. When we think about boxing rationally, however, we might wonder why it evokes fear. After all, boxing has many safety measures. People get hit with padded gloves, there are strict rules (head butts and groin strikes are illegal) along with a referee to protect both boxers, and amateur boxers even wear protective headgear.

Consider how afraid people are of boxing, even with these safety measures, and then compare boxing to fighting the Roman army. In boxing you cannot punch, kick, or knee your opponent in the groin, but the Roman Empire would train its soldiers to stab people in the crotch. Instead of facing a single person in a boxing match with a referee and strict rules to protect you, imagine being outnumbered in a battle by forty thousand well-trained Roman soldiers, who are going to do everything in their power to stab you in the crotch and kill you. Would that scare you?

The Roman historian Dionysius of Halicarnassus explains how the Romans fought the Gauls, who lived in a region that included modern-day France: "While their enemies were still raising their swords aloft, they would duck under the Gauls' arms, and holding up their shields while stooping and crouching down low, would render impotent the blows of the enemy which were aimed too high. The Romans, on the other hand, held their swords straight out and would strike their opponents in the groin, pierce their sides and drive their thrusts through their chests into their vitals. If the Romans saw any of them keeping these parts of their bodies protected, they would cut the tendons of the knees or ankles and topple them to the ground."[2]

I have heard many people compare American football to war, but football has extremely strict rules. In football you are not allowed to grab someone's helmet, let alone stab a human being to death. Unlike boxing and football, war has no referees who enforce rules. In war people maim and kill each other with every available means, because war is not a game. Military history is a long record of people doing what they must to survive and win in combat, regardless of the rules suggested by "just war theory," because losing in war is not like losing in a boxing match or football game. If you are a soldier who loses in war, you may not only lose your life, but also destroy the lives of your comrades and family.

In our society, the consequences of losing in war are mostly hidden from us. When I grew up watching action movies as a child, I saw the "hero" kill countless "bad guys," but I never saw the consequences. I never saw the families of the bad guys grieve for their deceased loved ones. I realize American media is focused largely on entertainment, but I have met so many people who base their understanding of war on the entertainment they see in movies. Lieutenant Colonel Dave Grossman says, "You think you know all about combat. You've seen all the TV shows. You've seen all the movies. Basing what you think you know about combat on what you've seen in Hollywood, is like basing what you think you know about elephants on Walt Disney's *Dumbo*, and you walk away convinced that elephants can fly."[3]

As a child I never saw an action movie where the hero kills his enemy and the enemy's parents are shown grieving over the death of their child. But this is shown in the *Iliad*, an epic poem about the Trojan War written nearly three thousand years ago by the Greek poet Homer.* The *Iliad* relates how an invading Greek army tried to conquer the city Troy. In a climactic scene toward the end of the *Iliad*, the Greek hero Achilles fights the Trojan warrior Hector in front of the gates of Troy. Homer then describes how Hector's father (Priam) and mother (Hecuba), the king and queen of Troy, react when they see Achilles kill Hector outside the city's walls, tie their son's corpse to a Greek chariot, and drag his lifeless body through the dirt.

To understand how remarkable the *Iliad* is, imagine if an American war movie showed an American soldier killing a German, Japanese, or Iraqi soldier, and then showed a detailed account of the dead soldier's parents grieving for their child. Even though Hector was an enemy of Greece, the Greek poet Homer described the consequences of his death.

Art is often paradoxical, because many artists use beautiful forms of expression to communicate painful experiences. Homer's art was also paradoxical, because he used beautiful poetry to express extreme human

* The authorship of the *Iliad* is still debated, and we may never know the identity of its author. I will refer to this mysterious author as Homer.

suffering. Robert Fagles translates Homer's depiction of Hector's death from ancient Greek to English:

> So he [Achilles] triumphed and now he was bent on outrage, on shaming [the corpse of] noble Hector. Piercing the tendons, ankle to heel behind both feet, he knotted straps of rawhide through them both, lashed them to his chariot, left the head to drag . . . And a thick cloud of dust rose up from the man they dragged, his dark hair swirling round that head so handsome once, all tumbled low in the dust . . .
>
> So his whole head was dragged down in the dust. And now his mother [Hecuba] began to tear her hair . . . she flung her shining veil to the ground and raised a high, shattering scream, looking down at her son. Pitifully his loving father [Priam] groaned and round the king his people cried with grief and wailing seized the city—for all the world as if all Troy were torched and smoldering down from the looming brows of the citadel to her roots. Priam's people could hardly hold the old man back, frantic, mad to go rushing out the Dardan Gates [to ask Achilles to return his son's body for a proper burial]. He begged them all, groveling in the filth, crying out to them, calling each man by name, "Let go, my friends! Much as you care for me, let me hurry out of the city, make my way . . . I must implore that terrible, violent man [Achilles] . . . Perhaps—who knows?—he may respect my age, may pity an old man. He has a father too, as old as I am . . . Stabbing grief for him [Hector] will take me down to Death . . ."
>
> So the voice of the king rang out in tears, the citizens wailed in answer, and noble Hecuba led the wives of Troy in a throbbing chant of sorrow: "O my child—my desolation! How can I go on living? What agonies must I suffer now, now *you* are dead and gone? You were my pride

throughout the city night and day—a blessing to us all, the men and women of Troy . . ."

Her voice rang out in tears, but [Andromache] the wife of Hector had not heard a thing. No messenger brought the truth of how her husband made his stand outside the gates. She was weaving at her loom, deep in the high halls, working flowered braiding into a dark red folding robe . . . But she heard the groans and wails of grief from the rampart now and her body shook, her shuttle dropped to the ground, she called out to her lovely waiting women, "Quickly—two of you follow me—I must see what's happened. That cry—that was Hector's honored mother I heard! My heart's pounding, leaping up in my throat, the knees beneath me paralyzed—Oh I know it . . . something terrible's coming down on Priam's children . . ."

So she cried, dashing out of the royal halls like a madwoman, her heart racing hard, her women close behind her. But once she reached the tower where soldiers massed she stopped on the rampart, looked down and saw it all— saw him dragged before the city, stallions galloping, dragging Hector back to Achaea's beaked warships—ruthless work. The world went black as night before her eyes, she fainted, falling backward, gasping away her life breath . . .

But crowding round her now her husband's sisters and brothers' wives supported her in their midst, and she, terrified, stunned to the point of death, struggling for breath now and coming back to life, burst out in grief among the Trojan women: "O Hector—I am destroyed! . . . Now you go down to the House of Death, the dark depths of the earth, and leave me here to waste away in grief, a widow lost in the royal halls—and the boy only a baby, the son we bore together, you and I so doomed. Hector, what help are you to him, now you are dead? . . . The day that orphans a youngster cuts him off from friends. And he hangs his head low, humiliated in every way . . . his cheeks stained with tears, and pressed by hunger the boy goes up to his father's old companions, tugging at one man's cloak, another's tunic, and some will pity him, true, and one will give him a little cup to drink, enough to wet his lips, not quench his thirst. But then some bully with both his parents living beats him from the banquet, fists and abuses flying: 'You, get out—you've got no father feasting with us here!' And the boy, sobbing, trails home to his widowed mother . . . And years ago, propped on his father's knee, he would only eat the marrow, the richest cuts of lamb, and when sleep came on him and he had quit his play, cradled warm in his nurse's arms he'd drowse off, snug in a soft bed, his heart brimmed with joy. Now what suffering, now he's lost his father."[4]

Remarkably, the *Iliad* not only shows how the parents of an enemy soldier are devastated by the death of their child, but also how the enemy's wife and child suffer tremendously. Throughout history, when armies conquered cities they often enslaved the women, and slaughtered or enslaved the children. A conflict occurs at the beginning of the *Iliad* when King Agamemnon, the commander of the Greek army, argues with Achilles over a slave. Agamemnon wants to claim one of Achilles's female slaves, a woman named Briseus who was taken into slavery during the war. Briseus's situation shows the reality of war and slavery.

Homer later humanizes the female slaves. Toward the end of the *Iliad*, he writes from the perspective of Hector's wife, Andromache, as she realizes Troy will be captured by the Greeks and she will become a slave. Andromache's agony shows the reality of war and slavery at a much deeper level.

Andromache realizes that because of her husband's death not only will she be enslaved, but her child will be murdered by the Greeks. From a practical perspective, the last thing the Greeks wanted was for Hector's infant son to grow up and become a fierce warrior, seeking revenge for his father's death. Because Hector was the best Trojan warrior and the "great guardian" of Troy, his wife Andromache knows that Troy will soon be conquered by the Greeks (whom Homer calls "Achaeans"). Then she will be raped, and her infant son killed. Speaking to her deceased husband and living son, she says:

> Because you are dead, her great guardian, you who always defended Troy, who kept her loyal wives and help-less children safe, all who will soon be carried off in the hollow ships and I with them—And you, my child, will follow me to labor, somewhere, at harsh, degrading work, slaving under some heartless master's eye—that, or some Achaean marauder will seize you by the arm and hurl you headlong down from the ramparts—horrible death —enraged at *you* because Hector once cut down his brother, his father or his son, yes, hundreds of armed Achaeans gnawed the dust of the world, crushed by Hector's hands![5]

Homer revealed the tragedy of war in many ways. Because he depicted powerful warriors panicking, having psychological breakdowns, and even crying, the Greek philosopher Plato wanted to censor the *Iliad*, because he thought it would give young men a negative impression of war. Poets such as Homer portrayed the psychological horror of war, while propagandists sanitize the image of war so that people will more willingly rush to battle. Like a propagandist, Plato wanted to sanitize the way people perceived war by concealing its ugliness. Describing how an ideal government must censor Homer's poetry, Plato said: "We'd be right, then, to delete the lamentations of famous men [in the *Iliad*], leaving them to women (and not even to good women, either) and to cowardly men, so that those we say we are training to guard our city will disdain to act like that."[6]

Because the soldiers who win a war so often suffer from trauma and watch their comrades die, war is the only competition in the world where the winning side can lose so much.* Homer reveals that the soldiers who succeed in war can lose their friends, humanity, and sanity.** In addition, war is the only competition where hundreds, thousands, and sometimes even millions of people on the winning side are killed in violent and agonizing ways. In the Bible Jesus says, "For all who draw the sword will die by the sword."[7] Like the Bible, the *Iliad* also expresses how war can cause destruction to both the winners and losers. Nearly a thousand years before Jesus lived, Homer said, "The god of war is impartial: he hands out death to the man who hands out death."[8]

Most parents are devastated when their children die. Although the *Iliad* was written nearly three thousand years ago, the suffering of Hector's parents is not too different from the way many American parents reacted when learning that their child died in the Vietnam War, Iraq War, or from a tragic incident not related to war. Furthermore, Hector's parents actually *watch* Achilles kill their son and mutilate his corpse. The *Iliad* captures the timelessness of the human condition, because a loving parent who witnesses such an atrocity, either today or three thousand years ago, would be horrified to the brink of madness. This is true of loving parents, no matter what country they are from, even if they are the parents of our enemies.

Through its intimate and gruesome depictions of war, the *Iliad* reveals that *every enemy soldier killed in war is someone's child.* According to the *Iliad*, this is not a political statement. It is simply the reality of war.

Unlike American action movies, in the *Iliad* the enemy soldiers killed in combat are not nameless abstractions, but human beings with names, parents, and families. The *Iliad* describes how Telamonian Ajax, the biggest and strongest Greek warrior, killed a Trojan soldier named Simoisius. Even though Simoisius was an enemy of Greece, he had parents who would be

---

\* This is demonstrated throughout military history and powerfully depicted at the end of the film *Seven Samurai.*

\*\* If the *Iliad* has some antiwar themes, how could Alexander the Great wage war after reading the *Iliad*? To look at this another way, how could the medieval European kings wage war after hearing the teachings of the New Testament? The antiwar messages in the New Testament (such as "love your enemies" and "turn the other cheek") are much more overt than the antiwar themes in the *Iliad*. These kinds of paradoxes can be caused by people deriving different meanings from the same source, not internalizing its message, or simply being hypocritical. Later in this chapter we will explore this further when discussing the paradox of Christianity.

devastated by his death: "Telamonian Ajax struck Anthemion's son, the hardy stripling Simoisius, still unwed . . . His mother had borne him along the Simois' [river] banks when she trailed her parents down the slopes of Ida to tend their flocks, and so they called him Simoisius. But never would he repay his loving parents now for the gift of rearing—his life cut short so soon, brought down by the spear of lionhearted Ajax."[9]

When soldiers on either side of the Trojan War die in the *Iliad*, their names are frequently mentioned, often with their father's name.* This reminds us that every dead soldier is someone's child, which sheds light on the consequences of war.** If we want to end war, we must resist the *sanitized depictions of war* that ignore the consequences of violence and portray war as a simplistic battle of good versus evil. When war is sanitized, the blindness of brutality is inevitable. In the twenty-first century, the *Iliad* can help us combat brutality by uncovering the reality of war. Uncovering this reality is a necessary step on the path to ending war.

Discussing how the *Iliad* does not sanitize war but instead shows the degrading reality of violence, classics scholar Bernard Knox tells us: "[In the *Iliad*] there is no attempt to gloss over the harsh realities of the work of killing . . . and no attempt, either, to sentimentalize the pain and degradation of violent death . . . Men die in the *Iliad* in agony; they drop, screaming, to their knees, reaching out to beloved companions, gasping their life out, clawing the ground with their hands; they die roaring, like Asius, raging, like the great Sarpedon, bellowing, like Hippodamas, moaning, like Polydorus. And death is the end: Homer offers no comforting vision of life beyond the grave."[10]

Instead of sanitizing war, Homer describes the agony of the Trojan soldier Harpalion, who bled to death when his bladder was ruptured by an arrow:

* There was also an ancient custom where men identified themselves with their father's name, but Homer could have chosen not to mention the names of the dead Trojan soldiers at all. It is also possible that Homer's poem resonated with people who believed they were descended from Trojan warriors.

** Even if someone's parents are deceased, that person can still be seen as a child at heart, and the *Iliad* skillfully portrays fierce warriors such as Hector and Achilles as children, such as when Achilles needs the comfort and compassion of his mother. The *Iliad* shows that almost every soldier who dies in war has at least one family member, friend, or comrade who will be devastated by that soldier's death.

"But Meriones caught him in full retreat, he let fly with a bronze-tipped arrow, hitting his right buttock up under the pelvic bone so the lance pierced the bladder. He sank on the spot, hunched in his dear companion's arms, gasping out his life as he writhed along the ground like an earthworm stretched out in death, blood pooling, soaking the earth dark red . . . [His comrades lifted his corpse] onto a chariot, bore him back to the sacred walls of Troy . . . deep in grief while his father, weeping freely, walked beside them now. No blood-price came his way. Not for his son who breathed his last in battle."[11]

In the *Iliad*, the Greek hero Odysseus, the main character in Homer's other epic poem the *Odyssey*, kills a Trojan soldier named Chersidamas by stabbing him in the crotch with a spear. Further depicting the horror of war, Homer tells us, "Odysseus caught him up under the bulging shield with a jabbing spear that split him crotch to navel—the man writhed in the dust, hands clutching the earth."[12]

According to the *Iliad*, the worst wound a human being could receive in battle was getting stabbed between the genitals and belly button. Describing the death of a Trojan soldier named Adamas, Homer says: "[During the battle] Adamas, Asius' son missed nothing, he saw it all . . . Meriones speared him between the genitals and the navel—hideous wound, the worst the god of battles deals to wretched men. There the spear stuck. Hugging the shaft he writhed, gasping, shuddering like some wild bull in the hills that herdsmen shackle."[13]

These excerpts from the *Iliad* are important, because they make us question the myth that human beings are naturally violent. Nearly every human being would be filled with terror and panic if an attacker pulled out a large knife and tried to stab that person in the crotch. When mass shootings happen, by far the most common human reaction is panic. But if human beings were naturally violent, why would violence, when it is up close and personal, be so terrifying to us?

A phobia is an irrational fear, but what is the most common phobia? Although human beings can have a phobia of snakes, spiders, or heights, around 98 percent of people have a phobia of human aggression. Lieutenant Colonel Dave Grossman calls this the *universal human phobia*. In fact, this is one reason fear of public speaking is so common: we might say something that triggers an audience's aggression. What if the worst-case scenario happens and the audience shouts at us angrily or laughs cruelly at our expense? Much of our fear of public speaking results from our fear of being judged or ridiculed in an aggressive and hurtful way.

Frederick Douglass, one of the greatest public speakers in American history, experienced the universal human phobia when he spoke in public for the first time. Douglass tells us, "It was with the utmost difficulty that I could stand erect, or that I could command and articulate two words without hesitation and stammering. I trembled in every limb. I am not sure that my embarrassment was not the most effective part of my speech, if speech it could be called. At any rate, this is about the only part of my performance that I now distinctly remember."[14]

Mark Twain, the famous American writer, also experienced the universal human phobia during his first public lecture: "I was in the middle of the stage, bewildered by the fierce glare of the lights, and quaking in every limb with a terror that seemed like to take my life away. The house was full, aisles and all. The tumult in my heart and brain and legs continued a full minute before I could gain any command over myself. Then, little by little, my fright melted away, and I began to talk."[15]

Consider how much an irrational fear such as public speaking frightened Frederick Douglass and Mark Twain, and how it continues to scare so many people today.* Also consider what my West Point boxing instructor and Mike Tyson said about people being naturally afraid of boxing. When we realize that most people are afraid of public speaking and boxing (because of the universal human phobia), it becomes obvious that human beings would be far more terrified of attackers trying to stab or shoot them to death. In action movies the heroes are almost never afraid, which can distort our understanding of how terrifying violence truly is.

One cause of the universal human phobia is our susceptibility to psychological trauma. As I explained in chapter 1, the most traumatizing event

---

* Aggression can take the form of physical attack, verbal abuse, or someone trying to humiliate us. The fear of public speaking is simply the fear of *possible* aggression, rather than a response to *actual* aggression. Compared to actual aggression, public speaking really isn't that terrifying, and one thing I teach during my Peace Leadership course is how to overcome the fear of public speaking.

we can experience is harm inflicted by our fellow human beings. Because the trauma inflicted by a human being can be so difficult to overcome, we have an unconscious fear of people hurting us. What is more psychologically traumatizing, falling off your bike and breaking your leg, or a group of attackers holding you down and breaking your leg with a baseball bat? Even though the physical outcome—a broken leg—is the same in both scenarios, an injury caused by a hateful human being is more traumatizing than the same injury resulting from an accident.

Fear of human aggression can be even more terrifying than fear of death. For example, every year in America hundreds of thousands die from the effects of smoking, but every day millions of people smoke without worrying. Every year in America tens of thousands die in car accidents, but every day millions of people drive casually to work. However, a few murders by a serial killer can cause a city to go on alert, striking terror in many of its citizens. The September 11 attacks, even though they killed far fewer people than car accidents and smoking related deaths annually, created so much fear that our country has never been the same since.

In an article in the *Atlantic* titled "Americans Are as Likely to Be Killed by Their Own Furniture as by Terrorism," Micah Zenko wrote: "Of the 13,288 people killed by terrorist attacks [around the world] last year [2011], seventeen were private U.S. citizens, or .001 percent . . . The number of U.S. citizens who died in terrorist attacks increased by two between 2010 and 2011; overall, a comparable number of Americans are crushed to death by their televisions or furniture each year. This is not to diminish the real—albeit shrinking—threat of terrorism, or to minimize the loss and suffering of the 13,000 killed and over 45,000 injured around the world. For Americans, however, it should emphasize that an irrational fear of terrorism is both unwarranted and a poor basis for public policy decisions."[16]

The death of every person killed by terrorism is tragic, yet if fifteen thousand Americans were killed by terrorism every year (a thousand times the fifteen Americans killed in 2010), this would still be less than half the number of Americans killed in car accidents annually (usually between thirty and forty thousand). If Americans during the ten years after the September 11 attacks were about as likely to be killed by their furniture as by a terrorist, why did Americans spend so much time worrying about being killed by a terrorist rather than their furniture?

The answer to this question can be found in the universal human phobia, and the way governments manipulate this phobia to serve their own interests. Fear mongering can occur over a variety of issues, but the most effective fear mongering occurs when people in authority positions make us afraid of our fellow human beings.

When I give lectures around the country, people often say, "The reason we are more afraid of terrorism than furniture or car accidents, even though car accidents kill so many more Americans every year, is because when we are driving we have control. Our fear of terrorism has nothing to do with the fact that people are harming us. It has to do with lack of control."

I usually say, "That is a good point, but if we look deeper we can see that it is not really about control. First of all, when we drive we don't really have control. We may have control over our own vehicle, but we don't have control over other drivers not paying attention, falling asleep at the wheel, driving drunk, or texting and driving. You might say that holding the steering wheel gives us the *illusion* of control, but what about riding in a taxi, where we are in the back seat and have little to no control? Why aren't most people as afraid of taxis as they are of terrorism? Furthermore, let's look at a situation where you completely give up control. How many of you have been in the passenger seat on a long road trip and gone to sleep? Do you realize how dangerous that is? You might never wake up. The driver might crash the car and kill you while you are sleeping. But do most people have a phobia of sleeping as passengers on long road trips, even though they are completely giving up control and have a much higher chance of being killed in a car accident than a terrorist attack, mass shooting, or violent home invasion?"

In the U.S. military we were not supposed to sleep as passengers on a convoy, even when driving in the United States, because when we are awake we can help protect the driver from falling asleep, and being awake also gives the driver an extra pair of eyes to watch the road. When civilians are on a long road trip, the passenger may be sleeping to rest up for his or her turn to drive. Nevertheless, the fear of completely giving up control by sleeping as a passenger is slim to nonexistent for most people.

People also lack control when natural disasters strike. Tornadoes, earthquakes, tsunamis, hurricanes, and wildfires can make us feel very helpless. But as I asked in chapter 1, what is more traumatizing, being a black family in the South and having your house burned down by a wildfire, or being a black family in the South and having your house burned down by the Ku Klux Klan? Even though the physical outcome—a destroyed house—is the same in both scenarios, the Ku Klux Klan exceeds natural disasters in the ability to inflict psychological trauma on human beings.

The universal human phobia is a reason school shooting massacres generate so much attention, even though many other dangers pose a statistically greater threat to children's lives. The universal human phobia is also a reason people on both sides of the gun control debate can be emotional and have difficulty dialoguing. I know people on both sides of the debate, and if I ask those I know who oppose gun control to list the reasons for owning a gun, one reason will be, "I don't want a crazy person to shoot me and my family." If I ask those I know who support gun control to list the reasons for restricting access to guns, one reason will be, "I don't want a crazy person to shoot me and my family."

Even though both sides of the gun control debate can have difficulty dialoguing, they actually share common ground. They are both afraid of their family members being murdered, but they react differently to this threat. People against gun control tend to favor owning guns, while those who support gun control favor restricting access to guns.*

As I mentioned in chapter 1, we are so vulnerable to human-induced trauma that a person does not even have to physically touch us to traumatize us. A person can harm our long-term psychological health by betraying us, humiliating us, calling us a racial slur, spitting in our face, verbally abusing us, spreading malicious rumors about us, and even shunning us. Many people would prefer to break their leg in an accident rather than be publically humiliated or betrayed by those closest to them. The universal human

---

* Gun owners and gun control supporters are often stereotyped, but there are many different opinions among gun control supporters regarding how restricted the access to guns should be. A person can also own guns and support certain restrictions on access to guns. Owning guns and supporting gun control are not mutually exclusive positions, yet the fear of violent human beings is one cause of both positions.

phobia is a symptom of our vulnerability to malicious human harm.*

The ancient Greeks knew about the universal human phobia. Many mythological stories are metaphors for reality, and the reality of war is reflected in the story of Ares, the Greek god of war. According to Greek mythology, Ares was a destroyer of cities who went into battle with his vicious sons Deimos and Phobos standing beside him.[17] Deimos was the god of fear, and Phobos was the god of panic and retreat.

The word "phobia" derives from Phobos. In Greek mythology, Phobos is a metaphor for the universal human phobia. The ancient Greeks knew that nothing fills us with more panic than an aggressive human being trying desperately to hurt us.

To explain why people are so terrified of combat, the Greeks believed that Deimos and Phobos were ruthless twins who could break the strongest battle formations by causing even combat-hardened veterans to panic and flee in fear. In the *Iliad*, Homer says, "Murderous Ares, his good son Panic [Phobos] stalking beside him, tough, fearless, striking terror in even the combat-hardened veteran . . . they turn deaf ears to the prayers of both sides at once, handing glory to either side they choose."[18]

Ares and his twin sons are metaphors for the reality of war, and the Greek poet Hesiod described these metaphors in vivid detail. According to Hesiod, one of the images engraved on the mythical shield of Heracles (who is better known by his Latin name, Hercules) was Deimos, the god of fear, who had "eyes that glowed with fire. His mouth was full of teeth in a white row, fearful and daunting."[19] Other images engraved on the shield of Heracles included "deadly Ares [who] held a spear in his hands and was urging on the footmen: he was red with blood as if he were slaying living men, and he stood in his chariot. Beside him stood Fear [Deimos] and Flight [Phobos], eager to plunge amidst the fighting men."[20]

The ancient Greeks knew that fear and panic are inseparable features of war, just as Deimos (Fear) and Phobos (Panic) are inseparable sons of Ares.

* The universal human phobia does not mean that around 98 percent of human beings have a phobia of terrorism, but that around 98 percent have a phobia of human aggression when it is up close, personal, and directed at them. This phobia makes the fear mongering over violent human beings more effective than other forms of fear mongering.

Even modern astronomy acknowledges the inseparable link between war, fear, and panic. The god of war Ares played a major role in Roman mythology, but the Romans called him Mars. The planet Mars has two moons, which the American astronomer Asaph Hall discovered in 1877. Following the advice of scientist Henry Madan, he named the moons Deimos and Phobos.

As mere mortals, not even the Spartans were immune to the power of Deimos and Phobos, succumbing numerous times to the fear and panic these mythological gods represented. At the height of their military power, the Spartans retreated in three battles against Thebes, a rival Greek city-state. In the Battle of Tegyra in 375 BC, the Greek historian Plutarch tells us that a Spartan army numbering between a thousand and eighteen hundred soldiers attacked a small Theban army of only three hundred.[21] Although the Spartan army greatly outnumbered the Thebans, the Theban soldiers made the Spartans panic and retreat.

After making the Spartans retreat during the Battle of Tegyra, the Thebans also made the Spartans retreat during the Battle of Leuctra in 371 BC, even though the Spartan army again outnumbered the Thebans. And the Spartans retreated yet again during the Battle of Mantinea in 362 BC, when the Theban politician and general Epaminondas charged the Spartan army with a small group of his best soldiers.* On many occasions, the Spartans proved themselves to be exceptionally courageous soldiers, but they had one major shortcoming that made them vulnerable on the battlefield. They were human.

An inevitable question we must ask is, if the universal human phobia exists, how were ancient armies able to make soldiers fight and not retreat? By answering this question we can understand why war, despite its traumatizing taste, has such a seductive scent that lures people to battle.

As I discussed in chapter 1, love is the most effective way to instill courage in war. The *Iliad* reveals how love of family, country, and comrades (along with other motivators besides love that we will explore later in this

---

* We do not know what percentage of these Spartan armies were comprised of Spartiates, the most well-trained Spartan soldiers. Thucydides tells us that among the Spartan soldiers who surrendered at the Battle of Sphacteria in 425 BC, nearly half (about 120 of 292) were Spartiates. So the Spartiates were not superhuman as pop culture depicts them, but were vulnerable to fear like all human beings.

chapter) compel people to willingly risk their lives in battle. In the *Iliad*, the Greeks are invaders trying to destroy Troy, and Hector is fighting to protect his family. Prior to battle, he reminds his army why they are fighting the Argives (who are from the city of Argos in Greece): "What I needed was men to shield our helpless children, fighting men to defend our Trojan women—all out—against these savage Argives."[22] Hector also uses love of country to encourage his men in battle, saying, "Fight for your country— that is the best, the only omen!"[23]

Determined to stop the invading Greeks from raping Trojan women and enslaving Trojan children, Hector also combines love of family and love of country into a single battle cry. Homer tells us, " [Hector shouted to the Trojan soldiers] 'And that comrade who meets his death and destiny, speared or stabbed, let him die! He dies fighting for fatherland—no dishonor there! He'll leave behind him wife and sons unscathed, his house and estate unharmed—once these Argives sail for home, the fatherland they love.' That was his cry as Hector put fresh fighting spirit in each man."[24]

By fighting at the front rank and risking his life for his people, Hector leads by example. In the heat of combat he says to his soldiers, "Follow me now. No more standing back, no fighting these Argives at a distance—kill them hand-to-hand. Now—before they topple towering Ilium [Troy] down, all our people slaughtered!"[25] And during battle Hector shouts at the Greeks, "I'll never yield, you'll never mount our towers, never drag our women back to your ships of war—I'll pack you off to the god of darkness first!"[26]

Although the Greeks are invaders, even they use the battle cry of love to motivate their soldiers to fight. In the *Iliad*, Homer describes how a Greek leader named Nestor encouraged the Greeks to fight by appealing to their pride and love of family: "Noble Nestor was first . . . pleading, begging each man for his parents' sake. 'Be men, my friends! Discipline fill your hearts, maintain your pride in the eyes of other men! Remember, each of you, sons, wives, wealth, parents . . . I beg you for *their* sakes, loved ones far away— now stand and fight, no turning back, no panic.' With that he put new strength in each man's spirit."[27]

In addition to love of family and love of country, West Point taught me that another powerful motivator that prevents people from retreating in combat is love of comrades. When the U.S. Army uses words such as "brotherhood," "camaraderie," and "cohesion," it is really talking about love. The military tends not to use the word "love," because in our society there are so many misconceptions associated with this word.

Jonathan Shay explains how love increases bravery in the military. Shay was the 2009 Omar Bradley Chair of Strategic Leadership at the U.S. Army War College and a MacArthur Fellow. As a psychiatrist he has dedicated his life to helping traumatized veterans and improving the military. The author of *Achilles in Vietnam* and *Odysseus in America*, from 1999 to 2000 he also performed the Commandant of the Marine Corps Trust Study. In it he says:

> When you talk to active American military officers and NCOs [noncommissioned officers] about love—they squirm. They are embarrassed. On the one hand, their organizational culture highly values rationality, which has been packaged to them as emotion-free—and love is clearly emotional. On the other hand, they instantly start worrying about sex, which in modern forces is *always* prohibited within a [deployed] unit, whether heterosexual or homosexual. In present-day America, the ideas of love and sex have gotten mashed together...
>
> *Of all groups in America today, military people have the greatest right to, and will benefit most, if they reclaim the word "love" as a part of what they are and what they do . . .*
>
> Bluntly put: The result of creating well-trained, well-led, cohesive units is—love. These Marines are "tight." They regard each other—as explained in Aristotle's discussion of *philía*, love—as "another myself" . . . The importance of mutual love in military units is no sentimental claptrap—it goes to the heart of the indispensable military virtue, courage . . . As von Clausewitz pointed out almost two centuries ago, fear is the main viscous medium that the Marine must struggle through . . . the urge to protect comrades directly reduces psychological and physiological fear,

which frees the Marine's cognitive and motivational resources to perform military tasks . . . The fictional Spartan NCO named Dienikes, in the acclaimed novel *Gates of Fire*, puts it very compactly: "The opposite of fear . . . is love."[28]

In the modern American military, the words "friend" and "comrade" have become synonymous with "brother." At West Point I learned a famous passage from Shakespeare's *Henry V*, which reads: "We few, we happy few, we band of brothers; for he today that sheds his blood with me shall be my brother."[29] Military history shows that fighting for one's brothers (and now sisters) on the battlefield, in addition to fighting for one's family at home, leads to courage in combat.

Over two thousand years before Shakespeare was born, Homer knew that love of comrades can cause people to risk and even sacrifice their lives in battle. Homer conveyed this when he depicted King Agamemnon, the commander of the invading Greek army, killing two sons of the Trojan Antenor. Although Antenor's sons are actual brothers, effective armies strive to transform soldiers, whether they are related to each other by blood or not, into a band of brothers. Homer describes the courage that can arise when people fight for their brothers:

> Iphidamas, the rough and rangy son of Antenor . . . came now, up against Agamemnon . . . [Agamemnon] hacked his neck with a sword and loosed his limbs. And there he dropped and slept the sleep of bronze, poor soldier, striving to help his fellow Trojans, far from his wedded wife, his new bride . . . But Coon marked him, Coon, Antenor's eldest son, a distinguished man-at-arms, and stinging grief went misting down his eyes for his fallen brother . . . Coon was just dragging his brother footfirst, wild now to retrieve his own father's son, calling for help from all the bravest men—but as Coon hauled the body through the press Agamemnon lunged up, under his bossed shield, thrust home hard with the polished bronze

point, unstrung his limbs and reared and lopped his head
and the head tumbled onto his fallen brother's corpse. So
then and there under royal Agamemnon's hands the two
sons of Antenor filled out their fates and down they
plunged to the strong House of Death.[30]

In addition to love of family, country, and comrades, another motivator
that compels people to fight on the battlefield is money. However, military
history shows that money is less effective than love at motivating people to
fight and die in battle. People will often die for their family, country, and
comrades, but they are less likely to die for money. After all, dying defeats
the main purpose of having money, because a dead person cannot spend
any money.

Although soldiers throughout history have been paid for risking their
lives in battle, soldiers in ancient Greece who fought *only* for money had a
reputation of being untrustworthy and unreliable. Soldiers who fought for
family, country, or any noble cause were considered much more reliable.
Greek philosopher Aristotle said, "Mercenaries prove cowards and when
the danger proves too great and when they are at a disadvantage in numbers
and equipment they are the first to flee, while citizen troops stand and die
fighting."[31]

In the *Iliad*, one of the Greeks tells a story about a powerful warrior
named Meleager who was unwilling to fight and die for vast riches, but
fought when he realized that his people would be raped and slaughtered if
the invaders successfully conquered his city. This story illustrates how love
is a more powerful motivator in war than money:

> And Aetolia's elders begged Meleager, sent high priests
> of the gods, pleading, "Come out now! Defend your peo-
> ple now!"—and they vowed a princely gift. Wherever the
> richest land of green Calydon lay, there they urged him to
> choose a grand estate, full fifty acres, half of it turned to
> vineyards, half to open plowland, and carve it from the
> plain. And over and over the old horseman [King] Oeneus

begged him, he took a stand at the vaulted chamber's
threshold, shaking the bolted doors, begging his own son!
Over and over his brothers and noble mother implored
him—he refused them all the more—and troops of comrades, devoted, dearest friends. Not even they could bring
his fighting spirit round until, at last, rocks were raining
down on the [royal] chamber . . . And then, finally, Meleager's bride, beautiful Cleopatra begged him, streaming
tears, recounting all the griefs that fall to people whose
city's seized and plundered—the men slaughtered, citadel
burned to rubble, enemies dragging the children [into
slavery], raping the sashed and lovely women. How his
spirit leapt when he heard those horrors—and buckling
his gleaming armor round his body, out he rushed to war.
And so he saved them all from the fatal day, he gave way
to his own feelings, but too late. No longer would they
make good the gifts, those troves of gifts to warm his heart,
and even so he beat off that disaster . . . empty-handed.[32]

In the *Iliad*, the Greek hero Achilles says money may be worth fighting
for, but it is not worth dying for: "I say no wealth is worth my life! Not all
they claim was stored in the depths of Troy, that city built on riches . . .
Cattle and fat sheep can all be had for the raiding . . . But a man's life breath
cannot come back again—no raiders in force, no trading brings it back, once
it slips through a man's clenched teeth."[33]

Many people may ask, "But isn't Achilles nearly invincible? Why would
he be afraid of dying?" According to a popular legend, Achilles is nearly
invincible because his mother dipped him in the magical river Styx when he
was a baby. Every part of his body that descended into the water became
indestructible, but since his mother held him by his heel when she dipped
him in the river, that part of his body did not touch the water. Another popular legend tells us that Hector's brother Paris killed Achilles toward the end
of the Trojan War by shooting him in the heel with an arrow. This is why
the fragile tendon near our heel is called our "Achilles tendon," and why the

term "Achilles heel" is used as a metaphor for weakness or vulnerability.

The legend about Achilles having an invincible body except for his heel is not in the *Iliad*, because Homer depicts Achilles as someone who can be wounded like every other soldier in the Greek and Trojan armies. The story of Achilles being dipped in the river Styx seems to have originated much later, possibly around the first century AD in Rome,* nearly a thousand years after Homer wrote the *Iliad*.

Homer depicts Achilles's mortality, vulnerability, and fear in several ways. First, Achilles says he cannot fight unless he has armor to protect his body: "How can I go to war? The Trojans have my gear . . . I know of no other armor. Whose gear could I wear?"[34] Furthermore, Homer describes Achilles being wounded in battle: "But the other [spear] grazed Achilles' strong right arm and dark blood gushed as the spear shot past his back."[35]

In addition, at the beginning of the *Iliad* Achilles is afraid of fighting Hector. When King Agamemnon's brother, a Greek named Menelaus, wants to fight Hector, Agamemnon tells him, "Don't rush to fight with a better man, with Hector the son of Priam. Many others shrink before him. Even Achilles dreads to pit himself against him out on the battle lines where men win glory—Achilles, far and away a stronger man than you."[36]

These quotes help dispel the myth that war is an inevitable part of human nature, because Homer's reflections on the human condition reveal that we have a motivation to stay alive and not die a gruesome death in combat, and generals must find a way to overcome our natural motivation to run away from lethal violence. Instead of putting soldiers on the battlefield and expecting them to naturally fight, generals put enormous effort into training their armies for battle and offer soldiers outside motivators such as money and love (of family, country, and comrades) to encourage them to risk their lives in war.

Generals know that soldiers cannot fight well in combat unless they are willing to die. In the movie *Patton*, actor George C. Scott, playing General George S. Patton, says, "Now I want you to remember that no bastard ever

---

* Achilles being nearly invincible because his mother dipped him in the river Styx is mentioned in the *Achilleid*, written in the first century AD by Publius Papinius Statius.

won a war by dying for his country. He won it by making the other poor dumb bastard die for his country."[37] When I called the General George Patton Museum in Fort Knox, Kentucky, and asked them about the authenticity of this quote, they said it is probably not a real Patton quote, but something made up for the movie. Patton actually said the exact opposite during a filmed speech he gave during World War II. With tears in his eyes, the real-life Patton said, "It's no fun to say to men that you've loved, 'Go out and get killed,' and we've had to say it, and by God they have gone, and they have won."[38]

The fact that Patton's eyes filled with tears when he spoke those words tells us something else about the reality of war, because one of the most interesting things about the Iliad is that the soldiers cry so often. It is remarkable how frequently Homer depicts fierce warriors crying. To offer one example, Homer says, "[King] Agamemnon rose up in their midst, streaming tears like a dark spring running down some desolate rock face, its shaded currents flowing."[39]

Because the soldiers in the Iliad cry so often, we might assume that it was socially acceptable for male soldiers to cry in ancient Greece. On the contrary, crying was often inappropriate for men, and there is evidence that many Greeks during Homer's era saw crying as unmanly and weak,* which is how many Americans see crying today. This makes it even more interesting that Homer chose to depict Greek and Trojan soldiers crying.

As a child I don't remember ever seeing a hero in an American action movie cry, but General Patton's tears reflect the reality of war. Homer's decision to include crying in his writing also reflects the reality of war, but why did Homer do this? Since citizens in ancient Greece were required to serve in the military, it is extremely likely that some of the poets who passed down the oral tradition of the Iliad to Homer, and maybe even Homer himself, were war veterans. Could people who have never experienced war or military service capture the raw emotions of soldiers as well as the poets who created the Iliad? As I explained in the previous chapter, creating art is one way to

* Pericles, Plato, Plutarch, and many other men in the ancient world seemed to view crying as unmanly. Attitudes in the eras of Homer and Pericles were complex, however, and not every Greek had this attitude toward crying. The interpretations I have read on Homer's depiction of crying are limited, because they do not include an analysis of war trauma.

communicate our painful life experiences, and it is very likely that some of the people who sculpted the story of the *Iliad* were not just poets, but warrior-poets.

The negative attitude toward crying in the ancient world is demonstrated when Priam, the king of Troy, forbids his soldiers to cry aloud as they recover the corpses of their fallen comrades from the battlefield: "And hard as it was to recognize each man, each body, with clear water they washed the clotted blood away and lifted them onto wagons, weeping warm tears. Priam forbade his people to wail aloud. In silence they piled the corpses on the pyre, their hearts breaking, burned them down to ash and returned to sacred Troy. And just so on the other side Achaean men-at-arms piled the corpses on the pyre, their hearts breaking, burned them down to ash and returned to the hollow ships."[40]

The Greek attitude that crying is unmanly and weak can be seen when Achilles pities and mocks his closest comrade, the Greek warrior Patroclus, for crying. When Patroclus cries after seeing so many of his comrades wounded and killed in battle, Achilles says: "Why in tears, Patroclus? Like a girl, a baby running after her mother, begging to be picked up, and she tugs her skirts, holding her back as she tries to hurry off—all tears, fawning up at her, till she takes her in her arms . . . That's how you look, Patroclus, streaming live tears."[41]

Of course, Achilles mocking Patroclus for crying is ironic, because no soldier cries more in the *Iliad* than Achilles. When Hector kills Patroclus, Achilles cries so uncontrollably that his mother, the sea goddess Thetis, hears his pain and rushes to comfort him. Nobody doubts the manhood of Achilles, because he is the most dangerous and powerful soldier in the world. Yet the image of the world's mightiest warrior crying while his mother comforts him is one of the most iconic moments in the *Iliad*. Because Achilles's tears are mixed with rage, the messenger Antilochus who tells Achilles of his comrade's death is terrified that Achilles will murder him for being the bearer of bad news. Homer describes how Achilles reacts when he learns that his dear friend Patroclus is dead:

A black cloud of grief came shrouding over Achilles. Both hands clawing the ground for soot and filth, he poured it over his head, fouled his handsome face and black ashes settled onto his fresh clean war-shirt. Overpowered in all his power, sprawled in the dust, Achilles lay there, fallen . . . tearing his hair, defiling it with his own hands . . . Antilochus kneeling near, weeping uncontrollably, clutched Achilles' hands as he wept his proud heart out—for fear he would slash his throat with an iron blade. Achilles suddenly loosed a terrible, wrenching cry and his noble mother [the sea goddess Thetis] heard him, seated near her father, the Old Man of the Sea in the salt green depths, and she cried out in turn . . .

[Thetis said] "Hear me, sisters, daughters of Nereus, so you all will know it well—listen to all the sorrows welling in my heart! I am agony—mother of grief and greatness—O my child! Yes, I gave birth to a flawless, mighty son . . . He is racked with anguish. And I, I go to his side—nothing I do can help him. Nothing. But go I shall, to see my darling boy, to hear what grief has come to break his heart while he holds back from battle."

So Thetis cried as she left the cave and her sisters swam up with her, all in a tide of tears, and billowing round them now the ground swell heaved open. And once they reached the fertile land of Troy they all streamed ashore . . . As he [Achilles] groaned from the depths his mother rose before him and sobbing a sharp cry, cradled her son's head in her hands and her words were all compassion, winging pity: "My child—why in tears? What sorrow has touched your heart? Tell me, please. Don't harbor it deep inside you . . ."

[Achilles replied] "My dear comrade's dead—Patroclus—the man I loved beyond all other comrades, loved as my own life—I've lost him—Hector's killed him,

stripped the gigantic armor off his back . . . I've lost the
will to live, to take my stand in the world of men—unless,
before all else, Hector's battered down by my spear and
gasps away his life."[42]

In his groundbreaking book, *Achilles in Vietnam*, Jonathan Shay
describes how avenging the death of a comrade is another motivator that
allows soldiers to overcome the universal human phobia and risk their lives
in battle. Like Achilles, many Vietnam veterans were so anguished by the
death of a comrade that they lost the will to live and cared only about
revenge. Shay explains:

> "I died in Vietnam" is a common utterance of our
> patients. Most viewed themselves as already dead at some
> point in their combat service, often after a close friend was
> killed. Homer shows Achilles as "already dead" before his
> death in a series of fine poetic stratagems. The transfor-
> mation begins as soon as Achilles hears the news of Patro-
> clus's death . . .
>    Speaking of the time after his closest friend-in-arms
> was killed, a [Vietnam] veteran said: "And it wasn't that I
> couldn't be killed. I didn't *care* if I was killed . . . I just
> didn't care if I lived or died. I just wanted blood. I just
> wanted revenge, and I didn't care. I didn't see myself going
> home. No . . . nope . . . no, I didn't . . ."
>    Another veteran in our [treatment] program wrote:
> "In my wildest thoughts I never expected or wanted to
> return home alive, and emotionally never have."[43]

Achilles is not willing to die for money, yet he is willing to die to avenge
his dead friend. Although money is a common motivator in war, military history shows that avenging comrades is often a stronger motivator. By seeking
revenge against Hector, Achilles can achieve a distorted sense of justice. Because
the vehicle of violence is the most effective way to communicate the experience

of trauma, inflicting violence will allow Achilles to share his pain with Hector. Another motivator in war is rage, the offspring of hatred. In *The Art of Waging Peace* I thoroughly discuss the experience of berserker rage, its seductive siren song. Berserker rage is a drug that makes you feel invincible, godlike, and desperate for death and destruction. As I say in *Peaceful Revolution*, "With the same desperation as a drowning person gasping for air, sometimes I sink so deeply into rage that inflicting pain seems like the only way to breathe."

In the *Iliad*, Greek soldiers such as Achilles, Odysseus, Ajax, and Diomedes are filled with so much berserker rage that they often seem insane.* Achilles is a useful metaphor for understanding violence and war, because in the *Iliad* he is called the "most violent man alive"[44] and the "most terrifying man alive."[45] As I mentioned earlier, Mike Tyson said, "If somebody tells you they're not afraid when they go in the [boxing] ring, either they're lying or they're totally insane."[46] There are times in the *Iliad* when Achilles and other ruthless soldiers, because of their lust to kill and lack of fear on the deadly battlefield, seem *totally insane*.

Another motivator that helps soldiers overcome the universal human phobia and risk their lives in battle is taking an oath. Every society admires people who keep their promises, because human communities rely on trust to survive, and promises are bonds of trust. If you ever find a friend or spouse who always keeps a promise, you are very fortunate. An oath is the highest form of promise. As a soldier I swore an oath to protect the U.S. Constitution, and it is not taken lightly. I knew soldiers in the U.S. Army who would rather die than break their oaths.

Never underestimate the power of oaths. In the *Iliad*, when the Greek army is considering ending the war and returning home to Greece, the Greek leader Nestor says, "What disgrace! Look at you, carrying on in the armies' muster just like boys—fools! Not a thought in your heads for works of battle.

---

* In the *Iliad* the Greek "heroes" are assisted by the gods, and many are descended from the gods. Most soldiers in battle are not nearly as courageous as Achilles and Odysseus. That is one reason why these characters were considered heroes, because unlike our modern view that heroes selflessly help others, the Greek heroes were not considered heroic because they were ethical (many of them behaved immorally), but because they were *exceptional*.

What becomes of them now, the pacts and oaths we swore? . . . Agamemnon—never swerve, hold to your first plan of action, lead your armies headlong into war!"[47]

Yet another motivator that helps soldiers overcome the universal human phobia and risk their lives in battle is ideas. Human beings are the only species on the planet that will die for an idea. These ideas can include freedom, democracy, justice, and peace. In the *Grapes of Wrath*, John Steinbeck says dying for ideas is a defining characteristic of humanity. Referring to humanity as "Manself," Steinbeck says, "And this you can know—fear the time when Manself will not suffer and die for a concept, for this one quality is the foundation of Manself, and this one quality is man, distinctive in the universe."[48]

The following diagram illustrates the various motivations that help soldiers overcome the universal human phobia and risk their lives in battle:

```
              ┌──────────────┐
              │   Love of     │
              │   Family,     │
              │   Country,    │
              │   Comrades    │
              └──────────────┘

┌─────────┐ ┌─────────┐ ┌─────────┐ ┌─────────┐ ┌─────────┐
│  Money  │ │ Revenge │ │  Rage   │ │  Oaths  │ │  Ideas  │
└─────────┘ └─────────┘ └─────────┘ └─────────┘ └─────────┘
```

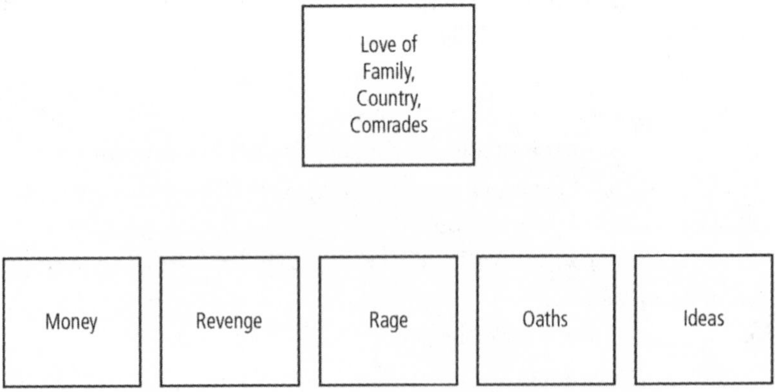

Figure 4.1: The motivations that help soldiers overcome the universal human phobia and risk their lives in battle.

Love fills the largest box in the diagram, because love is the most effective motivator that compels people to overcome the universal human phobia, confront lethal violence, and risk their lives. Love is so powerful that it can motivate people to risk their lives in the struggle to wage war or wage peace. Viewing all of humanity as their family, Gandhi and Martin Luther King Jr. were motivated by *love of humanity* to risk their lives, despite being threatened with lethal violence. Eventually both were assassinated.

Throughout history, countless soldiers have been forced against their will to fight in wars, but this diagram lists the motivations that cause people to *willingly* risk their lives in battle. So far in this chapter I have focused on how armies *motivate* soldiers to fight, but if you would like information on the many ways armies *condition* soldiers to fight, I highly recommend Lieutenant Colonel Dave Grossman's excellent book *On Killing*.

The preceding diagram is not yet complete, because later in this book I will list other motivations that compel soldiers to willingly risk their lives in battle, such as the desire for glory, fame, honor, belonging, and immortality. Since many people who start wars do not risk their lives in combat, the motivations to fight in battle are different from the causes of war, which I list in *The End of War*. One of the causes of war is manipulation. When politicians manipulate our love by telling us "our country is in danger" or "innocent people need our help and protection," they can recruit many conscientious human beings to willingly fight in combat.

Although love is the most effective way to motivate soldiers to risk their lives in battle, a person can experience all of these motivations at the same time, to varying degrees. These motivations are like ingredients in a soup. In the *Iliad* Hector tastes the sweet flavor of love for his family along with the burning spice of rage against the Greeks. Gandhi and Martin Luther King Jr. were motivated by a psychological soup that contained ingredients such as love and the willingness to die for ideas such as freedom, democracy, justice, and peace. But their psychological soup did not contain rage or a desire for money and revenge.

Although the Trojan soldiers are fighting to protect their families, many of them are also motivated by money. During combat some of the Trojan soldiers seem less interested in defending Troy and more interested in collecting "spoils"—valuable items such as armor and weapons dropped by the Greek soldiers. When the Greek soldiers panic and retreat to their ships, the Trojan army is on the verge of defeating the Greeks and forcing them to sail home. Enraged that some of the Trojans are collecting spoils rather than pursuing the retreating Greek army, Hector tells his soldiers, "Now storm the ships! Drop those bloody spoils! Any straggler I catch, hanging back from the fleet, right here on the spot I'll put that man to death."[49]

Human motivation is complex. Just as soup can contain more than one ingredient, human beings can be compelled toward action by more than one motivation. To explain how a person can join the military for various reasons, I must discuss why people go to West Point.

Unlike other colleges in America, West Point requires its cadets to serve five years in the army after graduating. During their service they may be required to fight and die in war. If people are naturally afraid of being violently attacked by other human beings, why would someone choose West Point over a university that does not require mandatory military service?

Many go to West Point for love of country, because they want to serve and protect America. Many also go to West Point because they want to fight for ideas such as freedom and democracy. Unlike the ancient Greek armies, where military service was mandatory for male citizens, some also go to West Point because serving in the military is a family tradition. Another common ingredient in the psychological soup that motivates people to attend West Point is financial opportunity.

Only a small fraction of army officers are West Point graduates, and only a small fraction of soldiers are officers. But many soldiers, whether they are officers or not, join the military looking for better opportunities in life. During a conversation I listened to between a peace studies professor and an army officer, the professor said, "The Iraq and Afghanistan wars allow the American government to kill young black men. Far more black Americans die in modern wars than whites."

The army officer replied, "Actually, studies have shown that a white man in the army today is more than twice as likely to die than a black man. This is because most black people join the army to gain college money and job skills, tending to stay away from combat arms branches such as the infantry.

A lot of white men join combat arms branches such as the infantry because it is a family tradition, because their grandfather fought during World War II." In an article in *Stars and Stripes*, Leo Shane III explains:

> In 1994, blacks comprised nearly 25 percent of all Army infantry units. By 2009, that figure had dropped to 10 percent. Today, there are four times more blacks serving in administrative or supply positions in the Army than in infantry posts, according to service statistics. Marine Corps statistics show similar trends . . .
>
> Why are fewer African-Americans electing to serve in combat units? [Former assistant secretary of defense Edwin] Dorn said it's a combination of factors, most pointing toward why many African-Americans are drawn to the military in the first place.
>
> "Some of it has to do with racial trends in society," he said. "[African-Americans] join the military because they see it as a place they can get a leg up, with more opportunity than the civilian economy. So they think about it as a career, or think about the kind of jobs that can translate into a civilian job later on."
>
> That means gravitating to administrative jobs that provide a long-term career track or are easier to translate into resume-friendly job skills . . . There's also a long-held perception inside the black community that more minorities were forced to the front lines during the Vietnam War than their white counterparts, [author John Sibley] Butler noted . . . Thus, parents who have encouraged their children to join the military in the last 20 years have also pushed them to seek jobs outside of combat specialties.
>
> "So, while Vietnam was fought disproportionately by blacks," Butler said, today's wars "are being fought disproportionately by whites."
>
> In fact, only about 9 percent of the troops killed in

Iraq and Afghanistan have been black, even though they make up more than 17 percent of the total active-duty force. In contrast, Hispanics make up roughly 10 percent of the active-duty force and 10 percent of the deaths from the current wars.[50]

Earlier in this book I described how my father pressured me to join the army because when he was my age, civilian job opportunities for black men were very limited, and he saw the military as the only place in America that gives black men a fair chance. In *Peaceful Revolution* I discussed my deployment to Iraq and role as an officer in the Air and Missile Defense branch, which has a self-defense mission that includes intercepting missiles, rockets, and mortars before they can strike American targets. My father, who fought in the Korean and Vietnam Wars, encouraged me to join this branch because it did not involve killing.

I realized the Air and Missile Defense branch was a better fit for my personality than the infantry, because my childhood trauma has given me a lot of berserker rage, which I describe in *The Art of Waging Peace*. West Point taught me the importance of not killing civilians in war, but when I feel threatened I can become so enraged and out of control that I can imagine myself shooting everyone around me.

Jo Ann Deck, my mentor whom I discussed in the previous chapter, once asked me, "Because of your berserker rage, you seem like a dangerous person to be in the infantry, and the army is lucky that you ended up in Air and Missile Defense. Doesn't the army give people psychological tests to keep people like you out of the infantry?"

I said, "No, and think of the people who are berserk prone like me, who can explode with so much rage that they become a threat to civilians as well as enemy soldiers, who do end up in the infantry."

Although *Stars and Stripes* says many black people join the military for financial reasons, West Pointers are often stereotyped as joining the military for similar reasons. When anyone asked one of my West Point roommates (who was white) why he went to West Point, he would always respond, "Because it's free." When I was a cadet at West Point, I heard that most West

Pointers leave the army after their five-year commitment to make more money as civilians.

During an era of escalating college debt, West Point provides a free college education worth over three hundred thousand dollars. West Point graduates have no college loans to pay back and a guaranteed job as an army officer. As a West Point cadet, you also receive a small monthly salary. Because West Point is often compared to Ivy League universities in terms of prestige and quality of education, many West Point graduates receive high-paying corporate jobs after leaving the military.

*Forbes*, one of the leading business magazines, listed West Point as the best college in the country in 2009. According to *Forbes*: "The best college in America has an 11:30 p.m. curfew. It doesn't allow alcohol in the dorms, which must be kept meticulously clean. Students have to keep their hair neat, their shoes shined, their clothes crisply pressed. They also receive a world-class education, at no cost, and incur no debt—except for a duty to their country. The college, of course, is the U.S. Military Academy, or West Point, and it tops our second-annual ranking of America's Best Colleges . . . Last year's No. 1 school, Princeton University, moved to No. 2 in the rankings, followed by the California Institute of Technology, Williams College, Harvard and Wellesley."[51]

About 80 percent of cadets who enter West Point end up graduating. Some choose to leave because they don't like the strict environment or for other reasons, but many are kicked out for a variety of infractions such as using drugs, drinking alcohol in the dorms, not meeting physical fitness requirements, failing a class (West Point cadets who fail a class are considered for expulsion by an academic board), and breaking the honor code by lying, cheating, or stealing. Aside from West Point's world-class education, *Forbes* further explains how West Point recruits people by providing personal development, prestige, and increased opportunities:

> College senior Raymond Vetter gets up at dawn to fit in a run or a workout. Then, hair shorn neatly and pants pressed, he marches into breakfast, where he sits in an assigned seat. After six hours of instruction in such

subjects as Japanese literature and systems engineering, two hours of intramural sports and another family-style meal with underclassmen, Vetter rushes to return to his room by the 11:30 p.m. curfew.

Most college students, we think, do not march to meals. A goodly number of them drink into the wee hours, duck morning classes and fail to hit the gym with any regularity. But Vetter, 21, is a cadet at the U.S. Military Academy in West Point, N.Y., where college life is a bit different.

According to students, alumni, faculty and higher education experts, the undergraduate experience at West Point and the other service academies is defined by an intense work ethic and a drive to succeed on all fronts. "We face challenges and obstacles that not every college student has to face, but we are able to be competitive in all the different areas, from sports to academics," Vetter says.

No alcohol is allowed in the dorms and freshmen are given only one weekend leave per semester. That rigor, combined with the virtue of a free education, has made West Point tops in FORBES' list of the best colleges in the country, up from sixth place last year . . .

West Point excels in most measures. It graduates 80% of its students in four years. It is fourth in winners of Rhodes scholarships since 1923 (ahead of Stanford), sixth in Marshalls since 1982 (ahead of Columbia and Cornell) and fourth in Trumans since 1992 (ahead of Princeton and Duke). This year 4 out of 37 Gates scholars, who earn a full ride to study at the University of Cambridge in England, graduated from the service academies. The Gates roster includes four Yale grads, one from Harvard and none from Princeton.

"I think I got a lot out of it," says Joseph M. DePinto,

USMA class of '86 and chief executive of 7-Eleven. "Just the discipline, the approach I take to leadership, the understanding of the importance of teamwork. All of that stuff I learned at West Point, and I think that's what helped me be successful."

Classes are small, with no more than 18 students. Cadets work their way through a core curriculum in which an English major has to take calculus and a chemist has to take a philosophy course . . . "If you really look at Brown University or Boston College or Stanford, their number one mission is likely not to teach. It's to bring research dollars to the campus to write the next book that will get them on CNN," says James Forest, an associate professor at West Point who is the director of terrorism studies . . .

[West Point offers] job security. Leadership training. Lifelong friendships. "A West Point diploma is at least as impressive as a Harvard diploma for a lot of things," says Robert Farley, an assistant professor of national security at the University of Kentucky. "Were I an employer, I'd have utter faith in a graduate of the service academies."[52]

Just as soldiers in the *Iliad* serve in war for various reasons, the same is true of people in the military today, along with those outside the military. When I was deployed to Baghdad in 2006, there were more civilian contractors in Iraq than soldiers. Civilian contractors are often paid a lot more than military personnel, and soldiers commonly refer to these contractors as "mercenaries." The *American Heritage Dictionary* defines a mercenary as someone who is "motivated solely by a desire for monetary or material gain."[53]

Most of the contractors I worked with did not fit this definition of a mercenary. Many of them were American citizens who believed in the war effort. They saw their work as a way of serving their country. I met some contractors who disagreed with the war, but risked their lives in Iraq to financially support their families. Most of them would have preferred a high-paying job on the safety of U.S. soil, rather than spending a year in Iraq away from their loved ones. Most of the contractors I met who were foreigners also preferred to be home with their families rather than overseas in a dangerous area, but economic needs drove them to the war zone. In *The Art of Waging Peace* I describe the various motivations of "mercenaries" in ancient history, and that few soldiers back then, or today, were driven only by greed.

By exploring ancient history, war, and the *Iliad*, we can find light in darkness. The *Iliad* is an ingenious work of art, and its lessons are timeless. The dark setting of war in the *Iliad* contains light, because it helps us increase our empathy for the soldiers who die in battle and the families who suffer the consequences of violence. The *Iliad* also deepens our understanding of the reality of war, the complexity of human motivation, and the truth of the human condition.

Although people can be compelled to fight by dark and selfish motivations, the *Iliad* shows that the light of love is the most effective motivator in war or peace. By understanding the power of love, we can learn why soldiers have become Christ figures and war has become a world religion. The god of war wears many masks to disguise its true nature. To overcome the problems that threaten humanity and our planet, we must reveal the face beneath the masks.

## The Paradox of Christianity

I was raised as a Christian. Some of my earliest memories include going to a Baptist church, and I later attended a Catholic middle school. But growing up in a violent household and witnessing my father's war trauma caused me to wonder why, through no apparent fault of my own, I had been born into such frightening circumstances. My agony set my curiosity on fire, like a flame igniting fuel. To understand the causes of my pain and the meaning of human existence, I felt the urge to question everything. During early adolescence I began to question Christianity, the nature of religion, and the existence of God. As the inferno of agony and curiosity burned within me, I also asked myself, "What does it mean to be a Christian?" To explore this question I had to embark on a spiritual journey that revealed the light of love within the darkness of madness and war.

I have heard anti-war activists criticize Christianity in many ways. I have heard them say things such as, "Christianity has been the leading cause of war and murder in human history. The Christians massacred countless Jews and Muslims during the Crusades, murdered thousands during the Inquisition, and burned innocent people suspected of being witches. Monarchs of Christian nations, such as King Leopold II of Belgium, killed millions of Africans during colonialism. Christians massacred millions of indigenous people in North and South America. And Christians enslaved millions of African Americans, whom they were legally allowed to beat, rape, and murder. Western Christian conquerors have caused more violence around the world than anyone else."

These are all facts of history, but psychologist Erich Fromm, who was raised Jewish, challenges us with a critical question. What if one reason Western Christian conquerors inflicted so much violence on other human beings is not because they were Christians, but because they never truly became Christians? After all, it's difficult to imagine that someone like Jesus, who said "blessed are the peacemakers" and "love your enemies," would condone the massacre of millions of Native Americans or slave owners raping their female slaves.

Erich Fromm points out an important historical fact: most of Europe became Christian in name after Emperor Constantine converted the Roman Empire to Christianity, but not Christian in behavior according to the ideals of Jesus. Fromm asks, "According to the history books and the opinion of most people, Europe's conversion to Christianity took place first within the Roman Empire under Constantine . . . But was Europe ever truly Christianized?"[54]

As I explain in *The Art of Waging Peace*, Europe was the most violent place on earth for over five hundred years. This violence culminated in two world wars during the twentieth century, which killed tens of millions of people. A lot of the violence during this period in European history was religious—Catholics killing Protestants and vice versa.

When people today tell me there will always be war in the Middle East and Africa, I often say, "Europe was the bloodiest place on earth for centuries, and a lot of that was religious violence. But could you imagine a war in Western Europe today? Could you imagine Germany and France going to war with each other in the twenty-first century? It's possible, but not very likely. If Western Europe, the bloodiest place in human history, could stop warring with itself, then any place on earth has the potential of stopping its bloodbaths."

It's difficult to imagine Jesus condoning the horrific wars and religious massacres that occurred in Western Europe. Sayings such as "What would Jesus do?" have become common today as a way of encouraging us to behave lovingly and peacefully toward each other. I have even seen bumper stickers that read WHO WOULD JESUS BOMB?

To many people Christianity seems like a paradox, because how can Jesus, one of humanity's greatest peacemakers who inspired both Gandhi and Martin Luther King Jr. to wage peace, be the central figure in a religion that seems to have caused so much violence? How can people who worship Jesus, the "Prince of Peace," be capable of so much cruelty and brutality? Discussing the contradiction between the peaceful ideals of Jesus and the violent historical reality of Europe, Fromm contrasts Jesus as the "hero of love" with the cruel and brutal history of Christianity:

> However the concepts [of Christianity] may differ, one belief defines any branch of Christianity: the belief in Jesus Christ as the Savior who gave his life out of love for his fellow creatures. He was the *hero of love* [emphasis added], a hero without power, who did not use force, who did not want to rule, who did not want to *have* anything. He was a hero of being, of giving, of sharing. These qualities deeply appealed to the Roman poor as well as to some of the rich, who choked on their selfishness . . . This belief in the hero of love won hundreds of thousands of adherents, many of whom changed their practice of life, or became martyrs themselves.

*The Christian hero was the martyr,* for as in the Jewish tradition, the highest achievement was to give one's life for God or for one's fellow beings. The martyr is the exact opposite of the pagan hero personified in the Greek and Germanic heroes. The heroes' aim was to conquer, to be victorious, to destroy, to rob; their fulfillment of life was pride, power, fame, and superior skill in killing (St. Augustine compared Roman history with that of a band of robbers) . . . Homer's *Iliad* is the poetically magnificent description of glorified conquerors and robbers. The martyr's characteristics are *being,* giving, sharing; the hero's, *having,* exploiting, forcing . . .

The history of Europe is a history of conquest, exploitation, force, subjugation. Hardly any period is not characterized by these factors, no race or class exempted, often including genocide, as with the American Indians, and even such religious enterprises as the Crusades are no exception. Was this behavior only outwardly economically or politically motivated, and were the slave traders, the [colonial] rulers of India, the killers of Indians, the British who forced the Chinese to open their land to the import of opium, the instigators of two World Wars and those who prepare the next war, were all these Christians in their hearts?[55]

During the eighteenth and nineteenth centuries, the Christians who dedicated their lives to abolishing slavery also wondered what it meant to be a Christian. If a slave owner who calls himself a Christian rapes his female slaves and murders resisters among his slave population, is that slave owner really a Christian? What if a slave owner who commits rape and murder not only calls himself a Christian, but also believes that Jesus Christ is his lord and savior? Does that make him a Christian? Can people be Christians if their lifestyle opposes the ideals of Jesus? Obviously, the ideals of Jesus tell us not to rape or murder. They also tell us not to hate, and to love our neighbors and enemies.

Frederick Douglass grew up as a slave among Christian slave owners, whom he saw as fake Christians. He said the essence of religion is not belief, but "a vital principle, requiring active benevolence, justice, love, and good will towards man."[56] The Bible agrees with Douglass. As I mentioned in the previous chapter, the book of 1 Corinthians states: "If I speak in the tongues of men or of angels, but do not have love, I am only a resounding gong or a clanging cymbal . . . If I have a faith that can move mountains, but do not have love, I am nothing . . . And now these three remain: faith, hope and love. But the greatest of these is love."[57]

Frederick Douglass, who called himself a Christian, realized that being a Christian does not mean simply believing in Jesus, but aspiring toward Christ's highest ideals. In a similar way, West Point taught me that being a soldier does not mean simply believing in warrior ideals such as integrity, but aspiring toward those high ideals. Illustrating the paradox of Christianity, Douglass described the hypocrisy of Christian slave owners and the Christlike actions of the Christians who risked their lives to abolish slavery:

> The church [in America] regards religion simply as a form of worship, an empty ceremony, and not *a vital principle, requiring active benevolence, justice, love, and good will towards man* [emphasis added] . . . But the church of this country is not only indifferent to the wrongs of the slave, it actually takes sides with the oppressors. It has made itself the bulwark of American slavery, and the shield of American slave hunters. Many of its most eloquent Divines, who stand as the very lights of the church, have shamelessly given the sanction of religion and the Bible to the whole slave system. They have taught that man may, properly, be a slave; that the relation of master and slave is ordained of God; that to send back an escaped bondman to his master is clearly the duty of all the followers of the Lord Jesus Christ; and this horrible blasphemy is palmed off upon the world for Christianity! For my part, I would say, welcome infidelity! Welcome atheism! They convert

the very name of religion into an engine of tyranny and barbarous cruelty . . .

Noble men [who are Christian ministers] may be found, scattered all over these Northern States, of whom Henry Ward Beecher, of Brooklyn, Samuel J. May, of Syracuse, and my esteemed friend, Rev. R. R. Raymond, on the platform, are shining examples, and let me say further, that, upon these men lies the duty to inspire our ranks with high religious faith and zeal, and to cheer us on in the great mission of the slave's redemption from his chains.[58]

Erich Fromm said some Europeans and Americans, such as the men and women who dedicated their lives to abolishing slavery and opposing injustice, lived according to the ideals of Jesus. Fromm said there were two types of Christians. The first type tried their best to become peacemakers, not be hateful, and love their neighbors and enemies as Jesus instructed them to do. The second type believed they did not have to love their fellow human beings, because Jesus would do all of their loving for them. Fromm explained:

[If so many Europeans and Americans do not live according to the ideals of Jesus], why do not Europeans and Americans frankly abandon Christianity as not fitting our times? There are several reasons: for example, religious ideology is needed in order to keep people from losing discipline and thus threatening social coherence. But there is a still more important reason: people who are firm believers in Christ as the great lover, the self-sacrificing God, can turn this belief, in an alienated way, into the experience that it is Jesus who loves *for them* . . . the belief in him becomes the substitute for one's own act of loving.

In a simple, unconscious formula: "Christ does all the loving for us; we can go on in the pattern of the Greek [conquering] hero, yet we are saved because the alienated

'faith' in Christ is a substitute for the *imitation* of Christ."
That Christian belief is also a cheap cover for one's own
rapacious attitude goes without saying. Finally, I believe
that human beings are so deeply endowed with a need to
love that acting as wolves causes us necessarily to have a
guilty conscience. Our professed belief in love anesthetizes
us to some degree against the pain of the unconscious feeling of guilt for being entirely without love.[59]

Frederick Douglass, Erich Fromm, and countless religious theologians
have said being a Christian means striving to emulate Jesus, not simply calling oneself a follower of Jesus. Martin Luther King Jr., for example, saw
Christianity not merely as a word or blind belief, but a lifestyle of love, peace,
and service to others. To make his point, King called Gandhi "the greatest
Christian of the modern world."[60]

This is a remarkable statement, because Gandhi was a Hindu. King said,
"It is ironic, yet inescapably true that the greatest Christian of the modern
world was a man who never embraced Christianity. This is not an indictment
on Christ but a tribute to Him—a tribute to his universality and His Lord-
ship. When I think of Gandhi, I think of the Master's words in the fourth
gospel: 'I have other sheep that are not of this fold.'"[61]

To many Christians, it is common sense that Christianity should include
striving to live a peaceful and loving life as Jesus did. Who was more of a
Christian, a person such as Gandhi who embodied Christ's highest ideals,
or an opponent of the civil rights movement who called himself a Christian
while bombing an African American church? Commenting on Gandhi's love
and his other Christ-like qualities, Albert Einstein said: "Generations to
come, it may well be, will scarce believe that such a one as this ever in flesh
and blood walked upon this earth."[62]

This raises another interesting question. Who was more of a Christian,
a person such as Henry David Thoreau who loved his fellow human beings
and worked to abolish slavery and war, yet did not adhere to organized
religion, or a slave owner who raped his female slaves and murdered resisters
within his slave population, yet went to church every Sunday? What is the

essence of Christianity? Is it a name, belief, or the *lifestyle of love*?

Citing the supporters of slavery as an example of people who called themselves Christians might seem like an obscure and extreme example, but millions of Christians in American history have supported the institution of slavery. For most of the nineteenth century this was not obscure or extreme; it was the norm. Martin Luther King Jr. did not hate these people or believe they were evil, but saw them as trapped within an "evil system."

Although King was empathetic toward those who perpetuated racism, even seeing them as fellow victims of an evil system, he did not believe that being trapped within an evil system excused their Christian duty to treat their fellow human beings with love, peace, and justice. On the contrary, King believed that living within an evil system made it even more important for Christians to embrace love and oppose injustice. King believed that when Christians are trapped in an evil system, it is their Christian duty to change the system.

Although the paradox of Christianity has many causes, a primary cause is that the highest ideals of Jesus are very difficult to attain, requiring dedicated practice in the art of living and the art of waging peace. Most people have never received training in these essential arts. One purpose of this book series is to give people from all walks of life and religious beliefs essential tools we can use to live fully and wage peace effectively.

Who was Jesus, and what does he teach us about waging peace? What does history tell us about this man who encouraged us to embrace love, peace, and justice? Christian theologian Albert Schweitzer realized there is so much about the "historical Jesus" we will never know, because much of his biographical information has been lost in the primordial past. Historian Elizabeth Castelli explains why authors who try to create a historical account of Jesus's life fall short of their goal:

> In 1906, Albert Schweitzer . . . published a book-length review of dozens upon dozens of lives of Jesus produced from the eighteenth century through the very beginning of the twentieth . . . which appeared a few years later in English as *The Quest of the Historical Jesus* . . .

Schweitzer's Quest makes the decisive and incontrovertible point, through careful analysis of dozens of lives of Jesus written over a 200-year period, that efforts to reconstruct the life of Jesus are bound to fail both because the historical archive is so irreparably fragmentary and because every life of Jesus inevitably emerges as a portrait with an uncanny resemblance to its author. Schweitzer didn't use these terms, but his point is that lives of Jesus are theological Rorschach tests that tell us far more about those who create them than about the elusive historical Jesus.[63]

Jesus exerts his greatest power as a symbol that inspires us to become better human beings. What I realized during my spiritual journey is that much of Jesus's appeal has less to do with his role as a historical figure, and more to do with his role as a *symbol of our highest human potential.* Most people I have met, whether they are Christians, Jews, Hindus, Muslims, Buddhists, or atheists, agree that our world would be a lot better off if more of us behaved like Jesus.

Jesus is a symbol that can live within all people, because everyone can strive to achieve their highest human potential. In Buddhism our highest human potential is often called "Buddha-nature," and in Taoism those who achieve their highest human potential are said to experience the "Tao." How are Buddha-nature and the Tao similar to the ideals of Jesus? They all involve the mindset of unconditional love.

Around five hundred years before Jesus said, "Love your enemies," Lao-tzu (who became known as the founder of Taoism) said a military victory should be treated like a funeral: "Weapons are instruments of ill omen; they are not the instruments of the princely man, who uses them only when he must. Peace and tranquility are what he prizes . . . He who rejoices in the slaughter of human beings is not fit to work his will . . . He who has exterminated a great multitude of men should bewail them with tears and lamentation. It is well that those who are victorious in battle should be placed in the order of funeral rites."[64]

To strive toward our highest human potential, to become *fully human*, we must be inspired. The military taught me that people need inspiration. Inspiration can assume many forms,* and one of the most powerful forms of inspiration is role models. Psychology reveals the importance of role models for healthy human development, because children and adults learn both good and bad habits from observing the attitudes and actions of others.

People from many time periods, cultures, and walks of life can serve as role models who embody our highest ideals. But Christ figures such as Jesus have a unique pull on our human nature. What is a Christ figure, and why does depicting soldiers as Christ figures benefit the war system? When our society combines the Greek conquering hero and the Christian martyr into a Christ figure who dies for our freedom, why does this create the perception that war is holy?

## The Religion of War

What does Hector, the Trojan warrior from the *Iliad*, have in common with Jesus? They are both Christ figures. But what is a Christ figure? I did not truly understand what this term meant until I became a soldier.** In the military I learned that armies are most powerful when their soldiers possess the strength of Christ figures.

Prometheus is the first Christ figure—a savior who sacrifices him- or herself for others—to appear in the annals of literature, history, or mythology.*** In Greek mythology, Prometheus was the wisest of the Titans. Descended from Gaia, goddess of the earth, and brother of Atlas, who held

---

* People can also be inspired by a song, ideal, the beauty of nature, the mystery of the universe, and many other sources.

** Christ figures can have other attributes, but in this chapter we are discussing courage and self-sacrifice, the central elements of Christ figures.

*** There may have been other Christ figures in mythology before Prometheus, and the Greek story of Prometheus may have been based on an earlier myth from another culture. But because the historical record before 1000 BC is so fragmentary, Prometheus is the first confirmed Christ figure that we know of in the annals of literature, history, or mythology. There were certainly deities in ancient Sumer and Egypt that seemed to resemble some aspects of Christ figures, but were these figures motivated by compassion for humanity? This is debatable, because the historical record from that early time period is so incomplete.

the sky on his shoulders, Prometheus's compassion for humanity led to an act of supreme sacrifice.

Against the wishes of Zeus, king of the gods, Prometheus stole the gift of fire from the gods and gave it to humanity. As punishment, Zeus had him chained to a rock where he remained helpless while a giant eagle ate his liver. Every night his liver grew back so that the eagle could consume it again the next day.

According to the Greek poet Hesiod, Prometheus was the only Greek deity willing to help all of humanity, even at great personal risk. Professor Elizabeth Vandiver, who teaches mythology and the classics, explains: "Hesiod doesn't tell us why Prometheus wants to help humans. Other [Greek] gods, as I've said, don't seem particularly interested in helping us or being kind to us. Prometheus goes out of his way and risks dreadful punishment, and suffers dreadful punishment, for helping us. Hesiod doesn't tell us why. Later authors said that Prometheus was the creator of men [and] that's why he tried to help them . . . That may be. It may be that Hesiod assumes we know this, so he doesn't say it. Or it may be that later authors made that version up to account for Hesiod's portrayal. We just don't know."[65]

When lions and hyenas hunted our early nomadic ancestors on the African savannah, people occasionally died while protecting their tribe from these predators. During a crisis, people willing to serve and sacrifice for their tribe were vital to human survival. This part of our primordial past remains with us, because today we often admire those who perform genuine acts of service and sacrifice. One example is the Medal of Honor—the highest award in the American military. As I explain in *Will War Ever End?*, at West Point I was surprised to learn that many Medal of Honor recipients never killed anyone, but received the award because they died trying to save their comrades.

A Christ figure is someone portrayed as a *savior*. It is not an exaggeration to call soldiers Christ figures, because soldiers throughout history have been portrayed as saviors, venerated by their society with intense admiration that resembles religious reverence. For example, the Battle of Thermopylae occurred in 480 BC, when three hundred Spartan soldiers and their allies defended Greece against an invading Persian army. Since then, Thermopylae has become a greater source of inspiration than perhaps any other battle in history. When I first learned about Thermopylae at West Point, I found it interesting that this battle did not inspire countless people because the Spartans won, but because they lost.

Although the Persians greatly outnumbered the Spartans and their allies during the battle, Leonidas (a Spartan king) and his Spartan soldiers fought and died to the last man. This is very rare in military history, because many soldiers surrender when threatened by near-certain death in combat, and as I mentioned earlier, the greatest problem of every army has been that when a battle begins, how do you stop soldiers from running away?

Richard Glover, an eighteenth-century English poet, wrote an epic poem to honor Leonidas and his Spartan soldiers who sacrificed their lives at Thermopylae. Like many writers throughout history, Glover depicts these men as saviors who died to protect Western civilization. In the preface to his epic poem about the Spartans, he says:

> All must admire the virtue of these men, who . . . cheerfully renounced their lives for the common safety of Greece, and esteemed a glorious death more eligible than to live with dishonour . . . Wherefore shall not all posterity reflect on the virtue of these men, as the object of imitation, who, though the loss of their lives was the necessary consequence of their undertaking, were yet unconquered in their spirit; and among all the great names, delivered down to remembrance, are the only heroes, who obtained more glory in their fall than others from the brightest victories? With justice may they be deemed the preservers of the Grecian liberty . . .
>
> Upon the whole, there never were any before these, who attained to immortality through the mere excess of virtue; whence the praise of their fortitude hath not been recorded by historians only, but hath been celebrated by numbers of poets . . . To conclude, the fall of Leonidas and his brave companions, so meritorious to their country,

and so glorious to themselves, hath obtained such a high
degree of veneration and applause from past ages, that
few among the ancient compilers of history have been
silent on this amazing instance of magnanimity, and zeal
for liberty.[66]

Like many people who idolize the Spartans, Glover hero-worshipped
Leonidas and his soldiers, neglecting the fact that they were vicious slave
owners (in *The Art of Waging Peace* I discuss slavery in Sparta, and how a
primary mission of the Spartan military was to suppress their slave population). When people are portrayed as saviors, we tend to overlook their flaws.
In the eighteenth century, Glover wrote his hero-worshipping poem to the
Spartans, over two thousand years after the Battle of Thermopylae. Even in
the twenty-first century, the Spartans are still admired as saviors. The popular
film *300* (based on the comic book of the same name) and novel *Gates of
Fire* echo this hero worship today.

Glover called the Spartans the "preservers of Grecian liberty," even
though they lost the battle by not accomplishing the military objective of
the Greek allies, which was to prevent the Persians from crossing the narrow
pass at Thermopylae. Although the Spartans, by fighting and dying to the
last man, allowed their allies to withdraw from the battlefield and fight
another day, many military historians do not see this as a decisive reason
why the Greeks later defeated the invading Persian military.

Historical evidence shows that the depictions of the Spartans created by
the poet Richard Glover, the film *300*, and the novel *Gates of Fire* are more
mythical than factual. In the film *300*, the Greek allies who fought with the
Spartans are portrayed as cowards who retreated prior to the last stand against
the Persians, while the Spartans fought and died heroically. But according
to historical accounts, many Greek allies fought with the Spartans until the
very end, and the Greek allies probably outnumbered the Spartans during
the last stand. Historian J. F. Lazenby discusses the mythical depictions of
the Battle of Thermopylae:

But it is also a battle that passed so rapidly into the realm of legend that it is easy to forget how little we know about it—we do not know, for example, how many men Leonidas had, what his intentions were, or what led to the final catastrophe. The outcome is particularly liable to distort our view of the role played by the Spartans: admiration for their courage may lead us to forget that they formed only a small part of the total number of Greeks engaged, though their king held the supreme command of the Greek army, and that even at the end they were probably outnumbered by the men of Thespiai and of Thebes.

Their deaths, moreover, created a myth—*the myth of the doomed army that prefers death to surrender* [emphasis added]. In reality, there is no reason to believe that Leonidas and his men thought that they were doomed, except perhaps on the morning of the final day, and even then they may have thought more of the military reasons for holding on as long as possible than of heroic gestures.

It is true that Greeks of a later generation believed that the notion of "death before dishonour" was part of the Spartan military code, but this was a belief very largely created by Thermopylai itself: the fact of the matter is that since the Spartans very rarely lost battles, and even more rarely were not in a position where retreat was feasible, the question of surrender seldom arose—[Spartan] prisoners were allegedly taken at the "Battle of the Fetters" early in the sixth century [BC], on Sphakteria in 425 [BC], and again at Kromnos in 365 [BC], so in this respect Thermopylai was the exception rather than the rule.[67]

To further debunk the myth that the Spartans lived by a strict code of "death before dishonor," we can look at how the Spartan government reacted when their soldiers were trapped on an island at the Battle of Sphacteria in

425 BC. During some of my lectures I ask the audience, "When Spartan soldiers were trapped by the Athenians at the Battle of Sphacteria, the Athenian government informed the Spartan government that their soldiers were trapped and at the mercy of the Athenians. How do you think the Spartan government responded?"

The audience always says something like, "The Spartan government must have replied, 'They will never surrender! Go ahead and kill them!'"

Actually, the Spartan government tried to sign a peace treaty with Athens to get the men back. And when the Spartan soldiers finally surrendered, the Athenians knew that the Spartan people did not want their soldiers—their sons and brothers—to die. So the Athenians kept the Spartan prisoners as hostages, threatening to execute them if the Spartans invaded Athens. According to Greek historian Thucydides, who lived during these events in the fifth century BC:

> [When the Spartan soldiers were trapped on the island, representatives from the Spartan government told the Athenians] "The [Spartans] accordingly invite you to make a treaty and to end the war, and offer peace and alliance and the most friendly and intimate relations in every way and on every occasion between us; and in return ask for the men on the island, thinking it better for both parties not to stand out to the end, on the chance of some favourable accident enabling the men to force their way out, or of their being compelled to succumb under the pressure of blockade. Indeed if great enmities are ever to be really settled, we think it will be, not by the system of revenge and military success, and by forcing an opponent to swear to a treaty to his disadvantage, but when the more fortunate combatant waives these his privileges, to be guided by gentler feelings conquers his rival in generosity, and accords peace on more moderate conditions than he expected. From that moment, instead of the debt of revenge which violence must entail, his adversary owes a

debt of generosity to be paid in kind, and is inclined by
honour to stand to his agreement . . ."

Such were the words of the [Spartans], their idea
being that the Athenians, already desirous of a truce and
only kept back by their opposition, would joyfully accept
a peace freely offered, and give back the men . . . [When
the Spartan soldiers surrendered] the Athenians determined to keep them in prison until the peace, and if the
[Spartans] invaded their country in the interval, to bring
them out and put them to death . . .[68]

Contrary to the mythical depiction that Spartan law completely forbade
surrender or retreat under all circumstances, Thucydides further describes
how the Spartan soldiers trapped on the island asked their government for
advice, and were given a vague answer that caused them to believe surrender
was warranted. This shows that the Spartan people valued the lives of their
soldiers who had been captured in combat, just as the American people valued the lives of American soldiers captured during the Vietnam War.*
Thucydides explains:

[The Athenians] made a proclamation [to the trapped
Spartan soldiers] through a herald, asking if they would
surrender themselves and their arms to the Athenians to be
dealt with at their discretion. When the Spartans heard the
words of the herald, most of them lowered their shields and
waved their hands to show that they accepted the offer. The
fighting now came to an end, and a meeting took place
between [the Athenian commanders] Cleon and Demos-
thenes and the Spartan commander Styphon . . .

Now Styphon and his advisers said that they wished
to send a herald to the Spartans on the mainland to ask

---

* Although this evidence shows that the Spartan people cared about their sons, brothers, husbands,
and fathers captured as prisoners of war, it is unlikely that the Spartan people viewed them as heroes,
which is the way many modern Americans viewed American POWs from the Vietnam War.

what they should do. The Athenians refused to let any of them go, but themselves invited heralds to come from the mainland . . . The Spartans on the mainland brought the following message: "The Spartans order you to make your own decision about yourselves, so long as you do nothing dishonourable." They, after discussing the matter among themselves, surrendered themselves and their arms . . . The numbers of those killed and captured alive on the island were as follows. Altogether 440 [Spartan soldiers] had crossed over, and of these 292 were taken alive to Athens, the rest having been killed. About 120 of the prisoners were of the Spartan officer class . . .

[In 421 BC, four years after the Spartan soldiers surrendered] Spartan opinion was, in fact, in favour of peace . . . Both sides, therefore, had cogent reasons for making peace, the Spartans, perhaps, most of all, since they were extremely anxious to get back the men who had been captured on the island. Among these men were Spartans of the officer class, important people themselves and related to members of the government. Sparta had begun to negotiate directly after their capture, but the Athenians were then doing so well [in the war against Sparta] that they would not listen to any reasonable proposals. After the [Athenian] defeat at Delium, however, the Spartans, realizing that Athens would now be more inclined to come to terms, immediately concluded the armistice for one year, in which it was provided that meetings should take place to see whether this period could be extended . . . [An alliance between Athens and Sparta] was made soon after the peace treaty. The Athenians gave back to the Spartans the men captured on the island.[69]

Because the Spartan people desperately wanted their soldiers returned safely, this passage from Thucydides contradicts the popular view that

Spartan mothers wanted their sons to die honorably in combat rather than surrender or retreat. There is a famous story of a Spartan mother telling her son before a battle, "Come back with your shield or on it." What does this mean? When a soldier retreated in an ancient battle, he often threw down his helmet, armor, and shield so he could run faster. A Spartan who retreated in combat usually lost his shield, and a Spartan who died in combat was returned lying on his shield.

Was it true that Spartan mothers told their sons to "come back with your shield or on it" as a way of telling their sons to die in battle rather than retreat or surrender? If this story is true, the saying may have had a deeper meaning, because the Spartans fought shoulder to shoulder. The Spartan army fought in such a tight formation that the shield a Spartan soldier held in his left hand protected the man standing to his left.

Military historian Nick Sekunda describes how the saying "Come back with your shield or on it" more likely meant "Don't abandon your comrades," rather than death before dishonor. Sedunka explains: "Many know the anecdote preserved by Plutarch *(Mor. 241 F)* that one Spartan mother when handing her son his shield before battle admonished him to return 'either with it or on it.' After the spear, the shield was the most important item of hoplite equipment. Warriors who threw away their shields were severely punished. When someone asked the exiled Spartan king Demaratos *(r. 510–491)* why people who lost their shields were dishonoured but those who lost their helmets or cuirasses [body armor] were not, he replied: 'Because the latter they put on for their own protection, but the shield for the common good of the whole line' *(Plut., Mor. 220 A)*."[70]

Although many modern depictions of the Spartans are more mythical than factual, the Spartans certainly fought courageously and selflessly on numerous occasions. The admiration heaped on the Spartans at Thermopylae is largely due to our belief that they demonstrated incredible courage and selflessness when facing certain death. This behavior greatly inspires people. We also attribute courageous and selfless heroism to Socrates, Jesus, Gandhi, and Martin Luther King Jr., which is one reason why they are admired by so many.

At West Point I initially found it odd that Thermopylae, which the Spartans lost, is perhaps the most celebrated battle in history. But when I realized how much human beings admire *saviors who sacrifice themselves for others,* also known as Christ figures, I understood why this battle has become so inspiring and influential. I also saw how soldiers are hero-worshipped as saviors today.

Today, many Americans hero-worship U.S. military personnel as saviors. Just as there are mythical accounts of Spartan battles that sanitize the terror of combat, there are mythical accounts of American wars that sanitize the horror of war. The myths of the ancient Spartans distort our understanding of humanity's natural fear of lethal violence, but the myths of the modern American military have far more dangerous consequences.

The September 11 attacks occurred during my senior year at West Point, and soon afterward I noticed that many Americans viewed the U.S. military with an attitude resembling religious reverence. Many other people in the military also noticed this. In an op-ed in the *Los Angeles Times,* Lieutenant Colonel William Astore explains why venerating soldiers as "demigods" and labeling everyone in the military as a hero is dangerous:

> Ever since the events of 9/11, there's been an almost religious veneration of U.S. service members as "Our American Heroes" (as a well-intentioned sign puts it at my local post office). But a snappy uniform—or even dented body armor—is not a magical shortcut to hero status.
>
> A hero is someone who behaves selflessly, usually at considerable personal risk and sacrifice, to comfort or empower others and to make the world a better place. Heroes, of course, come in all sizes, shapes, ages and colors, most of them looking nothing like John Wayne or John Rambo or GI Joe (or Jane) . . .
>
> But does elevating our troops to hero status really cause any harm? What's wrong with praising our troops to the rafters and adding them to our pantheon of heroes?
>
> A lot.
>
> By making our military a league of heroes, we ensure

that the brutalizing aspects and effects of war will be played down. In celebrating isolated heroic feats, we often forget that war is guaranteed to degrade humanity as well. "War," as writer and cultural historian Louis Menand noted, "is specially terrible not because it destroys human beings, who can be destroyed in plenty of other ways, but because it turns human beings into destroyers . . ."

In rejecting blanket "hero" labels today, we would not be insulting our troops. Quite the opposite: We'd be making common cause with them. Most of them already know the difference between real heroism and everyday military service . . . Even as our media and our culture seek to elevate them into the pantheon of demigods, the men and women at the front are focused on doing their jobs and returning home with their bodies, their minds and their buddies intact.[71]

After reading Lieutenant Colonel Astore's op-ed, I saw an American wearing a T-shirt with the following message printed on it: ONLY TWO DEFINING FORCES HAVE EVER OFFERED TO DIE FOR YOU: JESUS CHRIST AND THE AMERICAN SOLDIER. ONE DIED FOR YOUR SOUL, THE OTHER DIED FOR YOUR FREEDOM! The message on this T-shirt represents an extremely popular viewpoint in America. Just as Christians see Jesus as a Christ figure who died for their sins, most Americans see soldiers as Christ figures who died for their freedom.

The relationship between the American people and their veterans is complex. Veterans have been revered and venerated, but at the same time discarded and ignored. There are a variety of reasons for this. One reason for the contradictory treatment of veterans is that many Christ figures are widely revered only after they die. Christ figures such as Socrates and Martin Luther King Jr. are more widely revered as deceased martyrs than they ever were while alive. In fact, Socrates and King were often treated badly while alive (Socrates was executed and King was assassinated). A comprehensive biography of Martin Luther King Jr., written by David Garrow, is titled

256 OUR PRIMORDIAL PAST

*Bearing the Cross.* This title emphasizes that King, like Jesus, was often treated badly during his life, but became widely revered after his death.

Lieutenant Colonel Astore recognizes that some people in the military truly are heroes, but is everyone? During my junior year at West Point, Vietnam veteran Hugh Thompson gave a lecture to my entire class of around one thousand cadets. My professors called him an "American hero." Thompson was an American helicopter pilot awarded the Soldier's Medal for his heroism at the My Lai massacre, where U.S. soldiers executed several hundred unarmed Vietnamese children, women, and elderly. But Thompson was not awarded the Soldier's Medal for killing Vietnamese civilians, but for risking his life to save these civilians from the Americans.

Horrified by the massacre he was witnessing, Thompson landed his helicopter and went into the village to save the remaining Vietnamese civilians. He told his door gunner Larry Colburn and crew chief Glenn Andreotta that if the Americans killed any more civilians during the rescue attempt, they must open fire on the Americans to protect the innocent. Colburn and Andreotta were not forced to shoot at their fellow American soldiers as Thompson risked his life to save as many civilians as he could.

Describing the actions of the American soldiers during the massacre, Colburn said, "They raped the women with M16s, bayonets. They sodomized children. They decapitated people. They killed a monk, threw him down a well with hand grenades. It was so obscene. They did everything but eat the people."[72] In *Four Hours at My Lai*, a documentary I saw at West Point, Colburn described Thompson's attempt to rescue around a dozen Vietnamese civilians hiding in a bunker, who were about to be killed by the Americans:

> Warrant Officer Thompson was desperate to get these civilians . . . out of this bunker and into a safe area . . . He was convinced that the [American] ground forces would kill these people if he couldn't get to them first. He landed the aircraft in-between the American forces and the Vietnamese people in the bunker, got out of the aircraft, had us get out of the aircraft with our weapons to cover him,

and he went and had words with the lieutenant on the ground. He asked the lieutenant how he could get these people out of the bunker. The lieutenant said the only way he knew was with hand grenades. So when Warrant Officer Thompson came back to the aircraft he was furious and he was desperate to get these people out of the bunker.

He told us he was going over to the bunker himself, to see if he could get them out. I don't even think he took a rifle with him. Besides a sidearm, he was relatively unarmed. He told us, if the Americans were to open fire on these Vietnamese as he was getting them out of the bunker, that we should return fire on the Americans.[73]

In the documentary *Four Hours at My Lai*, Vietnamese civilian Sa Thi Qui, who barely survived the My Lai massacre, described what happened:

The first time the Americans came, the children followed them. They gave the children sweets to eat. Then they smiled and left. We don't know their language—they smiled and said "O.K." And so we learned the word "O.K." The second time they came, we poured them water to drink. They didn't say anything. The third time they killed everyone. Killed everybody, destroyed everything. Nothing was left.

The people were chased into the ditch like ducks, they fell head first, they were crying, "Oh God, have pity, please let me up, we're innocent, have pity!" They shot all the people dead. Then silence. Tiny children crawling along the edge of the ditch, it broke your heart. I thought I was going to die, I couldn't breathe, I was injured, so I crawled here back home. Over there was a naked woman who had been raped, and a virgin girl with her vagina slit open. We don't know why they behaved like that.[74]

In *The Art of Waging Peace* I discuss the causes of berserker rage, and the documentary *Four Hours at My Lai* describes some of the other factors that led to the massacre. Only a small fraction of American soldiers in Vietnam participated in these kinds of massacres. However, according to Nick Turse's extensive research in his book *Kill Everything That Moves*, the My Lai massacre was not an isolated incident, and American forces massacred other groups of Vietnamese civilians during the Vietnam War.

Hugh Thompson was certainly a hero, but were the soldiers at My Lai who used bayonets to rape women also heroes? If not, then how can anyone possibly say that all soldiers, or all veterans, are heroes?

After Thompson risked his life to protect the innocent Vietnamese civilians at My Lai, many Americans saw him not as a hero, but a traitor. In a 2004 interview on *60 Minutes*, Thompson said that when he returned home from Vietnam, "I'd received death threats over the phone . . . Dead animals on your porch, mutilated animals on your porch some mornings when you get up. So I was not [seen as] a good guy."[75]

West Point honored Thompson as a hero, even though he turned against his comrades. This illustrated West Point's teaching that we must do what is right, not what is popular. West Point also emphasized that Thompson, Colburn, and Andreotta were not awarded the Soldier's Medal until 1998, thirty years after the My Lai massacre. The lesson I learned from this was to do the right thing and in thirty years people might appreciate it.

Hugh Thompson told the Associated Press in 2004, "Don't do the right thing looking for a reward, because it might not come."[76] Thompson did not expect to receive an award for his actions during the My Lai massacre, and many people did not become aware of his story until he received the Soldier's Medal. I first learned about him in 1998, when my father showed me a newspaper article about how Thompson had finally received the Soldier's Medal after years of being treated as a traitor. Although my father almost never talked about the Vietnam War, Thompson became one of his biggest heroes.

Thompson died in 2006 from cancer at the age of sixty-two, Andreotta died three weeks after the My Lai massacre in a helicopter crash, and Colburn is still alive as I write this. West Point made it clear to me that their actions at My Lai made them ideal soldiers, heroes who were willing to die for others, even those they did not know.

Christ figures suffer for noble causes larger than themselves, and there are many kinds of Christ figures. Hector died trying to protect his people from a Greek invasion. The Spartans at the Battle of Thermopylae died trying to protect Greece from a Persian invasion. Socrates died for justice and intellectual freedom. Gandhi, Martin Luther King Jr., and Archbishop Oscar Romero died for justice, peace, and humanity.

People such as Buddha, Harriet Tubman, Khan Abdul Ghaffar Khan, Mother Teresa, Nelson Mandela, and Cesar Chavez can resemble Christ figures because although they did not die for others, they overcame immense adversity and dedicated their lives to *living for others*. Lieutenant Colonel Dave Grossman reminds us, "Sometimes the ultimate love is not to sacrifice your life, but to live a life of sacrifice."[77] Countless Christ figures who lived a life of sacrifice did not become famous. I have met many unsung heroes of peace and justice who exhibit the qualities of Christ figures by living for others. Their lives can speak in a language louder than fame, because their unconditional love creates ripples of peace and justice in the cosmic ocean.

Jesus is often seen as the ultimate Christ figure, because according to the Bible, he died for all of humanity. He even died for the people who killed him. Unlike Hector, who was motivated partly by the desire for glory (in a later chapter I discuss glory as a motivating factor in combat), Jesus is depicted in the Bible as truly selfless.

As I mentioned earlier in this chapter, Jesus is a symbol for our highest human potential. Jesus symbolizes the highest human expression of service to others, which is one reason selfless figures who preceded him, such as Prometheus in Greek mythology, are referred to as Christ figures.* According to Catholic priest Michael Gallagher, "A whole tradition of Christian commentators—from Tertullian to William Lynch—interpreted Prometheus as a Christ figure suffering for humanity and inviting people into creative freedom."[78]

---

* Not only have Christian theologians referred to Prometheus as a Christ figure, but so have Buddhists and even atheists. I have heard Buddhists and atheists refer to Prometheus as a Christ figure, rather than calling Jesus a Prometheus figure, because Jesus seems to take the archetype of Prometheus to a higher level.

But why do Americans revere U.S. military personnel as Christ figures? During my lectures around the country people have asked me, "Why do Americans worship soldiers? Why do Americans worship the military?" There are two main reasons Americans view the military with an attitude resembling religious reverence. The first reason is that our society has conditioned us to venerate the military, because this veneration benefits the war system. In the excerpt from Lieutenant Colonel Astore that I quoted earlier, he said: "By making our military a league of heroes, we ensure that the brutalizing aspects and effects of war will be played down. In celebrating isolated heroic feats, we often forget that war is guaranteed to degrade humanity as well . . . Our media and our culture seek to elevate them [military personnel] into the pantheon of demigods."[79]

Omar Bradley, a West Point graduate and five-star general, also realized that revering military personnel as demigods benefits the war system. He said: "It is easy for us who are living to honor the sacrifices of those who are dead. For it helps us to assuage the guilt we should feel in their presence. Wars can be prevented just as surely as they are provoked, and therefore we who fail to prevent them share in guilt for the dead."[80]

Every competent war propagandist knows that when a government glorifies the heroism of soldiers, it is an effective way to reduce public opposition to war. Gazing at the horror of war is like staring at the sun. The blinding light of the sun burns our eyes, and truly learning about the horror of war burns our conscience. But when war propagandists glorify all soldiers as heroes, they create a *war eclipse*.

Just as a solar eclipse occurs when the moon is positioned between the sun and the earth, preventing us from seeing the sun's blinding light, a war eclipse occurs when war propagandists position military heroism between the horror of war and their population's awareness, preventing us from seeing war's cruelty and brutality. And just as a solar eclipse covers the earth in darkness, war propagandists use war eclipses to cover their own people in the darkness of ignorance. The moon cannot fully hide the blinding light of the sun, however, and no propaganda can fully hide the painful reality of war.

The second reason soldiers are revered as Christ figures is due to the ancient practice of human sacrifice that still affects us today. Human sacrifice—a religious ritual where people murdered their fellow human beings because they believed it pleased the gods—was widespread in ancient history, yet it has become a taboo subject rarely discussed today. A peace studies professor once told me, "My students often ask me about human sacrifice, but I don't want to talk about it or think about it."

Nearly every agricultural civilization practiced human sacrifice at one time, but why? Studying the causes of human sacrifice gives us more insights into the human condition, along with additional evidence that human beings are not naturally violent.

As I explained in chapter 2, during my childhood I wondered, if human beings are not naturally violent, why did so many people worship violent, cruel, and psychotic deities such as the Greek gods? In chapter 2 I also discussed the violent Hindu goddess Kali, a destroyer of human beings who symbolizes time and death. She wears a necklace of decapitated heads, a girdle of hacked-off arms, and earrings made from children's corpses. If human beings are not naturally violent, why would a sect of Hindus worship such a violent deity?

Life was extremely difficult for many people living in ancient India—difficult in ways most of us today cannot comprehend—and life continues to be harsh for many Indians today. Worshippers of Kali recognize that the world is filled with severe suffering. Mark Muesse, a professor of religious studies, describes how a worshipper's devotion to violent Kali is similar to a traumatized child's devotion to an abusive parent:

> Although human sacrifices in honor of Kali have almost completely disappeared, animals are regularly offered to her at the Kalighat temple in Kolkata. The animals nonetheless are only a substitute for humans. The *Puranas* say that the goddess is pleased for a while with the sacrifice of goats or buffaloes, but a human sacrifice pleases her for a thousand years. Even today, on extremely rare occasions, there are reports of human sacrifice or self-immolation in honor of the goddess . . . In view of Kali's love for blood and her erratic temperament, one might

justly wonder what would motivate a Hindu to worship such a deity. Perhaps this hymn, written by Ramprasad Sen, an eighteenth-century Bengali poet and devotee . . . [of Kali] can illuminate this question:

> Though the mother beat him,
> The child cries, "Mother, O Mother!"
> And clings still tighter to her garment.
> True, I cannot see thee,
> Yet I am not a lost child.
> I still cry, "Mother, Mother."
> All the miseries I have suffered
> And am suffering, I know, O Mother,
> To be your mercy alone.

To be Kali's child is to suffer, but to know the source of that suffering. The Shakta tradition holds that Kali does not always give what one wants or expects. What devotees experience as cruelty forces them to reflect on the true nature of the phenomenal world, as well as of their own selves, and ultimately to transcend them. Thus, in Ramprasad's view, the sufferings one endures in this life are the chastisements of an ultimately loving mother, to whom one must cling in all circumstances. If she is ultimate reality, what other refuge is there?[81]

Kali reminds me of my childhood. Growing up as a Christian in Alabama, I worshipped a violent and vengeful Old Testament God (still worshipped by some Christians around the world today) who loved humanity despite treating us cruelly. Just as some Hindus cling to violent Kali the way traumatized children can cling to an abusive parent, perhaps I was fond of the Old Testament God because I had a violent father. As a young child I believed that the Christian God could punish people in horrific ways. It might seem odd that I believed this, but God in the Old Testament caused natural disasters, plagues, and other tragedies.

The ancient Israelites who worshipped the Old Testament God probably did not practice routine human sacrifice as the worshippers of Kali did long ago, but conducted this religious ritual only during rare emergencies. Theologian Norman Gottwald explains:

> It is clearly stated that Jephthah sacrificed his daughter (Judg. 11:30–40) and that, in the late monarchy in national emergency, the kings Ahaz and Manasseh sacrificed their sons by fire (2 Kgs. 16:3; 21:6). Ancient cultic stipulations to give all the firstborn to Yahweh (Exod. 22:28–29), or to allow firstborn children to be ransomed while firstborn animals were to be sacrificed (Exod. 34:19–20), are construed by some interpreters to mean that human sacrifice was a mandated feature of the earliest Yahwism, later tempered by animal substitutions. In that context, the near-sacrifice of Isaac by Abraham is seen as a polemic against widely accepted human sacrifice (Gen. 22:1–14).
>
> Evidence on human sacrifice from the immediate Canaanite environment of Israel is blurred . . . In sum, it is unlikely that either Canaanite or Israelite religion directly mandated or normally required human sacrifice. The notion, however, that all life belonged to the deity and that even human life could be efficaciously returned to the deity in order to resolve an extreme crisis seems to have hovered in the background waiting to be activated in times of desperation.[82]

This information about Kali and the Old Testament helps us understand the possible link between trauma and the worship of violent deities, but it does not reveal why human sacrifice in the primordial past helps to sustain the war system today. I better understood why human sacrifice was practiced among the ancient Greeks, Indians, and Israelites—and how it relates to modern war—when I looked at this question not from the perspective of human nature, but the nature of reality itself.

The Greek gods were personifications of nature, and when we project a human personality onto nature, it behaves in ways that seem fickle, unpredictable, and even psychotic. Imagine living in ancient Greece. You might be savoring a peaceful evening with your family today, and tomorrow your family might be killed by a natural disaster. This month your city might be enjoying prosperity, and next month your city might be ravaged by plague. This year your family might have abundant food because of a plentiful harvest, and next year your family might be starving to death because your crops were destroyed by drought.

When human beings live in small nomadic tribes, nature tends to seem reliable, even benevolent. If there is drought, you can move to another place and find water. If there is lack of food, you can move to another place and find something to eat. If your small nomadic tribe is unable to find food or water, then you will die out, unable to pass on your beliefs to the next generation. The nomadic tribes that do survive tend to pass on beliefs about nature's abundance, because when they move they always find what they need to survive. But when our ancestors started living in large agricultural communities, nature tended to seem dangerously fickle—capable of both enormous generosity and violent rage.

To understand how fickle nature can seem to people who are not nomadic, we can look at sacrificial religious rituals in China and other parts of the world. When agricultural people settle near a river, the river can nourish them with fresh water or destroy their villages with a flood. Scholar Tamra Andrews explains: "River and lake deities demanded regular sacrifices because, benevolent or not, they did have the power to pull people into the depths of their waters. They also had the power to send their waters surging over the land. Many myths of lakes and rivers involved drowning and flooding. So Ho Po in China received human sacrifices and gifts of jade. The Kawa-no-Kami in Japan received offerings, as did Ganga in India, Osiris in Egypt, and deities in other bodies of freshwater throughout the world."[83]

As I explained in chapter 2, our ancient ancestors did not understand why natural disasters and plagues happened. However, these people were far from stupid. Because they had a *craving to understand underlying causes*, they created very imaginative explanations for the world around them. The scientific understanding that earthquakes are caused by plate tectonics was not developed until the twentieth century, so if we are ever tempted to look down on our ancient ancestors for their lack of knowledge, we should ask ourselves, "If I had lived twenty-five hundred years ago, could I have come up with the scientific explanation of plate tectonics?"

Human sacrifice occurred because intelligent and imaginative people did not understand the forces of nature or causes of catastrophes. When they explained these forces by personifying nature, they tried to prevent nature's wrath and win divine favors by offering sacrifices to what they perceived were fickle and wrathful gods. Using simple logic, these people reasoned that a big favor from the gods required a big sacrifice on their behalf.

Human sacrifice usually had more to do with feelings of panic and desperation rather than human stupidity. The ancient Greek historian Plutarch tells us about the Athenian general Themistocles, who supposedly sacrificed several human beings because the Persians had invaded Greece and the Athenians were terrified and desperate:

> [As] Themistocles was offering [animal] sacrifice . . .
> three remarkably handsome prisoners were brought before
> him, magnificently dressed and wearing gold ornaments .
> . . At the very moment that Euphrantides the prophet saw
> them, a great bright flame shot up from the [animal] vic-
> tims awaiting sacrifice at the altar and a sneeze was heard
> on the right, which is a good omen. At this, Euphrantides
> clasped Themistocles by the right hand and commanded
> him to dedicate the young men by cutting off their fore-
> locks and then to offer up a prayer and sacrifice them all
> to [the god] Dionysus, the Eater of Flesh, for if this were
> done, it would bring deliverance and victory to the Greeks.
> Themistocles was appalled at this terrible and monstrous
> command from the prophet, as it seemed to him. *But the
> people, as so often happens at moments of crisis, were ready to*

*find salvation in the miraculous rather than in a rational
course of action* [emphasis added]. And so they called upon
the name of the god with one voice, dragged the prisoners
to the altar, and compelled the sacrifice to be carried out
as the prophet had demanded.[84]

In her book *Dying for the Gods*, archaeologist Miranda Aldhouse-Green
describes some of the desperate situations that caused people in the ancient
world to conduct human sacrifice:

> Human sacrifice was only outlawed in Rome in 97
> BC and—according to certain early Christian and Neo-
> Platonist writers—it was not officially banned in the
> empire as a whole until the reign of Hadrian in the early
> second century AD. During the period of the Roman
> Republic, human sacrifice was the occasional response to
> critical situations, when the security of the city-state itself
> was under a threat that required dire means to avert or
> neutralize it. Such was the context for the ritual murder,
> by burial alive, of Greek and Gaulish couples in the Forum
> Boarium, during the Second Punic War [third century
> BC], after Rome suffered a severe defeat at the hands of
> the Carthaginians. The foreign-ness of the victims proba-
> bly salved the consciences of those responsible; aliens were
> not quite as human as Romans. Indeed, it is recorded in
> the third-century compilation known as the *Augustan His-
> tories* that the emperor Aurelian is alleged to have
> demanded that a supply of prisoners from different
> nations (foreigners again) be kept in case of sacrificial
> need.
>     The aversion of catastrophes by appeasement of the
> divine was a common pretext for human sacrifice in antiq-
> uity. Thus the Old Testament king, Mesha of the
> Moabites, pledged his son as a sacrifice when the city of

Moab was besieged by the Israelites, and Jephthah's daughter was similarly promised as the price of victory. [Historian] Diodorus describes how in 310 BC, when the [Carthaginian] army was facing defeat by the Syracusans, the Carthaginians believed that their god Kronos was angry because he had been cheated of his due of child-sacrifices, which the people had withheld by deception and replaced by substitute gifts. Under the threat of disaster, 200 children from the noblest families were ritually slaughtered for Kronos, and 300 more were offered. In the context of Carthaginian child-sacrifice, three main reasons for such practice are given in the literary sources: to placate the gods, to appease or avert their displeasure and for personal gain; the bigger the favour asked, the more valuable the sacrifice had to be.

In discussing Gaulish ritual practice, Julius Caesar makes a similar point, observing that those suffering from life-threatening illness, or facing the dangers of war, conducted human sacrifices in order to persuade the gods to protect them . . . The aversion of earthquakes was an important context for ritual murder in Oaxaca [Mexico], just as seems to have been the case at the temple of Anemospila in ancient Crete . . .

[Human sacrifice is] a form of cognitive response to a world perceived as being inhabited by supernatural forces that might be malign or benign, depending on how they were treated . . . Ritual human killing was a rare but persistent aspect of this cognitive response, something that communities practiced at times of great stress, crisis or relief, a form of behaviour designed to appease or control the spirits residing in the natural and supranatural worlds.[85]

Human sacrifice was conducted not only to prevent nature's wrath and win divine favors such as victory in war, but to also show gratitude to the gods, and even to save the world. For example, the Aztecs believed that if they did not sacrifice human beings to the gods, the world would end. To understand why people in a particular society believed human sacrifice was necessary, we should ask ourselves, "What did these people think would happen if they did not sacrifice human beings?" As historian Manuel Aguilar-Moreno explains, the Aztecs believed terrible things would happen:

> Perhaps considered the most gruesome and violent aspect of the Aztec civilization, and certainly one of the most misinterpreted aspects, ritual human sacrifice had a place of honor and duty in Aztec cosmovision. It was a payment of debt (*tlaxtlaualiztli*) long ago owed to their astral rulers, a blood sacrifice (*nextlaualli*). Most indigenous cultures practiced a way of life that was efficient, not wasteful. Similarly, human sacrifice, in the vision of the Aztec people, was not a gratuitous act of killing; it was purposeful to the degree that they believed it to sustain their very existence . . .
>
> According to Aztec beliefs, human sacrifice was not a frivolous act of cruelty, nor did it stem from a narcissistic need to exert power over other peoples (although captives were often those sacrificed). It was, in fact, a ritual of survival that ensured their existence by nourishing their gods in acknowledgement of the sacrifices made by the gods themselves. As the gods had sacrificed themselves to create the world and human beings, then humans needed to give thanks to them with the most precious substance they had, their own blood (the essence of life) . . .
>
> An underlying fear that everything would cease to exist—the Sun would stop shining and moving across the sky, and life would come to a halting end—if the gods did not receive an adequate amount of human blood impelled

the Aztec to war. Blood nourished and fortified the gods and, in particular, the Sun. It was the ultimate sacrifice to the gods . . .

A variety of sources indicate a fundamental Aztec belief that envisioned a shared cosmic energy between all living things—plants, animals, humans, and gods—that need to be exchanged regularly. This energy was transported from humans to the gods through various forms of sacrifice, human and otherwise. The gods returned it in the form of light and warmth (from the Sun), water, and food, especially maize. The Sun was the supreme recipient in this exchange of energy, for the Sun provided the key elements to the sustenance of life . . .

Those sacrificed included warriors, captives, slaves, children (sacrificed to Tlaloc), noblewomen, and certain criminals. Most sacrifices were conducted on a sacrificial stone called a *techcatl* at a temple or other sacred place with an obsidian knife, or *tecpatl*, used to remove the heart. Before the sacrifice took place, a series of rituals were performed . . . The victims were treated as if they were the gods themselves and lived in a manner befitting this god for a period of time that could be as long as a year . . .

Sacrifice, and the blood that poured from it, ensured that the Aztec would continue to have access to the necessary elements—sun, water, earth, and air—and all the fruits resulting from these. It was another expression of the idea that life energy was dynamic and mutable. It was in constant motion, traveling between the gods and the living—people, animals, and plants.[86]

As I explained at the beginning of this book, *unjust policies always result from an inaccurate belief.* The Aztecs believed that human blood offered to the gods fueled the sun's movement across the sky, and this inaccurate belief led to the unjust policy of human sacrifice. This reminds me of a famous quote attributed to French philosopher Voltaire: "As long as people believe in absurdities, they will continue to commit atrocities."[87]

Professor Grant Voth, who teaches mythology, describes the Aztec creation myth that led them to kill human beings in religious rituals. The Aztec gods were saviors (Christ figures) who died so humanity could live, and the Aztecs believed they had to repay this divine sacrifice by sacrificing their fellow human beings. This Aztec creation myth is filled with poetic images, demonstrating the impressive imaginations of the Aztecs, but because this myth was believed literally, it resulted in the horror of human sacrifice. Professor Voth tells us:

> In one version [the gods Tezcatlipoca and Quetzalcoatl] create the universe out of the dismembered body of the great earth mother . . . They tear her apart [and] everything that humans need comes from her body. Her hair becomes trees, flowers, and herbs. Her skin makes grasses and smaller flowers. Her eyes produce wells and springs and small caves. From her mouth come the great rivers and canyons. From her nose mountain ridges and valleys. She is still thus in the earth. She *is* the earth. And ancient Aztecs said you could hear her screaming at night, screaming for sacrificial flesh and blood that can soothe her, so that she can keep producing what humans need to survive . . .
>
> The creation of the sun involves more sacrifice. Two gods have to leap onto a flaming pyre to make the sun and the moon, and then a group of gods have to have their own hearts cut out to make the sun and the moon move . . . A steady diet of blood and human hearts is required to keep this delicate cosmos alive, and hence the horror stories we have about the capture and sacrifice of thousands of human beings, their beating hearts cut out on the great temple steps to keep this creation alive.[88]

Through no fault of our own, humanity emerged into the world in such a state of ignorance that the origin of the sun, moon, and earth were a mystery to our early ancestors. When the Aztecs lacked scientific explanations for the mysterious reality around them, their craving to understand underlying causes urged them to invent explanations.

But science has revealed that human sacrifice is not needed to propel the sun across the sky. In fact, science has revealed that the sun does not really move across the sky. It is an illusion, because the earth is actually moving around the sun. Unlike our early ancestors who were born into ignorance, people in the twenty-first century have inherited critical scientific discoveries from our ancestors, like gifts passed through the generations.

In elementary school I was taught that the Aztecs were cruel practitioners of human sacrifice while the Mayans were peaceful people who did not practice human sacrifice. Neither claim is true. The Aztecs did not see human sacrifice as cruel, but as a necessary ritual to protect the survival of the world, and the Mayans conducted human sacrifice almost as much as the Aztecs. According to religious historian Charles Long, "At one period of scholarship on Meso-America, the Aztecs were portrayed as a horrible bloodthirsty culture that demanded innumerable human sacrifices whereas the Maya were seen as a more passive, docile culture that abhorred bloody human sacrifices. This was indeed an aberration of scholarship for we now know that the Mayan sacrificed almost as much as the Aztecs."[89]

In *Peaceful Revolution* I discuss *moral distance* as a form of dehumanization. Moral distance creates a sense of moral superiority over others. As Christianity spread throughout Europe and the Americas, Christians dehumanized "pagans" who conducted human sacrifice, which was an attempt to demonstrate Christian moral superiority. This is ironic, because prior to the rise of Christianity, the pagan Romans dehumanized foreign "barbarians" who conducted human sacrifice, which was an attempt to demonstrate Roman moral superiority.

The Romans also dehumanized the early Christians as cannibals, because the Christian communion ritual is a symbolic act of cannibalism. Just as some cannibals believe that ingesting the blood and flesh of another human being allows you to absorb that person's powers, the Christian communion ritual is a symbolic cannibal ceremony where people consume the blood and flesh of Jesus. For most Christians, however, communion has nothing to do with cannibalism and is instead a powerful spiritual metaphor. Miranda Aldhouse-Green tells us: "The Christian message is clear: human sacrifice was an outrageous practice, fit only for pagans. Ironically, this was precisely the same argument used by earlier Graeco-Roman writers about the uncouth ritual customs of 'barbarians' like Gauls, Britons and Phoenicians . . . Cicero accused the Gauls of practicing human sacrifice, implying the involvement of the Druids, and making the point that the word of people capable of such barbarity should not be taken seriously . . . The context in which the early Christian writers attacked pagan human sacrifice was in defense of their own faith which, according to its detractors, included the killing and consumption of people."[90]

Many people today have a condescending attitude toward those who practiced human sacrifice thousands of years ago, but what if we are not so different from them? What if people in the modern world continue to die in massive ceremonies of human sacrifice? What if you supported the ritual of human sacrifice at some point in your life, without even realizing it? I certainly did, when I, like so many other people around the world, practiced the religion of war and supported the sacrifice of human beings to the god of war. Erich Fromm discusses the similarities between the ancient practice of human sacrifice and the modern war system:

> Let us consider . . . the sacrifice of children, as it was practiced in Canaan at the time of the Hebrew conquest and in Carthage down to its destruction by the Romans, in the third century B.C. Were these parents motivated by the destructive and cruel passion to kill their own children? Surely this is very unlikely. The story of Abraham's attempt to sacrifice Isaac, a story meant to speak against sacrifice of children, movingly emphasizes Abraham's love for Isaac; nevertheless Abraham does not waver in his decision to kill his son. Quite obviously we deal here with a religious motivation which is stronger than even the love for the

child. The man in such a culture is completely devoted to his religious system, and he is not cruel, even though he appears so to a person outside this system.

It may help to see this point if we think of a modern phenomenon which can be compared with child sacrifice, that of war. Take the first World War. A mixture of economic interests, ambition, and vanity on the part of the leaders, and a good deal of stupid blundering on all sides brought about the war. But once it had broken out (or even a little bit earlier), it became a "religious" phenomenon. The state, the nation, national honor, became the idols, and both sides voluntarily sacrificed their children to these idols.

A large percentage of the young men of the British and of the German upper classes which are responsible for the war were wiped out in the early days of the fighting. Surely they were loved by their parents. Yet, especially for those who were most deeply imbued with the traditional concepts, their love did not make them hesitate in sending their children to death, nor did the young ones who were going to die have any hesitation. The fact that, in the case of child sacrifice, the father kills the child directly while, in the case of war, both sides have an arrangement to kill each other's children makes little difference.[91]

Although Fromm points out the similarities between ancient human sacrifice and the modern war system, he does not mention several important differences. The most significant difference is that unlike the Carthaginian god Kronos, the Aztec gods, and other ancient deities that demanded human sacrifice, the war system is not imaginary, but real. And sometimes, the reasons for going to war are also real. As I said in *The Art of Waging Peace*, Frederick Douglass makes a strong case for the necessity of the American Civil War, and as I discussed in *The End of War*, Nazi Germany was so militarily powerful in the early 1940s that a strong argument can be made for

American military intervention in World War II.

But as I thoroughly explain in *The Art of Waging Peace*, the war system is the *master of deception*. In the *Iliad*, Homer calls Ares (the Greek god of war) the "lying two-faced god."[92] And in *The Art of War*, written over two thousand years ago, Sun Tzu says, "All warfare is based on deception."[93]

Military history contains countless examples of governments lying to their people. One reason the war system is so powerful is because there have been some just wars in the past. This allows war propagandists to depict every unjust war as a just war. If the American government wants to go to war for an unjust reason, as it did during the Vietnam War, it makes the war seem like the struggle against Nazi fascism.

War propaganda is the oxygen all wars breathe in order to survive and thrive. To sustain the war system, war propaganda creates illusions as imaginary as ancient bloodthirsty gods. To show the similarities between ancient human sacrifice and the modern war system, we can compare the Carthaginians in the fourth century BC to the Germans in the twentieth century. The Carthaginians believed that their god Kronos was enraged because they had not sacrificed their children to him. As a result, they believed he had punished them by sending foreign invaders to destroy Carthage. Desperate and terrified, the Carthaginians sacrificed a couple hundred of their children to appease their wrathful god.*

Of course, most people today would agree that Kronos does not exist and the Carthaginian children died for something imaginary rather than real. In a similar way, when the German government in World Wars I and II told the German people they had to support the invasion of other countries in the name of "peace" and "self-defense," most people today would agree these soldiers died for political lies and propaganda—illusions as imaginary as Kronos.

---

* The existence of child sacrifice in Carthage has been debated, but Josephine Quinn, a lecturer in ancient history at Oxford University, describes the conclusions of a new and comprehensive study: "When you pull together all the evidence—archaeological, epigraphic and literary—it is overwhelming and, we believe, conclusive: they [the Carthaginians] did kill their children, and on the evidence of the inscriptions, not just as an offering for future favours [from the gods] but fulfilling a promise that had already been made." You can read more about the study in this article: http://www.theguardian.com/science/2014/jan/21/carthaginians-sacrificed-own-children-study.

Just as the ancient Aztecs believed the sun would cease to move if human beings were not sacrificed to the gods, American politicians said the United States would cease to exist* if thousands of American soldiers were not sent to fight and die in the Vietnam War. Both beliefs were figments of the human imagination. And just as the ancient Romans sacrificed foreigners to the gods, believing it would protect Roman freedom, many Americans believe we must sacrifice foreign civilians in drone strikes to protect our freedom. As I explain in chapter 11 of *The Art of Waging Peace*, the notion that drone strikes make our country safer is an illusion.

The American people want to believe in goodness, especially when greed and selfishness are causing so much harm in our society. Immediately after the September 11 terrorist attacks, Americans admired first responders and firefighters—in addition to soldiers—as selfless heroes. Since then, politicians have repeatedly told us that American troops are dying for our freedom and sacrificing themselves to liberate Iraqi and Afghan civilians from oppression. American troops are portrayed as Christ figures sacrificing themselves for people they don't even know. This story inspires many Americans, but when soldiers are depicted as Christ figures, violence becomes our savior and war becomes holy.

People throughout history have worshipped what the Old Testament refers to as false idols. The Old Testament describes Moses becoming angry when Hebrews worshipped the golden calf—a false idol. Other false idols have included the Egyptian pharaohs and Roman emperors, who were worshipped as divine beings. But perhaps the most powerful false idol in history has been war. The god of war is the only deity that Christians, Jews, Muslims, Hindus, atheists, agnostics, and even Buddhists all worship together. Unlike the false idol of money, which people will kill for but rarely die for, millions of people have died for the false idol of war.

At the beginning of this book I explained that human beings crave

---

* This fear was based partly on the inaccurate "domino theory," which did not reflect reality. The domino theory claimed that the United States would eventually be destroyed if we did not invade Vietnam. The domino theory has been thoroughly debunked. Some politicians might have known that the domino theory was an illusion, but many politicians were truly afraid of communism and believed the myths of the domino theory.

purpose and meaning. If so many American soldiers did not believe the U.S. government's reasons for the Vietnam War, how did these soldiers find purpose and meaning during the war? Historian Christian Appy explains how American soldiers fighting in Vietnam found purpose and meaning in love for their comrades:

> One [Vietnam] veteran put it this way: "We realized collectively we had nothing to fight for, that nobody cared about us, and we didn't give a shit about them. Our sense of motivation was a buddy system: 'we are in this and nobody cares, but at least we can care about each other.'"
>
> A soldier in Vietnam used almost the same language: "We fight for each other. We're really tight here. Nobody else cares for us." Vietnam was certainly not unique in drawing men together and motivating men to fight for their buddies. The Stouffer study of GIs in World War II argues that primary group cohesion was the major motivating force among the soldiers of that war; but there is a distinct character to the unity felt by Vietnam soldiers. It was shaped not only by the common dangers of war but also by a common sense of the war's pointlessness. In World War II, by contrast, most soldiers rarely doubted the worth or significance of their sacrifices . . . In Vietnam, however, soldiers drew together around the shared assumption that the war itself had no meaningful purpose, that the only meaning was located in the collective unity necessary to survive.
>
> Robert Sanders, a black infantryman who served in 1968, describes his feelings . . . "I felt closer to everybody in that unit at the time than I do my own blood sisters and brothers . . . It was THE family . . . We was so close it was unreal. That was the first time in my life I saw that type of unity, and I haven't seen it since. And that was ten years ago. It was beautiful. It sort of chills you, brings

goose bumps just to see it, just to feel it, cause the family is guys from all over the states, from New York and California, Chicago, Mississippi, 'Bama, everywhere . . . That was the only thing that really turned me on in Vietnam. That was the only thing in Vietnam that had any meaning." [94]

Because the war system is the master of deception, many people (especially in the civilian population) do not even realize they worship war. But history gives us overwhelming evidence that war is similar to religion. War does not resemble every single aspect of religion, but it resembles enough aspects of religion to become what Fromm called "a religious phenomenon." Like major world religions, the religion of war has heretics and behavior deemed sacrilegious. When a government is mobilizing its people for war, opposition to the war system is often seen as sacrilegious, and peace activists are treated as "unpatriotic" heretics.

Furthermore, many Americans show more reverence on Veterans Day than on religious holidays such as Christmas. And just as the ancient Carthaginians sacrificed their children to the god Kronos in exchange for protection, we sacrifice children to the god of war in exchange for freedom and security. As I mentioned earlier, the *Iliad* reminds us that every soldier killed in war is someone's child. According to the *Iliad* this is not a political statement. It is simply the reality of war.

Perhaps the most striking similarity between major world religions and the religion of war is the hostility directed at those who question and criticize war, similar to the hostility directed at those who question and criticize a religious practice. Telling people the war system does not truly give us freedom and security in the twenty-first century, but in fact harms our freedom and security today,* can incite as much aggression as telling an ancient Carthaginian or Aztec that human sacrifice was based on illusion.

If more people criticize rather than sanitize war, the war system will have

---

* In chapter 11 of *The Art of Waging Peace*, I explain how the war system in the twenty-first century does not give us freedom and security, but harms our freedom and security.

a harder time fooling people with the illusions of war. If more Americans learn about the full deception of war propaganda and the hidden reality of war, the war system will lose much of its power. But disagreeing with popular support of the war system can be as controversial as disagreeing with popular support of a dominant religious faith. In many societies, to oppose the war system is to be a heretic. Because the war system is able to evoke so much reverence for war, throughout history the most fanatical form of patriotism always occurs around war.

Like Martin Luther King Jr., we can honor the sacrifices of soldiers—respecting them as human beings rather than demigods—while resisting the war system. When King opposed the Vietnam War, he said, "I have nothing but admiration for the bravery of those [soldiers] who are engaged in the kind of sacrificial and suffering situation that they are in . . . I think that the things that I'm saying and the things that I'm trying to do, and all of the people in the peace movement are trying to do, are really geared toward bringing the boys back home. In other words, we are trying to prove to be their best friends by doing something to bring about the climate that will bring an end to this war."[95]

My exploration of human sacrifice and the religion of war has greatly increased my empathy for all human beings. It has also increased my hope that we can end war. But I am not naive about the immense challenge of defeating the war system. War, especially in America, is a powerful religious force that can seduce atheists, agnostics, and people from all religions. But if we increase our empathy, hope, and understanding, we can become strong enough to overthrow the god of war. If we train ourselves to wage peace, we can replace the religion of war with the religion of peace. If we understand our primordial past, we can save our fragile future.

# PART II

# Our Fragile Future

# CHAPTER 5

# Beauty and Belonging

## *The Tightrope of Beauty*

Suffering is combustible, like gasoline, gunpowder, or rocket fuel. And like any combustible substance, suffering can hurt or help us. Our suffering can explode violently, harming us and those we care about. Our suffering can also choke us quietly with its smoke and toxic fumes, gradually suffocating our zest for life and making us bitter shadows of who we once were. Or we can benefit from our suffering. Similar to people who use rocket fuel to journey beyond perceived limitations, we can use our suffering to fuel our spiritual journey toward empathy, hope, and peace. To explain how I used my suffering to propel me to the transcendent spiritual realm of radical empathy, I must discuss my experiences as an Asian-looking black child in Alabama.

Although I am part black and my father taught me to think like a black man from his generation, I looked Asian as a child. Growing up mostly around white children, I was bullied because I looked Asian. In fifth grade when I was walking to class one day, a boy who often made fun of me said in front of the other students, "Paul is so ugly, I can't imagine a woman ever wanting to marry him. Paul will never get married because he is too ugly." I felt humiliated and did not know what to say. I was also deeply confused, because why would he say something so cruel? Was it true?

Because I was bullied for looking Asian, as a child I desperately wanted to look white, but I came to the painful realization that I could not change the shape of my eyes or the tan color of my skin. Like many people with racial features deemed unattractive, I began to hate the parts of my appearance I could not change. I cannot count the number of times I stared in the mirror as a child, hating my facial features, hating myself, wishing I looked different.

As we discussed earlier, in modern society virtually all human beings have shared this experience to some extent. How many people, especially in American society, have stared in a mirror and wished they looked different? How many have wanted to be taller, slimmer, more muscular, or younger? How many have gazed at their reflection and desired a nicer head of hair, clearer skin, less wrinkles, a flatter stomach, or the ability to change the shape and size of their facial features and body parts? How many have been tormented by the feeling that they are not pretty enough, handsome enough, or good enough?

As I explained in chapter 2, the Tree of the Knowledge of Good and Evil is a metaphor for our *heightened human awareness*. We are the only species on the planet, as far as we know, who looks in the mirror and thinks, "I hate my body. I hate my face. I hate myself." No other species suffers from self-destructive eating disorders because it perceives itself as being too fat. No other species hates its body because it does not look like a supermodel, or feels so ugly that it ponders suicide.

A person might assume that Asian facial features are considered ugly only in America, but this perception also exists in Asia. According to an article from ABC News, the country with the highest proportion of plastic surgeries among its population is South Korea:

> The plastic surgery industry has stormed Asia, and South Korea has the continent's biggest clientele. The *Economist* first reported that a 2009 survey by a market-research firm known as Trend Monitor found that about one in five women from Seoul have undergone some sort of plastic surgery. According to the report, more than 360,000 total procedures were performed in 2010, with the most common procedures being liposuction, nose jobs and blepharoplasty, or double eyelid surgery [to make their eyes look more European]. More than 44,000 double eyelid surgeries were performed in 2010.
>
> "In Asia, it's very common for patients to want more Western-looking eyes," said Dr. Malcolm Roth, president

of the American Society of Plastic Surgeons. "So that's really no surprise there."[1]

In middle school one of my teachers said beauty's only function is to attract a mate, but beauty has much deeper significance. Beauty is also about belonging. So far in this book I have explained that human beings crave purpose, meaning, and explanations for why things happen. But human beings also crave belonging. In the previous chapter I described numerous motivators that compel people to fight in battle, and another motivator I can add to that list is the urge for belonging. The strong urge to belong to a community of comrades, along with the fear of being treated as an outcast if one behaves like a coward, can increase a soldier's courage in combat.

When children are labeled as "ugly," they are often bullied and treated as outcasts who do not belong. Children can also be bullied and treated as outcasts because they are different. To mention just a few examples, children in school can be bullied because of their weight, height, skin color, facial features, hair color, the way they talk, and the kinds of clothes and shoes they wear. But is it human nature to bully those who seem different from the group?

My first childhood home in Alabama was located in a poor neighborhood and had a lot of cockroaches, spiders, and crickets. I remember being three years old and seeing a cricket one evening with a missing hind leg. The cricket was all by itself. Feeling empathy for the small insect, I sat next to it, talking to it to keep it company. Of the four dogs my parents had, three had similar patterns of black and white fur, while one had brown fur that looked different from the others. My favorite dog was the brown one—the one who looked unique.

Many children's stories reveal that young boys and girls can feel empathy for those who look different, because some of the most popular children's stories are about outcasts. "The Ugly Duckling," written by Hans Christian Andersen in 1843, is just one example of a children's story that teaches empathy for outcasts. Mette Norgaard gives us a concise summary of "The Ugly Duckling":

One summer, close to the moat of a manor house, a mother duck was nesting. One by one the eggs cracked, but an uncommonly large one remained. An old duck insisted it was a turkey egg and warned the mother that turkeys were afraid of water. When it finally cracked, a large, ugly duckling tumbled out. Fearing he was indeed a turkey, the mother thought, "Into the water with him, even if I have to kick him in."

She brought her brood down to the moat, and one after the other the ducklings plopped in and they all floated splendidly, including the ugly one. "No, that's no turkey!" thought the mother, "He's my own all right!"

Once in the duck yard, the others picked on the ugly one for he was so different. The ducks bit him, the hens pecked him, and even the girl who came to feed them kicked him. His sisters and brothers said they hoped the cat would take him, and eventually even the mother wished him far away. In desperation, the duckling fled over the fence and escaped to the marshland . . .

One fall evening the duckling noticed a flock of beautiful white birds with long, graceful necks: They were swans! The majestic creatures spread their wings and flew away toward warmer climates. The duckling felt strangely connected. Although they soon disappeared from sight, there was no way he could forget those stunning creatures.

Winter came and the poor little duckling had to swim about to keep the water from freezing completely. But in the end he got tired and was trapped in the ice. Fortunately a farmer saw him and rescued him.

Finally spring returned and the duckling tested his wings. They made a strong swooshing sound as they carried him to a beautiful garden. When he landed on the water, he saw the majestic birds again, but this time they were coming toward him with their feathers all puffed up. He feared they might hack him to death for being so hideous. Accepting his fate, he bowed his head toward the surface of the still water and suddenly he saw his own reflection—he was himself a swan![2]

Like "The Ugly Duckling," films such as *Dumbo* (about an elephant with large ears) and *Finding Nemo* (about a fish with a disproportionately small fin) have been very popular among children, showing that humanity has a natural capacity to feel empathy for those who do not belong. Popular comic books such as *X-Men* are also about outcasts. The premise of *X-Men* poses a hypothetical question. What if the outcasts persecuted by society had superpowers? Would they destroy or protect humanity?

In the early *X-Men* comic books, Magneto, the character with the strongest "physical" superpower (he can control magnetic fields and manipulate metal with his mind), tries to destroy humanity. Professor X, the character with the strongest "mental" superpower (he can control people's minds), tries to protect humanity.* Professor X is a Christ figure who loves and is willing to die for humanity, despite being hated and persecuted by human beings.

The superheroes in *X-Men* are called "mutants." The mutants are metaphors for outcasts such as homosexuals, African Americans, and people with HIV. For example, the character Beast is blue. Like persecuted African Americans, Beast is judged by his color and seen as a subhuman animal, even though he is exceptionally smart. Rogue's mutant superpower causes her to kill people if she has intimate physical contact with them, which is a metaphor for the way Americans feared HIV patients during the 1980s.** Like many mutants, Rogue is rejected by her family and society.

When children relate to a story such as "The Ugly Duckling," *Dumbo*,

---

* When I say that Magneto and Professor X have the strongest "physical" and "mental" superpowers respectively, I am referring only to the early comics. More powerful mutants have been introduced later in the comic series.

** Although Rogue's character debuted in the X-Men comic books before HIV was discovered, this metaphor is illustrated in the X-Men films, where Rogue is unable to have intimate contact with men without potentially killing them.

*Finding Nemo*, or *X-Men*, they show a natural capacity to feel empathy for those who do not belong. Many other popular stories also have outcasts as main characters. But if children are capable of feeling so much empathy for outcasts, why is bullying so common in schools?

This is a complex question, because bullying has many causes. One cause is an abusive upbringing. I know children who became bullies because they had abusive parents. But perhaps a more common cause of bullying is the way our society conditions us to treat people. A friend told me that his Jewish father was constantly bullied by non-Jews while growing up in New York during the 1930s, because Jews in America were demonized and seen as subhuman. Part of the reason I was bullied in the 1980s was because American society had demonized people who look Asian, especially when fighting the Japanese in World War II, North Koreans and Chinese in the Korean War, and Vietnamese in the Vietnam War. Today many students of Middle Eastern descent are bullied in school because American society has demonized people in the Middle East.

It is a myth that children are bullied simply because they are unusual. If a high school boy looks like a muscular supermodel, that is certainly unusual, but he will probably not be bullied for it. Instead of being bullied for just being unusual, children are often bullied for possessing characteristics that society deems unattractive. When I was a child, boys were bullied for being short, wearing glasses, displaying "feminine" behavior, or being physically weak—characteristics that adults in our society had labeled as flaws to be rejected. When I was a child, I noticed that girls were much more likely to be teased for being smart or poor, rather than pretty and rich.

I am not saying a child cannot be bullied for being attractive, because children can also bully someone because they feel insecure and envious. However, even though the high school students considered physically imperfect by our society far outnumber those who look like supermodels, a high school student is much more likely to be bullied for being physically imperfect (by societal standards) than for looking like a supermodel. Some children attempt to diminish the anxiety they feel over their own imperfections by making fun of and emphasizing the imperfections of others.

This shows that a lot of bullying occurs because adults teach children to despise certain characteristics in other human beings. When I hear adults talk about the need to stop bullying, I have never heard them take responsibility by discussing how our adult-run society labels so many characteristics as undesirable flaws that should be shunned. Nelson Mandela offered us hope, because he realized that just as children can be taught by adults to hate, they can also be taught to love. Years before recent discoveries in neuroscience revealed the power of empathy, Mandela realized empathy is a natural part of being human. He said, "People must learn to hate, and if they can learn to hate, they can be taught to love, *for love comes more naturally to the human heart than its opposite* [emphasis added]."[3]

Although I have listed some common causes of bullying, there are certainly other causes. Whatever the cause may be, however, bullying has similar effects on all people. Being bullied tends to make us feel *alienated*, and alienation is the opposite of belonging. Alienation is the feeling of not belonging to the community of human beings who receive respect and empathy. Because our early ancestors relied on cooperation and community to survive, human beings crave belonging as much as they crave purpose and meaning. And we are tormented by alienation, just as we are tormented by a meaningless life with no purpose.

A woman told me that she was trying to explain to her husband (who sees himself as a nonconformist) that human beings crave belonging, yet he insisted that he does not care about belonging. I asked her, "How would he feel if you and every single one of his friends and family members decided to never speak to him again and treated him like an outcast?" She replied, "Obviously he would be devastated." I said, "Maybe he doesn't care about conformity, but there are many ways to feed our craving for belonging, and a strict sense of conformity is only one of those ways. All human beings, unless they are severely mentally ill, want to belong to some group of people, or nature, or something."

Someone might disagree by saying, "But the craving for belonging is childish. Great philosophers such as Socrates, Gandhi, and Martin Luther King Jr. overcame the silly need to belong. They were comfortable as outcasts and did not feel alienated, no matter how much their community rejected them." But Socrates, Gandhi, and King did not lose their craving to belong. Instead, they fulfilled it in a different way, by embracing the vision that they belonged to the entire human race. Socrates said, "I am not an Athenian or a Greek, but a citizen of the world."[4]

Gandhi felt a strong sense of belonging not only to humanity, but also to high ideals, nature, other forms of life, and the mysterious universe I call the cosmic ocean. Gandhi's strong sense of belonging transcended national boundaries and transformed his way of living. To him, belonging to humanity was not simply a belief, but a lifestyle. Gandhi's deep understanding of belonging caused him to see true religion as the *lifestyle of love* that emulates the lives of Buddha, Jesus, and other spiritual icons.

Gandhi felt he belonged to humanity *because he loved humanity*. For him the highest sense of belonging occurred through love's power to create deep connections with others. Gandhi scholar Bhikhu Parekh describes Gandhi's views on belonging:

> [According to Gandhi] all human beings are therefore sacred, inviolable, equal, and part of a single human family. The natural world too must be approached in a spirit of reverence and cosmic piety. Since we cannot survive without making demands on it, we must ensure that these are minimum and do not disturb its inner rhythm. A religion that encourages violence against outsiders, treats them as inferior human beings, or views the natural world as mere raw material to be exploited for human greed is guilty of "sin against God." As Gandhi puts it, "the greater the scope for compassion is a way of life, the more religion it has."[5]

Our societal standard of beauty is very narrow, like a tightrope where few people can stand without falling off. Because the few people who fit within this narrow standard of beauty surround us on billboards and other forms of advertising, nearly everyone in our society has shared a similar painful experience: feeling insecure about a physical feature we cannot change. Those considered attractive by societal standards can also feel insecure about their appearance, because if they base their self-worth on how they look, then growing old or being around someone considered more attractive can threaten their self-worth.

Also, just because we stand on the narrow tightrope of beauty at one moment in our life does not mean we will be there forever. A supermodel who stands on the tightrope of beauty during her youth might fall off as she grows older, because society no longer considers her aging face attractive. And a man admired for his toned and muscular body will notice his flesh beginning to sag as he ages. We are mistaken if we believe that any form of plastic surgery can truly defeat nature's most powerful force—the passage of time.

My painful childhood experiences have fueled my empathy for all human beings, regardless of whether they are deemed attractive or unattractive by societal standards, because we all share a common humanity. We all crave to belong, to not feel alienated, to possess self-worth, and to be treated with respect and empathy. Yet we hurt each other unnecessarily when we are confused, insecure, angered by our own suffering, and taught to hate. Together we must turn the tightrope of beauty into a wide road where we can all walk side by side as one human family. The survival of our fragile future depends on it.

## Expand Our Perception of Beauty

The first part of this book is titled Our Primordial Past and the second part is titled Our Fragile Future, because we must understand our past to protect our future. The four chapters in Our Primordial Past provided new answers that can help us overcome trauma, injustice, war, and the confusion of human existence. The four chapters in Our Fragile Future answer more questions about the human condition and list four practical steps (each chapter describes a different step) that can help us solve a wide variety of human problems and bring our civilization to its highest potential.

When people discuss serious issues such as racism, sexism, environmental destruction, and war, they rarely discuss how these issues are symptoms of much deeper problems. Racism, sexism, environmental destruction, and war are caused by problems of understanding, perception, values, and society. We can overcome these problems by embarking on a journey to understand human nature (which I discuss in *Will War Ever End?* and *The End of War*), strengthening the muscles of our shared humanity (which I discuss in *Peaceful Revolution*), learning how to wage peace (which I discuss in *The Art of Waging Peace*), and understanding the human condition and putting these four practical steps into action (which I discuss in *The Cosmic Ocean*).*

The first practical step for improving our world is to *expand our perception of beauty*. Is it possible to see all human races and skin colors as beautiful? Is it possible to see beauty not only in physical youth, but also in physical maturity? Can we see beauty in a greater variety of body types? Can we see beauty in Asian eyes? I first pondered this as a child watching the science-fiction television series *Star Trek: The Next Generation*, which is about the starship *Enterprise*'s mission to explore the galaxy.

Created by Gene Roddenberry and first airing on television in 1987, *Star Trek: The Next Generation* takes place in the twenty-fourth century. To me, one of the most inspiring aspects of Roddenberry's vision of the future is that human beings of all races have inherent dignity. Furthermore, among the starship *Enterprise*'s crew are alien crewmembers who look so diverse, they make the shape of my Korean eyes and differences in human skin color look relatively insignificant. Growing up in Alabama during the 1980s, my mixed-race background caused me to feel like an abomination, an outcast, a freak of nature. But if I had been a crewmember on the starship *Enterprise*, nobody would have looked down on me for being part African American and part Asian. I would have belonged to the human race.

*Star Trek: The Next Generation*'s acceptance of racial diversity is similar to the American dream's implication that we should be judged by our character, not by who our parents were. Roddenberry's vision of the future is also similar to Martin Luther King Jr.'s dream of the future expressed in his "I Have a Dream" speech: "I have a dream that my four little children will one

---

* "Human nature" and "the human condition" are both terms that describe our internal universe, but is there a difference between these two terms? Although there is some overlap between these terms, "human nature" deals more with the principles that govern human behavior, while "the human condition" deals more with the problem of human existence.

day live in a nation where they will not be judged by the color of their skin but by the content of their character."[6]

In 1976 the first women were admitted to West Point, where they would be trained to serve as officers. But in 1966, the original *Star Trek* television series featured a black female officer who graduated from Starfleet Academy, Roddenberry's science fiction version of West Point.* During the 1960s in the United States, black women graduating from military service academies truly was fiction, but today it has become a reality.

Nichelle Nichols, the actress who played the black female officer named Lieutenant Uhura, explains how she wanted to leave the original *Star Trek* series after the first season ended in 1967, but was convinced to stay by one of the show's fans:

> I told Gene [Roddenberry] after the end of the first season that I would not be returning to the show, that I wanted to return to my first love, which was musical theater. But I didn't know that meeting a *Star Trek* fan would change my life. [At a party] I was told that a fan wanted to meet me, and I turned and looked into the face of Dr. Martin Luther King. I was breathless.
>
> He says, "Yes, I'm a trekker. I'm a *Star Trek* fan." And he told me that *Star Trek* was one of the only shows that his wife Coretta and he would allow their little children to stay up and watch . . .
>
> I told him that I was leaving the show. All the smile came off his face and he said, "You can't do that." He said, "Don't you understand that for the first time we are seen as we should be seen. You don't have a black role. You have an equal role."
>
> And I went back to work on Monday morning. I went to Gene's office and I told him what had happened

---

* Starfleet Academy is based on military service academies such as the U.S. Naval Academy and West Point. According to www.startrek.com, Commander Uhura graduated from Starfleet Academy in 2261.

over the weekend, and he says, "Welcome home. We've got a lot of work to do."[7]

Roddenberry's vision of the future included respecting not only the dignity of all races, but also the dignity of all human beings, regardless of whether they are short, tall, old, young, or even bald. In *Star Trek: The Next Generation*, actor Patrick Stewart played Captain Picard, the officer in charge of the starship *Enterprise*. A bald actor, he describes how during the first press conference, a reporter criticized Roddenberry for having a bald captain in the twenty-fourth century:

> [My bald head] came up at the very first press conference. A reporter asked Gene Roddenberry, "Look, it doesn't make any sense, you've got a bald actor playing this part. Surely by the twenty-fourth century they will have found a cure for male-pattern baldness."
>
> And Gene Roddenberry said, "No, by the twenty-fourth century no one will care."
>
> It was one of the nicest things that's ever been said about men like me.[8]

History shows that societal standards of beauty are largely subjective, because physical characteristics once considered beautiful are now depicted as ugly. Hundreds of years ago, women were considered beautiful during the European Renaissance if they had some visible fat around their stomach and hips. But today, many women are so worried about having any visible fat around these areas that they suffer from dangerous eating disorders such as anorexia and bulimia.

Having some visible fat was an acceptable standard of beauty during the European Renaissance, and this body type is still viewed as beautiful in some countries today. But in modern America and many other parts of the world, things are different. Today the epitome of beauty for American women is to be tan with no visible fat around their bellies. And the epitome of beauty for American men is to be tan and muscular, with a small percentage of body fat so that their abdominal muscles show.

Even when men's magazines today feature a woman with a "curvy" body type, she is depicted with a flat stomach, unlike many of the women depicted in Renaissance paintings. And although a male body with muscle tone and low body fat was idealized in ancient Greece, muscle magazines and action movies in modern America idealize a male body that is a lot more muscular than the epitome of male beauty in ancient Greece. Standards of beauty can be subjective, because having some body fat was not the only standard of beauty during the Renaissance. Some Renaissance painters preferred to feature women who were thin.

Standards of beauty throughout history have been influenced by wealth. Hundreds of years ago, poor peasants were thin. Because so much of the inexpensive food in America contributes to weight gain and bad health, however, the poor in modern America are stereotyped as being overweight. Wealthier people are more likely to have the time and money necessary to eat well, stay in shape, and get a good tan. A tan and muscular body, which many American men desire today, used to be a body type common to slaves around the world. When I traveled to Uganda to teach a Peace Leadership workshop, the participants told me that a lot of men in Uganda want to have a receding hairline and a potbelly, because these features are often associated with status.

In cultures around the world, beauty is not only about belonging, but also self-worth. Because human beings deeply crave belonging and self-worth, we can prioritize beauty above our health. Excessive tanning is unhealthy for our skin, because it increases the risk of skin cancer and causes premature aging. Anorexia and bulimia also create significant health risks. Yet some people would rather damage their health than fall off the narrow tightrope of beauty.

I know many people who are proud of the hard work they have put into losing weight and getting in shape, and I admire their achievements. Obesity is certainly not good for our health, and the motivation to be healthy can encourage people to diet and exercise. But people can be very healthy without having the body of an ultra-thin supermodel, and extreme thinness can actually be unhealthy. If standards of beauty can change, as history proves, why can't we transform the narrow tightrope of beauty into a wide road where many different skin tones, facial features, and body types are considered beautiful?

Why is the tightrope of beauty in our society so narrow? One reason is because there are many ways to profit from a narrow standard of beauty. All societies have standards of beauty, but beauty standards in modern America are extremely narrow because making people believe they have physical defects can be very profitable. When people believe they have a physical defect that threatens their potential to attract a mate, ability to belong, or sense of self-worth, they will often spend a lot of money to correct that defect.

These physical defects include features that are not defects at all, such as the depiction of coarse African American hair as ugly. In comedian Chris Rock's documentary *Good Hair*, he shows the multibillion-dollar industry that has risen from the depiction of African American hair as defective. He also compassionately explores the trouble people go through to straighten their hair and the large amounts of money African American women spend on weaves.

It is easier to perceive ourselves as physically defective when computers greatly modify the images we see in advertisements. Because photographs in advertisements are digitally altered to give people flawless skin and perfect bodies, an unattainable standard of beauty is created. An unattainable standard of beauty can be very profitable because it makes nearly everyone seem physically defective as they normally appear. Advertisers know a simple truth: the more dissatisfied people are with their appearance, the easier it is to sell them products that promise to make them beautiful.

Expanding our perception of beauty beyond narrow and unattainable standards should not be used as an excuse for neglecting our personal responsibility to maintain a clean and dignified appearance. Some of the poorest people during the civil rights movement, along with Christian and Buddhist monks throughout history who embraced a simple life, still maintained cleanliness and dignity in their appearance. Expanding our perception of beauty means appreciating many forms of beauty and seeing the dignity that transcends distinctions. But as Susan B. Anthony, Frederick Douglass,

Mahatma Gandhi, and Martin Luther King Jr. demonstrated while struggling to attain their human rights, people are more likely to treat us with dignity when we make an effort to present ourselves in a dignified way.

Our society has narrowed the standard of beauty in a way that denies human dignity. Throughout history, elders were revered in many societies and admired for their life experience, but our society's extremely narrow standard of beauty tells us, "If you do not look young, you are defective." Because the negative attitude toward aging is getting so extreme, many people in our society are disturbed by the thought of having any wrinkles or a single gray hair. From an advertising perspective, that is a brilliant way to sell products. Other cultural influences also cause people to disrespect the elderly, and this problem will persist unless conscientious people wage peace to resolve it. Psychologist Susan Fiske tells us how widespread this disrespect is today:

> Well we've done our work on [studying] stereotyping across a lot of different countries, and I'm sorry to say that the sort of default stereotype of old people is the same in three dozen countries, that they're kind of pathetic and useless but well-intentioned. Here's the one exception: African Americans talking about [older] African Americans. So that's the one community in which we find respect for elders. One place that we thought we would find respect for elders was in East Asian cultures, and to our big surprise we did not in our own data . . . Looking at stereotypes of old people across the world, it's actually worse in East Asia. So that was not intuitive to us, but the data are what the data are. And in talking to people the explanation that we've come up with is that in East Asian cultures in particular, you respect your parents, you respect your teacher, you respect your promoter, but you don't have to respect old people in general because it's too much of a burden . . . [African American elders tend to be respected] because of the community role that they play,

and that's been very important in keeping families together and keeping communities together.[9]

The standard of beauty in our society is more flexible for men than for women. To offer one example, men are under less pressure than women to look young, because a male actor can have wrinkles and gray hair, yet still be considered a sex symbol. However, men in our society face other pressures, such as the pressure to be tall and wealthy.

As Patrick Stewart mentioned earlier, men are also pressured to have hair. When he was interviewed in 2010 on *The Tavis Smiley Show*, Smiley said, "There is something serious I want to pick up on, which as you well know, this hair business for men is a billion dollar industry worldwide. Saving it, putting it back, replacing it, holding on to it, making it grow. It's a billion dollar business. When you say you lost your hair at the age of nineteen . . . how did you navigate past that at nineteen?"[10]

Patrick Stewart responded, "At nineteen . . . I thought that a large part of my life had ended, certainly any romantic aspect of my life would be over. Who could possibly go for a guy who is nineteen and has no hair? The prospects were grim."[11]

There is evidence that our society's standard of beauty is widening in some ways. In a reader's poll conducted by the magazine *TV Guide*, Patrick Stewart was chosen as Sexiest Man on TV in 1992, and Most Bodacious Man on TV in 1993.[12] He would never have imagined this was possible when he was nineteen and depressed over his baldness. Nevertheless, the massive increase in plastic surgery procedures, escalating obsession with youth, and prevalence of anorexia and bulimia are just a few examples that reveal how our society's standard of beauty is narrowing in other ways.

What I find most surprising about our society's narrow standard of beauty is that it seems geared more toward making us feel defective and insecure about our appearance, rather than revealing what most people prefer in a mate. Advertisements directed at women can make them feel defective and insecure for not being thin enough, while advertisements directed at men can make them feel defective and insecure for not being muscular and masculine enough.

Although I have met men who are most attracted to very thin women, studies show that the majority of men do not prefer women with the ultra-thin bodies of runway models. In a similar way, I have met women who are most attracted to men with gigantic bodybuilder physiques, but the majority of women do not prefer men with the massive muscles and bulging veins of a professional bodybuilder. Anthropologist John Marshall Townsend describes how women's desire to be thin can have more to do with belonging and self-worth than appearing desirable to men:

> In the contemporary United States, women and men may disagree on how much body fat is attractive. Psychologists April Fallon and Paul Rozin found that college women generally believe that they are heavier than men prefer, and they want to be thinner than the figures they believe are most attractive to men. But men actually prefer heavier body types than what women believe they prefer—which makes women's preference for thinness two steps removed from what men actually consider the most attractive. These results suggest that women's standards are not simply a response to what men actually want. There are other influences at work. First, keeping thin and controlling weight help to give some women a feeling of control over their own lives. Second, women believe that thinness is generally considered a very positive personal feature over and above its possible effect on men. One of the reasons that thinness is generally considered a positive characteristic is that in Western societies upper-class women are thinner.
>
> In any era, the standards of the upper classes determine what is fashionable and acceptable in dress, appearance, and aesthetics. In our society, these standards are disseminated by the mass media—television, movies, fashion advertising, newspapers, and magazines—and depict what the rich and famous are doing. Whether they know

it or not, the middle classes tend to emulate these standards and adopt many of them. Top fashion designers, for example, create expensive couture originals for their upper-class clientele; in time, cheaper versions of these originals will appear in department stores. The ideal of female thinness appears to have followed this same trickle-down pattern: it began in the upper classes and has now been affected by the middle classes as well.

Given the Fallon and Rozin findings, it may be likely that many women know what men prefer, but because women emphasize status more in their standards for partners than men do, they disregard to some extent what men actually prefer because they want to look like upper-class women . . . Evidently, some psychological research and the persistence of curvier women in men's magazines suggest that many men refuse to follow the dictates of high fashion.[13]

To show how flexible standards of beauty can be, Japanese men used to shave the tops of their heads in a way that mimicked male-pattern baldness. This fashion did not involve shaving their entire heads, but only enough of their hair so that it looked like they were balding. This fashion derived from the samurai—members of the upper class—who shaved the tops of their heads (while leaving their topknots intact) so that their helmets would fit more comfortably. In a society where wisdom and experience were admired and people often died young, balding could also be seen as a symbol of maturity and status.

Historian Anthony Bryant tells us: "Shaving the top of the head, something often believed to be an indicator of *samurai* status, was more widespread [in Japan] than often realized. Commoners—farmers, merchants, townsmen—all sported shaved pates and topknots. The fashion certainly originated with the *samurai*, but it caught on with the populace at large. Its origin is believed to have something to do with wearing helmets so often that a shaved head was simply more comfortable."[14]

Our discussion of past standards of beauty and today's especially narrow standard of beauty reveals there are two kinds of beauty. The first kind is *commodified beauty*, which occurs when beauty is reduced so much to a commodity that we cannot see beyond the surface. This surface can consist of skin color, facial features, body type, or the clothes we wear. There is nothing wrong with people enjoying how they look in a new set of clothes, but many people in our society judge and even dehumanize those who wear cheap clothes and unfashionable shoes.

Tim Gunn, a fashion consultant who appeared on the reality television show *Project Runway*, seems like an unlikely person to support school uniforms that restrict students' fashion choices. But he explains, "I have recalibrated [my] thinking about the [school] uniform. I find it's very democratizing. You don't have to get up in the morning and think about what am I going to wear. And for girls in particular, I love a uniform, because the fashion pressures on teenagers and younger women are extraordinary. And living in New York City, I love the private schools that have a uniform, and I have to say I have something of a disdain for those that don't, because the fashion competition [in schools] is ridiculously stupid. In fact it's absurd."[15]

The Dr. Seuss children's book *The Sneetches and Other Stories* contains a metaphor for commodified beauty. The Sneetches are yellow creatures. A group of them, known as the Star-Belly Sneetches, have a green star on their bellies. The green star is considered a feature of beauty and elite status. The Plain-Belly Sneetches lack a green star on their bellies. Similar to racial segregation, the Star-Belly Sneetches treat the Plain-Belly Sneetches as unattractive and inferior.

One day a salesman named Sylvester McMonkey McBean tells the Plain-Belly Sneetches that he can put a green star on their bellies with his Star-On machine. This procedure costs three dollars, and the Plain-Belly Sneetches line up to give McBean their money. The original Star-Belly Sneetches become angry that they no longer look distinct and exceptional, so McBean tells them he will remove their green stars with his Star-Off machine. This procedure costs ten dollars, and the original Star-Belly Sneetches line up to give McBean their money.

The Sneetches run back and forth between the two machines, repeatedly getting their green stars removed and replaced, until all their money is gone and McBean is rich. McBean drives away laughing. The Sneetches learn from the experience, however, by expanding their perception of beauty. Realizing how trivial the green stars truly were, they learn to respect each other's dignity, regardless of whether they have green stars or not.

This story is a metaphor for commodified beauty and the trivial nature of prejudice. This story also shows how fickle fashion can be. The green stars symbolize the shallow surface features that hide our common humanity and inherent dignity. A second kind of beauty, *priceless beauty*, occurs when we see beyond the green stars.

Priceless beauty is not a commodity we can buy. It is a perception, an attitude, a vision, a way of seeing what is both visible and invisible to the eyes. When I look at human beings, animals, and nature through the *perception of priceless beauty*, I see beyond the shallow surface and a profound new world opens up to me. I feel deeply connected to human beings, animals, and nature in meaningful and fulfilling ways. When we see with the perception of priceless beauty, our suppressed human powers such as empathy, appreciation, and sublime joy burst out of us like a roaring fire, enveloping our world with love's light.

If we truly want to solve problems such as racism, sexism, environmental destruction, and war, we must develop our perception of priceless beauty by strengthening the muscles of our humanity (which I discuss in *Peaceful Revolution*). Expanding our perception of beauty is a challenging and gradual struggle, like climbing a tall mountain. But this journey is well worth the effort, because the perception of priceless beauty allows us to live the lifestyle of love symbolized by Jesus, Buddha, and other spiritual icons.

Protecting our fragile future requires us to develop our perception of priceless beauty, because seeing beyond the shallow surface allows us to experience deep connection with others and transcend the boundaries that divide us. Any system that dehumanizes us based on how we look produces both cruelty and brutality. To combat these unjust systems, the perception of priceless beauty repels dehumanization like light casting out shadow. Because the perception of priceless beauty recognizes the dignity inherent to the mystery of life, the more we expand our perception of beauty, the more we threaten all unjust systems, including the war system. It's difficult to bomb people when we perceive them as beautiful.

A common theme in every chapter of this book is the *expansion of empathy*, especially for those we do not understand. Increasing our understanding allows us to enter the transcendent spiritual realm of radical empathy where priceless beauty is all around us. In our daily lives, we can all spread the message of priceless beauty not only by seeing deep and diverse forms of beauty, but also by speaking to each other with respect and treating each other with dignity. We can also spread the message of priceless beauty by creating art and social norms that recognize the dignity of life, and working to transform the narrow tightrope of commodified beauty into the wide road of priceless beauty.

In my early twenties I had a dream about a part of myself I once hated. In my dream I was looking at a door that led to freedom, but between me and the door was a winding path. The path was several hundred feet long, but extremely narrow—only a few inches wide. If I slipped I would fall into a dark pit below and plunge to my death. Navigating this dangerous path would be very difficult, I realized, because I was holding a heavy box, and for some strange reason I was not allowed to put it down. When I turned to my right I saw a Korean boy, shorter than me, whose Asian features were more pronounced than my own. I realized he symbolized a part of me. He looked at me without saying anything, and I stared back, also silent.

Within that silence, I acknowledged his existence, accepting him as a part of myself. When I did that, he reached out gently and took the heavy box from me. Holding it over his head, he led me down the narrow, winding, dangerous path toward the door, toward freedom. After we safely traversed the path I could not see him anymore, but I felt like we had merged into one being. I reached out my hand to open the door, and then I woke up.

# CHAPTER 6

# The Sanity of Humanity

## *The Art of Fighting Demons*

The most difficult opponent a human being will ever face is the demon in one's own heart. Many kinds of demons can make their home in the human heart; we call them by names such as fear, hatred, greed, selfishness, self-loathing, alienation, addiction, trauma, hopelessness, cynicism, bitterness, and rage.

In some religions and mythologies, a supernatural demon can be exorcised through a ceremony, but the psychological demons that reside in the human heart are not as easily defeated. Psychological demons such as hatred, trauma, and bitterness cannot be exorcised through a quick religious ceremony performed by someone else. They must be overcome by embarking on a lifelong spiritual journey that leads deep within us. The only person who can defeat the demons within me, is me, and the only one who can defeat the demons within you, is you. But we don't have to battle demons alone, and I am proof that demons can be confronted, understood, and transformed.

Despite all the suffering I have endured, I have resisted the temptation to become cynical about humanity. My hope, empathy, and positive outlook do not result from being naive, but from winning many battles against the demons within me. When we confront the demons within us, we can gain spiritual treasures such as realistic hope and radical empathy. A life focused on cultivating these spiritual treasures gives us far greater purpose, meaning, and joy than a life obsessed with pursuing excessive material wealth. Anyone who learns the art of fighting demons can become wealthy with realistic hope, radical empathy, and other spiritual riches that open the gateway to bliss.

When I say "the art of fighting demons," I am addressing a paradox about the process of inner healing. My spiritual journey has taught me that I should not hate my psychological demons, nor see them as evil. The paradox of inner healing is that when we stop running from our demons and instead fight them effectively, we no longer perceive them as demons, but as teachers. Martial arts and Buddhist philosophy taught me that our fiercest opponents are often our greatest teachers.

When we confront and understand our demons, only then can we transform them into teachers. When we avoid rather than confront our demons, however, psychologist John Welwood calls this *spiritual bypassing*. He explains:

> Spiritual bypassing is a term I coined to describe a process I saw happening in the Buddhist community I was in, and also in myself. Although most of us were sincerely trying to work on ourselves, I noticed a widespread tendency to use spiritual ideas and practices to sidestep or avoid facing unresolved emotional issues, psychological wounds, and unfinished developmental tasks.

> When we are spiritually bypassing, we often use the goal of awakening or liberation to rationalize what I call *premature transcendence*: trying to rise above the raw and messy side of our humanness before we have fully faced and made peace with it . . . Trying to move beyond our psychological and emotional issues by sidestepping them is dangerous . . .

> I'm interested in how it plays out in relationships, where spiritual bypassing often wreaks its worst havoc. If you were a yogi in a cave doing years of solo retreat, your psychological wounding might not show up so much because your focus would be entirely on your practice, in an environment that may not aggravate your relational wounds. It's in relationships that our unresolved psychological issues tend to show up most intensely. That's

because psychological wounds are always relational—they form in and through our relationships with our early caretakers.

The basic human wound, which is prevalent in the modern world, forms around not feeling loved or intrinsically lovable as we are. Inadequate love or attunement is shocking and traumatic for a child's developing and highly sensitive nervous system. And as we internalize how we were parented, our capacity to value ourselves, which is also the basis for valuing others, becomes damaged. I call this a "relational wound" or the "wound of the heart."[1]

My way of dealing with trauma is different from the way it is often dealt with today. My approach is not to repress trauma, but to learn from it. My approach is to transform my trauma into a teacher. When we learn from our painful life experiences, those experiences gain new purpose and meaning. To offer one example, if we use our painful life experiences to develop more empathy for people who have shared similar experiences, our pain becomes fuel that propels us to greater heights of awareness, understanding, and connectedness.

At West Point I learned to confront rather than run away from my suffering, and to transform my pain into progress. Just as the physical adversity of exercise makes our bodies stronger, West Point taught me that overcoming psychological adversity can make our minds stronger. Before attending West Point, I first learned this philosophy of *strength through adversity* from an unlikely source—the video games I played during my childhood.

Living in a violent household and being bullied as a child gave me an obsession with video games. For me, video games were portals into other worlds. In these other worlds I was not a helpless child being beaten by my father or a racial outcast alienated from society. Instead, I was a powerful warrior who could not only defend myself, but I could also protect others. I am certainly not alone in my childhood obsession with video games, because video games give many children a sense of power, control, freedom, adventure, and purpose that they do not experience in the real world.

Video games taught me an important life lesson. A common theme in video games is descending into a dark and dangerous place such as a dungeon, cave, or labyrinth in order to defeat an evil force. This descent into danger allows your character in the game to grow stronger and your skills as a player to improve. In the video game *The Legend of Zelda*, for example, I would descend into dark labyrinths filled with monsters, and in those foreboding places I would retrieve treasures, in the form of weapons and useful items that I needed to succeed in the game. Video games such as this taught me that great treasures are hidden in the darkest places, and that I have the power to find bright light in the deepest darkness.

This theme in video games reflects human psychology and ancient mythology. Joseph Campbell tells us, "The goal . . . is to find those [deepest] levels in the psyche that open, open, open, and finally open to the mystery of your Self being Buddha consciousness or the Christ. That's the [spiritual] journey . . . It is by going down into the abyss that we recover the treasures of life. Where you stumble, there lies your treasure. The very cave you are afraid to enter turns out to be the source of what you are looking for. The damned thing in the cave that was so dreaded has become the center . . . The goal is to bring the jewel [from the cave] back to the world, to join the two things together."[2]

By analyzing mythology, Joseph Campbell gives us guidance into *the art of living* and *the art of waging peace*,* which are other ways of saying the art of fighting demons. Many other psychologists, spiritual teachers, and scholars of mythology also give us insights into these art forms. Professor of mythology Grant Voth discusses how the greatest human treasures are often buried in the darkest places of the human mind—a place that seems filled with metaphorical demons and dragons. Professor Voth explains how ancient mythology contains metaphors for the psychological monsters we must overcome during our spiritual journey:

> The underworld or the dragon or the monster that
> later heroes will have to face is really one's own fear, which

---

* I discuss *the art of living* and *the art of waging peace* in my other books.

has to be mastered in order to achieve individuation [personal growth]. Bearing and Cashford say that in all myths the hero's quest is a kind of symbolic drama of what is really an inner conflict and it's valid in any age for men and women alike.

They quote Carl Jung on this issue, and this is what Jung says about this particular kind of reading [of mythology]: "In myths the hero is the one who conquers the dragon, not the one who is devoured by it. Also he is no hero who never met the dragon or who, if he once saw it, declared afterwards that he saw nothing. Equally, only one who has risked the fight with the dragon and is not overcome by it wins the hoard, the treasure hard to attain. He alone has a genuine claim to self-confidence, for he has faced the dark ground of himself, and has thereby gained himself. This experience gives him faith and trust . . . For everything that menaced him from inside has been made his own . . ."

[According to Joseph Campbell] the journey taken by the hero [in ancient mythology] is not a geographic or literal one, but it's rather a psychological journey. It's a quest not into the world out there, but into the world [within us], specifically a quest into one's own unconscious. It's in the unconscious, Campbell says, that we meet the dragons and demons that we have to fight and slay, we meet the goddess, and we have to become reconciled with our father. All of this is an internal thing. It happens within ourselves. The boon that one brings back from a Campbell quest is an enhanced awareness of one's self, making life richer, and also we bring back an enhanced understanding of how all psyches work, so that we can bring back enlightenment both for the individual and for the community.[3]

Like ancient mythology, modern video games can offer us guidance for overcoming the struggles of life. In *The Legend of Zelda*, the items needed to overcome evil are hidden in dark labyrinths. In a similar way, the ideas needed to overcome war, injustice, and the confusion of human existence are hidden in dark subjects such as trauma, cruelty, brutality, and violence, which we have explored in this book.

Just as doctors who want to promote health must confront rather than run away from the causes of illness, those of us who want to promote peace must confront rather than run away from the causes of violence. We must not be afraid to explore and understand trauma, war, and injustice, just as doctors must not be afraid to explore and understand illnesses, diseases, and injuries. A peace activist unwilling to learn about trauma is like a doctor unwilling to look at a cancer patient or broken bone.

Trauma and many other forms of adversity can teach us, but when we run away from our problems for our entire lives, we cannot learn and grow stronger. There are numerous ways to retreat from our suffering. Many people try to drown their suffering in excessive amounts of alcohol, not realizing that suffering can hold its breath forever. People also hide from their suffering behind a wall of endless distractions, not realizing that suffering can walk through walls. And some people flee from their suffering by escaping into fantasy worlds, not realizing that suffering has the power to invade and destroy worlds.

Because I could not physically escape the pain of living with my father, as a child I often escaped into the fantasy worlds of video games. I used video games as a form of escapism throughout my childhood, but my suffering was always close behind me, stalking me like my shadow. At West Point I decided to apply the lesson of confronting darkness, a common theme in the fantasy worlds of video games, to my real life.

The perception of radical empathy teaches us to not look down on people who don't confront their suffering, because every person walks a unique spiritual path, and sometimes the agonies experienced through alcoholism, drug addiction, and escapism also serve as great teachers. Another reason to not look down on those who don't confront their suffering is because most of us have never been taught how to confront, understand, and transform our suffering. To help remedy this problem, every book in this series offers guidance for living well and achieving our highest human potential.

Another reason I do not look down on people who don't confront their suffering is because descending into darkness can be dangerous, like entering a metaphorical dragon's lair. Since my violent upbringing has made me berserk prone, descending into darkness to find hidden sources of light has been very dangerous for me. You must do what you think is best for yourself and carve your own unique spiritual journey out of your experiences, like a sculptor carving a unique masterpiece out of stone. As long as your empathy continues to grow, and you notice an increase in your sense of purpose, meaning, belonging, and self-worth, then you are making progress on the spiritual path. However, always remember that the spiritual path is a *winding path*. It does not travel in a straight line.

The winding path of spiritual development means we all have emotional highs and lows, so we should not hate ourselves when we temporarily regress into our old painful habits. Many people despise themselves when they regress into old habits they are trying to get rid of, but we should learn from our setbacks, keep the progress we have made in perspective, and be kind to ourselves. I don't experience radical empathy or the perception of priceless beauty during every minute of every day, but practicing the art of living has allowed me to experience these treasures for more minutes on more days.

Even the Fourteenth Dalai Lama (who is widely regarded as a spiritual master) still occasionally gets angry. Describing the pain caused by anger, he said, "If we live our lives continually motivated by anger and hatred, even our physical health deteriorates . . . Happiness cannot come from hatred or anger. Nobody can say, 'Today I am happy because this morning I was very angry.' On the contrary, people feel uneasy and sad and say, 'Today I am not very happy, because I lost my temper this morning.'"[4]

In a 2010 interview, at the age of seventy-five, the Fourteenth Dalai Lama discussed his anger and our incredible human ability to heal our anger through the power of compassion and calm:

> Mostly . . . my mental state is quite calm and then also
> I consider every soul as human being, basically we are all

the same, nothing different, physically we are the same. Of course there is a little difference in colour, or size of the nose, otherwise you see we are completely same . . . So I never look at human beings as the President or King or Prime Minister or beggar . . . in my eyes all are the same. So whenever I meet these people I say, "Look at them, they are just other human beings . . . our brothers and sisters." So this also creates more peace in my mind. But I may not be that level of mind not always, occasionally I burst . . .

If you ask some silly question repeatedly, then I may lose my temper . . . Actually once it happened in America, I think most probably in New Jersey . . . one *New York Times* columnist, one lady, she asked me, first some other questions, then she asked me, what I want my name or legacy to be in future. And I told her, I am a Buddhist practitioner and I do not think of my name like that. Then we had some other discussion, then again she asked me the same question, and I answered in the same way, then again after some time she asked me the same question . . . then I lost my temper . . .

Sometime when it is a more serious form of anger, I try to separate myself from anger, then watch my anger, that emotion . . . then immediately the strength of anger diminishes, according to my own experience. And then, I also share [by discussing my problems] with my friends . . . in order to bring more calmness to my mind. You cannot have some sort of special practice for each case, but you must build your basic mental attitude in a healthy way, like in the case of a healthy body if the immune system is strong then some virus or germs can't disturb you much, so similarly, your mental attitude has to be calm, then if some disturbances come, even if some negative emotions come, they remain for very short period, all the emotions remain on the surface, and do not disturb much

in depth . . . So there is no point in neglecting taking care
of our mind. Spirituality does not necessarily mean God,
Buddha, but just about mental calmness. So that practice
of compassion is very very helpful for a calm mind.[5]

Radical empathy means having compassion not only for others, but also
for ourselves. When we suffer from trauma, developing compassion for ourselves can be as difficult as developing compassion for those who have hurt
us, because trauma can severely damage our self-worth, making us feel like
we don't deserve compassion. As we heal our traumatic wounds, psychological scar tissue can still remain, which I continue to struggle with. When my
psychological demons seem to turn against me long after I thought I had
befriended them, I realize I still have something to learn from them.

By learning from and helping each other, we do not have to fight
demons alone. I have learned from celebrated figures such as Gandhi, but I
have also learned from the unsung heroes of peace and justice—people I col-
laborate with on the mission of peace who continue to inspire me. And I
have learned by transforming my agonies, setbacks, and mistakes into learning experiences. Teachers can be found in the most unlikely places when we
listen to the world around us and the reality within us. When we walk the
road to peace with an open mind and willing heart, we all gain the power to
transform demons and darkness into teachers and strength.

## Feed Our Spiritual Organs

I use darkness as a metaphor for psychological agony, not only because
darkness conveys the fear and danger associated with pain, but also because
the underworld of agony is a mysterious place. Psychological agony is mysterious like the dark depths of the ocean, a cave where sunlight barely enters,
and the night sky on a moonless night. The labyrinth of our unconscious
mind, where the beast of trauma resides, unable to rest, is even darker and
more mysterious than the pain of our conscious thoughts. Darkness symbolizes mystery, but what treasures do we find when we descend into darkness?

When I explored the dark underworld of my agony and descended deeper into the shadowy labyrinth of my unconscious trauma, I did not know what I would find. Would I find hopelessness and insanity? Or would I find solutions to my strife? After years of battling the darkness within me, I gradually befriended the shadows in my soul, learning from the sage that is human suffering. The light I found transcends the limits of language, erupting in rays of realistic hope, radical empathy, and revelatory understanding that must be experienced to truly be understood.

In my books, I have tried to communicate the light I gained during my spiritual journey, even though language has its limits. I have also tried to reflect this light in my daily life, even though I am not a bringer of light. Instead, I am merely a servant of the light that burns within you, me, and all human beings. Even though many of us have not learned how to see the light that illuminates our inner and outer worlds, Herman Hesse explained that it shines within us all:

> The author who has awakened you or given you an insight is neither a light nor a torch-bearer; he is at best a window through which light can shine on the reader . . . His only function is that of a window: not to stand in the way of the light but to let the light through. Possibly he will long to do noble deeds, to become a benefactor of mankind, and just as possibly such a longing will be his ruin, preventing him from admitting the light. He must not be guided and spurred on by pride or by a frantic striving for humility* but solely by love of light, by openness to reality and truth . . .
>
> A writer must believe in the light, he must know it through incontrovertible experience and must be as wide

---

* Herman Hesse makes an important point here, because true humility does not arise from "frantic striving," but understanding and appreciation. In *Peaceful Revolution* I discuss how humility is a vein in the muscle of appreciation. Unlike false humility (which can be common in our society), true humility flows naturally from sources such as a broad perspective that recognizes our interdependence with others.

open to it as possible, but he must not regard himself as a
bringer of light and surely not as the light itself. For, if he
does, the window will close and the light, which does not
need us, will go other ways.[6]

The light is a metaphor not only for a higher bliss than ignorance, but
also for truth. As I explained in chapter 2, I have met people who say, "All
truth is relative. We cannot really know what is true and what is untrue,
because there is no such thing as truth." *But there is such a thing as truth.* To
mention just a few examples, it is a scientific fact that African Americans are
not genetically subhuman and inferior to white people. It is a scientific fact
that women are not intellectually and morally inferior to men. And it is a
scientific fact that the earth and other planets in our solar system revolve
around the sun. Not long ago, people were imprisoned, beaten, and even
killed for promoting these truths.

The untruth of African Americans' racial inferiority was used to justify
state-sanctioned slavery, and the untruth of women's intellectual and moral
inferiority was used to rationalize laws denying American women the right
to vote. Truth is eternal, but the lies that sustain oppression and injustice
have a lifespan. Since the birth of humanity it has always been true that
women are not less than human and no race was designed for slavery, but
lies suppress these truths.

Another truth, which affects all of us regardless of our skin color or gender, is that *human beings crave self-worth.* We can witness this truth not only
within us, but all around us. As I mentioned earlier in this book, human
beings are capable of feeling worthless, despising themselves when they look
in the mirror, and hating their very existence. As far as we know, we are the
only species on the planet that can have freedom, companionship, good
health, and a belly full of food, yet still be so tortured by a sense of worth-
lessness that we seek comfort in addiction, destruction, or suicide.

When Greek warriors in the *Iliad* or Japanese samurai fought for honor,
they were really fighting for their sense of worth. In many past cultures,
honor was seen as a sense of worth based on what others said and thought
about us. To insult people's honor meant insulting their worth. Because

human beings crave a sense of worthiness, countless people throughout history have been willing to risk their lives to defend their sense of self-worth.

In modern society our sense of self-worth can be influenced by factors we have little control over, such as fickle changes in standards of beauty. Consequently, attaining self-worth is a challenging struggle for many people. Erich Fromm explains how low self-worth can result when our society conditions us to see ourselves not as human beings who possess inherent dignity, but as commodities:

> [In many cases in our society] a person is not concerned with his life and happiness, but with becoming salable. This feeling might be compared to that of a commodity, of handbags on a counter, for instance, could they feel and think. Each handbag would try to make itself as "attractive" as possible in order to attract customers and to look as expensive as possible in order to obtain a higher price than its rivals. The handbag sold for the highest price would feel elated, since that would mean it was the most "valuable" one; the one which was not sold would feel sad and convinced of its own worthlessness. This fate might befall a bag which, though excellent in appearance and usefulness, had the bad luck to be out of date because of a change in fashion . . .
>
> Since modern man experiences himself both as the seller and as the commodity to be sold on the market, his self-esteem depends on conditions beyond his control. If he is "successful," he is valuable; if he is not, he is worthless. The degree of insecurity which results from this orientation can hardly be overestimated. If one feels that one's own value is not constituted primarily by the human qualities one possesses, but by one's success on a competitive market with ever-changing conditions, one's self-esteem is bound to be shaky and in constant need of confirmation by others. Hence one is driven to strive relentlessly for suc-

cess, and any setback is a severe threat to one's self-esteem;
helplessness, insecurity, and inferiority feelings are the
result . . .

The way one experiences others is not different from
the way one experiences oneself. Others are experienced
[not as human beings with inherent dignity but] as commodities like oneself . . .[7]

Although many people have low self-worth due to the *commodification
of life* (in chapter 5 we discussed how life and beauty are reduced to commodities), as a child my self-worth became damaged due to my violent
upbringing and the racism I experienced. When children are abused, they
can rationalize their abuse by telling themselves, "I must deserve to be treated
like this. I must not deserve to be treated compassionately, because I have
low worth." When people who are physically, verbally, or sexually abused
lack a strong support network, feelings of low self-worth are common.

In addition to the commodification of life and the effects of abuse,
another cause of low self-worth is negative and positive stereotypes. Negative
stereotypes include myths such as "all women are emotionally unstable" and
"African Americans are not smart." Positive stereotypes include myths such
as "all Asians are good at math" and "all black men are extremely athletic."
If an Asian person isn't exceptionally skilled at math and a black man is not
a star athlete, yet society expects them to be this way, this can contribute to
feelings of low self-worth.

In an article in *Psychology Today*, Art Markman describes the other harmful effects of positive stereotypes:

In the United States, there are cultural stereotypes that
Asians are good at math and that women are nurturing. If
hearing a negative stereotype about your group gets you
upset, does hearing a positive stereotype have the opposite
effect? This question was explored in a series of studies by
John Oliver Siy and Sapna Cheryan in the January, 2013
issue of the *Journal of Personality and Social Psychology* . . .

In one study, Asian Americans were brought to the lab where they engaged in a task along with a White participant (who was actually one of the experimenters posing as a participant). In the experiment, each participant was going to fill out a packet. One packet had math problems in it, while the other had verbal problems in it. After a rigged coin flip to make the selection process appear random, the White participant was chosen to select who would fill out each packet.

In the control condition, the White participant handed the math packet to the Asian participant and said, "How about you take this packet, and I'll work on this one." In the positive stereotype condition, the White participant said, "I know all Asians are good at math, how about you take the math packet. I'll work on this one."

After completing the packets, participants rated how much they liked their partner and they filled out some other scales including a measure of how much they felt like their partner depersonalized them by reducing them to a member of their racial group.

Positive stereotypes did not make people feel good. When the White participant used a positive stereotype, the Asian participant liked them less and felt more depersonalized. The positive stereotype also made the participants angry. Statistically, the amount of depersonalization they felt explained the amount of dislike they felt for their partner.

Other studies in this series demonstrated a similar effect with women who were told that they were nurturing or cooperative because of their gender. These studies also ruled out some other explanations like the possibility that Asian Americans react negatively to the positive stereotype because it does not acknowledge that they are both Asians and Americans . . .

I suspect there is an additional factor at play in these studies. When someone uses a positive stereotype to judge you, it is reasonable to assume that it is only a matter of time until they apply negative stereotypes as well.[8]

During my childhood I actually liked positive stereotypes. Even though I did not enjoy math as a child, I liked hearing people say, "All Asians are good at math," because it made me proud of my racial background. When children bullied me because of my race, it gave me a strange sense of comfort to think, "You white kids can make fun of my Asian eyes all you want, but my race is smarter than your race." I never said this out loud, but it felt good to think it. Because I am part white, this was an odd thing to think, but when people insult our racial background, we can search for comfort in odd thinking.

In fifth grade I was the fastest sprinter in my grade, winning first place in both the sprinting event and long jump during the annual athletic competition. Years later when I experienced rapid muscle growth from lifting weights, I thought, "I am athletic because I am part black." Although there is evidence that slave owners bred their slaves to be muscular, all African Americans are not athletic, and the vast majority of African Americans are not athletic enough to play in the NBA and NFL, even though these organizations contain a high proportion of black men.

I liked the stereotype that black men are physically superior to other races, however, because this counterbalanced my painful experience of feeling like a racially inferior freak. It's difficult for people to understand how freakish I felt growing up in Alabama during the 1980s, being part black, white, and Asian. I took pride in positive stereotypes as a desperate attempt to counterbalance the negative stereotypes of Asians and black people. This approach did not heal my damaged self-worth at all. Instead, it delayed my later realization that we are a global human family.

To counter negative racial stereotypes, people such as Frederick Douglass had to work exceptionally hard to raise the self-worth of his race. The activists who wanted to abolish slavery ridiculed Douglass for wanting to start his own newspaper, because they did not think a former slave who lacked formal education would be smart enough to accomplish such a difficult task. Douglass explains:

> [When talking to white activists in the movement to abolish slavery] I told them that perhaps the greatest hindrance to the adoption of abolition principles by the people of the United States was the low estimate everywhere in that country placed upon the Negro as a man—that because of his assumed natural inferiority people reconciled themselves to his enslavement and oppression as being inevitable, if not desirable. The grand thing to be done, therefore, was to change this estimation by disproving his inferiority and demonstrating his capacity for a more exalted civilization than slavery and prejudice had assigned him.
>
> In my judgment, a tolerably well-conducted press in the hands of persons of the despised race would, by calling out and making them acquainted with their own latent powers, by enkindling their hope of a future and developing their moral force, prove a most powerful means of removing prejudice and awakening an interest in them. At that time there was not a single newspaper in the country regularly published by the colored people, though many attempts had been made to establish such, and had from one cause or another failed . . .
>
> My [white] friends in Boston had been informed of what I was intending, and I expected to find them favorably disposed toward my cherished enterprise. In this I was mistaken. They had many reasons against it . . . This opposition from a quarter so highly esteemed, and to which I had been accustomed to look for advice and direction, caused me not only to hesitate, but inclined me to abandon the undertaking. All previous attempts [by black people] to establish such a journal having failed, I feared lest

I should but add another to the list, and thus contribute another proof of the mental deficiencies of my race . . .

I can easily pardon those who saw in my persistence an unwarrantable ambition and presumption. I was but nine years from slavery . . . My American friends looked at me with astonishment. "A wood-sawyer" offering himself to the public as an editor! A slave, brought up in the depths of ignorance, assuming to instruct the highly civilized people of the North in the principles of liberty, justice, and humanity! The thing looked absurd. Nevertheless, I persevered. I felt that the want of education, great as it was, could be overcome by study, and that wisdom would come by experience . . .

The most distressing part of it all was the offense which I saw I must give my friends of the old anti-slavery organization, by what seemed to them a reckless disregard of their opinion and advice. I am not sure that I was not under the influence of something like a slavish adoration of these good people, and I labored hard to convince them that my way of thinking about the matter was the right one, but without success . . .

[My newspaper] *The North Star* was a large sheet, published weekly, at a cost of $80 per week, and an average circulation of 3,000 subscribers. There were many times when, in my experience as editor and publisher, I was very hard pressed for money, but by one means or another I succeeded so well as to keep my pecuniary engagements, and to keep my antislavery banner steadily flying during all the conflict from the autumn of 1847 till the union of the states was assured and emancipation was a fact accomplished.[9]

By asserting his dignity through his attitude and actions, Frederick Douglass was able to maintain his self-worth despite ridicule and racism. The concept of self-esteem, as it is widely understood today, is different from the self-worth Douglass possessed. Self-worth is a foundation we can stand on even when we are ridiculed. It is a foundation that does not require constant praise. There are productive and counterproductive ways to praise children (which we will discuss), and counterproductive forms of praise can actually damage our self-worth.

The life experiences that shaped my understanding of self-worth began when I was in preschool. When I was a three-year-old in preschool, the teacher divided us into different reading groups based on our ability. I was the only student in the "Mickey Mouse Group," the highest reading group, because I was the only child in the class able to read complete sentences. Reading was very easy for me, but the teacher never told me I was a good reader, nor did she compare me to the other children.

I do not recall the teacher ever saying, "The Mickey Mouse Group is the best group." Instead, children were divided into reading groups named after Mickey Mouse, Donald Duck, Pluto, and other popular Disney characters, all of whom were friends. The teacher had a creative approach, because she allowed her students to learn according to their ability, she did not overtly rank us as superior or inferior, and she did not inflate my impressionable three-year-old ego. Rather than overrelying on praise to make us read, she made reading a fun activity associated with cartoon characters.

At that time I did in fact realize I was the best reader in the class. Because all of the groups were named after popular Disney characters, however, everyone had worth and I did not become arrogant and narcissistic.

When I was five years old, I played in a youth soccer league. During a game I vividly remember, my team won three to zero, and I scored all three points for my team. When I scored the second and third goals, my coach knelt down, looked me in the eyes, and shouted enthusiastically, "You scored another one for us, buddy!" His joyful reaction filled me with excitement. After the game was over, nobody praised me, and I did not care. Knowing I had scored the goals and seeing my coach happy gave me sufficient gratification.

During a game later in the soccer season, I did not score a single goal during the entire game, and I thought I played terribly. At least half a dozen parents, including my mother, told me afterward, "You played so well!" This really confused me and made me a little angry. I wondered, "When I scored three goals, no one told me I played well, but now why is everyone telling me I did great?" The most confusing part of this experience was that I distinctly remember second-guessing myself and thinking, "Did I not play well when I scored those three goals, and did I play well when I thought I played terribly?"*

We must realize that some forms of praise can confuse us and even weaken our self-worth. Psychologist Carol Dweck explains how praising children by telling them, "You are so smart!" can make them feel anxious and insecure about their self-worth. If children base their self-worth on being praised for their intelligence, then getting a low grade or struggling intellectually with a problem can cause them to feel worthless. Her studies show that praising specific factors such as work ethic, which children have a lot of power to control, is more productive for a child's development than praising generalized attributes such as intelligence. Dweck explains:

> As a psychologist, I have studied student motivation for more than 35 years. My graduate students and I have looked at thousands of children, asking why some enjoy learning, even when it's hard, and why they are resilient in the face of obstacles. We have learned a great deal. Research shows us how to praise students in ways that yield motivation and resilience. In addition, specific interventions can reverse a student's slide into failure during the vulnerable period of adolescence . . .
>
> Many educators have hoped to maximize students' confidence in their abilities, their enjoyment of learning, and their ability to thrive in school by praising their intelligence. We've studied the effects of this kind of praise in

---

* When I thought I played terribly because I did not score any points, were the adults instead praising me for good teamwork? Teamwork was not a factor, because like many five-year-olds, the children in the league were not skilled enough to use team tactics but were instead playing "bunch ball," where all the kids bunch up and chase after the ball.

children as young as 4 years old and as old as adolescence, in students in inner-city and rural settings, and in students of different ethnicities—and we've consistently found the same thing: Praising students' intelligence gives them a short burst of pride, followed by a long string of negative consequences.

In many of our studies, 5th grade students worked on a task, and after the first set of problems, the teacher praised some of them for their intelligence ("You must be smart at these problems") and others for their effort ("You must have worked hard at these problems"). We then assessed the students' mind-sets. In one study, we asked students to agree or disagree with mind-set statements, such as, "Your intelligence is something basic about you that you can't really change." Students praised for intelligence agreed with statements like these more than students praised for effort did. In another study, we asked students to define intelligence. Students praised for intelligence made significantly more references to innate, fixed capacity, whereas the students praised for effort made more references to skills, knowledge, and areas they could change through effort and learning. Thus, we found that praise for intelligence tended to put students in a fixed mind-set (intelligence is fixed, and you have it), whereas praise for effort tended to put them in a growth mind-set (you're developing these skills because you're working hard).

We then offered students a chance to work on either a challenging task that they could learn from or an easy one that ensured error-free performance. Most of those praised for intelligence wanted the easy task, whereas most of those praised for effort wanted the challenging task and the opportunity to learn.

Next, the students worked on some challenging problems. As a group, students who had been praised for their intelligence *lost* their confidence in their ability and their enjoyment of the task as soon as they began to struggle with the problem. If success meant they were smart, then struggling meant they were not. The whole point of intelligence praise is to boost confidence and motivation, but both were gone in a flash. Only the effort-praised kids remained, on the whole, confident and eager.

When the problems were made somewhat easier again, students praised for intelligence did poorly, having lost their confidence and motivation. As a group, they did worse than they had done initially on these same types of problems. The students praised for effort showed excellent performance and continued to improve.

Finally, when asked to report their scores (anonymously), almost 40 percent of the intelligence-praised students lied. Apparently, their egos were so wrapped up in their performance that they couldn't admit mistakes. Only about 10 percent of the effort-praised students saw fit to falsify their results.

Praising students for their intelligence, then, hands them not motivation and resilience but a fixed mind-set with all its vulnerability. In contrast, effort or "process" praise (praise for engagement, perseverance, strategies, improvement, and the like) fosters hardy motivation. It tells students what they've done to be successful and what they need to do to be successful again in the future. Process praise sounds like this:

- You really studied for your English test, and your improvement shows it. You read the material over several times, outlined it, and tested yourself on it. That really worked!

- I like the way you tried all kinds of strategies on that math problem until you finally got it.

- It was a long, hard assignment, but you stuck to it and got it done. You stayed at your desk, kept up your concentration, and kept working. That's great!

- I like that you took on that challenging project for your science class. It will take a lot of work—doing the research, designing the machine, buying the parts, and building it. You're going to learn a lot of great things.

What about a student who gets an *A* without trying? I would say, "All right, that was too easy for you. Let's do something more challenging that you can learn from." We don't want to make something done quickly and easily the basis for our admiration.

What about a student who works hard and *doesn't* do well? I would say, "I liked the effort you put in. Let's work together some more and figure out what you don't understand." Process praise keeps students focused, not on something called ability that they may or may not have and that magically creates success or failure, but on processes they can all engage in to learn . . .

[We explained to the students] that the brain is like a muscle—the more they exercise it, the stronger it becomes. They learned that every time they try hard and learn something new, their brain forms new connections that, over time, make them smarter. They learned that intellectual development is not the natural unfolding of intelligence, but rather the formation of new connections brought about through effort and learning.

Students were riveted by this information. The idea that their intellectual growth was largely in their hands fascinated them. In fact, even the most disruptive students suddenly sat still and took notice, with the most unruly boy of the lot looking up at us and saying, "You mean I don't have to be dumb?"[10]

In *Peaceful Revolution* I described how discipline, work ethic, and determination are better indicators of success and happiness in life than intelligence, so it makes sense to praise these factors, which are within people's capacity to control. Certainly, we should not lie to children when praising them. If a child obviously does not work hard, we should not say, "You worked so hard on this!" It confuses children when we are dishonest with them, because they have a reasonable expectation that adults are telling them the truth.

If a child does something truly brilliant, it can be helpful to say, "That is brilliant!" If we call a child's *work* brilliant, rather than labeling the child as brilliant, our praise is much more specific, especially if we elaborate on the reasons we are impressed with the work. As military leadership taught me, people can also reach a mindset where their ego does not swell no matter how much they are complimented. When I was in the army, a colonel I worked for responded to the tasks I completed by sending me e-mails containing just three words, "YOU DA MAN!" Instead of letting those e-mails swell my ego, I felt appreciated and found them endearing, and I always enjoyed receiving them.

To more effectively combat low self-worth, we must understand its causes. The following diagram lists the five causes of low self-worth:

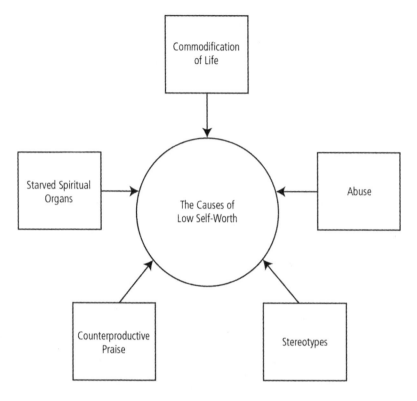

Figure 6.1: The Causes of Low Self-Worth

In the diagram, one cause of low self-worth that I have not yet discussed is *starved spiritual organs*. Before I can explain what this means, I must briefly summarize the "muscle metaphor" from *Peaceful Revolution*. In *Peaceful Revolution* I identify and outline the *seven muscles of our shared humanity*. These seven muscles are hope, empathy, appreciation, conscience, reason, discipline, and curiosity. There are two more muscles, the muscle of language and the muscle of imagination, not discussed in *Peaceful Revolution*. Because these two muscles are capable of so much destruction, I explore them in the last two books of this series. The muscle of language gives us endless cooperative power along with the ability to manipulate, and the muscle of imagination is our most mysterious and dangerous human power.

As I show in *Peaceful Revolution*, strengthening the muscles of our shared humanity allows us to become fully human, achieve our highest potential, and create the future needed for our survival. But in addition to the nine muscles of our shared humanity, we have nine cravings that transcend our physical needs. To help us better understand these cravings, I have conceptualized them metaphorically as the *nine spiritual organs of our shared humanity*. The preface and each chapter in this book reveals a different spiritual organ, which are listed in the following diagram:

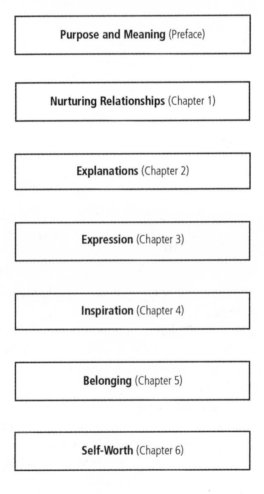

Figure 6.2: The Spiritual Organs of Our Shared Humanity

This diagram only lists seven of our nine spiritual organs. I will describe the last two in chapters 7 and 8, the last two chapters of this book. Why do I use the word "spiritual" to describe these cravings that transcend our physical needs? When I use the word "spiritual" in this way, I am referring to the powerful intersection between science, religion, and philosophy.

How does this intersection help us understand the human condition? As I explained at the beginning of this book, science reveals that human beings crave purpose and meaning.* This scientific fact affirms Jesus's statement, "Man does not live by bread alone."[11] In addition to Christianity, every major world religion reveals that human beings crave a higher purpose and meaning than merely eating, sleeping, and having sex. Countless philosophers also tell us the search for purpose and meaning is a timeless human struggle.

There are diverse views among scientists, religious thinkers, and philosophers, but when a large consensus from science, religion, and philosophy point toward the same truth, I call this "spirituality." The word "spirituality" has become so vague today that it can mean ten different things to ten different people. Vague words tend to create misunderstandings, but we can give the word "spirituality" a precise and useful meaning that will help us walk the road to peace.

When scientific evidence, timeless religious teachings, and philosophical wisdom intersect by agreeing on something, this intersection can serve as a compass pointing toward truth. As we journey together on the road to peace, spirituality is a compass that can help us find the hidden truth surrounding us, along with the deeper truth within us. People often say "ignorance is bliss," but the deeper truth within us gives us a higher bliss than ignorance. Spirituality is our search for this higher bliss.

Why not just ignore religion and philosophy by relying only on science? Religion and philosophy communicate through vivid metaphors and compelling stories that can make complex ideas accessible to the masses. Also,

---

* There is a strong consensus in psychology that human beings crave purpose and meaning. There are some disagreements about how powerful this craving is in relation to our physical urges, which I explore later in this book when discussing Abraham Maslow's *hierarchy of needs*.

religion and philosophy have given us timeless insights into the human condition that predate scientific discoveries by thousands of years. Long before neuroscientists began studying the importance of empathy, Jesus and Buddha showed us that empathy is essential to our humanity. Science helps us separate the untruths of religion (such as the belief that gods require human sacrifice or that earthquakes are caused by Poseidon) from the timeless truths of Jesus, Buddha, Lao-tzu, and other religious thinkers.

Although we must continue to expand our scientific and moral understanding if humanity is going to survive, physicist Robert Oppenheimer explained that science is discovering timeless truths expressed by ancient religious traditions: "The general notions about human understanding and community which are illustrated by discoveries in atomic physics are not in the nature of things wholly unfamiliar, wholly unheard of, or new. Even in our own culture they have a history, and in Buddhist and Hindu thought a more considerable and central place. What we shall find [through discoveries in atomic physics] is an exemplification, an encouragement, and a refinement of old wisdom."[12]

The intersection between science, religion, and philosophy challenges our preconceptions about religion, such as the popular myth that all religions require blind obedience. The Fourteenth Dalai Lama explains: "The scientific way of thinking, their method of investigating the reality is very important, very useful. I think basically some of my friends may already know, that Buddhism in general, particularly the Nalanda tradition, their way of thinking is very scientific. So Buddha himself has made it very clear in one of his quotations that all his followers should not accept his teachings out of faith but out of thorough investigation and experiment. So this is the scientific way of thinking."[13]

To offer another example of the intersection between science, religion, and philosophy, they all agree* that human beings crave nurturing relation-

* By "all agree," I am referring to an overwhelming consensus. It is a scientific fact that nurturing relationships are vital to a child's healthy development. Not only do religious traditions and philosophers support the idea that love is helpful for our development while cruelty is harmful, but the idea that human beings crave nurturing relationships (in the form of friendship or family) is so widely understood that it is considered common sense. Low self-worth is one among many factors that can cause people to end up in abusive rather than nurturing relationships.

ships, which I discussed in chapter 1. As I explained, the most serious forms of trauma occur when our interactions with people are not nurturing, but filled with cruelty, betrayal, and violence. Where chapter 2 is concerned, science, religion, and philosophy also agree that human beings crave explanations for events and phenomena. Obviously, a primary purpose of science, religion, and philosophy is to offer explanations for our human questions. In chapter 3 I showed that human beings crave expression. Expression does not have to be grandiose, because one of the most fulfilling forms of expression human beings can experience is a meaningful conversation with a friend. We can also express ourselves by playing music, dancing, creating art, having a positive impact on others through our job, voting, performing religious rituals, getting tattoos, playing a sport, or committing destructive acts. The section "Painting with Knives" explained my desire to communicate through destruction and how I found more productive ways to express myself. Science, religion, and philosophy all agree that human beings have a craving to communicate.

In chapter 4 I discussed our craving for inspiration. We can derive inspiration from many sources, but one of the most celebrated sources of inspiration is role models. Science, religion, and philosophy all have heroes that serve as role models and sources of inspiration. These role models include figures such as Isaac Newton, Marie Curie, Jesus, Buddha, Socrates, and Seneca, just to name a few. People in history have been inspired by Greek conquerors, but perhaps no one has more inspirational power than a Christ figure. A role model can also be an unsung hero of peace and justice such as a parent or member of our local community. Our craving for inspiration is so strong that if people do not have good role models to look up to, they can look up to bad role models. We live in a society where some celebrities who promote greed and extreme materialism have been viewed as role models.

In chapter 5 I showed that human beings crave belonging. Science, religion, and philosophy agree that human beings have a craving to belong to something larger than themselves, whether it is a community, nation, or our global human family. Religion offers many people a sense of belonging, and philosophers such as Socrates were aware of the dangers of unquestioning conformity, which can arise from our craving to belong.

In this chapter I am discussing our craving for self-worth. Science, religion, and philosophy agree that human beings crave a sense of worthiness. The evidence that human beings prefer to feel worthy rather than worthless, and that our self-worth can be severely damaged, is overwhelming. It is a scientific fact that children want to feel worthy of love. The ways we seek self-worth, however, can vary widely, resulting in behavior that is productive or self-destructive.

Why do I use the word "organs" to describe cravings such as purpose and meaning, nurturing relationships, explanations, expression, inspiration, belonging, and self-worth? Organs are a useful metaphor for these cravings that transcend our physical needs, because we must feed these cravings with psychological nutrients. In a similar way, we must feed our liver, heart, and other bodily organs with physical nutrients. If we do not feed our bodily organs with healthy nutrients, we will starve physically, and if we do not feed our spiritual organs with healthy nutrients, we will starve psychologically.

Where can we find healthy nutrients to satisfy the cravings of our spiritual organs? Hope, empathy, appreciation, and the other muscles of our shared humanity provide healthy nutrients for our organ of purpose and meaning, unlike tainted food such as fear, hatred, and greed. Respect and compassion provide healthy nutrients for our organ of nurturing relationships, unlike tainted food such as disrespect and cruelty. And ideas that promote truth and empathy provide healthy nutrients for our organ of explanations, unlike tainted food such as propaganda that promotes deception and division.

Furthermore, people who lead by example and inspire us through their courage and sacrifice provide healthy nutrients for our organ of inspiration, unlike those who are hypocritical, cowardly, and selfish. The truth of our shared humanity is a healthy nutrient for our organ of belonging, unlike the "us versus them" illusion that leads to fear, hatred, war, and fascism. And recognizing the inherent dignity of life is a healthy nutrient for our organ of self-worth, unlike an attitude that bases our self-worth on the commodification of life.

When our spiritual organs are well fed rather than deprived of proper nutrition, this can counterbalance low self-worth. To use the spiritual organ of explanations as an example, if a black child is told, "The true explanation for racism is not that you are subhuman and inferior, but that those with racist attitudes have been taught to hate, do not understand how our shared humanity makes all races equal, and do not yet accept your inherent dignity as a human being," this can boost a child's self-worth. If a child is fed an inaccurate explanation, such as "God made you to be inferior," this can decrease the child's self-worth.

To offer another example of how feeding our spiritual organs can increase our self-worth, when people have a job that truly fulfills their craving for purpose, meaning, nurturing relationships, expression, inspiration, and belonging, their self-worth depends less on how much money they make.

When we lack purpose and meaning, we will suffer from spiritual hunger pains. These pains also result when our relationships are abusive and traumatizing, we are fed explanations that promote hatred, we are unable to express ourselves in productive ways, we lack role models who embody empathy, our sense of belonging derives from illusions of superiority and the dehumanization of others, and our self-worth is severely damaged.

As history shows, these spiritual hunger pains cause more violence, cruelty, and brutality around the world than anything else. To protect our fragile future we must understand and feed our spiritual organs, which is not an easy task. The most challenging problem of humanity's fragile future is not how to provide food to billions of people on the planet, but how to feed billions of spiritually starved human beings who are hungry for purpose, meaning, belonging, self-worth, and so much more.

CHAPTER 7

# Sailing the Night Sky

## *The Secrets of Video Games*

I have many vivid memories from my early childhood. Most of these memories do not involve traumatic events, but everyday experiences, such as being in preschool. I remember sitting at my desk as a three-year-old, having a crush on the girl who sat next to me, and writing the alphabet. On the wall across from my desk, there was a large image of Snoopy sleeping on top of his red doghouse. Also on the wall were numerous paper dog bones. Each bone had a student's name written on it in big letters.

Every time a child misbehaved in class, the teacher moved the dog bone with the child's name one space closer to Snoopy. If someone misbehaved three times, that child's dog bone ended up in Snoopy's doghouse. When this happened, the student was sent to the principal's office and spanked with a paddle. All the bones went back to the starting position at the beginning of each week, and during the week it seemed like a big event whenever the teacher reprimanded a student by walking to the wall and moving his or her bone closer to Snoopy. Every time this happened, the children suddenly became quiet as tension filled the room.

This didn't really frighten me when I entered preschool at age two, because unlike my father's unpredictable rage, which caused him to attack me in the middle of the night when I was four, I knew how to keep my bone out of Snoopy's doghouse. I just had to follow a few simple rules, and if I made a mistake, I still had two more chances before I got a spanking. Although most of the children, including myself, never had our paper dog bone end up in Snoopy's doghouse, I remember Snoopy's ominous presence in the classroom. At that age I thought it was odd that Snoopy, a cartoon character that children loved, symbolized getting a spanking. I remember staring at the wall and wondering, "Why Snoopy?"

I don't know why I have so many vivid memories from my early childhood. I have several distinct memories of events that occurred before I was two years old. There are no photographs to remind me of these events, nor did my parents discuss these experiences with me, so I am not sure why I remember them. As an adult I asked my mother about those memories, and she said with surprise, "You remember that?"

According to an article in the *Wall Street Journal*, a child can form memories at a very early age, but most are forgotten as they grow older: "Researchers in Canada have demonstrated that some young children can remember events from even before age 2—but those memories are fragile, with many vanishing by about age 10, according to a study in the journal Child Development . . . Researchers asked 140 children, aged between 4 and 13, to describe their three earliest memories, and repeated the exercise two years later with the same children. On average, the 50 youngest children, aged 4 to 6 during the first interview, recalled events from when they were barely 2 years old, as verified by their parents. When they were interviewed two years later, only five of those 50 children mentioned the same earliest memory."[1]

I remember many experiences that occurred before I was four. Why do I have these memories? Is it because early childhood trauma rewired my brain? Did reading at a young age improve my memory, or did certain genes make it easier for me to remember events as a child? Or did those early memories, even the ones that seem mundane, haunt me in some way? If I could not make sense of an early childhood experience, did my brain refuse to let it go, like a puzzle that needed to be solved? Many children remember big events such as their birthday parties, but I cannot remember a single birthday celebration from my childhood. I remember only three Christmases, and two of them involved questions. When I was four I realized Santa Claus was not real, and I wondered, "Why did my parents lie to me?"

Many of my early childhood memories involve troubling questions I could not answer as a child. These questions refused to rest, like spirits in children's ghost stories who refuse to die. As a child I wondered why my preschool chose Snoopy to symbolize a spanking. Was it supposed to make spanking seem less frightening? When I started kindergarten at a different school, children were not spanked. In kindergarten I wondered, why were children spanked in preschool, but not in kindergarten?

When I started kindergarten, other unresolved questions entered my mind. Why was school so boring now? In kindergarten we spent most of the year learning the alphabet, but I had learned how to read two years earlier. Why was I learning A, B, C all over again? And why was I becoming a "bad" student with a growing hatred for school, when I had performed well with more challenging material during preschool? Why did I love going to preschool, despite Snoopy's ominous presence, and why did I hate elementary school so much? Many of these questions remained unanswered in my mind throughout my childhood. I did not realize how my father's violent attacks affected my happiness and concentration not only at home but also at school, until I became a young adult.

Other questions haunted me throughout my childhood. This book series shares my journey to exorcise the ghosts from my past and confront the broader questions that continue to haunt humanity. Through writing I have pursued my obsession to confront every perplexing question that ever troubled me as a human being. Many of these questions, such as how to end war, violence, injustice, racism, and suffering, trouble countless human beings.

If we want to find solutions to any problem, we first have to ask the right questions. Solutions to our problems are sometimes found in the most unlikely questions. For example, people often think the question "What is the meaning of life?" will give us the deepest answers to our human dilemmas, but a question that gives us far greater insight is "Why do human beings play video games?"

Video games reveal a lot about the human condition, because they uncover secrets about humanity's struggle for survival and craving for spiritual fulfillment. As I discussed in chapter 1, the cosmic ocean is a metaphor for the universe, and there are two ways to drown in the cosmic ocean. The first way is extinction. Most of the species that ever existed have drowned in this way. The second way is for our spiritual organs to starve, which occurs when we suffer from problems such as lack of purpose and meaning. Video games reveal some of the ways human beings learned to swim for survival and spiritual fulfillment.

The first video game I ever played was an arcade game called *Dig Dug*. I was around two years old, and the game was in a shopping center at Redstone Arsenal, a military base in Huntsville, Alabama. My father lifted me up so that I could reach the controls, and although I did not really understand how to play the game, I was mesmerized. *Dig Dug* allowed me to control a character on a screen as he dug underground. When he died fighting the monsters that lived underground, he came back to life, allowing me to try again. When he died several times, the game was over.

Video games have several elements that appeal to people, and all of these elements can be found in *Dig Dug*. The most important element is *good gameplay*. To understand why good gameplay makes video games so compelling and even addicting, we must realize that our early ancestors required a lot of physical coordination to survive. Hunting with weapons, making intricate tools with our hands, and the highly developed sense of balance needed to run on two legs all require complex bodily coordination.

To develop this bodily coordination, we must practice the necessary body movements over and over again. When human beings throw a spear hundreds of times, for example, they become much better at the coordination needed for spear throwing, because the neural connections in our brain required for this task become stronger. How does nature encourage us to practice something hundreds of times? Nature does this by creating an incentive for us to practice, which we know as *play*. When we play, we are willing to do something over and over again because it feels fun.

Nature uses the incentive of play to encourage other mammals to practice their survival abilities. Have you ever watched two puppies play with each other? Their play mimics abilities their ancestors (wolves) need to survive in the wild. By playing, puppies practice running, maneuvering, chasing, biting, and wrestling. When kittens play, they also mimic survival abilities their ancestors needed in the wild. To overcome the struggles of nature, playing not only allows young mammals to practice the survival abilities they will need as adults, but it is also used for social bonding. Human beings and many other mammals use play to bond.

The difference between play and violence is that the purpose of play is to bond socially, develop muscular strength, and build the neural connections in our brain needed to survive in the wild. The purpose of violence is to harm. If children are throwing pinecones for fun, and one child gets hit in the face and starts crying, the play stops. Dogs bite with minimal force when playing. If a dog bites hard enough to make another dog cry out in pain, the play stops.

Play is an incredibly complex behavior. This is true not only when humans play, but also when other mammals, such as dogs, play together. In a *Washington Post* article, David Grimm tells us:

> Watch a couple of dogs play, and you'll probably see seemingly random gestures, lots of frenetic activity and a whole lot of energy being expended. But decades of research suggest that beneath this apparently frivolous fun lies a hidden language of honesty and deceit, empathy and perhaps even a humanlike morality.
>
> Take those two dogs. That yogalike pose is known as a "play bow," and in the language of play it's one of the most commonly used words. It's an instigation and a clarification, a warning and an apology. Dogs often adopt this stance as an invitation to play right before they lunge at another dog; they also bow before they nip ("I'm going to bite you, but I'm just fooling around") or after some particularly aggressive roughhousing ("Sorry I knocked you over; I didn't mean it.") All of this suggests that dogs have a kind of moral code—one long hidden to humans until a cognitive ethologist named Marc Bekoff began to crack it . . .
>
> Few people had studied animal play, but Bekoff was intrigued. "Play is a major expenditure of energy, and it can be dangerous," he says. "You can twist a shoulder or break a leg, and it can increase your chances of being preyed upon. So why do they do it? It has to feel good." . . .

What's more, he found that canines "role-reverse" or "self-handicap" during play. When a big dog played with a smaller one, for example, the big dog often rolled on her back to give the smaller dog an advantage, and she allowed the other dog to jump on her far more often than she jumped on him.

Bekoff also spotted a number of other blink-and-you'd-miss-them behaviors, such as a sudden shift in the eyes—a squint that can mean "you're playing too rough"— and a particular wag of the tail that says, "I'm open to be approached." . . . Such signals are important during play; without them, a giddy tussle can quickly turn into a vicious fight. In the wild, coyotes ostracize pack members that don't play by the rules. Something similar happens in dog parks.

[Biological anthropologist Brian] Hare, one of the first scientists to show that dogs could understand human pointing while chimpanzees could not, says that Bekoff's studies add a new dimension to the canine personality: Dogs aren't just smart, they're also emotionally complex. "That's why we can have such a deep relationship with them," says Hare.[2]

One reason human beings invented sports is because nature incentivizes practice through play. Early sports, such as those in nomadic tribes and the Olympics in ancient Greece, involved simple activities such as running, wrestling, and throwing something. Throwing objects was a crucial survival ability for our ancestors, even before they became proficient hunters, because they had to protect their tribes from predators.

As I mentioned in chapter 1, our early nomadic ancestors were the most vulnerable mammals in Africa. We are too slow to outsprint predators and unable to quickly climb trees. Lions and leopards can climb trees much faster than the average human. We are also too big to burrow underground for safety, and because our large brains take so long to develop, human children remain helpless for a longer period of time than the offspring of any other mammal. To make matters worse, we have no natural weapons such as fangs, claws, tusks, or horns.

With no natural weapons, relatively weak bodies (in comparison to chimpanzees and gorillas), and the inability to outsprint much faster predators, how did our early ancestors survive when threatened by predators on the African savannah? In addition to posturing (a self-defense behavior that other animals possess), our early ancestors had a unique human gift: the ability to throw rocks with deadly force. Chimpanzees also throw objects when threatened by predators, but throwing is the only act of raw physical power where humanity greatly exceeds the ability of any other creature on the planet. Although chimpanzees are stronger than human beings, they cannot throw a rock with nearly as much force and accuracy as we can.

The physique of a human being is built much better for throwing rocks than the physique of a chimpanzee. A grown man can kill a hyena by throwing rocks. Although women do not have as much upper body strength as men, imagine the serious injuries you would suffer if a grown woman threw a rock the size of a baseball and hit you in the head. No animal wants to get hit by a rock thrown by a human male or female.

When people think of humanity's survival advantages, they often think of our large brains, opposable thumbs, advanced tool-making ability, high capacity for language, heavy reliance on cooperation, and ability to walk upright, but they rarely think of our powerful ability to throw objects. Just as an eagle is built and optimized for flying, the human body is built and optimized for throwing. Science writer Steve Connor explains:

> The ability to throw objects fast and accurately helped to turn humans from a second-rate primate into one of the most successful species on the planet, a study suggests. Throwing enabled the ancestors of modern humans to defend themselves against dangerous predators, hunt big game, expand their diet, boost brain power and colonise [sic] almost every corner of the globe, scientists said.
>
> The skills that today enable top-class bowlers to deliver

cricket balls at up to 100 mph are the result of key evolutionary adaptations to the torso, shoulders and arms which began nearly 2 million years ago, the researchers said . . .

The researchers tracked the upper-body movements of American college baseball pitchers using 3-D cameras and computer animations. This revealed how the human shoulder acts much like a slingshot during a throw by storing and then suddenly releasing large amounts of energy.

They found that compared to a chimpanzee, which can only throw objects at less than a third of the speed of a 12-year-old child, the human anatomy is finely tuned for the act of throwing.

Dr. [Neil] Roach [from George Washington University] and his colleagues found that three crucial adaptations—a wide waist, a lower position of the shoulders on the torso and the ability to twist the upper arm bone—all occurred as early as nearly 2 million years ago, during the time of Homo erectus, our hominin ancestor.

These three changes to the human anatomy enabled our early relatives to throw projectiles, such as rocks or wooden spears, at incredible speeds by storing and releasing energy in the tendons and ligaments crossing the shoulder . . .

"When humans throw, we first rotate our arms backwards away from the target. It is during this 'arm-cocking' phase that humans stretch the tendons and ligaments crossing their shoulder and store elastic energy," he [Dr. Roach] said. "When this energy is released, it accelerates the arm forward, generating the fastest motion the human body produces, resulting in a very fast throw," he added . . .

"Humans are remarkable throwers, and the only species that can throw objects fast and accurately. Chimpanzees, our closest living relatives, throw very poorly, despite being incredibly strong and athletic," Dr. Roach said. "Adult male chimps for instance can only throw objects at about 20 mph, one third of the speed of a 12-year-old little league pitcher," he said . . .

However, our innate throwing prowess is not to be abused. Premier league cricketers and baseball players throw far more frequently than our ancestor would ever have done during hunting and practising [sic].

This can lead to stretching and strains the human body is not able to cope with, Dr. Roach explained.

"At the end of the day, despite the fact that we evolved to throw, when we overuse this ability it can end up injuring us," he said.[3]

According to a *New York Times* article that discusses the same scientific study: "Throwing overhand, she [Dr. Susan Larson] said, is clearly an innate human ability, but not one that everyone uses. 'I throw like a girl,' she said, hastening to point out that many girls and women throw hard and fast with the classic cocked arm, sideways body turn and forward step of the overhand throw. There are no anatomical differences in the sexes, other than the obvious size and strength, that would make women less proficient at throwing. Dr. [David] Carrier said he also thought the overhand throw was an innate human behavior. 'It's like walking,' he said. 'You have to practice.' Everyone who is able practices walking, but not everyone practices throwing."[4]

Abundant evidence reveals that nature gave us an incentive to practice throwing. Hitting targets tends to be fun for human beings, because this allowed our early ancestors to survive. They survived by throwing objects (such as rocks and spears) toward a target, or using an acceleration tool (such as a sling, spear-thrower, or bow) to propel an object toward a target at greater speeds.

Consider how many games involve throwing objects (such as a ball) toward a target, or using an acceleration tool (such as a tennis racket, golf club, or hockey stick). Here are a few examples: basketball, golf, bowling, lacrosse, table tennis, darts, hockey, dodgeball, badminton, cricket, baseball, horseshoes, air hockey, foosball (table soccer), tennis, racquetball, pool, archery, beer pong, polo, a water-balloon fight, a snowball fight, skipping rocks, paintball, softball, American football, croquet, pinball, playing catch with a Frisbee, and water polo. Like many people, I sometimes feel an urge to throw objects in trash cans and recycling bins. When I hit the target, I feel a small sense of accomplishment and pleasure.

All of these games have something in common: the need for hand-eye coordination. What better way to incentivize improving our hand-eye coordination than to make it feel like play? As I realized when playing games as a child, there is something fun and satisfying about hitting a target. At West Point I took a tennis class during my senior year, and I was surprised by how much fun it was to not only successfully hit the ball with my racquet, but to also make the ball land in the exact spot where I wanted.

Although human beings can throw objects with greater speed and power than any other creature on the planet, we used our large brains to invent acceleration tools, such as the sling David used against Goliath, that allow us to propel objects even faster. In sports, golf clubs and tennis rackets function as acceleration tools by launching a ball much faster than it can be thrown. Of course, a far more complex acceleration tool is the gun, which propels tiny pieces of metal at lethal speeds, but acceleration tools can also be very simple.

The simplest acceleration tools are our own limbs. Volleyball players use their hand and arm like a racquet when they spike a ball at high speed, and soccer players use their leg as an acceleration tool when they kick a ball with tremendous force. It may seem odd to call the human leg an acceleration tool, but the truth is that the way soccer players use their leg to kick is similar to how golf players use their club to swing.

In the book *Two Steps to a Perfect Golf Swing*, Shawn Humphries and Brad Townsend describe some of the similarities among soccer, golf, tennis, and baseball: "Your [golf] swing works in a circular motion, because like tennis, soccer, and baseball, golf is a side-on sport. *Side-on* means you are standing to the side of the ball when you strike it. What happens when you hit a ground stroke in tennis? If you are a right-handed player, the ball generally curves from right to left. The same thing happens when you kick a soccer ball."[5]

Someone might argue, "But how could golf possibly relate to human survival? Golf seems completely different from throwing rocks and spears." To explain this, I will offer an analogy. Eating fresh fruit promotes our survival, because it contains a lot of natural sugar and nutrients. This is why fruit tastes good to most people. On the other hand, candy tastes good to most people, because it simulates fruit's high sugar content, tricking our brain into thinking we are eating something nutritious.

Golf is like candy, because just as people think a piece of candy is delicious, even though it contains little or no nutrients and does not promote human survival, many people think golf is fun, even though it contains little or no practical survival skills that would help us survive in the wild.* Because hitting a predator with a rock or spear requires accuracy, any game that develops hand-eye coordination can trick our brain into thinking we are doing something useful for our survival, just as any food that tastes sweet can trick our brain into thinking we are eating something packed with nutrients.

Just as people prefer different kinds of fruit, people also prefer different kinds of games. My favorite fruit may be different from your favorite. One of my favorite fruits is kiwi, and I have met people who think kiwi is disgusting. Nevertheless, virtually all human beings like at least some fruits, even though we have different preferences. In a similar way, my favorite game may be different from your favorite. You may even think my favorite game is boring. Nevertheless, virtually all human beings like at least some games. I have never heard a child say, "I hate all games! Sports, board games, video games, hide-and-seek, hop scotch, jump rope, competitive games, cooperative games, solo games, I hate them all!"**

Having different preferences for physical activities did not endanger the survival of our early ancestors, because they lived in cooperative communities

---

* I am not using this metaphor to say that golf is unhealthy to play (as candy is unhealthy to eat). On the contrary, many people use golf as a form of exercise. Instead, this metaphor shows that just as any food containing sugar can trick our brain into thinking we are eating something nutritious (since foods in nature that taste sweet to us also have nutrients), any game that involves hand-eye coordination can trick our brain into thinking we are practicing an essential survival ability. Later in this chapter I discuss deeper reasons why golf and other games appeal to us.

** Although people have different music preferences, there is a rare disorder that can cause someone to dislike every form of music. I have heard of some children with mental illness hating all games, but most children like at least some games.

we call tribes. If only five out of twenty people in an early nomadic tribe could throw rocks and spears with accuracy and deadly force, that tribe would still have been extremely dangerous to any predator. If a small tribe has only a few expert spear throwers, a pride of ferocious lions can go from being the predators to being prey.

Because of human creativity, a wide variety of games have been invented to satisfy our different preferences. Just as some children prefer bananas over oranges, when I was a child I preferred video games that allowed me to hit targets, rather than sports such as basketball and baseball. I liked hitting monsters with my magic boomerang in *The Legend of Zelda*, jumping on enemies* and shooting them with fireballs in *Super Mario Bros.*, and blasting bad guys with my gun in *Contra* and *Mega Man*. I also liked first-person shooters such as *Wolfenstein 3D*, *Doom*, *Quake*, and *Halo*.

I have heard many people say human beings like violent video games because we are naturally violent, but these games appeal to us not because we are natural warmongers, but *natural throwers*. As a child I didn't care what kind of targets I was hitting in video games, as long as the gameplay was good. In *The Legend of Zelda* I was destroying evil creatures, in *Super Mario Bros.* I was smashing "goombas" (walking mushrooms), in *Contra* I was killing aliens, and in *Mega Man* I was shooting robots. When first-person shooters are concerned, in *Wolfenstein 3D* I was killing Nazis, in *Doom* I was blasting demons, in *Quake* I was shooting zombies, and in *Halo* I was fighting aliens.

Why do so few video games focus on shooting a stationary target, and why do most of them involve shooting evil creatures, goombas, aliens, robots, Nazis, demons, or zombies? One reason is that it is much more challenging to hit a moving target than a stationary object. Hitting a moving target develops better hand-eye coordination skills. Another reason is that fighting demons, robots, and aliens allows video game designers to create a story that gets players emotionally invested in the game. What sounds like a more fun, challenging, and rewarding experience to you, shooting a

---

* In platform games such as *Super Mario Bros.*, your character becomes a projectile and the places you jump to become targets.

stationary round bull's-eye in a video game, or shooting invading aliens trying to destroy earth?

Many video games today are far more violent than those I played as a child. I cannot thoroughly discuss how violent video games can affect children's brains in this short chapter, but if you are interested in exploring this subject further, a useful place to start is Lieutenant Colonel Dave Grossman's book *On Killing* (the last chapter discusses video games and media violence). Some video games certainly increased my aggression as a child, but the violence in video games varies widely. Some video games involve massacring human beings, and others are about as violent as chess.

Why are chess and other strategy games fun if they don't involve hitting a target? In addition to hitting a target, another survival ability our early ancestors relied on, which is found in many games, is *strategic thinking*. Games that involve strategic thinking include chess, checkers, poker, and nearly every board game ever invented. Furthermore, many professional sports such as golf, basketball, and American football also require strategic thinking. There is something fun and satisfying about making a strategic decision that gives us a positive outcome. At West Point my roommates and I used to play chess, and it felt good to make strategic decisions that led to success. As a child some of my favorite video games were strategy games that did not involve any shooting at all.

Team games such as American football add *cooperation*, another survival ability. To allow the quarterback to throw the ball and hit his intended target, a football team must rely heavily on cooperation, strategic thinking, and the camaraderie that comes from social bonding. If a pride of lions confronted an early human tribe that possessed the high level of cooperation, strategic thinking, and camaraderie of a football team, the lions would be in severe danger.

Modern games are fun because they allow us to practice abilities our early ancestors needed to survive in the wild. These survival abilities include: hitting a target, strategic thinking, cooperation, social interaction and bonding, creativity, communication, knowledge, exploration, and physical prowess (balance, reflexes, strength, speed, endurance, flexibility, and sensory perceptions such as sight or hearing).

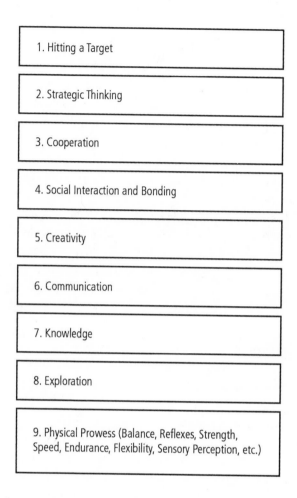

1. Hitting a Target

2. Strategic Thinking

3. Cooperation

4. Social Interaction and Bonding

5. Creativity

6. Communication

7. Knowledge

8. Exploration

9. Physical Prowess (Balance, Reflexes, Strength, Speed, Endurance, Flexibility, Sensory Perception, etc.)

Figure 7.1: The Nine Survival Abilities in Games

When we play a game, we are stimulating one or more of these nine survival abilities. Puzzle games require strategic thinking and creativity. Games such as charades require creativity, cooperation, and communication. Wrestling requires strategic thinking and physical prowess. Golf, basketball, and fencing require strategic thinking, physical prowess, and hitting a target. Trivia games test our knowledge (because our early nomadic ancestors had not yet invented writing, memorization was an ability they relied on to survive). Children's games such as house, tea party, and playing with an imaginary friend mimic the skills needed for social interaction and bonding. Our early ancestors had to explore their environment to gather resources and survive, and many of my favorite video games as a child, such as *The Legend of Zelda*, stimulated my sense of exploration. In addition to serving a survival function, exploration can also invoke a sense of awe and transcendence.

Even a seemingly innocent children's game like hide-and-seek stimulates our survival abilities. When children playing hide-and-seek look for a place to conceal themselves, they use strategic thinking to pick the best hiding spot. The child chosen to search for the hidden children relies on visual perception (a form of physical prowess), mimicking hunting skills such as observation and tracking. This child is actually functioning somewhat like a hunter. When I was a child, we played a form of hide-and-seek that required running (another form of physical prowess). When the hunter spotted the children, they had to run back to a certain spot as the hunter chased after them, trying to tag them.*

Competition can strengthen these survival abilities. West Point makes every cadet participate in mandatory competitive sports to increase cooperation, because a high degree of cooperation is needed when competing against a group of skilled human beings. When training in jiu-jitsu, I was taught that the best way to improve my skills is to compete against someone more skilled than me, because this person will be able to challenge and teach me.

I know some peace activists who want to ban all forms of competition, including all sports competitions, because they see competition as inherently destructive. But competition is like fire. When we use fire responsibly, it can

---

* Games that rely entirely on luck, such as the modern-day American version of Snakes and Ladders (the traditional Indian version has a deeper cultural meaning), typically appeal to very young children, since many older children and adults find games based entirely on luck to be boring. The modern-day version of Snakes and Ladders stimulates social interaction among young children and some hand-eye coordination through rolling the dice and moving the pieces around the board. Some adults may find these luck-based games relaxing because they spark social interaction without the stress caused by decision making and relying on a skill.

help us, just as competition can help develop our abilities. We must be cautious and thoughtful about how we use competition, however, because like a mismanaged fire it can spiral out of control and become extremely destructive. West Point's sports philosophy is based on the ideal of *friendly competition*, rather than the attitude of destructive competition.

Competition is sometimes useful like fire, but cooperation is absolutely essential like the air we breathe. In *Will War Ever End?* I explain that human beings, more than any other mammal, rely on cooperation to survive. Albert Einstein also discussed why cooperation is more important for human survival than competition:

> Darwin's theory of the struggle for existence and the selectivity connected with it has by many people been cited as authorization of the encouragement of the spirit of competition. Some people also in such a way have tried to prove pseudoscientifically the necessity of the destructive economic struggle of competition between individuals. But this is wrong, because man owes his strength in the struggle for existence to the fact that he is a socially living animal. As little as a battle between single ants of an ant hill is essential for survival, just so little is this the case with the individual members of a human community.[6]

Although the *act* of playing games stimulates one or more of our nine survival abilities, the *reasons* for playing games are far more diverse. Many people play games simply as distractions, and during my childhood I played some games to vent my anger and frustration. Games can also feed people's starving spiritual organs. Athletes can gain a sense of purpose, meaning, belonging, and self-worth from participating in a sport,* and spectators can

---

* Although games are supposed to be fun, an athlete can experience so much pressure to succeed in a sport that it is no longer enjoyable. If an athlete's self-worth is tied to success, this can also create a great deal of stress. On the other hand, if we want to perform any sport (or activity such as writing or playing a musical instrument) with the highest degree of skill possible, it may not always feel enjoyable because pushing our human abilities to their utmost limits requires thousands of hours of practice, which are filled with hard work and often monotonous repetition.

feed these same spiritual organs by watching their favorite team. For many people, sports share similarities with religion. In his book *Baseball as a Road to God*, president of New York University John Sexton explains:

> In the basement of my family's home, my friend Bobby "Dougie" Douglas and I knelt and prayed with all the intensity we could muster, grasping between us in dynamic tension each end of a twelve-inch crucifix we had removed from the wall.
>
> We prayed before a radio instead of an altar, which broadcast the sounds of Game Seven of the 1955 World Series instead of hymns . . . For the two of us, baseball and our still-forming Catholic faith were not connected literally; nonetheless, though we did not appreciate it at the time, baseball that day displayed some of the profound and complex elements that constitute religion. We were transported to a plane familiar to "the faithful"—to a place where faith, hope, and love were as much on display as [baseball pitcher Johnny] Podre's arm.
>
> October 4, 1955. For me and millions of others, a sacred day. Why? Hard to put into words. Impossible to capture completely in our limited vocabulary. But we do have a word for something that defies reduction to words: *ineffable*. We cannot define the ineffable, even though we can experience and "know" it profoundly.[7]

One reason for the popularity of spectator sports is our yearning to feed spiritual organs such as belonging and self-worth. When people cheer for their favorite team during a spectator sport, this can give them a sense of belonging. When their team loses badly (and they identify strongly with their team), this can threaten their self-worth, just as their team winning a championship can feed their self-worth.

Even though fans are not actually playing a professional sport, by being a spectator they can still find a way to exercise the survival abilities involved in playing games. Fans exercise strategic thinking by discussing various strategies their favorite team can use. Fans also watch games as a way to bond socially with their friends. And many fans memorize an impressive amount of statistics and player-related information. Sports trivia is a game that fans can enjoy, and fantasy sports leagues are another way for fans to exercise their brains.

Cooperation is an essential survival ability that games can stimulate, and when fans cheer during live sporting events, they are in a way cooperating with their team. Screaming fans can encourage their players and disrupt the concentration of the opposing side, which is one reason why football fans are called the "twelfth man." All of this shows that just because fans are spectators does not mean they are passive.

Watching and participating in sports allow many people to feel a range of intense emotions such as exhilaration, excitement, triumph, and transcendence, which they do not often experience in their daily lives. As I will explain in the next chapter, spiritual transcendence is a sublime experience that many scientists, religious teachers, and philosophers have written about, but few of us living today understand.

Like bees craving pollen that are lured to different kinds of flowers, our craving for spiritual transcendence lures us to different flowers of human fulfillment, such as science, religion, philosophy, sports, creative art-forms, and even video games. Like bees that mistake carnivorous plants for flowers, we can mistake war and harmful drugs for flowers of human fulfillment.

After playing my first video game, *Dig Dug*, at the age of two, the question "Why do people enjoy video games?" gradually formed in my mind, haunting me more intensely as the years passed. By exploring this question with an obsession to understand, video games helped me learn many secrets about the human condition. I learned how human beings survived on the harsh African savannah, why games are fun, and how games as diverse as baseball and *The Legend of Zelda* can appeal to our spiritual cravings. Video games also taught me a secret about our fragile future. If we look closely, defeating enemies in video games gives us a secret insight into defeating our greatest enemies in the real world. Enemies such as injustice, environmental destruction, and war.

## *Increase the Clarity of Communication*

All human inventions have a dark side. A hammer can be used to build a house, or to murder. Writing can be used to spread love and truth, or hatred and lies. Electricity can be used to provide heat in winter, or to torture someone. An airplane can deliver food, or drop bombs. We can use tools to educate and protect us, or enslave and destroy us.

Like all human inventions, games also have a dark side. Video games taught me secrets about the human condition, but some of these games increased my aggressive and antisocial tendencies. A sport can teach resilience, perseverance, fair play, and cooperation, or domination, ruthlessness, cheating, and destructive competition. A sport can instill ideals that help us solve our global problems, or it can distract us from these problems.

As I explain in *Peaceful Revolution*, to overcome the dark side of any human invention, we must strengthen the muscles of our shared humanity. When we use muscles such as empathy, conscience, and reason to wield an invention, we become strong enough to use it in responsible ways that promote more good than harm.* Our tools can be guided by empathy and truth, or hatred and illusion. We can use our tools to carve light out of darkness, or to serve the darkness.

To survive in the twenty-first century and beyond, we must learn to throw more than just physical objects. We must learn to propel truth, love, and justice with enough accuracy and force to shatter unjust systems. This kind of throwing does not rely on the muscles of our body, but the muscles of our shared humanity. Only by cultivating this kind of strength can we become powerful enough to defeat an enemy as mighty as war.

In many ways, the war system is similar to a mythological Greek god. In my other books I explain why humanity can end war on a global scale. But what I did not reveal in those books is that the war system is immortal. The war system cannot be killed, but this is simply another reason why we can end war. At first this seems like an absurd contradiction, a paradox, but if we look deeper we will see new layers of truth. To clarify this

---

* In *Peaceful Revolution* I discuss why some inventions, such as nuclear weapons, should be abolished.

paradox, I must explain why ancient Greek gods are useful metaphors for fierce opponents such as injustice, environmental destruction, and modern war.

In ancient Greek mythology there were two races of gods. The first race, the Titans, included the goddess of the earth Gaia, the god of time[8] Cronus, and Prometheus, who sacrificed himself to give the gift of fire to humanity. The second race, the Olympians, included Zeus, his brothers Poseidon and Hades, his wife Hera, and his children Athena, Ares, and Heracles (who is better known by his Latin name, Hercules).* I have listed only a few of the many Titans and Olympians, who were organized as large families. The Olympians descended from the Titans.

When Zeus tried to overthrow his father, the Titan Cronus, many of the Titans declared war against the Olympians. The Titan Atlas, brother of Prometheus, led the Titans in a war against Zeus and the Olympians. Although the Titans had ruled the world for a long time, the younger Olympians grew in power, and the Titans lost the war. Because the Titans were immortal and could not be killed, however, they did not die during the conflict, but were imprisoned by Zeus. Atlas was punished with the burden of holding the sky on his shoulders, and other Titans were imprisoned in Tartarus, a dark underworld in Greek mythology similar to the Christian concept of hell.

In his book, *The Myths and Legends of Ancient Greece and Rome*, E. M. Berens describes the War of the Titans, which lasted for ten years:

> Zeus, with his brothers and sisters, took his stand on Mount Olympus, where he was joined by Oceanus, and others of the Titans, who had forsaken Cronus on account of his oppressions. Cronus and his brother-Titans took possession of Mount Othrys, and prepared for battle. The struggle was long and fierce, and at length Zeus, finding that he was no nearer victory than before, bethought

---

* Heracles was a demigod, half human and half divine, who became an Olympian after dying. This occurred after the War of the Titans. He is the only Greek hero to become an Olympian.

himself of the existence of the imprisoned Giants, and knowing that they would be able to render him most powerful assistance, he hastened to liberate them. He also called to his aid the Cyclops . . . who had only one eye each in the middle of their foreheads, and were called Brontes (Thunder), Steropes (Lightning), and Pyracmon (Fire-anvil). They promptly responded to his summons for help, and brought with them tremendous thunderbolts [which they later gave to Zeus] . . .

Aided by these new and powerful allies, Zeus now made a furious onslaught on his enemies, and so tremendous was the encounter that all nature is said to have throbbed in accord with this mighty effort of the celestial deities. The sea rose mountains high, and its angry billows hissed and foamed; the earth shook to its foundations, the heavens sent forth rolling thunder, and flash after flash of death-bringing lightning, whilst a blinding mist enveloped Cronus and his allies.

And now the fortunes of war began to turn, and victory smiled on Zeus. Cronus and his army were completely overthrown, his brothers dispatched to the gloomy depths of the lower world, and Cronus himself was banished from his kingdom and deprived for ever of the supreme power, which now became vested in his son Zeus . . . With the defeat of Cronus and his banishment from his dominions, his career as a ruling Greek divinity entirely ceases. But being, like all the gods, immortal, he was supposed to be still in existence, though possessing no longer either influence or authority.[9]

Like the two races of immortal Greek gods, opponents such as injustice, environmental destruction, and war cannot be killed. But this does not mean they cannot be overthrown and imprisoned. Just as Zeus deprived Cronus of his influence and authority, we can do the same to ideologies of injustice, environmental destruction, and war. And just as the Olympians overthrew and imprisoned the Titans, we can overthrow and imprison what the Olympians symbolize in the modern world.

Zeus is a metaphor for injustice, because he represents the old paradigm of "might makes right" that constructs the foundation of every unjust system. Heracles is a metaphor for environmental destruction, because in Greek mythology he represents the conquest of Greek civilization over nature.*

Heracles is a paradox, because although he symbolizes Greek civilization, he is very uncivilized according to Greek standards. Heracles is not a highly trained soldier, but a brute wielding a club. Wearing a lion's skin, he relies on big muscles and enormous physical power to get what he wants. Heracles protects humans from nature by defeating monsters and wild animals, yet he behaves wildly with excessive gluttony, greed, and violence. Ironically, his uncivilized behavior shows that our attempt to conquer and "civilize" nature is in many ways uncivilized.

Before his transformation from a mortal demigod into an immortal Olympian, an acidic poison burns his entire body, leading to his death. In a similar way, our destruction of the environment poisons our soil, air, and water in ways that can harm and kill us. Professor of mythology Elizabeth Vandiver further describes the story and symbolism of Heracles:

> Heracles, who may be more familiar in the Latin form of his name, Hercules, is not just the greatest hero within Greek myth itself. He is also, I think it's fair to say, the most famous hero of classical myth on into the modern day . . . When he reached maturity, Heracles was characterized not only by exceptional strength and courage, but also by exceptional or excessive appetites and powers in other regards as well. He's characterized by extremes of

---

* Mythology has many interpretations. My interpretation of Heracles is based partly on Professor Elizabeth Vandiver's lecture series *Classical Mythology*, a DVD set in The Great Courses series. In addition to offering interpretations of Heracles, she also discusses how Zeus is an arbiter of justice between humans, although he often treats human beings unjustly. I have added new meaning to these metaphors so they can help us solve our modern problems.

sexual appetite, of hunger and thirst, and of rage . . .

There are various stories, particularly by [ancient] comic authors, that refer to Heracles as a kind of proto-typical glutton and drunkard, someone who eats and drinks . . . very excessively. On a less comic level, Heracles is also noted for excessive passions, including the passion of rage. There are various times when he gives way to excessive rage, even to the extent of madness . . . [In] the most famous such episode of madness, Heracles kills his own children by his first wife, Megara, and perhaps kills the wife as well. Authorities differ on that. And so Heracles is susceptible to extreme rage in which he does things that normally he would not do . . .

Unlike most other heroes that we encounter in Greek myth, Heracles is neither primarily a warrior, nor prima-rily a king . . . His primary role, his main reason for exis-tence, is to be a fighter of animals and of mythical monsters. That seems to be what he is there for. Unlike Achilles, who is a great warrior, or a king such as Oedipus, Theseus, Agamemnon, and others, Heracles exists to fight animals . . .

One primary interpretation of this is that Heracles represents the spread of Greek culture, that as Greek civi-lization came into contact with other civilizations throughout the ancient world, and as Greek civilization spread through colonies that were planted in other places, so Heracles is imagined as traveling . . . away from Greece, and during these travels killing monsters and overcoming wild animals as he goes . . . The Greek assumption was that their civilization was superior, that when they took Greek civilization to other lands, they were somehow improving, civilizing, humanizing those other lands . . .

There are many different ways in which he is in him-self, a contradictory character . . . [Heracles] is both

admirable and horrifying . . . The hero who overcomes
monsters, marks out the civilized world, is also the madman who kills his own children.[10]

In chapter 2 I discussed how Greek mythology, the Bible, Chinese
philosopher Lao-tzu, and science all depict nature as dangerous to early agricultural civilizations. When early agricultural people personified nature's
forces, they tended to see nature as fickle and even psychotic. These people
did not understand why their families were being killed by plague, famine,
and natural disasters. Nature's destructive forces have threatened not only
ancient agricultural people, but all forms of life. As I mentioned in chapter
1, many scientists estimate that over 99 percent of the species that ever
existed have gone extinct.

By defeating monsters that devour innocent people, Heracles symbolizes
humanity's admirable struggle to protect our families from nature's devouring
destruction, but he also represents the gluttony, greed, and madness that
result from humanity's war with nature. In the end, our war with nature is
a war against ourselves, because we are a part of nature, just as a drop of
water is one with the ocean.

Heracles is a useful metaphor for humanity's conquest of nature, because
his behavior and humanity's effort to conquer nature are both paradoxes.
Like us, Heracles is a part of nature, but he is also at war with nature. If we
enjoy any of the luxuries that modern technology gives us, however, we
should not be so quick to see what Heracles symbolizes as pure evil, because
every person alive today has benefitted in some way from our ancestors' conquest of nature.

Just as Heracles captures and defeats wild animals, humanity has learned
to capture and defeat many of nature's forces. We can manipulate fire and
electricity as easily as Heracles outwrestled the Nemean lion. Just as Heracles
has enormous physical strength, modern technology makes us strong enough
to lift massive objects into the clouds. In a feat of incredible physical power,
we can send an airplane carrying a hundred thousand pounds of food and
medical supplies across the world.

Our might extends far beyond flight. We can overpower scorching heat with air conditioning, freezing temperatures with fire and warm clothes, drought with irrigation, high child mortality rates with medical technology, and predators with weapons carved out of stone and metal. Despite our power to conquer many of nature's forces, however, we are far from all powerful. We cannot conquer time and death, or prevent most natural disasters. And we cannot survive if we conquer nature to the point where we destroy our fragile ecosystem. We need oxygen, water, and the other gifts of nature much more than nature needs us.

By strengthening the muscles of our shared humanity, waging peace with the infinite shield and the sword that heals (which I discuss in *The Art of Waging Peace*), and feeding our starved spiritual organs, we can end our war with nature. We must end this war, because when we poison and destroy our environment, we also poison and destroy ourselves, along with the other struggling species that share this planet with us. Humanity is a manifestation of nature's grandeur, which makes our destruction of the environment an act of self-destruction, and our war with nature a civil war.

I first contemplated this when studying war in the military, because if science tells us all human beings are related and every person on the planet shares about 99.9 percent of the same DNA, then isn't every war among humans a civil war? Isn't every war between countries a war between brothers, like Cain killing his brother Abel? And if we are a part of nature, then isn't our war with nature also a civil war? If our war with nature is not a civil war, then why does our destruction of the environment harm us, poison us, and threaten to drive us extinct?

Human beings have spent thousands of years trying to protect their children, but our destruction of the environment now threatens every child, just as Heracles is a madman who kills his own offspring. Humanity's conquest of nature, which began innocently as the shaping of stone and the manipulation of fire, gradually escalated into a kind of madness, in the form of an all-out war to conquer every aspect of nature. By deepening our understanding, expanding our empathy, waging peace, and using our tools to carve light out of darkness rather than to serve the darkness, we can end this madness and create a sane civilization.

Just as Heracles can help us better understand environmental destruction, the war god Ares and war goddess Athena can help us better understand the reality of war. As I explain in *The Art of Waging Peace*, Ares and Athena are effective metaphors for the deception and destruction of war. In my other books I use these kinds of metaphors to discuss the illusions and reality of war, along with the strengths and weaknesses of the war system.

Using mythological Greek gods (who can be imprisoned but never killed) as metaphors for opponents such as injustice, environmental destruction, and war gives us important insights. This metaphorical understanding shows that we cannot kill these opponents, but we can imprison them. The reason we cannot kill injustice, environmental destruction, and war is because they are ideas, and violence cannot kill an idea. Ideas based on ignorance and illusion cannot be destroyed with bullets and bombs. They can only be imprisoned with the chains of love and truth.

If humanity someday abolishes wars between countries on a global scale, yet a single generation forgets how war deceives us, then the ideology of war can escape from its prison and once again wreak havoc on the world. A political leader simply has to say, "Evil people who are not like us want to kill our family, and we have no choice but to defend ourselves in the name of self-defense, freedom, and peace." As I discussed earlier in this book, Hitler used this kind of argument to support his aggressive wars.

Imprisoning an idea does not mean censorship. On the contrary, the only jail strong enough to imprison war must be made of awareness, education, and just laws. War can break every chain but the ones made of love and truth. I know a few well-intentioned peace activists who attempt to end war by telling people not to think about war and the military, but this encourages ignorance. To imprison war, we must truly educate people on the illusions and reality of war. War runs freely through the fields of ignorance, but loses its freedom as more people become educated on war's true nature.

As I explain in my other books, this will not be easy, because the struggle to end war is an underdog journey. It is extremely challenging to defeat the god of war, especially when it is supported by the seductive religion of war. But we can win, because all unjust systems have weaknesses that can lead to their downfall.

Video games taught me that all opponents have weak spots. Defeating enemy bosses in video games required me to learn what their weaknesses were. My study of military strategy at West Point also showed me the importance of finding an opponent's weak spots, and studying waging peace taught me that one weak spot of all unjust systems is that they are built on myths. If we wage peace strategically and confront the weak spots of an unjust system, we can win victories for justice. Our ancestors showed this is possible when they ended state-sanctioned slavery, gained American women the right to vote, and defeated racial segregation laws in the South and apartheid in South Africa.

Because the creation of enduring positive change is always an underdog struggle, overcoming any unjust system is a significant challenge, and we must rise to meet this challenge. The eighth spiritual organ of our shared humanity is *challenge*, because we need challenge to grow. Challenge strengthens our mind, sharpens our skills, and builds character. For artists to excel at their art form, they must be challenged. For human beings to grow physically, mentally, or spiritually, we must be challenged.

When I discuss "spirituality" in terms of personal growth, I am referring not only to the intersection of truth between science, religion, and philosophy, but also the intersection of peace between our internal and external universes. I use the term *spiritual growth* to represent our journey to make peace with our internal universe (the human condition) and create peace in our external universe (the world around us). A defining feature of the human condition is our craving for purpose, meaning, nurturing relationships, explanations, expression, inspiration, belonging, and self-worth. Making peace with these cravings and creating a more peaceful world through spiritual growth is not only a timeless human challenge. It is also the greatest human challenge.

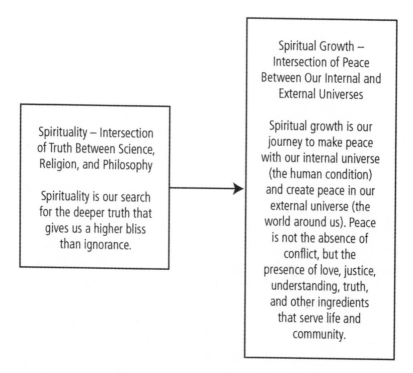

Spirituality – Intersection of Truth Between Science, Religion, and Philosophy

Spirituality is our search for the deeper truth that gives us a higher bliss than ignorance.

Spiritual Growth – Intersection of Peace Between Our Internal and External Universes

Spiritual growth is our journey to make peace with our internal universe (the human condition) and create peace in our external universe (the world around us). Peace is not the absence of conflict, but the presence of love, justice, understanding, truth, and other ingredients that serve life and community.

Figure 7.2: Definitions of Spirituality and Spiritual Growth

Purpose, meaning, and self-worth taste sweet like fresh fruit, but challenge tastes more like vegetables. Just as vegetables are nutritious for our body, challenge is nutritious for the human spirit. As an adult I have learned to enjoy the taste of vegetables, but as a child I preferred the sweet flavor of candy over the taste of vegetables. In a similar way, many people prefer the sweet flavor of ease over the taste of challenge. Like vegetables, challenge can be an acquired taste.

Challenge can be both delicious and deeply fulfilling. For me, the challenge of journeying within myself and unlocking the secrets of the human condition has given me immense spiritual fulfillment. In his book *Olympic Marathon*, Charles Lovett discusses how people can be drawn to many forms of challenge: "For there is something in man that seeks out challenge, especially the challenge of a single man taking on a task in which all the forces of nature, and often the opinions of men, are arrayed against him; a task in which his own solitude may become his greatest enemy . . . There is something in man that seeks out the challenge of the unknown. As the world around us became more and more known in this century, man increasingly turned to the unknown within himself and sought to challenge the limits of his very being."[11]

Many people misinterpret the biblical concept of "original sin" to mean that humanity is naturally evil, but we are much more empowered to solve our problems when we see original sin as humanity's *tendency to take the easy path*. What if most of the harm humans inflict on each other is caused not by hatred, but by our tendency to take the easy path?

West Point taught me that "taking the easier wrong over the harder right" creates many of the problems around the world. It can be easier to lie and cheat than to maintain our integrity. It can be easier to avoid confrontation and tolerate injustice than to improve our society. It can be easier to be complacent than to work hard. It can be easier to remain stuck in old ways of doing things than to change for the better. It can be easier to be judgmental than to have empathy. It can be easier to be apathetic than to care deeply.

When we constantly choose the easier wrong over the harder right, we will starve spiritually, because spiritual growth often occurs in the cauldron of challenge. Just as challenging forms of exercise can grow our muscles, challenging life experiences can grow our radical empathy, realistic hope, and revelatory understanding.

Our exploration of challenge gives us essential insights, because it reveals that embracing challenge is necessary for truly ethical behavior, whereas taking the path of least resistance can cause us to do what is easier in the short term, but not what is right. Many people do not realize that the temptation to take the easy path, which seems so innocent and harmless at times, can cause so much harm around the world. Because it is much easier to have a slave do all of our work for us, slavery is just one example of the injustices that can arise when people choose easier wrongs over harder rights. Taking the easy path is also a cause of brutality, because it can be easier to close our eyes and hearts to the suffering of others than to confront the causes of injustice.

West Point taught me that other forms of choosing the easier wrong over the harder right include not standing up for what is right due to fear of consequences, cutting corners when we work rather than paying attention to detail, surrendering to bad habits rather than developing good habits, and not taking responsibility for our actions. Humanity's tendency to take the easy path also causes us to seek quick fixes over real solutions and instant gratification over long-term goals that require sacrifice.

Taking the easy path can also lead to murder. Sometimes it can just seem easier to kill someone who bothers us, especially if we do not know how to resolve conflict peacefully. In many religious and philosophical systems, taking the easy path is closely linked with the kinds of temptations that often cause harm. People who interpret the Garden of Eden story literally or metaphorically can view Adam and Eve as submitting to temptation. Resisting temptation requires discipline, self-control, and in many cases empathy and conscience.

Wild animals also exhibit some behavior that demonstrates the tendency to take the easy path. When wolves, lions, hyenas, and other predators hunt, what prey do they often pursue? The weak, the vulnerable, and the very young. Many people today consider killing the weak, vulnerable, and very young (even when waging war) as the height of immorality, but these predators do not behave this way because they are evil, but because they are taking the easy path—the path of least resistance. We can see the tendency to take the easy path not only in humans and wild animals, but also in other aspects of nature. The laws of physics cause water to find the path of least resistance when it flows downhill.

Many fables reveal the harm caused by the easy path. In Aesop's "The Grasshopper and the Ant," a lazy grasshopper plays and procrastinates while a disciplined ant saves enough food to last through the winter. When winter arrives the grasshopper starves while the ant survives. In "The Three Little Pigs," one pig works hard to build his house out of bricks while another pig builds a house made of sticks, and another uses straw. When a wolf blows down the stick and straw houses, the two lazy pigs seek safety in the hard-working pig's house of bricks.

The ant in Aesop's fable and the pig with the brick house embrace challenge by being disciplined and hard working, which requires sacrifice in the short term but benefits them in the long term. The path of least resistance tends to be easy in the short term, like a child effortlessly rolling downhill on a sled, but at the end of this downhill journey there may be a cliff that causes us to fall to our demise. These fables reveal that the easy path can cause harm and endanger our survival, which is why I have a chapter on discipline in *Peaceful Revolution*. I am not suggesting that human beings are naturally lazy, but that discipline is a muscle of our shared humanity that we must develop.

Expressing the importance of discipline and hard work, General George Patton said, "A pint of sweat saves a gallon of blood."[12] Contrary to this ideal of hard work, as a child I often heard a popular saying, "Work smart, not hard." But working smart can sometimes be unethical. Some people consider cheating on a test or in professional sports (if they don't get caught) to be working smart. We can become more effective at solving our human problems and creating a more peaceful and just world if we *work smart and hard with integrity*.

There are many examples where the easy path is in fact the best way, but when we maintain our integrity and are willing to work hard, we protect ourselves from those easy paths that may lead us off a cliff, and we become an example to those around us. One reason there is such a lack of integrity in our society is that so many people are not exposed to role models who embody integrity.

When we wage peace by confronting an unjust system's weak spots, we should not do this simply because it is the easy way, but the smart way that promotes truth and makes the most of our hard work. Like vegetables, hard work and discipline can also be acquired tastes. But they are among the best spiritual flavors a human being can experience. In *Peaceful Revolution* I describe how working hard for something can give us a greater sense of appreciation and fulfillment when we finally attain it. Discipline and hard work can have an aftertaste of deep appreciation and lasting fulfillment.

The Latin saying "*Per aspera ad astra*" means "Through hardship to the stars." This saying expresses the importance of challenge for human development. Roman philosopher Seneca said something similar, "*Non est ad astra mollis e terris via*," which means "There is no easy way to the stars from earth."[13] When we feed our spiritual organ of challenge, we can sail our internal night sky—the darkness within—to find the stars in our soul that lead to inner and outer peace. Since my earliest memories, I have been sailing my internal night sky, haunted by questions, searching for the star of truth.

Ending war is the kind of significant challenge that can bring out the best in us. Only a struggle against adversity can reveal the greatness human beings are truly capable of achieving. If we overcome adversity by ending war and solving our other global problems, humanity will still need to be challenged in the future. Two great challenges, which we must pursue to achieve our highest human potential, are exploring our internal universe (the mysterious reality within us) and our external universe (the mysterious reality that surrounds us). *Sailing the internal night sky* is a metaphor for our journey through the darkness within, while *sailing the external night sky* is a metaphor for space travel.

Sailing the night sky of the cosmic ocean by sending people beyond our planet's atmosphere is challenging, dangerous, and adventurous. Space travel is such an immense challenge that it requires humanity's greatest intellectual, creative, and cooperative powers. Space travel can also provide alternative jobs to the engineers who make missiles and other weapons, because it takes a lot of brilliance to create acceleration tools that propel people far beyond the earth. Furthermore, when we expand our awareness to include outer space, we are reminded that we are truly a global human family.

During our challenging struggle to imprison unjust systems with the chains of love and truth, we must realize that unjust systems imprison us by limiting our ability to communicate. To escape from this prison and effectively fight injustice, we must *increase the clarity of communication*. In chapter 5 I explained that the second part of this book describes four practical steps that can help us solve a wide variety of human problems and bring our civilization to its highest potential.

Although it can be challenging to make progress in these four steps, they are practical because we can begin applying them to our daily lives right now. We can make gradual and persistent progress, and doing so will benefit us and everyone around us. We don't have to wait for the world to change to begin living these steps. In fact, applying these steps to our daily lives will help change the world. In addition to expanding our perception of beauty (which I discussed in chapter 5) and feeding our spiritual organs (which I discussed in chapter 6), increasing the clarity of communication is the third practical step.

A problem with the English language is that we often use one word to mean too many things. As I explained in chapter 3, when we use the word "love" to mean a thousand different things, this decreases the clarity of communication. In a similar way, when we use the word "violence" to mean a thousand different things, this also decreases the clarity of communication.

Some of my fellow peace activists use the word "violence" to describe a thousand different things. One well-intentioned peace activist told me clapping is violent, and another said that when I give a lecture by standing in front of a sitting audience, I am committing a violent act against them, because I am placing myself above them. But I am not trying to place myself above anyone. Instead, many people find it easier to see and hear a speaker when the person is standing up rather than sitting, and I can more effectively project my voice and use body language when I stand.

Calling these things violent decreases the clarity of communication and trivializes the word "violence." In a similar way, someone who claims, "I didn't sell my car for as much as I wanted; the buyer raped me" is something I would never say, because it trivializes rape.

Some activists label every unjust act as "violence," even when physical abuse is not involved, but we can use many far more precise words to describe injustice. To list just a few options, we can describe injustice as degrading, dehumanizing, demeaning, brutal, cruel, oppressive, destructive, and humiliating. These words are specific and increase the clarity of communication, yet they also carry a lot of weight and do not diminish the seriousness of injustice.*

The following diagram lists a few behaviors that are commonly labeled with the word "violence," but are different from violence in ways we should understand. My definitions of violence, cruelty, and verbal abuse are similar

---

* There is a famous quote attributed to Gandhi: "Poverty is the worst form of violence." However, I think we gain a much better understanding of the attitudes that sustain poverty when we say, "Poverty is the worst form of brutality." Poverty certainly contains prominent elements of violence and cruelty, but as terrible as poverty can be, is it accurate to say poverty is a worse form of violence than war, state-sanctioned slavery, or genocide?

to most people's current understanding of these terms, but as far as I know, there are no words in the English language to describe the dangerous form of apathy I call brutality. A destructive phenomenon like brutality needs a name if we are going to better understand it, clearly talk about it, and cooperate to defeat it.

A person can be both cruel and violent, or cruel in some ways and brutal in other ways. This diagram defines these various behaviors, which can exist separately or blend together:

**Violence**
(The use of physical force
to inflict injury.)

**Direct Cruelty**
(Enjoying the act of inflicting and watching someone's pain. Cruelty can be verbal, physical, or both.)

**Indirect Cruelty**
(Enjoying someone's suffering, whether observing it or merely being aware of it. An example is someone who enjoys watching a person being bullied, but does not actually do the bullying.)

**Direct Brutality**
(Directly causing others to suffer, but preferring not to see them suffer.)

**Indirect Brutality**
(Not directly causing others to suffer, while being apathetic to the agony and injustices around the world.)

**Verbal Abuse**
(Verbally attacking someone. Cruelty is only one among many reasons why we can verbally abuse someone. We can also abuse people with words because we are venting or feel insulted by them.)

Figure 7.3: Definitions of Violence, Cruelty, Brutality, and Verbal Abuse

People can be violent, cruel, brutal, and abusive to varying degrees. To combat these behaviors in all their forms, this diagram is just a start. As a next step, increasing the clarity of communication requires us to cooperate to improve the accuracy and force of our words. Our ancestors protected their families from predators by throwing objects with a high degree of accuracy and force, and if we want to protect humanity from unjust systems, we must propel our words with even greater accuracy and force. The war system conceals its weaknesses in the fog of cloudy communication, but we can expose these weaknesses when we become skilled in the art of clear communication.

Writer George Orwell explains why increasing the clarity of communication is necessary for clear thinking and a healthy democracy: "Modern English, especially written English, is full of bad habits which spread by imitation and which can be avoided if one is willing to take the necessary trouble. If one gets rid of these habits one can think more clearly, and to think clearly is a necessary first step toward political regeneration: so that the fight against bad English is not frivolous and is not the exclusive concern of professional writers."[14]

According to Orwell, propaganda always benefits when we do not clearly define our words, because propaganda relies on vague words and cloudy communication. One reason I use metaphors when I write is because human beings intuitively understand symbolic language (I discussed this in chapter 1), and effective metaphors increase the clarity of communication. My use of metaphors in this chapter provides greater clarity regarding why the war system is so difficult to overcome, and how we can defeat it. Orwell explains how vague words and cloudy communication serve the war system:

> In our time, political speech and writing are largely the defense of the indefensible . . . [To justify unjust policies] political language has to consist largely of euphemism, question-begging and sheer cloudy vagueness.
>
> Defenseless villages are bombarded from the air, the inhabitants driven out into the countryside, the cattle machine-gunned, the huts set on fire with incendiary bullets: this is called *pacification*. Millions of peasants are robbed of their farms and sent trudging along the roads with

no more than they can carry: this is called *transfer of population* or *rectification of frontiers*. People are imprisoned for
years without trial, or shot in the back of the neck or sent
to die of scurvy in Arctic lumber camps: this is called *elim-
ination of unreliable elements*. Such phraseology is needed if
one wants to name things without calling up mental pictures of them. Consider for instance some comfortable English professor defending Russian totalitarianism. He cannot
say outright, "I believe in killing off your opponents when
you can get good results by doing so."

Probably, therefore, he will say something like this:
"While freely conceding that the Soviet regime exhibits certain features which the humanitarian may be inclined to
deplore, we must, I think, agree that a certain curtailment of
the right to political opposition is an unavoidable concomi-
tant of transitional periods, and that the rigors which the
Russian people have been called upon to undergo have been
amply justified in the sphere of concrete achievement."[15]

When I learned how to communicate more clearly, many of the violent
tendencies I had as a child diminished, because I had a more effective way to
express myself. I felt less inclined to throw my fists with accuracy and force,
because I could propel my words with accuracy and force. Countless children
learn cloudy or abusive communication techniques from their parents,
because a child's brain absorbs language as easily as a sponge soaks up water.

Just as children absorb language easily, they also absorb the communication techniques exhibited by their parents and other adults. Many parents
in our society do not practice respectful communication techniques. In addition, how often do you see people on television resolve conflict in a loving
and peaceful way?* Conflict resolution that is respectful, loving, and peaceful

---

* When I watch debates on cable news, I often see a lot of yelling and disrespect. During my childhood, *Star Trek: The Next Generation* was one of the few television shows where people resolved conflict in peaceful ways. There have been other television shows that depict peaceful conflict resolution,
but today reality shows (which usually involve abusive and cruel communication techniques) are
more common.

requires clear communication, and many people have never seen this form of communication in action. Instead, they see adults yelling, being disrespectful, and insulting each other.

In her book *Social Aggression Among Girls*, Marion K. Underwood explains how the angry and abusive communication techniques of adults can make children more aggressive: "Chronic exposure to parents' anger has negative consequences for preschool children, some of which persist long term. Research on marriage conflict shows that children exposed to interparental anger have higher rates of physically aggressive behavior . . . Even if parents are not divorced, exposure to their anger can have negative consequences. In a sample of 4- to 8-year-olds, children exposed to angry marital conflict were rated as more aggressive by peers, teachers, and mothers, and were observed to show more angry responses in peer interactions . . . Cognitive contextual theories suggest that watching parents engage in heated, intense, unresolved conflict may be disorganizing and distressing for youth, causing them to have poor social adjustment and to behave aggressively with peers."[16]

Men, women, and people of every race and religion are capable of displaying the harmful behaviors in the preceding diagram. There is no conclusive evidence that women are less prone than men to being cruel, brutal, or verbally abusive. Earlier in this book I explained the difference between warning aggression (also known as posturing) and hostile aggression (physical violence). Women also posture and commit acts of hostile aggression, and there is abundant evidence that women can be just as aggressive as men. In his book *Female Serial Killers*, Peter Vronsky tells us:

> Newly emerging studies of female violence in various societies, both primitive and modern, reveal that preschool-age girls are as violent as their brothers. They are equally prepared to push and punch and use physical force to achieve their goals. But when they reach the age of ten or eleven it appears that females become less physically aggressive.
>
> This does not mean that females are no longer aggres-

sive at that age, but that their aggression begins to take a different form than it does in males. In the male a public display of aggressive prowess is encouraged, while the female begins to use her newly acquired linguistic and social skills to practice aggression surreptitiously. Females begin to use indirect or "masked" aggression, manipulating others to attack or somehow using the social structure to harm their intended victim. The use of gossiping, exchanging derogatory notes, and excluding a victim from groups, the forming of hate clubs and recently hate websites are common media for adolescent female aggression and sometimes these forms can lead to serious physical repercussions.

Anthropologist Ilsa Glazer observed that in both Zambia and Israel, female leaders tended to scapegoat and gossip about other ambitious subordinate women in an attempt to exclude them from power. In nearby Palestine, where often women are murdered by their fathers or brothers to "defend family honor," Glazer discovered that the killing was actually instigated by women who first insistently spread accusatory gossip [about the victim], which spurred the men to act. In North American youth gangs, girls sometimes instigate violence by deliberately calculated acts of "bad-mouthing" that compel their boyfriends to commit acts of violence . . .

Aggression in females slips below the radar because they tend to express early aggression through social and verbal forms. Today few would deny that girls commit physical bullying: Schoolgirl bullies are a huge juvenile issue these days. In the past, females tended to first use gossip and social exclusion as a form of aggression among their peers, but today that expression is frequently a prelude to conventional physical violence.[17]

As a child I was haunted by questions that caused me to look for wisdom and answers in unexpected places. Since then I have been sailing through the storms of struggle in search of the star of truth. Humanity continues to be haunted by the question of how to imprison the unjust systems that harm us. If we look deeply, we can find wisdom and answers in video games, sports, mythology, military strategy, the history of waging peace, the mysterious universe within us, the deepest darkness, and the timelessness of truth.

# CHAPTER 8

# The Mystery Beneath the Waves

## *The Tree of Life*

I have spent most of my life searching for immortality. I remember an early childhood experience that ignited this search. I was around two years old, and my parents had just parked their car. We were walking to church in the evening during a thunderstorm, and I was wearing a pair of Smurf flip-flops, based on the Saturday morning cartoon that had just debuted on American television.

To reach the church we had to cross a road. No cars were passing, and the only sound was the rhythm of rain. Along the curb on the other side of the road, rainwater accumulating in the gutter flowed rapidly downhill like a small stream. My father held my hand while we crossed the street, but as he gently pulled my hand to help me step onto the sidewalk, my foot passed too close to the gutter and the surging water seized one of my flip-flops. I watched helplessly as my flip-flop sped away from me, carried down the gutter by the rushing rainwater, and disappeared into a sewer drain. I started crying as most children do, but a few seconds later I began to cry as I never had before.

My father picked me up in his arms and carried me toward the church, but instead of calming down when my father held me, I began to cry louder. It was my only way to express a new kind of pain I had never experienced before. I could not articulate my conflicted thoughts in words at such a young age, but I clearly remember what went through my mind during those moments. I was crying not simply because I lost my flip-flop, but because I suddenly had a terrifying realization. As my father carried me away, I realized he was powerless and unable to rescue something I had cherished. It had disappeared forever, and there was nothing he could do.

Before seeing my flip-flop disappear into the dark sewer drain, my father had seemed like an all-powerful protective presence in my life. But the loss of a simple object destroyed this illusion. During that moment of loss, I learned how something I cared about could disappear forever, and my father was powerless to stop it. This was the beginning of my journey to understand loss and the limits of human power.

Several years later at the age of four I experienced another kind of loss, when I witnessed how the storm of trauma could submerge my kind and gentle father in madness. A man I had trusted with all my heart now seemed lost in darkness and gone forever. A man who had seemed like an all-powerful protective presence in my life now made me fear for my life. As I watched my father struggle with rage and suicidal urges throughout my childhood, I became increasingly haunted by questions about loss and immortality. I wanted to know whether it is possible to prevent loss, overcome death, and live forever.

We all ask these questions at some point in our lives. Humanity has a natural fascination with immortality, and this fascination expresses itself in numerous ways. Countless people around the world are drawn to stories about reincarnation and the afterlife. People in history even dreamed of a "fountain of youth" that would keep them forever young. Many people today dream of a future when scientists will discover a way to indefinitely extend human life. And countless people seek immortality through fame, nationalism, and the struggle for transcendence (which we will discuss later in this chapter).

We can better understand humanity's fascination with immortality by exploring the metaphor of the Tree of Life from the Bible. According to the Bible, there are two forbidden trees in the Garden of Eden. The first is the Tree of the Knowledge of Good and Evil, a metaphor for our heightened human awareness, which we discussed in chapter 2. The second forbidden tree is the Tree of Life.

Many people in our culture know the story of Adam and Eve eating from the Tree of the Knowledge of Good and Evil, yet the Tree of Life is often left out of the story. The Bible says that Adam and Eve were banished from the Garden of Eden not only because they ate from the first forbidden tree, but also because God did not want them to eat from the second forbidden tree: the Tree of Life. According to the book of Genesis, if human beings ate from both trees, we would become like gods, because we would not only have heightened awareness, but immortality.

The book of Genesis describes what happens when Adam and Eve eat from the Tree of the Knowledge of Good and Evil, and how the Tree of Life can be seen as the real reason for their banishment:

> And the LORD God said, "The man has now become like one of us, knowing good and evil. He must not be allowed to reach out his hand and take also from the tree of life and eat, and live forever." So the LORD God banished him from the Garden of Eden to work the ground from which he had been taken. After he drove the man out, he placed on the east side of the Garden of Eden cherubim and a flaming sword flashing back and forth to guard the way to the tree of life.[1]

The Tree of Life is not a metaphor for immortality. Instead, it is a metaphor for human *mortality*, because it symbolizes how eternal life is beyond our reach. Just as Adam and Eve cannot eat from the Tree of Life, human beings have developed ingenious ways to delay death, but despite all our brilliance, we are powerless to prevent death's inevitability.

The Tree of Life also symbolizes our craving for immortality. Just as the flaming sword and cherubim (a kind of angel) prevent Adam and Eve from fulfilling their desire to consume the Tree of Life, the laws of nature prevent us from consuming immortality. Unlike laws made by governments, the passage of time and inevitability of death are laws of nature that no human being can break. Our fantasy that science will someday give us eternal life could very likely be a modern-day myth, similar to our ancestors' belief in the fountain of youth. Science and technology are certainly powerful, yet they are far from all powerful. In the end, science and technology are merely human inventions that may be incapable of granting us godlike eternal life.[2]

All animals are mortal, but human beings are unique, because our heightened awareness of our mortality can drive us to fanaticism, religious extremism, madness, violence, or self-destruction. As far as we know, human beings are the only species on the planet that can be terrified of growing old and anxious about the inevitability of death.

Because of our heightened human awareness, our ability to perceive mortality extends far beyond our understanding that all human beings eventually die. As far as we know, we are the only species on the planet that can imagine the extinction of all life, the destruction of our world, and the demise of the universe. Many religious figures, scientists, and philosophers have discussed the end of humanity, our planet, and the universe. No other species on earth seems fascinated by these apocalyptic stories. Science-fiction films and world religions are some of the ways human beings explore this fascination.

Not only can we imagine an apocalypse that would eradicate every human being on earth, but we can also make it happen. We are the only creatures on the planet capable of choosing between mass extinction and cooperative survival. We can use our technological brilliance to drive ourselves and most other species on earth extinct. Or we can use our large brains to protect our environment, sustain the habitats of other species, leave our planet to explore other worlds, and never go extinct as long as the universe exists. We can choose to destroy or save our planet.

During the twentieth century, the word "planet" gained a new meaning. People began using this word to signify the fragile and interconnected biosphere that makes life possible on earth. For example, when people talk about "saving our planet" today, they are not referring to the iron core of the earth, which is not threatened by nuclear weapons, war, and environmental destruction. Instead, modern uses of the word "planet" refer to our fragile and interconnected biosphere and the delicate web of life contained within it. Using the word "planet" in this way gives us a survival advantage, because it allows us to recognize that our biosphere, along with our future, are both very fragile.

Our heightened awareness of mortality allows us to recognize how fragile our future truly is. If we do not protect our fragile future by waging peace, humanity will destroy itself. In this book series I use our heightened human awareness to discuss why the road to peace is necessary for our survival, and how we can walk together on this peaceful path. Our heightened human awareness can aid our survival in many ways, but it can also be a significant source of psychological suffering for human beings.

Other animals can certainly suffer from excruciating psychological pain, including trauma. Numerous scientific studies, books, and documentaries confirm the fact that many animals experience deep emotions. Science is also debunking the myth that animals cannot think. Temple Grandin, a professor of animal science, tells us: "Saying an animal is just sort of a robot that blindly does instinctual hardwired behaviors—that's just ridiculous. When it comes to some of the emotional things and cognition in animals, I think scientists are going to prove that little old ladies in tennis shoes, who say that [their dog] little Fifi really can think, are right. But that doesn't mean that an animal can think at our level."[3]

Other animal species are lower than human beings only if we value cognitive ability as the highest criteria for dignity and worth. Native American traditions realize that many species have exceptional intuitive and sensory abilities that exceed those of human beings. As I will explain later in this chapter, other species also seem to live in harmony with the eternal mystery of the universe. Because Native American traditions recognize humanity's heightened cognitive awareness, they teach that we must use this power to behave as stewards of the earth.

Although other animals can experience immense psychological pain, human beings can suffer in ways other animals cannot. To mention just a few of the many examples we have explored in this book, we can suffer enormously from a lack of purpose and meaning in our lives, even when we have freedom, good physical health, companionship, and a belly full of food. We can also hate ourselves, feel like outcasts from nature, dread the idea of getting wrinkles and gray hair, starve ourselves to look thin, suffer from alcoholism, be conditioned to believe we are part of an inferior race, go through a midlife crisis, and be tormented by feelings of low self-worth. If we want to reduce these problems in ourselves and throughout society, we must learn how to feed our spiritual cravings and make peace with the problem of human existence.

In school I was never taught how to feed our spiritual cravings and walk the path of inner and outer peace. Instead, in high school I learned about Maslow's *hierarchy of needs*, which states that our most important human needs are food, water, sex, and sleep. According to Maslow, when those physical needs are met we can satisfy our need for safety, and when that need is met we can satisfy our higher needs for love, belonging, self-worth, and self-actualization. In school I was taught that people must fulfill their lower needs before pursuing their higher needs:

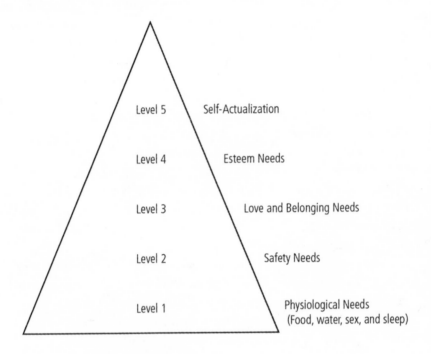

Figure 8.1: Maslow's Hierarchy of Needs[4]

Human behavior is much more complex than Maslow's hierarchy of needs suggests.* In the twenty-first century, we require a new and more accurate model of the human condition to help us solve our personal, national, and global problems. In my first book, *Will War Ever End?* I explain why cooperation is *the key to human survival.* Psychologist Pamela Rutledge discusses the flaws of Maslow's theory, explaining why our nomadic ancestors needed cooperation to survive as much as they needed food and water:

> Maslow's model, as its name suggests, organizes groups of human needs into levels in a hierarchical structure, forming a pyramid. It's similar in some senses to video games in that you have to fulfill the requirements of one set of needs before you can level up. But the same things that make Maslow's model cognitively appealing— that sense of order and predictability—also makes it wrong. If only life were so simple . . .
>
> But here's the problem with Maslow's hierarchy. None of these needs [such as food and safety]—starting with basic survival on up—are possible without social connection and collaboration. None of Maslow's needs can be met without social connection. Humans are social animals for good reason. Without collaboration, there is no survival. It was not possible to defeat a Woolly Mammoth, build a secure structure, or care for children while hunting without a team effort. It's more true now than then. Our reliance on each other grows as societies became more complex, interconnected, and specialized. Connection is a prerequisite for survival, physically and emotionally.
>
> Needs are not hierarchical. Life is messier than that. Needs are, like most other things in nature, an inter-

---

* Although Maslow's hierarchy is often taught in schools as a strict list of priorities, in Maslow's original paper he discussed how people can sometimes prioritize these needs in a variety of orders. Not only was Maslow's hierarchy taught to me (and many other students) incorrectly, but I later realized that he underestimated the amount of exceptions to his theory.

active, dynamic system, but they are anchored in our ability to make social connections.* Maslow's model needs rewiring so it matches our brains. Belongingness is the driving force of human behavior, not a third tier activity. The system of human needs from bottom to top . . . are dependent on our ability to connect with others. Belonging to a community provides the sense of security and agency that makes our brains happy and helps keep us safe.[5]

In high school I did not think Maslow's hierarchy of needs made sense, because human beings frequently turn this hierarchy upside down. People often prioritize love, belonging, esteem (self-worth), and self-actualization (achieving our full potential) above food, safety, and even survival. For example, people with anorexia will prioritize belonging and self-worth above food by starving themselves—risking their health and lives. People on hunger strike will also starve themselves, because they are willing to suffer and die for a cause. Hindu ascetics will voluntarily live in the wilderness, subjecting themselves to thirst, hunger, and danger during their quest for enlightenment. And many parents living in poverty prioritize love over food by feeding their child even when their own stomachs are empty.

In her book *Hunger*, Sharman Russell describes how Gandhi's hunger strike for justice nearly killed him:

Hunger is a form of communication. When we fast for health, we are having a conversation with the body. When we fast as a Jew or Catholic, Moslem or Hindu, we are having a conversation with God. These are private discussions and often silent. Hunger strikes are different. Almost always, they are loud and public, like a messy

---

* I define *connection* as the experience a person has when relating to another lifeform and having one or more of the following cravings fed: purpose and meaning, nurturing relationships, expression, belonging, and transcendence. Empathy builds a foundation for the strongest form of belonging— which is solidarity.

family argument the whole neighborhood can hear. The man or woman fasting for change wants the world to know and judge. To know and act. The conversation is with the world . . .

In Ireland, nationalists who opposed the British occupation of their country had begun to use the hunger strike as well. In 1917, a nationalist died in prison after being force-fed. Forty thousand people followed his funeral procession through the streets of Dublin. In 1920, the lord mayor of Cork died of a hunger strike after seventy-four days without food. His words became a touchstone for future strikers, "It is not those who inflict the most but those who will suffer the most who will conquer . . ."

In 1932, Indian and British leaders began working on a form of Indian self-government. Gandhi declared a fast to the death when the British suggested a constitution that would establish three separate electorates for Moslems, Hindus, and Untouchables [a population of Indians treated as subhumans by the caste system]. Gandhi believed that to give the Untouchables a separate electorate would divide them further from their fellow Hindus and undo what work had been done to get rid of the caste system . . .

Gandhi was now sixty-two years old and in a British jail. Early on, this fast badly affected him. He drank little water and seemed listless. He could not stand nor walk, but had to be carried to his bath on a stretcher. He complained of sharp pains, and his blood pressure rose alarmingly high.

The news media in India followed every detail. Those who could read told the story to those who could not, and they told others. All over the country, Hindus prayed for their beloved Great Soul [Mahatma Gandhi]. His desire had been to make each one of them feel responsible for his life, and they seemed to understand. From the first day of the fast, Hindu temples that had previously denied entrance to Untouchables opened their doors. Hindu schoolchildren sat next to Untouchables during class. Untouchables could now use wells and roads once forbidden . . .

[Journalist] Louis Fischer wrote, "The fast could not kill the curse of untouchability which was more than three thousand years old ... [But Gandhi's fast] snapped a long chain that stretched back into antiquity and had enslaved tens of millions. Some links of the chain remained . . . But nobody would forge new links . . ."

By the fifth day of the fast, Gandhi seemed near death. He whispered to his wife who should inherit his few personal belongings. By now, Hindu and Untouchable leaders had worked out an agreement, but nothing could be official until the British government consented as well. The new pact was telegraphed to London on a Sunday. Ministers left their homes, hurried to Downing Street, poured over the documents, and telegraphed back their approval early Monday morning. That afternoon, Gandhi accepted a glass of orange juice.[6]

People not only starve themselves to serve their ideals, but they also face violent attacks. Many civil rights activists sacrificed safety because they were willing to die for justice, and countless activists have preferred to be beaten, imprisoned, and killed rather than abandon their ideals. Early Christians executed by the Romans, along with people from many religious faiths, have also died for their beliefs. Maslow lists sex as a basic need that must be satisfied before a person can become self-actualized, but what about self-actualized people such as Gandhi, the Fourteenth Dalai Lama, Thich Nhat Hanh, and all those who choose temporary or lifelong celibacy?

When I teach courses on peace leadership, I often ask people what our human needs are. Every time, they start out by saying things such as food, water, and shelter. Most of the time, they do not even mention purpose, meaning, belonging, self-worth, or our other spiritual cravings.

When teaching a peace leadership course in northern Uganda, I wrote humanity's spiritual cravings on a board. I then asked the group of about twenty-five participants, "What is more important, food or purpose and meaning?" They all said, "Purpose and meaning." One of the participants raised her hand and explained, "Purpose and meaning are more important than food, because if you have food but don't have any purpose and meaning, you won't want to eat. You won't want to live."

If you don't have any food, but you have a lot of purpose and meaning, you will work hard to find some food. But if you have a lot of food, and you don't have any purpose and meaning, you will lose the will to live. Someone could say, "Food is more important than purpose and meaning, because if every single human being was completely deprived of food, our species would go extinct." However, isn't this also true for purpose and meaning? If every single human being was completely deprived of purpose and meaning, wouldn't our species also go extinct?

Although people today rarely discuss humanity's spiritual cravings, and Maslow's paradigm still dominates our society's understanding, we must journey beyond Maslow's theory by recognizing humanity's spiritual cravings. Only then can we solve our national and global problems, because many of these problems are caused by spiritual hunger pains. Nationalism, for example, is caused by humanity's spiritual cravings. Hitler gave Germans a sense of belonging through his message of national identity, a sense of self-worth through his rhetoric of German superiority, a sense of purpose and meaning through his vision for Germany's future, a sense of inspiration through the skillful use of propaganda, and explanations for Germany's economic problems through a worldview. Nationalism can even feed our craving for transcendence when we identify with icons that seem immortal such as a nation-state, flag, and ideology.

In *The End of War* and *The Art of Waging Peace*, I describe how we can create a healthy form of patriotism (where love of country motivates us to challenge injustice) that resists the most destructive forms of nationalism. Hitler did not invent nationalism, but manipulated humanity's spiritual cravings, just as Roman emperors, Greek politicians, and many other rulers have done. Nationalism appeals to people from all economic backgrounds—the poor as well as the rich—which refutes Maslow's theory that people who are hungry tend to care only about food. As Jesus, who spent much of his time preaching to the poor, noticed, "Man does not live by bread alone."

If we want to understand why fascist ideologies and violent fundamentalist religious sects appeal to people, we should ask ourselves, "How do these groups feed people's spiritual organs? How do these groups offer people purpose, meaning, explanations for how our world works, expression, inspiration, belonging, self-worth, and transcendence? When spiritual organs such as nurturing relationships and the acquired taste of challenge are concerned, do these groups lure people with the illusion of nurturing relationships and provide easy answers rather than real challenge? How do these groups give people an outlet for rage and trauma?"

The materialism of secular society tends to create a spiritual void that can be filled by fascist ideologies and violent fundamentalism. However, the *road to peace* offers a more fulfilling way than materialism, fascism, and violent fundamentalism to feed our spiritual organs and deal with rage and trauma. When our fragile future is concerned, only the way of peace can create the global solidarity that is necessary for human survival and the protection of our delicate biosphere.

There are numerous interpretations of Maslow's hierarchy of needs, and Maslow's views changed over the years. However, his basic theory lacks sufficient evidence to support it. Fiona Wilson, a professor of organizational behavior, tells us: "Maslow's theory lacks empirical support (Wahba and Bridwell, 1976), as Maslow himself admitted when, in 1962, he wrote: 'My motivation theory was published 20 years ago and in all that time nobody repeated it, or tested it, or really analysed [*sic*] it or criticized it. They just used it, swallowed it whole with only the minor modifications.' (Lowry, 1982; 63)."[7]

The most obvious refutation of Maslow's theory is war. Although coercive methods are widely used to get soldiers to fight, many people in war voluntarily subject themselves to hunger, thirst, sleep deprivation, injury, and death because they are willing to sacrifice for their family, comrades,

country, or an idea. During my time in the army I met soldiers who voluntarily joined the military after the September 11 attacks, because they wanted
to serve their country and fight for democracy.

In *The End of War* I discuss greed as a cause of war, but this chapter will
take that idea a step further by discussing the many forms of greed. In addition to greed for money, people can also be greedy for glory, fame, recognition, power, and immortality. In the *Iliad*, Achilles must choose between
returning home to live a long and peaceful life by abandoning the war effort,
or dying young in battle and achieving immortality.

Achilles is not seeking immortality in the form of reincarnation or an
afterlife, but immortality in the form of being forever famous. For Achilles,
glory means a degree of fame that will cause future generations to recognize
and admire him. If his glory never dies, then he will achieve a form of
immortality. In the *Iliad*, Achilles says the following as he ponders leaving
the battlefields of Troy and returning home to Greece:

> Mother tells me, the immortal goddess Thetis with
> her glistening feet, that two fates bear me on to the day of
> death. If I hold out here and I lay siege to Troy, my journey
> home is gone, but my glory never dies. If I voyage back to
> the fatherland I love, my pride, my glory dies . . . true, but
> the life that's left me will be long, the stroke of death will
> not come on me quickly.[8]

When Achilles seeks revenge for the death of his friend Patroclus, he
chooses the glory that will result from dying young in battle over a long and
peaceful life. In chapter 4 I listed various motivations that cause soldiers to
willingly risk their lives in battle, and the desire for fame and glory is another
motivation. Although Achilles is a fictional character, historical figures such
as Alexander the Great desired everlasting fame and glory just like Achilles.

Alexander the Great turns Maslow's hierarchy of needs upside down.
He not only chose to endure hunger, thirst, and sleep deprivation during
long military campaigns, but he also sought the immortality of fame and
glory by repeatedly risking his life in battle. Anyone who risks dying for fame

OUR FRAGILE FUTURE

also turns Maslow's hierarchy upside down. Many mass shooters have committed bloody massacres that resulted in suicide as an attempt to express their pain and become famous. A conqueror such as Napoleon, who had statues built to portray himself as a divine hero, also risked his life for fame, glory, and immortality.

Maslow's hierarchical model oversimplifies the complexity of human behavior. I have met people who believe that middle-class workers are afraid of losing their jobs simply because Maslow's hierarchy of needs places food as humanity's most important priority. But are people motivated only by the desire for food when they fear losing their jobs, or is human behavior far more complex?

For many people, jobs are not just about food. Jobs can give us a sense of purpose and meaning in our lives. Jobs can also define our self-worth, causing those who lose their jobs to feel worthless and ashamed. Jobs can even create a sense of belonging and foster nurturing relationships (through a social network with workplace colleagues). When people work, they can also be motivated by love of family and the hope of giving their children a better future. Saying that jobs are just about food oversimplifies human behavior, which results in an oversimplification of reality.

A more realistic and practical model of human motivation is represented in the following diagram:

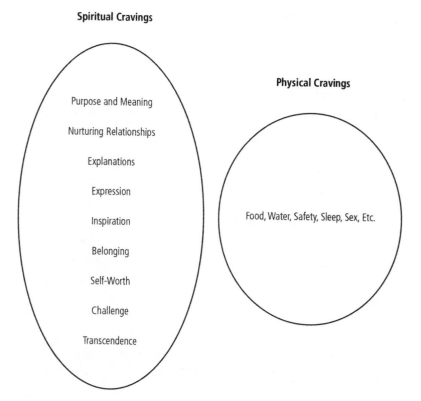

**Spiritual Cravings**

Purpose and Meaning

Nurturing Relationships

Explanations

Expression

Inspiration

Belonging

Self-Worth

Challenge

Transcendence

**Physical Cravings**

Food, Water, Safety, Sleep, Sex, Etc.

(These spiritual cravings are listed in the
order they were introduced in this book, not
in an order of priority. The priority of these
cravings varies from person to person.)

Figure 8.2: Spiritual and Physical Cravings

This diagram shows that human beings have spiritual and physical cravings, represented by an ellipse and circle respectively. The ellipse and circle are placed side by side as equals, because people can be motivated by both sets of cravings. Our early nomadic ancestors had to satisfy their spiritual and physical cravings to achieve their highest potential, cooperate fully as a group, and survive in the harsh African wilderness. The reason the ellipse is larger than the circle in the diagram is because our spiritual appetite is larger, more complex, and not as easy to satisfy as our physical appetite. For a full understanding of human motivation, the content in this book should be combined with the content in *Peaceful Revolution*, because we can also be motivated by the muscles of our shared humanity (such as hope, empathy, appreciation, and conscience), which I discuss in that book.

All human beings want to fulfill spiritual cravings such as purpose, meaning, belonging, and self-worth, yet the intensity and priority of these cravings can differ from person to person. Just as people's physical appetites can differ in size, our spiritual appetites can also differ in size. Because I have suffered from extreme trauma, my spiritual craving for explanations to the questions that haunted me as a child is especially large and voracious.

Understanding our spiritual and physical cravings gives us deeper insight into a wide variety of human behavior. People's motivation to satisfy a physical craving such as safety can be so powerful that they may accept their government's claim that basic liberties must be sacrificed to protect them from "enemies." Some people risk their lives to feed their craving for challenge when they participate in dangerous sports that push the human body and mind to its limits. Some people take risks to feed their craving for expression when they live as "starving artists" who struggle in poverty. Later in this chapter I will discuss how people take risks to satisfy their craving for transcendence—the one spiritual craving I have not yet discussed.

Of course, sports and art can fulfill more than one spiritual craving. Writing gives me a sense of purpose, meaning, expression, challenge, and transcendence. Writing also allows me to discover explanations to the questions that haunted me as a child, and by exploring who I am through writing I have developed a better sense of my self-worth and my belonging to the mystery of life. My writing relies heavily on research, and by researching our remarkable human ancestors and the other incredible species that share this planet with us, I also fulfill my craving for inspiration.

We do not have to be athletes or artists to place a high priority on fulfilling our spiritual cravings. Although religion can appeal to people from all backgrounds, religion has allowed many of the poorest people to feed their craving for purpose, meaning, nurturing relationships (in the form of a community), explanations, expression (in the form of music, rituals, etc.), inspiration, belonging, self-worth, challenge (for those who strive to become better people through religious ideals), and transcendence. In his book *Animal Farm*, George Orwell describes how oppressed people in desperate circumstances can be drawn more fiercely to religion, even if they have not fulfilled their most basic physical needs.

*Animal Farm* is an allegorical story about farm animals who overthrow their farmer. The farmer symbolizes oppressive rulers,* the animals symbolize oppressed people, and Sugarcandy Mountain represents how religion and the belief in an afterlife can have a unique appeal to people who are hungry. The following passage from *Animal Farm* shows how the hungry animals (a metaphor for starving people throughout history) yearn for justice and fairness through their belief in an afterlife:

> [The raven Moses] claimed to know of the existence of a mysterious country called Sugarcandy Mountain, to which all animals went when they died. It was situated somewhere up in the sky, a little distance beyond the clouds, Moses said. In Sugarcandy Mountain it was Sunday seven days a week, clover was in season all the year round, and lump sugar and linseed cake grew on the hedges. The animals hated Moses because he told tales and did no work, but some of them believed in Sugarcandy Mountain . . .
>
> He would perch on a stump, flap his black wings, and talk by the hour to anyone who would listen. "Up there, comrades," he would say solemnly, pointing to the sky with his large beak—"up there, just on the other side of that dark cloud that you can see—there it lies, Sugarcandy Mountain, that happy country where we poor animals shall rest forever from our labours!" He even claimed to have been there on one of his higher flights, and to have

---

* Although *Animal Farm* is an allegory of the Bolshevik Revolution in Russia, its metaphors apply to many other oppressive systems around the world and throughout history.

seen the everlasting fields of clover and the linseed cake and lump sugar growing on the hedges. Many of the animals believed him. Their lives now, they reasoned, were hungry and laborious; *was it not right and just that a better world should exist somewhere else?* [emphasis added][9]

People can seek to fulfill their spiritual cravings through religion, sports, art, friendship and family, scientific pursuits, philosophy, or a combination of these and other endeavors. The religion of war also offers to fulfill our spiritual cravings. In the army I gained purpose and meaning through a sense of mission, and I felt a deep sense of belonging through camaraderie. In the civilian world it is difficult to replicate the magnitude of purpose, meaning, and belonging I felt in the military. This is why, for so many soldiers, war has a seductive scent and a traumatizing taste.

War can be seductive, because it offers to feed our spiritual cravings. Not only did I feel purpose, meaning, and belonging in the army, but I also experienced an increased sense of self-worth, because I felt like my society needed and respected me. Although I had many bad leaders in the military, I also had great leaders and loyal comrades who fulfilled my craving for nurturing relationships. The military also gave me explanations for how the world works (by providing a worldview), and it challenged me physically and psychologically.

People can try to fulfill their spiritual cravings in surprising ways. Although I list food under physical cravings, people can eat excessively because they are depressed, lonely, or trying to fill a spiritual void. Sex can be categorized as a physical craving, but sex is often motivated by spiritual cravings such as nurturing relationships (in the form of a loving relationship with a partner), transcendence, and even self-worth. When exploring serial killers in chapter 3, we learned how sexual assault can be a cruel form of expressing one's rage.

How can sex be motivated by the craving for self-worth? In our society, a man who has sex with a lot of desirable women is often admired. If a man in our society is a virgin or has not had a lot of sexual partners, some may call him a "loser." In her book *Pornland*, Gail Dines describes how women can embrace being objectified as sex objects because it gives them an ephemeral sense of power and a fleeting sense of self-worth:

> Conforming to the image [of a sex object] is seductive as it not only offers women an identity that is in keeping with the majority but also confers a whole host of pleasures, since looking hot does garner the kind of male attention that can sometimes feel empowering. Indeed, getting people to consent to any system, even if it's inherently oppressive, is made easier if conformity brings with it psychological, social, and/or material gains. Many women know what it's like to be sexually wanted by a man: the way he holds you in his gaze, the way he finds everything you say worthy of attention, the way you suddenly become the most compelling person in the world . . . This is an attention men shower on women they want sexually, and it feels like real power, but it is ephemeral because it is being given to women by men who increasingly, thanks to the porn culture, see women as interchangeable hookup partners. To feel that sense of power, women need to keep sexing themselves up so they can become visible to the next man who is going to, for a short time, hold her in his lustful gaze.[10]

Obviously, sex can go beyond a mere physical craving by becoming intertwined with our complex spiritual cravings. When we do not understand the complexity of humanity's spiritual cravings, we cannot develop practical solutions to heal humanity's problems. To heal an illness, a doctor must know the cause and the cure. In a similar way, to heal epidemics such as war, injustice, and environmental destruction, we must understand the human condition by exploring what it means to be human, because we are the cause of these epidemics. And we are the cure.

What if humanity is suffering from problems that do not yet have a name? Would you agree that two of the biggest problems in human history have been racism and sexism? But did you know there was no word for racism in the English language until around the 1930s, and there was no word in the English language for sexism until the 1960s? Prior to 1900, racism and sexism were not words or even concepts for most people around the world. To make progress toward solving any large-scale problem, we must first conceptualize it and give it a name.

What if all of us in the twenty-first century are facing problems just as big as racism and sexism, but these problems are not yet words or even concepts for most people living today? As far as I know, there are currently no words in the English language that describe the behavior I call "brutality," nor is there a term that conveys the problem I call "spiritual hunger," which expands and deepens our understanding of the human existential problem. The psychological blindness of brutality is the apathy that sustains racism, sexism, poverty, war, abuse of animals, environmental destruction, and all the injustice in the world. Spiritual hunger, as I describe it, shows that religion, science, and philosophy are different languages that express the same human existential problem.* Brutality and spiritual hunger cause more human suffering than anything else.

Racism and sexism existed in our primordial past, long before they were given names, but we could not begin to fully confront these problems until we gave them names. Brutality and spiritual hunger also existed in our primordial past, but how we deal with these problems in our fragile future is up to us.

We have the power to solve our national and global problems. We can also solve timeless problems such as brutality and spiritual hunger by learning to cure our psychological blindness and heal our spiritual hunger pains. But is it possible to solve the problem symbolized by the Tree of Life? Is it possible to transcend time and death? Although the path to the Tree of Life is guarded by cherubim and a flaming sword, is it possible to overcome these obstacles and taste immortality?

---

* Today people tend to think of religion, science, and philosophy as different languages, but these languages often overlapped in the past, and we can find the intersection of truth between them as we move forward in the future.

## Change the Quality of Our Suffering

I am my father's son in more ways than one. Every moment my heart beats, his blood echoes in my veins. Every day I work for peace, his suffering whispers in my soul. His struggles did not die with him, but continue to sing through me. The more I progress on my spiritual journey, the more empathy and appreciation I gain for my father. He carried the heavy weight of war, racism, and trauma for most of his life. The burden he harbored in his heart weighed more than the human mind can imagine.

Unlike me, my father did not have access to mental health support, and he did not have a productive outlet such as writing to explore and reconcile his agony. His unresolved trauma shaped who I am, but because I have spent years growing empathy and understanding in the dark soil of suffering, I have given purpose and meaning to my suffering, ensuring neither of us suffered in vain. In some ways I now see my father as a comrade and brother, because all suffering people secretly yearn for peace, and I am determined to complete the journey to peace that he could not finish while he was alive.

We can all journey to peace by growing empathy and understanding in the dark soil of suffering. Soil, like suffering, has the potential to nourish life and growth. Plants grow underground in darkness, then emerge from soil and reach toward the sun. In a similar way, our empathy and understanding can grow in the darkness of suffering, then emerge from the soil of agony and reach toward the light of love and truth. When we grow empathy and understanding in the dark soil of suffering, our suffering serves a purpose and gains meaning. Just as the nutrients from plants can transform and improve the quality of soil, purpose and meaning can transform and improve the quality of our suffering. This ensures we do not suffer in vain.

Changing the quality of our suffering is the fourth practical step that can help us solve our most serious human problems and bring our civilization to its highest potential. As I explained in chapter 5, to solve our human problems we must embark on a journey to understand human nature (which I discuss in *Will War Ever End?* and *The End of War*), strengthen the muscles of our shared humanity (which I discuss in *Peaceful Revolution*), learn how to wage peace (which I discuss in *The Art of Waging Peace*), and understand the human condition and put these four practical steps into action (which I discuss in *The Cosmic Ocean*). Since each book in this series uncovers more hidden landmarks on the road to peace, I will discuss more solutions for solving our personal, national, and global problems when I write the next books in this series.

I have focused on these four practical steps in this book, however, because I rarely hear them discussed today. Expanding our perception of beauty, feeding our spiritual organs, increasing the clarity of communication, and changing the quality of our suffering are eternal challenges where we can make significant progress, but there is no clear finish line. Every person must embark on a journey to apply these four practical steps to their life, and doing so will improve their psychological well-being and local community. In fact, every country and our entire world will benefit immensely if we put these four practical steps into action, but as I write this these steps are largely neglected and not a topic of conversation for most people. Together we can change that.

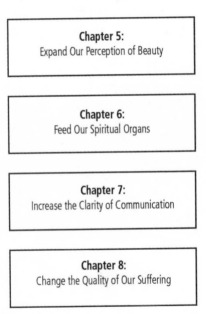

Figure 8.3: Four Practical (and Largely Neglected) Steps for Improving Our World

Changing the quality of our suffering does not consist of a simple decision to create change, but a spiritual journey that requires persistence and patience. Just as seeds do not emerge from soil as blooming plants overnight, it takes time before the seeds of empathy and understanding can emerge from the dark soil of suffering and fully bloom. I have experienced firsthand how challenging it can be to find light in darkness, and numerous unsung heroes of peace and justice have assisted me on my journey, such as my mentor Jo Ann Deck, English teachers Janice Vaughn and Jean Arndt who encouraged me to be a writer, and the many kind people I have met within and outside of the military.

Despite the adversity I have experienced, I am more fortunate than most, because acts of kindness are like raindrops, and throughout the years people have given me a lot of rain. When we change the quality of our suffering through empathy, understanding, purpose, and meaning, we increase our compassion for others who suffer, which makes us less judgmental. We should not look down on someone who remains bitter and has difficulty growing empathy and understanding in the dark soil of suffering, because everyone's struggles are unique, and we all receive different amounts of rain.

I did not fully realize how much this rain nurtured me until later in my life. When these raindrops of kindness fell on me as a child, my anger often prevented me from appreciating them. Because my father could be kind, then suddenly erupt in a storm of rage, I tended to view kindness not as nourishing rain, but as a potential flood that threatened to drown me. Our heightened human awareness gives us the power of introspection and self-reflection, and by using this awareness to reflect deeply on my life, I can see how even small acts of kindness I received helped my empathy and understanding to grow.

For every person like me who receives enough rain to transform trauma into an abundant harvest, countless people who suffer from trauma end up homeless, in prison, addicted to drugs, or dead before they have lived a full life. We can respond to their pain by working to prevent the causes of trauma and pouring more kindness into the world. Our world needs soldiers of peace to not only challenge injustice in all its forms, but to also serve as rainmakers.

The dark soil of suffering does not have to consist of extreme trauma for us to grow empathy and understanding. We can also grow empathy and understanding in another kind of psychological soil—the uncomfortable realization that life is fragile, vulnerable, and mortal. Children have a natural capacity to feel empathy for the vulnerable creatures that share this planet with us. In chapter 5 I discussed being a three-year-old child and feeling empathy for a cricket with a missing hind leg. I also have other memories of early childhood empathy.

When I was three, my mother found a sick baby bird on the ground. I named the bird Billy, and I remember my mother keeping him in our living room, trying to nurse him back to health, and feeding him with a tiny metal spoon. I was deeply concerned about the fragile bird's well-being. After we had Billy for a couple of days, I woke up and walked to the living room to see him, but he was gone. I asked my mother where he went, and she said, "His mother came to take him home."

When I was around seven, I asked my mother, "Do you remember when you told me Billy's mother came to get him? That didn't actually happen, did it? He died and you didn't want to tell me, right?" My mother said he died overnight, and she made up that story because she did not want to upset me.

Although children learn about the fragility, vulnerability, and mortality of life at different ages, we all learn about death eventually. According to science writer Virginia Hughes: "Children begin to grasp death's finality around age 4. In one typical study, researchers found that 10 percent of 3-year-olds understand [the] irreversibility [of death], compared with 58 percent of 4-year-olds."[11]

My first memory of pondering death occurred when I was around three years old. I remember seeing a skeleton on a television show, and feeling physically ill when I suddenly realized my parents and I would someday look like that. My parents asked me what was wrong and I simply told them I was sick, because I could not express the new and disturbing emotions I was experiencing.

Before I became an extremely traumatized child at the age of four, my empathy began growing in a psychological soil that all human beings share—the uncomfortable recognition that life is fragile, vulnerable, and mortal.

Science is revealing that this recognition provides fertile soil for the growth of empathy. In chapter 2 I quoted Jeremy Rifkin, who said:

> So when a child learns that life is vulnerable and frag-ile and that every moment is precious and that they have their own unique history, it allows the child then to expe-rience another's plight in the same way, that [another] per-son, or other being—it could be another creature—has a one and only life, it's tough to be alive, and the odds are not always good.
>
> So if you think about the times that we've empathized with each other—our fellow creatures—it's always because we've felt their struggle . . . and we show solidarity with our compassion. Empathy is the opposite of utopia. There is no empathy in heaven . . . There isn't any empathy in heaven because there's no mortality. There is no empathy in utopia because there is no suffering. Empathy is grounded in the acknowledgement of death and the cele-bration of life and rooting for each other to flourish and be. It's based on our frailties and our imperfections, so when we talk about building an empathic civilization, we're not talking about utopia, we're talking about the ability of human beings to show solidarity not only with each other, but our fellow creatures who have a one and only life on this little planet.[12]

When we recognize the fragility, vulnerability, and mortality of life, we can understand why life is so precious. What if this is our one and only life? If the children killed in war immediately go to an afterlife where they will live in eternal paradise, then someone could argue that war is not so tragic after all. A similar argument is used by many religious extremists, who tell their followers that dying in war guarantees entry to eternal paradise. Fur-thermore, if slaves will spend an eternity in paradise after dying, or live an infinite number of lives through reincarnation, then the fate of a slave doesn't seem as bad. But if children and slaves have only one very fragile life to live, then war and slavery are unacceptable, and we must do everything in our power to end these injustices.

Because no one can prove with 100 percent certainty that an afterlife or reincarnation exist, I strive to fully appreciate the precious moments of this life, rather than take the gift of life for granted. I also strive to treat people with respect and compassion as if this is their one and only life. Regardless of your religious beliefs, wouldn't you want to be treated with the kind of respect and compassion that views your life as precious?

As I explain in chapter 7 of *Peaceful Revolution*, a transcendent mystery underlies all life and the universe itself. "Reverence" is the word I use to describe the love, appreciation, and awe I experience when I feel connected to the transcendent mystery. Instead of fully answering all of humanity's questions, scientific discoveries lead us deeper and deeper into this mystery.

For example, the ancient Greeks were unable to explain the mystery of lightning, so they created stories of Zeus hurling lightning bolts across the sky. When scientists discovered that lightning is electricity, this led to an even deeper mystery. What is electricity? When scientists discovered that electricity is caused by charged particles at the subatomic level, this led to an even deeper mystery. Why do the laws of physics work like this? When scientists suggested that the laws of physics were created during the big bang—this led to even deeper mysteries. Where did the big bang come from? Why did it happen? What existed before the big bang?

Many of our ancestors saw lightning as a mysterious force of nature. Although our scientific discoveries have allowed us to harness the power of electricity, it still remains a mystery to us. We understand how the laws of physics cause lightning, but we don't know why these laws are arranged in such a precise way to make lightning possible. We don't know why the laws of physics exist in the first place, or why anything exists at all. Every scientific discovery that tries to answer these questions leads to deeper questions, causing the mysterious to seem even more mysterious. If the laws of physics were slightly different, lightning and every other phenomenon in the universe, including life itself, would cease to exist.

When many animals see themselves in a mirror they are unable to comprehend their own reflection. In a similar way, there are some things the human mind may never be able to grasp. Where the universe came from may be beyond our comprehension, just as a reflection is beyond the comprehension of many animals.

Scientists, philosophers, and religions acknowledge the transcendent mystery that underlies all life and the universe itself. Albert Einstein believed the human mind cannot fully comprehend the transcendent mystery of the universe. But experiencing this mystery and striving to unlock its secrets make us feel truly alive. He said: "The most beautiful thing we can experience is the mysterious. It is the fundamental emotion that stands at the cradle of true art and true science. He who does not know it and can no longer wonder, no longer feel amazement, is as good as dead, a snuffed-out candle."[13]

When the human mind tries to comprehend the transcendent mystery of the universe, it is like trying to pour the entire Pacific Ocean into a tiny cup. The cosmic ocean's transcendent mystery is too vast to fully fit into the cup of the human mind, but we can taste and savor this mystery through powers such as science, religion, philosophy, artistic expression, and love.

Many religions also acknowledge the incomprehensible mystery of the universe. According to the oldest Hindu text, the *Rig Veda*, not only do human beings lack the ability to comprehend the origin and ultimate mystery of the universe, but comprehending this mystery may even be beyond the ability of the gods. The *Rig Veda* states: "Who can tell whence and how arose this universe? The gods are later than its beginning: who knows therefore whence comes this creation? Only that god who sees in highest heaven: he only knows whence came this universe, and whether it was made or uncreated. He only knows, *or perhaps he knows not* [emphasis added]."[14]

In religions around the world, God is a metaphor for the transcendent mystery of the universe. Many Native American traditions refer to God as "The Great Mystery," and many Jewish, Christian, Muslim, Hindu, and Buddhist theologians also discuss the mysterious essence of God and the universe. Christian theologian Albert Schweitzer said, "The spirit of the universe is at once creative and destructive—it creates while it destroys and destroys while it creates, and therefore it remains to us a riddle."[15]

Buddhist monk Thich Nhat Hanh, whom Martin Luther King Jr. nominated for the Nobel Peace Prize, also acknowledged the mysterious essence of the universe. A miracle is a mystery that cannot be fully explained, and by recognizing the mystery of existence, Thich Nhat Hanh saw human beings, the blue sky, and even the act of walking as miracles. He explains:

> I like to walk alone on country paths, rice plants and wild grasses on both sides, putting each foot down on the earth in mindfulness, knowing that I walk on the wondrous earth. In such moments, existence is a miraculous and mysterious reality. People usually consider walking on water or in thin air a miracle. But I think the real miracle is not to walk either on water or in thin air, but to walk on earth. Every day we are engaged in a miracle which we don't even recognize: a blue sky, white clouds, green leaves, the black, curious eyes of a child—our own two eyes. All is a miracle.[16]

I use the word "transcendence" to describe our craving to connect deeply with the mysterious and the eternal. People often think of eternity as endless time, but eternity is also the experience of *timelessness* that occurs when we become fully absorbed in the present moment.[17] Transcendence occurs when we become so absorbed in the present moment that we lose our sense of time.

Our craving to experience a sense of timelessness where we become lost in the present moment, which I call "the search for transcendence," is one reason* people pursue drugs, sex, sports, music, religious worship, a sense of connection with nature, meditation, video games, art, spending time with a loved one, or even the most destructive forms of nationalism. Some of these sources of transcendence not only result in destructive behavior, but consist of unfulfilling experiences that do not feed our craving for transcendence in the deepest and most meaningful ways.

How can we feed our craving for transcendence in meaningful ways?

---

* People can also pursue drugs, sex, sports, music, etc. to feed other spiritual organs, to merely distract themselves, or to cope with the pain of life and reality.

As we endure the adversities of life, developing a deep connection with the mysterious universe around us results from our spiritual journey to explore the mysterious universe within us. To deeply connect with our outer world in the most meaningful ways, a first step is to connect with something deep within us—our shared humanity.

Our craving for transcendence is one reason for our fascination with immortality. We have a craving to transcend time, to no longer feel bound by mortality, to touch the eternal, to taste the metaphorical Tree of Life, to experience the transcendent mystery in every fiber of our being.

Why do people perceive animals as living in a state of transcendence? When we witness the behavior of wild animals in their natural environment, they seem to live in the present moment and be fully absorbed in their surroundings. Furthermore, many of us have seen dogs enjoying the outdoors, relishing nature, senses fully attuned to their surroundings, seeming happy just to be alive. I think one reason human beings are drawn to animals is because we can perceive in their behavior a kind of carefree joy, sense of belonging to their environment, and state of transcendence that we crave. They seem to live in peace with the deepest mysteries of the universe.

I have many memories of being two years old, before my brain developed a craving for purpose, meaning, belonging, self-worth, and transcendence. At this early age I was capable of feeling pain and fear, but I experienced transcendence effortlessly, viewing my surroundings with wonder and awe. The world seemed magical and mysterious, almost like a fairy tale. In this beautiful reality, I belonged and felt worthy without effort, and purpose and meaning were not a struggle. The more I progress on my spiritual journey, the more I feel like a small child again, except I have gained the realistic hope, radical empathy, and revelatory understanding that bloomed from a lifetime of searching and suffering, and I bear the psychological scars of extreme trauma.

The search for transcendence can allow us to feel at peace with ourselves and united with the universe, or it can cause us to stray down a variety of unfulfilling and destructive paths, like an arrow that strays off course and misses its target. If we make a wrong turn and wander from the road to peace, our craving for transcendence can cause us to slip into dark pits such as drug addiction, alcoholism, unquenchable hedonism, and the ruthless desire for immortality that seeks fame at all costs.

All of our spiritual cravings, not just our craving for transcendence, can stray from the road to peace and lure us down unfulfilling and destructive paths. Throughout this book I have described how our spiritual hunger, represented metaphorically by the nine spiritual organs of our shared humanity, can lead to harm and fanaticism, as well as empathy and understanding.

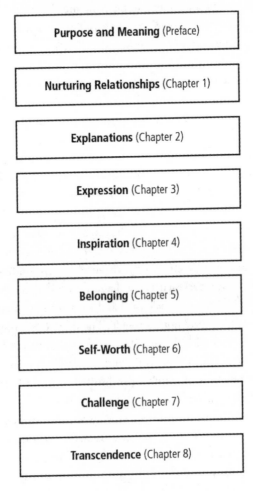

Figure 8.4: The Nine Spiritual Organs of Our Shared Humanity

What are religion, science, and philosophy? They have been difficult to define, since the meaning of these terms can vary widely from person to person. Yet we can reliably define religion, science, and philosophy in relation to the nine spiritual organs of our shared humanity. All religions, at a bare minimum, strive to feed our craving for purpose, meaning, explanations of how the world works, belonging, and transcendence. Science, at a bare minimum, strives to feed our craving for explanations of how the world works (which can agree with or conflict with religious explanations).* And philosophy (as it developed in ancient Greece and the East), at a bare minimum, strives to feed our craving for purpose and meaning.

Explanations of how the world works form the basis of our worldview, and our worldview is deeply intertwined with our political and social beliefs. Religion, science, and philosophy can go far beyond this bare minimum, and they can overlap with each other in numerous ways. But despite the wide variety of religions, scientific schools of thought, and philosophies of life, they all strive to feed some or all of our spiritual cravings. Because the spiritual organs of our shared humanity result from the problem of human existence,** we do not know of any other species on earth that has religion, science, or philosophy. We can have a worldview that feeds our spiritual organs well, or a worldview that leaves us deficient in the nutrients of love and truth.

Just as we will starve physically if we do not feed our bodily organs with healthy nutrients, we will starve psychologically if we do not feed our spiritual organs with healthy nutrients. One of the healthiest nutrients for spiritual fulfillment is love. Buddhism teaches the paradox that we cannot attain spiritual enlightenment when we desire enlightenment. In other words, our spiritual cravings find true satisfaction when we become loving, selfless, and

---

* For scientists, science can also go beyond this bare minimum by feeding many of their other spiritual cravings, giving their lives purpose, meaning, and much more.

** We do not have any evidence that other animals *crave* and therefore *actively seek* purpose, meaning, self-worth, and transcendence as we do. They seem to live in harmony with these aspects of their existence. As I explained in chapter 2, we also do not have any evidence that other animals crave explanations that reveal underlying causes. They seem to live in harmony with the mystery of the universe. However, there is abundant evidence that many animals *crave* and *actively seek* nurturing relationships and belonging. Arthropods such as spiders do not seem to do this, but many animals (such as dogs) behave in ways that reveal a craving for nurturing relationships and belonging.

mindful of our community, not when we are self-centered and so obsessed with spiritual enlightenment that we forget our global family.

When we walk the road to peace by strengthening the muscles of our shared humanity and by waging peace, we can feed our spiritual organs and experience the transcendent mystery of the universe in deep and meaningful ways. In the following excerpt from Martin Luther King Jr.'s book *Where Do We Go From Here?* he calls the transcendent mystery the "ultimate reality." He also describes how feeding our spiritual hunger with proper nutrition—such as love—is needed to end war and protect our fragile future. According to King, love connects us to the ultimate reality, which I call the transcendent mystery and many call God:

> Love is the key that unlocks the door which leads to ultimate reality. This Hindu-Muslim-Christian-Jewish-Buddhist belief about ultimate reality is beautifully summed up in the First Epistle of Saint John: "Let us love one another: for love is of God: and every one that loveth is born of God, and knoweth God. He that loveth not knoweth not God; for God is love . . . If we love one another, God dwelleth in us, and his love is perfected in us."
>
> Let us hope that this spirit will become the order of the day. We can no longer afford to worship the God of hate or bow before the altar of retaliation . . . We are now faced with the fact that tomorrow is today. We are confronted with the fierce urgency of *now*. In this unfolding conundrum of life and history there is such a thing as being too late. Procrastination is still the thief of time. Life often leaves us standing bare, naked and dejected with a lost opportunity . . .
>
> We may cry out desperately for time to pause in her passage, but time is deaf to every plea and rushes on. Over the bleached bones and jumbled residues of numerous civilizations are written the pathetic words: "Too late." . . .

We still have a choice today: nonviolent coexistence or violent coannihilation. This may well be mankind's last chance to choose between chaos and community.[18]

Throughout my life I have pondered humanity's choices and the ways they flow forward through time. Time has been an underlying theme throughout this book, because we must first learn from our primordial past before we can make the choices needed to protect our fragile future. The choices, people, historical events, and ideas I have discussed throughout this book are metaphorical waves on the surface of the cosmic ocean. Everything we see, hear, touch, taste, smell, and think is a wave floating in time and space. Beneath these waves is an eternal mystery that transcends human comprehension. I cannot describe the transcendent mystery within the limitations of language, but I have been able to experience it, and together we can point toward a path that reveals its hidden essence.

To overcome a force as powerful as the religion of war, we must point the way toward love, truth, and transcendence. However, we must point not with our fingers, but with our empathy, understanding, and actions. To imprison mighty systems such as war and environmental destruction, we must develop a deep spirituality that not only reflects the intersection of science, religion, and philosophy, but also helps people become aware of their shared humanity and connection to the mystery of life.

As human beings we share so many similarities, but perhaps what we share most is a choice. We are manifestations of the transcendent mystery that can choose between mass extinction or cooperative survival. We are waves of the cosmic ocean that can choose to remain in darkness or rise toward the mystery of eternal light.

# Notes

## Preface: The Human Condition

1. Frank Newport, "In U.S., 87% Approve of Black–White Marriage, vs. 4% in 1958," http://www.gallup.com/poll/163697/approve-marriage-blacks-whites.aspx.

2. Frederick Douglass, *Narrative of the Life of Frederick Douglass* (New York: Dover, 1995), xi–xiii.

3. Frederick Douglass, *The Life and Times of Frederick Douglass* (New York: Dover, 2003), 31, 32, 41, 42.

4. Ibid., 13.

5. Ta-Nehisi Coates, "Honoring CHM: One Drop," http://www.theatlantic.com/national/archive/2010/04/honoring-chm-one-drop/38952/.

6. Ibid.

7. Frederick Douglass, *Frederick Douglass on Slavery and the Civil War*, ed. Philip Foner, (Mineola, NY: Dover, 2003), 42.

8. *Frontline: The Interrupters*, PBS, 2012, DVD.

9. Erich Fromm, *Man for Himself* (New York: Henry Holt, 1990), 46.

10. Matthew 4:4, Holy Bible, New International Version (NIV).

11. *McGraw-Hill Dictionary of American Idioms and Phrasal Verbs*, "Man does not live by bread alone," http://idioms.thefreedictionary.com/Man+does+not+live+by+bread+alone.

12. Ibid.

13. *Mythology*, ed. C. Scott Littleton (London: Duncan Baird, 2002), 194–95.

14. Homer, *The Odyssey*, trans. Robert Fagles (New York: Penguin, 1997), 269.

15. Victor Frankl, *Man's Search for Meaning* (Boston: Beacon, 2006), x–xi.

16. Ibid., 76.

17. Michael Nojeim, *Gandhi and King: The Power of Nonviolent Resistance* (Westport, Connecticut, Praeger, 2004), 85–86.

18. *A Force More Powerful*, A Force More Powerful Films, 2002, DVD.

19. *Eyes on the Prize: Ain't Scared of Your Jails*, PBS, 2010, DVD.

20. Personal conversation with Bernard Lafayette, June 2013.

21. Army Code of Conduct, http://www.armystudyguide.com/content/army
_board_study_guide_topics/code_of_conduct/the-code-of-conduct.shtml.

22. Frankl, *Man's Search for Meaning*, 76.

23. Ibid., 107.

24. Personal conversation with Bernard Lafayette, June 2013.

25. Frederick Nietzsche, trans. Anthony M. Ludovici, *Ecce Homo* (New York: MacMillan, 1911) 13.

26. "Mozart of Chess: Magnus Carlsen," *60 Minutes*, http://www.youtube.com/watch?v=Qc_v9mTfhC8.

27. Edwin Mora, "Report: U.S. Veterans Struggle with Resurgence of Al-Qaeda in Iraq," http://www.breitbart.com/Big-Peace/2014/01/11/Report-U-S-Veterans-Struggle-With-Regeneration-of-Al-Qaeda-in-Iraq.

28. Henry David Thoreau, *Walden and Civil Disobedience* (New York: Penguin, 1986), 50.

## Chapter 1: A Dark Night Filled with Predators

1. Matthew 7:3–5, Holy Bible, NIV.

2. Eric Jaffe, "A Glimpse Inside the Brains of Trauma Survivors," http://www.psychologicalscience.org/index.php/publications/observer/2012/july-august-12/the-psychology-of-resilience.html.

3. Lt. Col. Dave Grossman discusses the tornado scenario in his DVD *The Bulletproof Mind.*

4. Dave Grossman, *On Killing* (Boston: Little, Brown, 1995), 77.

5. *Hearts and Minds*, Criterion, 2002, DVD.

6. Ibid., 78–79.

7. Bruce Perry and Maia Szalavitz, *The Boy Who Was Raised As a Dog* (New York: Basic Books, 2008), 38–39.

8. Jocelyn Kelly, "Rape Traumatizes All Congolese, Not Just Women," http://hhi.harvard.edu/sites/default/files/publications/publications%20-%20women%20-%20opinion.pdf.

9. *Trauma, Brain & Relationship: Helping Children Heal,* The Post Institute, https://www.youtube.com/watch?feature=player_embedded&v=jYy-EEMlMMb0#t=10m59s.

10. Phone conversation with Jonathan Shay in 2011.

11. "Back to School," This American Life, http://www.thisamericanlife.org/radio-archives/episode/474/transcript.

12. Ibid.

13. Jaffe, "A Glimpse Inside the Brains of Trauma Survivors."

14. Jonathan Shay, *Achilles in Vietnam* (New York: Scribner, 2003), 205–6.

15. Plutarch, *Of Banishment*. Online Library of Liberty, http://oll.liberty-fund.org/?option=com_staticxt&staticfile=show.php%3Ftitle=1213&chapter=91778&layout=html.

16. Rhodes Professorship: R. Spencer Wells, http://rhodesprofessors.cornell.edu/RhodesProfsWells.html.

17. Spencer Wells, *The Journey of Man* (New York: Random House, 2003), 9.

18. Stanford News Service: News Release, http://news.stanford.edu/pr/02/genetics18.html.

19. Spencer Wells, "Out of Africa," http://www.vanityfair.com/culture/features/2007/07/genographic200707.

20. Floyd H. Ross and Tynette Hills, *The Great Religions by Which Men Live* (New York: Beacon, 1956), 80.

21. William Shakespeare, *Henry V* (New York: Signet Classics, 1998), 89.

22. *Sun Tzu on the Art of War: The Oldest Military Treatise in the World*, trans. Lionel Giles (El Paso: El Paso Norte Press, 2005), 49.

23. Lucy Morgan, "Woman bites dog; twice, to be precise," http://www.sptimes.com/News/062101/news_pf/State/Woman_bites_dog_twice.shtml.

24. Hitler's Speech at Danzig, speech of September 19, 1939, http://www.humanitas-international.org/showcase/chronography/speeches/1939-09-19.html. Accessed on August 6, 2013.

25. Sue Hubbard, "The Kid's Doctor: Fear of the dark is a normal part of development," http://articles.chicagotribune.com/2012-04-11/lifestyle/sns-201204101630—tms—premhnstr—k-j20120411apr11_1_fear-dark-night-scary-thoughts.

26. *Naabi: A Hyena Princess,* BBC documentary, 2008.

27. Wells, *The Journey of Man,* 131.

28. Frederick Nietzsche, trans. Anthony M. Ludovici, *Ecce Homo* (New York: MacMillan, 1911), 13.

29. Lt. Col. Dave Grossman with Loren W. Christensen, *On Combat* (Milstadt, IL: Warrior Science Publications, 2008), 67–68.

30. *Sun Tzu on the Art of War*, 13.

31. A January 2002 interview with Gene Knudsen Hoffman, http://www.peaceheroes.com/PeaceHeroes/jeanknudsenhoffman.htm.

32. Erich Fromm, *The Art of Loving* (New York: Perennial Classics, 1956), 27.

33. Joseph Campbell, *The Power of Myth*, Athena, 2010, DVD.

## Chapter 2: Poseidon's Wrath

1. Erich Fromm, *Man for Himself* (New York: Henry Holt, 1990), 40.

2. G. R. Evans, *First Light* (London: I.B. Tauris, 2014), 130–31.

3. Homer, *The Iliad*, trans. Robert Fagles (New York: Viking, 1990), 457.

4. Jeremy Rifkin, *The Empathic Civilization*, RSA Animate, http://www.youtube.com/watch?v=l7AWnfFRc7g.

5. Marcus Aurelius, *Meditations* (New York: Oxford World Classics, 2011), 50.

6. Genesis 3:19, Holy Bible, NIV.

7. Homer, *The Iliad*, 393.

8. Andrew Robinson, *Earthquake* (London: Reaktion, 2012), 15.

9. Ibid.

10. Homer, *The Iliad*, 394.

11. Walter Burkert, *Greek Religion* (Cambridge: Harvard University Press, 1987), 139.

12. *Encyclopedia of Ancient Greece*, ed. Nigel Guy Wilson (New York: Routledge, 2006), 247.

13. Amos Nur with Dawn Burgess, *Apocalypse* (Princeton, NJ: Princeton University Press, 2008), 80.

14. Helen Scales, *Poseidon's Steed* (New York: Penguin, 2010), 23.

15. Hesiod, *The Theogany, Works and Days,* and *The Shield of Heracles*, trans. Hugh G. Evelyn-White (Stilwell, KS: Digireads, 2008), 44.

16. Kerry Emanuel, *Divine Wind* (New York: Oxford University Press, 2005), 3–5.

17. Alfred Bradford, *Leonidas and the Kings of Sparta* (Santa Barbara: Praeger, 2011), xvi.

18. Peter Krentz, *The Battle of Marathon* (New Haven: Yale University Press, 2010), 108–110.

19. Ibid., 181.

20. Xenophon, *The Persian Expedition*, trans. Rex Warner (Baltimore: Penguin, 1965), 107.

21. Jeremy Manier, "Baseball and Superstition," http://articles.chicagotribune.com/2008-10-03/news/0810020405_1_theories-batters-and-pitchers-ritual.

22. Carl von Clausewitz, *On War*, trans. J. J. Graham (New York: Penguin, 1982), 116.

23. Thucydides, *History of the Peloponnesian War*, trans. Rex Warner (New York: Penguin, 1972), 8182.

24. Ibid., 289.

25. Gene Dark, *The Brutality of War* (Gretna, LA: Pelican, 2009) 161.

26. Court Document from State of Missouri, http://localtvktvi.files.wordpress.com/2013/06/jessica-howell-redacted-complaint.pdf.

27. *Cosmos,* Episode 12 (Cosmos Studios, 2002), DVD.

28. Victoria Moore, "It's become the fastest-selling self-help book ever, but is *The Secret* doing more harm than good?," http://www.dailymail.co.uk/femail/article-450745/Its-fastest-selling-self-help-book-The-Secret-doing-harm-good.html.

29. Thucydides, *History of the Peloponnesian War*, 20.

30. Peter Tyson, *"The Hippocratic Oath Today,"* http://www.pbs.org/wgbh/nova/body/hippocratic-oath-today.html.

31. Mohandas K. Gandhi, *The Mind of Mahatma Gandhi,* ed. R. K. Prabhu and U. R. Rao (Ahmedabad, India: Navajivan, 2010), 44-45.

32. RSA Animate, "Smile or Die," http://www.youtube.com/watch?v=u5um8QWWRvo.

33. Frederick Douglass, *The Life and Times of Frederick Douglass* (New York: Dover, 2003), 29, 52, 53 54, 55.

34. George Thompson, *Lectures of George Thompson*, ed. William Lloyd Garrison (Boston: Isaac Knapp, 1836), 168, 169.

35. *Frontline: The Interrupters*, PBS, 2012, DVD.

36. Frederick Douglass, *Frederick Douglass on Slavery and the Civil War,* ed. Philip Foner, (Mineola, NY: Dover, 2003), 42.

37. Rabbi Michael Shire, *The Jewish Prophet* (Woodstock, VT: Jewish Lights, 2001), 121.

38. Joseph Patrick Byrne, *The Black Death* (Westport, CT: Greenwood Press, 2004), 59, 60, 93.

39. ———, *Encyclopedia of the Black Death* (Santa Barbara, CA: ABC-CLIO, 2012), 115, 116.

40. Suzanne Hatty and James Hatty, *The Disordered Body* (Albany: State University of New York Press, 1999), 94.

41. Byrne, *Encyclopedia of the Black Death*, 115, 116.

42. Spencer Wells, *The Journey of Man* (New York: Random House, 2003), 158–60.

43. Genesis 3, Holy Bible, NIV.

44. Wolf-Dieter Storl, *Shiva: The Wild God of Power and Ecstasy* (Rochester, VT: Inner Traditions, 2004), 122–24.

45. Thucydides, *History of the Peloponnesian War*, 21.

46. Lao-tzu, *Lao-tzu's Taoteching*, trans. Red Pine (Port Townsend, WA: Copper Canyon, 2009), 10.

47. Ibid.

48. Kenneth Hill, "The Decline of Child Mortality," Department of Population Dynamics, School of Hygiene and Public Health, John Hopkins University, 1.

49. Jonathan Dewald, *The European Nobility, 1400–1800*, (New York: Cambridge University Press, 1996), 17.

50. Hill, "The Decline of Child Mortality," 5.

51. *The Matrix*, Warner Home Video, 2007, DVD.

52. Deuteronomy 30:19, Holy Bible, English Standard Version.

## Chapter 3: Tools Made of Flesh, Blood, and Bones

1. Definition of "paradox," http://dictionary.reference.com/browse/paradox?s=t.

2. Darcy Morey, *Dogs* (New York: Cambridge University Press, 2010), 17–18.

3. Fran Dancing Feather and Rita Robinson, *Exploring Native American Wisdom* (Franklin Lakes, NJ: Career, 2003), 180, 210.

4. Frederick Douglass, *The Life and Times of Frederick Douglass* (New York: Dover, 2003), 25.

5. Ibid, 47–49.

6. Midas, http://www.theoi.com/Heros/Midas.html.

7. Ibid.

8. Herman Hesse, *My Belief* (New York: Farrar, Straus and Giroux, 1974), 37–38.

9. John 4, Holy Bible, NIV.

10. 1 Corinthians 13, Holy Bible, NIV.

11. Robert W. Shumaker, Kristina R. Valkup, Benjamin B. Beck, *Animal Tool Behavior* (Baltimore: John Hopkins University Press, 2011), 45.

12. Martin Luther King Jr., *Where Do We Go From Here?* (New York: Signet Classics, 2000), 132.

13. John Steinbeck, *The Grapes of Wrath* (New York, Knopf, 1993), 192–93.

14. J. S. Wacher, *The Roman World*, vol. 1 (London: Routledge, 1990), 48.

15. Micheline Ishay, *The History of Human Rights* (Berkeley: University of California Press, 2008), 337.

16. Jeremy Rifkin, *The Empathic Civilization* (New York: Tarcher, 2009), 8485.

17. Ben Thomas, "What's So Special About Mirror Neurons," http://blogs.scientificamerican.com/guest-blog/2012/11/06/whats-so-special-about-mirror-neurons/.

18. Herman Hesse, *Siddhartha*, trans. Hilda Rosner (New York: New Directions, 1951), 119.

19. Ecclesiastes 4:9–12, Holy Bible, NIV.

20. Philip S. Foner, ed., *Frederick Douglass on Women's Rights* (Cambridge, MA: Da Capo, 1992), 113.

21. According to *The Oxford Encyclopedia of American Social History*, it is believed that Frederick Douglass was the only African American at the convention, although it cannot be known for certain.

22. The Declaration of Sentiments, http://www.fordham.edu/halsall/mod/senecafalls.asp.

23. Ken Burns, *American Lives: Not for Ourselves Alone*, PBS, 2013, DVD.

24. Foner, *Frederick Douglass on Women's Rights*, 13–14.

25. Judith Wellman, *The Road to Seneca Falls* (Chicago: University of Illinois Press, 2004), 210-11.

26. Foner, *Frederick Douglass on Women's Rights*, 29, 32–41.

27. Ibid., 75.

28. Proverbs 16:24, Holy Bible, NIV.

29. Francis Bacon, *Sacred Meditations* (Radford, VA: Wilder, 2012), 22.

30. Malcolm X, *Malcolm X Speaks*, ed. George Breitman (New York: Grove, 1990), 10–12.

31. Henry Louis Gates Jr., "Were There Slaves Like Stephen in 'Django'?," http://www.theroot.com/views/were-there-slaves-stephen-django?page=0,1.

32. Douglass, *The Life and Times of Frederick Douglass*, 11, 12, 16, 17, 18.

33. Clayborne Carson and Kris Shepard, eds., *A Call to Conscience* (New York: Grand Central, 2002), 157–58.

34. Norman F. Cantor, *Alexander the Great* (New York: Harper Perennial, 2007), 40–41.

35. Rüdiger Safranski, *Nietzsche: A Philosophical Biography*, trans. Shelley Frisch (New York: W. W. Norton, 2002), 316.

36. Dave Grossman, *On Killing* (Boston: Little, Brown, 1995), 97, 98, 107, 108.

37. Christopher R. Browning, *Ordinary Men* (New York: Harper Perennial, 1998), 64.

38. Ibid.

39. Ibid., 66, 67, 68, 69.

40. Ibid, 74.

41. Ibid., 73.

42. Richard Breitman, *The Architect of Genocide* (Lebanon, NH: University Press of New England, 1991), 196–97.

43. Hannah Arendt, *Eichmann in Jerusalem* (New York: Penguin Classics, 2006), 87–89.

44. Browning, *Ordinary Men*, 25.

45. Martin Luther King Jr. speech: January 1965, http://www.hark.com/clips/ykflndhxhd-martin-luther-king-speech-january-1965.

46. Elie Wiesel, *From the Kingdom of Memory: Reminiscences* (New York: Schocken, 1995), 233.

47. Roy L. Swank and Walter E. Marchand, "Combat Neuroses: Development of Combat Exhaustion," American Medical Association: Archives of Neurology and Psychiatry, 1946, 244.

48. Joseph Campbell, *The Power of Myth*, Athena, 2010, DVD.

49. Erich Fromm, *The Anatomy of Human Destructiveness* (New York: Henry Holt, 1973), 145, 147.

50. Mohanadas Gandhi, *Autobiography: The Story of My Experiments with*

*Truth* (New York: Dover, 1983), 140.

51. Albert Schweitzer, *Out of My Life and Thought* (Baltimore: John Hopkins University Press, 1998), 235, 236, 238, 243.

52. Homer, *The Iliad*, trans. Robert Fagles (New York: Viking, 1990), 89.

53. Robert Kahn, *Beethoven and the Grosse Fuge* (Landham, MD: Scarecrow, 2010), 24–25.

54. Gwendolyn Brooks, "Boy Breaking Glass," http://www.poetryfounda-tion.org/poem/172094.

55. Mike Tyson YouTube video, https://www.youtube.com/watch?v=P0oxD-pJr8po.

56. *Carl Panzram: The Spirit of Hatred and Vengeance*, Virgil Films and Enter-tainment, 2012, DVD.

57. "Waging Peace: Katherine Rowland Interviews Paul Chappell," http://www.guernicamag.com/interviews/waging-peace/.

58. Erich Fromm, *The Art of Loving* (New York: Perennial Classics, 2000),

59. Peter Vronsky, *Female Serial Killers* (New York: Berkley Books, 2007), 33.

60. Ibid., 7, 33, 34, 35, 50, 51.

61. Ibid., 47.

62. *Frontline: The Interrupters*, PBS, 2012, DVD.

63. Victor Frankl, *Man's Search for Meaning* (Boston: Beacon, 2006), 23–24.

64. Mary Shelley, *Frankenstein* (Wilmington, DE: Montecristo, 2012, Kindle edition), 45.

65. Paraphrase of personal conversation with Ricardo Pitts-Wiley, June 2013.

66. Matthew 5:44, Holy Bible, NIV.

67. Homer, *The Iliad*, trans. Robert Fitzgerald (New York: Farrar, Straus and Giroux, 2004), 144.

68. Judith Wellman, *The Road to Seneca Falls* (Chicago: University of Illinois Press, 2004), 204.

69. Foner, *Frederick Douglass on Women's Rights*, 11.

70. Ibid., 159.

71. Personal conversation with Jo Ann.

## Chapter 4: Soldiers as Christ Figures

1. *Being: Mike Tyson*, episode 1,
https://www.youtube.com/watch?v=erxE0rQw9cI.

2. Ross Cowan, *For the Glory of Rome* (London: Greenhill, 2007), 141–42.

3. *The Bulletproof Mind*, Dave Grossman and Gavin de Becker, 2008, DVD.

4. Homer, *The Iliad*, trans. Robert Fagles (New York: Viking, 1990), 554–58.

5. Ibid., 612.

6. Plato, *Plato's Republic*, trans. G. M. A. Grube (Indianapolis: Hacket, 1992), 63.

7. Matthew 26:52, Holy Bible, NIV.

8. Homer, *The Iliad*, 477.

9. Ibid., 161.

10. Ibid., 26.

11. Ibid., 362.

12. Ibid., 310.

13. Ibid., 359.

14. Frederick Douglass, *The Life and Times of Frederick Douglass* (New York: Dover, 2003), 151.

15. *Mark Twain—A Film Directed by Ken Burns*, PBS, 2004, DVD.

16. Micah Zenko, "Americans Are As Likely to Be Killed by Their Own Furniture as by Terrorism," http://www.theatlantic.com/international/archive/2012/06/americans-are-as-likely-to-be-killed-by-their-own-furniture-as-by-terrorism/258156/.

17. Theoi Greek Mythology, "Deimos and Phobos," http://www.theoi.com/Daimon/Deimos.html.

18. Homer, *The Iliad*, 351.

19. Hesiod, *The Theogony, Works and Days, and The Shield of Heracles*, trans. Hugh G. Evelyn-White (Lawrence, KS: Digireads, 2009), 61.

20. Ibid, 62.

21. Plutarch, "Pelopidas," trans. John Dryden, The Internet Classics Archive, http://classics.mit.edu/Plutarch/pelopida.html.

22. Homer, *The Iliad*, 449.

23. Ibid., 333.

24. Ibid., 403.

25. Ibid., 405.

26. Ibid., 236.

27. Ibid., 409.

28. Commandant, U.S. Marine Corps Trust Study—Final Report, Appendix E: Cohesion Essay, 2000.

29. William Shakespeare, *Henry V* (New York: Signet Classics, 1998), 89.

30. Homer, *The Iliad*, 303–5.

31. Matthew Trundle, *Greek Mercenaries* (New York: Routledge, 2004), 31.

32. Homer, *The Iliad*, 271.

33. Ibid., 265.

34. Ibid., 473.

35. Ibid., 525.

36. Ibid., 218.

37. *Patton*, 20th Century Fox, 2001, DVD.

38. Actual Voice of General Patton, https://www.youtube.com/watch?v=d4_47O2Pfy8.

39. Homer, *The Iliad*, 252.

40. Ibid., 228.

41. Ibid., 412.

42. Ibid., 468–70.

43. Jonathan Shay, *Achilles in Vietnam* (New York: Scribner, 2003), 51–53.

44. Homer, *The Iliad*, 82.

45. Ibid., 473.

46. *Being: Mike Tyson*, episode 1.

47. Homer, *The Iliad*, 110.

48. John Steinbeck, *The Grapes of Wrath* (New York: Knopf, 1993), 192.

49. Homer, *The Iliad*, 398–99.

50. Leo Shane III, "Why do blacks receive fewer valor medals?," http://www.stripes.com/news/special-reports/heroes/heroes-2011/why-do-blacks-receive-fewer-valor-medals-1.146508.

51. Richard Vedder and David M. Ewalt, "America's Best Colleges 2009," http://www.forbes.com/2009/08/02/colleges-university-ratings-opinions-colleges-09-intro.html.

52. Hana R. Alberts, "America's Best College," http://www.forbes.com/forbes/2009/0824/colleges-09-education-west-point-america-best-college.html.

53. Definition of Mercenary,
http://ahdictionary.com/word/search.html?q=mercenary.

54. Erich Fromm, *To Have or To Be* (New York: Continuum, 1976), 139.

55. Ibid., 141–43.

56. Mason Lowance, ed., *Against Slavery: An Abolitionist Reader* (New York: Penguin Classics, 2000), 43.

57. 1 Corinthians 13, Holy Bible, NIV.

58. Mason Lowance, ed., *Against Slavery: An Abolitionist Reader* (New York: Penguin Classics, 2000), 43.

59. Erich Fromm, 143–44.

60. Martin Luther King on Gandhi as "Greatest Christian," https://people.stanford.edu/ccarson/martin-luther-king-gandhi-"greatest-christian."

61. Ibid.

62. *The Expanded Quotable Einstein*, trans. Alice Calaprice (Princeton: Princeton University Press, 2000), 82.

63. Elizabeth Castelli, "Reza Aslan—Historian?," *http://www.thenation.com/article/175688/reza-aslan-historian#.*

64. Lao-tzu, *The Sayings of Lao-tzu*, trans. Lionel Giles (New York: E. P. Dutton, 1905), 32.

65. *Classical Mythology*, Lecture 6, The Teaching Company, DVD.

66. Richard Glover, *Leonidas: A Poem*, https://archive.org/details/leonidasapoem05glovgoog.

67. J. F. Lazenby, *The Spartan Army* (Mechanicsburg, PA: Stackpole Books, 2012), 105.

68. Thucydides, *The History of the Peloponnesian War*, trans. Richard Crawley (Amazon Digital Services, Kindle Edition), Location 3862.

69. *Thucydides, History of the Peloponnesian War*, trans. Rex Warner (New York: Penguin, 1972), 288, 289, 356, 357, 363.

70. Nick Sekunda, *The Spartan Army* (Oxford: Osprey, 2008), 26.

71. William Astore, "Every soldier a hero? Hardly," http://articles.latimes.com/2010/jul/22/opinion/la-oe-astore-heroes-20100722.

72. Paula Bock, "The Choices Made," http://seattletimes.com/pacificnw/2002/0310/cover.html.

73. Four Hours at My Lai, https://www.youtube.com/watch?v=FYzb9DH7YAE.

74. Ibid.

75. Richard Goldstein, "Hugh Thompson, 62, Who Saved Civilians at My Lai, Dies,"
http://www.nytimes.com/2006/01/07/national/07thompson.html?_r=0.

76. Ibid.

77. Personal Defense Network: Sheepdog by Lieutenant Colonel Dave Grossman, https://www.youtube.com/watch?v=vk2Yx3VdbSo.

78. Michael Paul Gallagher, *What Are They Saying about Unbelief?* (New York: Paulist, 1995), 52.

79. William Astore, "Every soldier a hero? Hardly,"
http://articles.latimes.com/2010/jul/22/opinion/la-oe-astore-heroes-20100722.

80. General Omar Bradley, 1948 Memorial Day address at Long Meadow, MA, http://www.guidepostsmag.com/personal-change/ personal-change-archive/?i=2208&page=1.

81. Mark Muesse, *The Hindu Traditions* (Minneapolis: Fortune, 2011), 161,163.

82. Norman K. Gottwald, *The Hebrew Bible* (Minneapolis: Fortress, 2010), 122–23.

83. Tamra Andrews, *Dictionary of Nature Myths* (Oxford: Oxford University Press, 1998), 163.

84. Miranda Aldhouse Green, *Dying for the Gods* (Charleston, SC: Tempus, 2001), 141–42.

85. Ibid., 169, 201.

86. Manuel Aguilar-Moreno, *Handbook to Life in the Aztec World* (Oxford: Oxford University Press, 2006), 172–74.

87. This quote derives from the Voltaire quote "*Certainement qui est en droit de vous rendre absurde est en droit de vous rendre injuste,*" which means "Certainly he who is capable of making you absurd is also capable of making you unjust." My gratitude to Stephanie Van Hook for translating this for me.

88. *Myth in Human History*, Lecture 10, The Teaching Company, 2010, DVD.

89. Vincent James Stanzione, *Rituals of Sacrifice* (Albuquerque, NM: University of New Mexico Press, 2003), x.

90. Miranda Aldhouse Green, *Dying for the Gods* (Charleston, SC: Tempus, 2001), 174, 189.

91. Erich Fromm, *The Anatomy of Human Destructiveness* (New York: Henry Holt, 1973), 205–6.

92. Homer, *The Iliad*, trans. Robert Fagles (New York: Viking, 1990), 191.

93. *Sun Tzu on the Art of War: The Oldest Military Treatise in the World*, trans. Lionel Giles (El Paso: El Paso Norte Press, 2005), 5.

94. Christian Appy, *Working-Class War* (Chapel Hill: University of North Carolina Press, 1993), 242–43.

95. *King—Man of Peace in a Time of War*, Passport, 2007, DVD.

## *Chapter 5: Beauty and Belonging*

1. Mikaela Conley, "Nip/Tuck Nations: 7 Countries with Most Cosmetic Surgery," http://abcnews.go.com/Health/niptuck-nations-countries-cosmetic-surgery/story?id=16205231.

2. Mette Norgaard, *The Ugly Duckling Goes to Work* (New York: AMACOM, 2005), 42–43.

3. Jennifer Crwys-Williams, ed., *In the Words of Nelson Mandela* (New York: Walker, 2010), 65.

4. Plutarch, *Of Banishment.* Online Library of Liberty, http://oll.liberty-fund.org/?option=com_staticxt&staticfile=show.p hp%3Ftitle=1213&chap-ter=91778&layout=html&Itemid=27.

5. Douglas Allen, ed., *The Philosophy of Mahatma Gandhi for the Twenty-First Century* (New York: Lexington Books, 2008), 11.

6. Clayborne Carson and Kris Shepard, eds., *A Call to Conscience* (New York: Grand Central, 2002), 85.

7. Nichelle Nichols Met Martin Luther King, http://www.youtube.com/watch?v=pqoZ0C0cnRE.

8. BBC interview: Patrick Stewart, https://www.youtube.com/watch?v=pXOK-ZVJMaU.

9. Attitudes of Aging, http://whyy.org/cms/radiotimes/2013/09/05/24892/.

10. Tavis Smiley Interview: Patrick Stewart, https://www.youtube.com/watch?v=VRZUy6S2hfM.

11. Ibid.

12. Patrick Stewart: Biography, http://www.tvguide.com/celebrities/patrick-stewart/bio/169205.

13. John Marshall Townsend, *What Women Want, What Men Want—What Men Want* (Oxford: Oxford University Press, 1998), 112–13.

14. Anthony Bryant, *Samurai* (Oxford: Osprey, 1998), 14.

15. Tim Gunn Interview, NPR, http://www.npr.org/2014/02/05/271997689/tim-gunn-on-and-off-the-runway-life-is-a-big-collaboration.

## Chapter 6: The Sanity of Humanity

1. Human Nature, Buddha Nature: An interview with John Welwood by Tina Fossella, www.johnwelwood.com/articles/TRIC_interview_uncut.doc.

2. Joseph Campbell, *A Joseph Campbell Companion: Reflections on the Art of Living* (San Anselmo, CA: Joseph Campbell Foundation, 2011), Kindle Edition, Location 152–65.

3. Grant Voth, *Myth in Human History*, Lectures 14 and 21, The Teaching Company, 2010, DVD.

4. Mary Craig, ed., *The Pocket Dalai Lama* (Boston: Shambhala, 2002), 13, 16.

5. In conversation with the Dalai Lama, http://www.ndtv.com/article/india/in-conversation-with-the-dalai-lama-35955.

6. Herman Hesse, *If the War Goes On* (New York: Farrar, Straus and Giroux, 1971), 177–78.

7. Erich Fromm, *Man for Himself* (New York: Henry Holt and Company, 1990), 70–73.

8. Art Markman, "The Pain of Positive Stereotypes," http://www.psychologytoday.com/blog/ulterior-motives/201302/the-pain-positive-stereotypes.

9. Frederick Douglass, *The Life and Times of Frederick Douglass* (New York: Dover, 2003), 183–85, 187.

10. Carol S. Dweck, "The Perils and Promises of Praise, " *Educational Leadership* 65, no. 2 (October 2007), 34–39.

11. Matthew 4:4, Holy Bible, New International Version.

12. J. Robert Oppenheimer, *Science and the Common Understanding* (New York: Simon and Schuster, 1954), 9–10.

13. In conversation with the Dalai Lama, http://www.ndtv.com/article/india/in-conversation-with-the-dalai-lama-35955.

## Chapter 7: Sailing the Night Sky

1. Melinda Beck, "Blanks for the Memories," http://online.wsj.com/news/articles/SB10001424052702304520804576341482658082052.

2. David Grimm, "In dogs' play, researchers see honesty and deceit, perhaps something like morality," http://www.washingtonpost.com/national/health-science/in-dogs-play-morality/2014/05/19/d8367214-ccb3-11e3-95f7-7ecdde72d2ea_story.html.

3. Steve Connor, "Throwing ability 'helped turn humans from second-rate primate into most successful species on the planet,'" http://www.independent.co.uk/news/science/throwing-ability-helped-tu...ate-primate-into-most-successful-species-on-the-planet-8675395.html.

4. James Gorman, "Scientists Unlock Mystery in Evolution of Pitchers," http://www.nytimes.com/2013/06/27/science/evolution-on-the-mound-why-humans-throw-so-well.html?pagewanted=2&_r=0.

5. Shawn Humphries and Brad Townsend, *Two Steps to a Perfect Golf Swing* (New York: McGraw-Hill, 2004), 42.

6. Albert Einstein, *Ideas and Opinions*, ed. Cal Seelig (New York: Three Rivers Press, 1982), 62.

7. John Sexton, *Baseball As a Road to God* (New York: Gotham Books, 2013), 1–3.

8. The *Encyclopedia of Time*, edited by Samuel L. Macey, discusses how Plutarch and perhaps some ancient Greeks such as Pindar identified Cronus with the god of time (Chronos). So many of the written records from the ancient world were destroyed that we may never know how widespread this view was.

9. E. M. Berens, *The Myths and Legends of Ancient Greece and Rome* (Radford, VA: Wilder, 2013), 15, 16.

10. *Classical Mythology*, Lecture 16, The Teaching Company, 2007, DVD.

11. Charles Lovett, *Olympic Marathon* (Westport, CT: Praeger, 1997), xii.

12. George S. Patton, *War As I Knew It* (Boston: Houghton Mifflin, 1995), 108.

13. Victor Shea and William Whitla, eds., *Essays and Reviews: The 1860 Text and Its Reading* (Charlottesville, VA: University of Virginia Press, 2000), 128.

14. George Orwell, "Politics and the English Language," https://www.mtholyoke.edu/acad/intrel/orwell46.htm.

15. Ibid.

16. Marion K. Underwood, *Social Aggression Among Girls* (New York: Guilford, 2003), 83, 84, 122.

17. Peter Vronsky, *Female Serial Killers* (New York: Berkley, 2007), 46, 47, 61.

## Chapter 8: The Mystery Beneath the Waves

1. Genesis 3:22–24, Holy Bible, New International Version.

2. Here are a few additional notes regarding the Garden of Eden metaphor. God does not seem concerned about humans eating from the Tree of Life until after they eat from the Tree of the Knowledge of Good and Evil, since the Tree of Life would make them immortal even outside of the garden. The story implies that eating from both forbidden trees would make humans into godlike creatures, and God's use of the cherubim and flaming sword implies that Adam and Eve desire fruit from the Tree of Life. If we think about this story metaphorically, if human beings *never* died wouldn't we be godlike? After all, we have technology that mimics the powers of the Greek gods (just as Zeus controlled lightning bolts, we have transformed electricity into our servant). We also have satellites and surveillance systems that give us a degree of omnipresence similar to many mythological deities.

3. *Animal Odd Couples*, PBS Nature, 2013, DVD.

4. Rod Plotnik and Haig Kouyoumdjian, *Introduction to Psychology* (Stamford, CT: Cengage Learning, 2010), 333.

5. Pamela Rutledge, "Social Networks: What Maslow Misses," http://www.psychologytoday.com/blog/positively-media/201111/social-networks-what-maslow-misses-0.

6. Sharman Russell, *Hunger* (New York: Basic Books, 2005),73, 78, 79, 82, 83.

7. Fiona M. Wilson, *Organizational Behavior* (Oxford: Oxford University Press, 2010), 125.

8. Homer, *The Iliad*, trans. Robert Fagles (New York: Viking, 1990), 265.

9. George Orwell, *Animal Farm* (New York: Signet Classics, 1996), 17, 18, 117, 118.

10. Gail Dines, *Pornland* (Boston: Beacon, 2010), 112–13.

11. Virginia Hughes, "When Do Kids Understand Death?," http://phenomena.nationalgeographic.com/2013/07/26/when-do-kids-understand-death/.

12. RSA Animate—The Empathic Civilization, http://www.youtube.com/watch?v=l7AWnfFRc7g.

13. *The Expanded Quotable Einstein*, trans. Alice Calaprice (Princeton: Princeton University Press, 2000), 295.

14. *The Upanishads*, trans. Juan Mascaró (New York: Penguin, 1965), 10.

15. David L. Dungan, "Reconsidering Albert Schweitzer," http://www.religion-online.org/showarticle.asp?title=1864.

16. Thich Nhat Hanh, *The Miracle of Mindfulness*, trans. Mobi Ho (Boston: Beacon, 1999), 12.

17. Erich Fromm discusses the experience of "being" and its relation to eternity in *To Have or To Be?*

18. Martin Luther King Jr., *Where Do We Go from Here?* (Boston: Beacon, 2010), 201–2.

# Index

increase, 107–108

angels of, 186, 195–200

for animals, 180–183

author's personal experiences, 24, 61, 195–198

brain processes, 141–142

cynicism's interference with, 25

expansion of beauty as way to increase, 301

human beings' unique capacity for, 66–68

methods for bombing, 156–157

neuroscience of, 141–142

for ourselves, 310

for outcasts, 283–287

painful experiences as source of, 61

recognition of fragility, vulnerability, mortality of life and, 394–395

satisfaction of life devoted to, 23

shared humanity as source of, 50, 61

solidarity as highest expression of, 142–143

suffering as tool for gaining, 281

as threat to oppressive systems, 139–140

understanding aggression as way to increase, 65–66

understanding human fragility as way to increase, 75–76

for violence reduction, 195

*The End of War* (Chappell), 29, 62, 97, 98, 177, 178, 179, 273–274, 290, 383

Enemies, knowing or loving, 65–66, 136, 195

Environmental destruction, 58–59, 122, 289–290, 350–357

Eternity, 398

Europe, history of violence in, 237–238

Evans, G. R., 73–74

Evil

personification through superstitious

rituals, 93

as tragedy explanation, 82, 97, 98–99

war propaganda dehumanizing enemies as, 54, 55

Explanations

author's personal experiences, 386, 388

human beings' craving for, 108, 265, 329, 330, 358

human beings' uniqueness in search for, 69–77

inaccurate beliefs and, 98–109

for laws of nature, 109–122

reasons for seeking, 78–98

religion's role in feeding craving for, 401

self-worth and, 331

for slavery, 130

worldview formation and, 401

*Exploring Native American Wisdom* (Dancing Feather and Robinson), 126–127

Expression. *See also* Metaphors

art as, 203–204

human being's craving for, 183–184, 329, 330, 358, 386

psychological and physical benefits of, 184

vehicles of, 184–185

violence as, 185–195

Extinction, 51, 57, 121–122

**F**

Fagles, Robert, 204–206

False idols, worship of, 275

Fascism, 382

Fear

of aggression, 210–217

of combat, 201–202

of darkness, 55–56

of death, 71

fighting demon of, 302–310

of public speaking, 210–212

The Cosmic Ocean